# The New Third World

# The New Third World

SECOND EDITION

edited by
## Alfonso Gonzalez
**University of Calgary**

## Jim Norwine
**Texas A&M University**

 WestviewPress
*A Division of* HarperCollins*Publishers*

Copyright © 1998 by Alfonso Gonzalez and Jim Norwine

Published in 1998 in the United States of America by Westview Press, 5500 Central Avenue, Boulder, Colorado 80301-2877, and in the United Kingdom by Westview Press, 12 Hid's Copse Road, Cumnor Hill, Oxford OX2 9JJ

Library of Congress Cataloging-in-Publication Data
The new Third World / edited by Alfonso Gonzalez and Jim Norwine. — 2nd ed.
    p.  cm.
Rev. ed. of: The Third World, 1988.
Includes bibliographical references and index.
ISBN 0-8133-2250-2 (hc). — ISBN 0-8133-2251-0 (pb)
    1. Developing countries—Economic conditions.   2. Natural resources—Developing countries.   3. Developing countries—Social conditions.   4. Developing countries—Politics and government.
I. Gonzalez, Alfonso, 1927–  .  II. Norwine, Jim.  III. Third World.
HC59.7.N377   1998
330.9172'4—dc21                                                                98-2634
                                                                                CIP

The paper used in this publication meets the requirements of the American National Standard for Permanence of Paper for Printed Library Materials Z39.48-1984.

10     9     8     7     6     5     4     3     2     1

# Contents

# Tables, Figures, and Maps

# *Preface*

This book aspires to characterize the Third World at the close of the twentieth century. It is *The New Third World* because, truism or not, the world *is* changing, and these changes are not only immense, they are incoherent and contradictory. Every description seems inadequate, which indicates the magnitude of this ongoing paradigm shift and our consequent confusion. Consider just a few examples:

- We are at once converging and fragmenting (i.e., becoming more placeless *and* more local, or at least more anxious to recapture or reify a local identity).
- The developing world fast becomes more Western (e.g., skeptical of convention and constraint) while the postmodern demographics, gated communities, and beyond-the-pale underclass enclaves of places like Los Angeles more and more resemble Third World cities.
- Skin color declines in social import as appearance, being attractive, and "cool," for instance, ascends.
- The skilled overclass and the redundant unskilled underclass expand while the ranks of the middle class become, if not thinner, less secure.
- Possession of natural resources (other than water) now means far less than the geography of intellectual resources.
- We are context-free postmoderns in our everyday attitudes and behaviors yet often consider ourselves "traditional" or even fundamentalist, and this conflict within our own individual, personal valuescapes makes us uneasy.
- We are masters of a largely humanified natural world, which yet lurks, we intuit, awaiting its vengeance.

In 1940, the global population was almost evenly divided (40–60 roughly) between the developed and the developing worlds. Now, only a half century later, three-quarters of all people live in the Third World and most births occur somewhere in that realm.

One might even ask whether there will *be* a First World by the next *fin de siècle*. After about 2050, for example, so-called minority subgroups—

notably Hispanics, African Americans, and Asian Americans—will together constitute a majority of the U.S. population. In color, "complexion," or ethnicity, and even culture, the United States will soon resemble the world in miniature, and by the second or third generation of the new century, Europe will have experienced the same profoundly exciting and challenging transformation. From a perspective based on changing demographics and their possible consequences, then, the Third World seems fast on its way to being, simply, the world.

The First World seems to be disappearing before our very eyes. Or is it merely going underground? What manner of Third World will in fact inherit the world? It is obvious that modern and even postmodern outlooks are in the ascension in the developing world. Egalitarianism is in, hierarchy is out, or at least is on the ropes. For example, most newly arrived immigrants to southern Texas, where I live and teach, are already about half-Americanized (or globalized, if you insist). I am thinking not so much of the nearly universal assumption of the necessity of personal freedom and access to the good material life (e.g., "owning stuff"), but of attitudes and behaviors tied to worldview, particularly among the young: popular rather than high or low culture; self-referential rather than deferential; choice over constraints; maybe even image over reality.

(Irony may be the only postmodern attribute that has yet to make serious inroads among ordinary people in the developing world. Third World consumerism, for example, remains modern or sincere or genuine, for ownership of something like a first home or car or even a nice dress or baseball glove can give genuine pleasure, even joy. In the First World, on the other hand, even our shop-till-you-drop consumerism—even that!—is ironic and *faux*: We would like for new stuff to make us happy, we hope against hope that it does, but we do not expect it to, and it does not.)

The new Third World is coming into its own, is becoming the world, and is transforming in ways—democracies, market economies, modern/postmodern *Weltanshauungen*—that potentially could mean the loss of formerly highly prized traditional virtues. More important, perhaps, traditional outlooks as diverse as those of Black Elk, Saint Francis, and Charles Darwin have assumed that authentic personal identity can only be attained via a submission or a deference of individuals to something larger than self. This notion stands in direct opposition to the contemporary paradigm, already dominant in the First World and rising in the Third, that the self is and must be central because it is the only center that has held.

I hope that *The New Third World* fairly portrays the developing world as it is. As to what it will be, the people of the Third World will have to decide—as those in the rich world seem long since to have done–where their hearts' desires lie. To exaggerate a bit, much of the developing world is shifting almost directly from traditionality to postmodernity with only a bare minimum of a "modern" phase in between. The profundity of the contrast is fantastically destabilizing. However, it is just possible that the abruptness of this transition (and the lingering resonance of traditional truths—e.g., radical personal autonomy is not synonymous with freedom, happiness and pleasure are not equivalent, submission is not always oppression) might make it easier to avoid the extreme self-referentiality (the phrase "being jerks" comes to mind) that already seems normal, perhaps even hegemonic, in the postmodern West.

*Jim Norwine*

# Introduction

## Alfonso Gonzalez

THE PROBLEM OF SOCIOECONOMIC DEVELOPMENT and the concomitant improvements of levels of living or the quality of life is certainly one of the outstanding issues confronting mankind. Virtually all aspects regarding the problem of development are subject to controversy, and there appears to be little general agreement on anything. Nevertheless, we endeavor to provide perspectives from a variety of specialists on different aspects of this ever-present critical problem.

Development does not appear to be a question of national endowment, such as natural resources or population size, but of capabilities, such as the utilization of resources, technology, and socioeconomic institutions. A definition of development would include the processes of more effective use of resources and increased efficiency in production and distribution, which result in a greater volume and diversity of goods and services for less human physical labor. Some argue that the distributional aspects within society are of major, perhaps primary, concern. To these advocates, the redistribution of wealth or the more egalitarian distribution of income constitutes "true" development. To this same group, and to others, "true" or "real" development consists of "human rights." Human rights generally consist of (1) political and civil rights (i.e., civil liberties and political freedom; this is the concept that is probably most frequently used in Western democracies), and (2) socioeconomic rights (i.e., the right to health care, an adequate diet, education, decent housing, and even the right to employment and rights for women and minorities). In most Western democracies, the socioeconomic aspect of human rights are generally considered to be highly desirable objectives of social justice and government policy rather than "rights." However, this aspect of human rights is most frequently advocated by the underdeveloped world in general, and by radicals and former Marxist regimes in particular, where political and civil rights are about the most restricted anywhere.

The causes of the status of development in the underdeveloped regions are also a subject of great controversy. Some groups, and even specialists, expound on one particular cause or another, including the social system and structure, culture, limited education and technology, inadequate resources, population growth and pressure, inadequate capital accumulation, colonial and neocolonial exploitation, dependency on other countries or source regions, sociocultural isolation, the capitalist system (nationally and/or internationally), restraints on private enterprise, and so forth. Despite the conventional wisdom that development is a complex issue, many appear to argue that the cause, and therefore presumably the cure, for the condition of the Third World is due essentially to a single dominant factor. Since there is clearly no agreement on that factor, then perhaps another perspective would be that the issue *is* really complex and involves various elements perhaps differing in importance through time and countries.

Some have taken their lack of national development as an implication of lessened national prestige and thereby compensate by alleging that their culture has spiritual and ethical values not found in the higher technological societies. Unquestionably, all cultures have some merit; but in the cultural competition that is occurring—and competition always occurs when cultures come into contact with each other—the trend toward highly urbanized, educated, and industrial-commercial societies is relentless and cannot be denied.

In the national quest for development, the traditional indigenous cultures virtually everywhere are at a serious disadvantage. Many in these cultures (and some from the outside) wish to preserve some or all of their ancient traditions in the face of this cultural onslaught. Since development requires fundamental changes in society and the economy, these more traditional cultures in reality face the options of adjusting in some important degree or paying the price of slower change—less economic growth, lower material well-being, and falling ever further behind the more technological cultures. The choice should be theirs to make, but the consequences must be weighed with extreme caution.

There is a great diversity of approaches to development in the form of economic systems operating in the Third World. These range from capitalist economies, in which there is relatively minor government intervention in the operation of the economy, to varying degrees of state intervention and ownership, to the near-total elimination of private enterprise and virtually full governmental control of the economy seen in "socialist"/communist regimes, few of which now remain. On the basis of recent economic growth, no one economic system appears to have a clear advantage over the others. Nevertheless, beginning in the early 1980s the world trend has clearly been in the direction of less government ownership and intervention in the economy. This movement toward more open economic and political societies accelerated with the collapse of the Soviet system at the end of the 1980s.

Political systems also exhibit a great range within the Third World. There are relatively open multiparty democracies, semidemocracies or partly free societies, and authoritarian and totalitarian regimes. Again, no one political system appeared to provide a greater benefit in terms of economic growth than the others until the 1980s. The only clear association that can be made between economic and political systems is that Marxist-based economies (of diverse types) permit no political competitiveness and very limited civil liberties.

By 1991 the ideologically bipolarized world, which had dominated the post–World War II period, had collapsed. The end of the Cold War had an impressive impact on the Third World, creating a new and changing political, economic, and social environment—in essence, a New Third World. The competition between the two superpowers for allies and favored status along with foreign aid and surrogate wars came to an end. Increases, or even the maintenance, of assistance became problematic with budget restraints and trade imbalances in the leading industrial countries. The economies and political structures of the former Second World, notably the Soviet bloc, began to disintegrate and eliminated the continuation of assistance to the Third World. Even earlier, the decline of oil revenues necessitated reductions in aid contributions by the OPEC countries of the Middle East.

The collapse of the Second World also accelerated the demise, perhaps only temporarily, of alternative paths to development. With the debt crisis, starting in 1982, neoliberal/conservative policies for economic development began to gain favor, aided by the elections of Margaret Thatcher in the United Kingdom and Ronald Reagan in the United States a few years earlier. These policies generally entailed government deregulation, privatization, and open economies in terms of foreign investment and imports along with greater stress on exports. It was emphasized that the government was to be a less active participant in the development process and that the private sector would be the driving force ("engine") in a more competitive and export-oriented economy.

Lagging somewhat behind was the movement toward greater democracy and human rights, in the Western tradition (political competitiveness and freedom along with civil liberties). Both of these elements—a market economy and democracy—have been received somewhat grudgingly by much of the Third World. In many cases, tough economic measures imposed by international and national lending agencies created hardship as Third World countries attempted to shift their economies. Much of the Third World had a tradition of government ownership and intervention in the economy and authoritarian political rule. These newer measures were supposed to bring about a transformation of the Third World in their economic, political, and social structures.

Furthermore, with the deteriorating economic situation in many countries and the "New World Order" (the disappearance of the Communist threat), military expenditures declined somewhat but even more so did spending on health, education, and other social programs. This weakening of the social-support system had a severe impact in many countries, especially among the poor, and did not bode well for future political stability.

The great attention to economic restructuring and stability and the push for economic development have resulted in perhaps an even greater neglect in social investments. Education, health, and nutrition have undoubtedly sustained significant setbacks in many countries. However, there seems to be a recent growing awareness of social conditions, and perhaps rectifying measures will be implemented.

Another manifestation of change has been the resurgence of ethnic conflict, which has displaced ideology as the major determinant of warfare in the Third World. Ethnic conflict is certainly not new, but it has become even more common recently. The major conflicts have shifted from the more advanced world up to the mid–twentieth century to the Third World in the post–World War II period. With deteriorating economic and social conditions and the weakening of authoritarian rule, the prospects for both ethnic and political conflict will certainly not diminish.

There has also been a move toward regional trading blocs. This originated with Western Europe in the immediate post–World War II period and has spread, with lesser degrees of involvement, to areas of the Third World. For the first time a Third World country, Mexico, has been incorporated into a close trading bloc with advanced industrial countries, the United States and Canada in the North American Free Trade Agreement. At the same time, many Third World countries, particularly those in Africa, have been cut off from traditional trade with previous colonial partners due to new exclusive trading arrangements such as the European Union.

Despite all these recent momentous changes affecting the Third World the more traditional patterns remain, although with some modifications. Some of these continuing features include the following:

1. continued rapid population growth, with a gradual decrease in the rate of growth (but not the absolute annual increase), except for the poorest region, Sub-Saharan Africa, where the potential for even faster growth exists;
2. increasing attention to the protection and preservation of the environment, although this has not near the priority it has in the First World;
3. the uneven distribution of wealth and income, probably most severe in Latin America and Sub-Saharan Africa and most reasonably balanced in the Orient;

4. the entrenched power of elite groups, who generally resist change, especially that which they cannot control or they consider detrimental to their perceived interests;
5. lack of sufficient economic growth to overcome the pervasive poverty of most of the population;
6. dependency on the First World for technology and assistance;
7. cultural resistance to change and to the general development process in many areas by different groups;
8. the continuing historical pattern that innovations are adapted by societies that are more receptive and able to incorporate changes means that many Third World countries will fall further behind as they do not have the resources to adapt innovations, such as the "information revolution," or they wish to restrict, in part, the effects and consequences of such changes;
9. as the gap continues to grow between the First and Third Worlds, there is *within* the Third World a growing gap between those countries that continue to modernize and grow rapidly, best exemplified by the newly industrialized countries (NICs), and those that are changing gradually or exhibit little growth or transformation.

The diverse and controversial solutions or approaches to development that have been advocated make it clear that there is little overall consensus, and the evidence indicates there is no sure "solution." In the developmental process there are certain policies ("fads") that attain ascendancy at particular times. Currently we are experiencing an emphasis on open economies and political systems, and there are many protestations that improvement cannot be accomplished without both, despite the historical evidence to the contrary. Probably no theory, and few concepts, with regard to the development process has been accepted by the majority of specialists. Furthermore, the situation in many parts of the Third World is desperate and it is not getting better. The time for resolution is not endless.

It is hoped that the following chapters will provide insight into the complex nature of the problem of development. No simplistic solutions have been put forward. Differing options are available and contrasting perspectives are presented. No attempt at conformity or unity of approach has been attempted in these presentations because in the real world these do not exist unless imposed by authorities on a country. We have tried to present as balanced an approach as possible. The reader may assess, interpret, and judge from the writings of these specialists and so choose the perspective he or she prefers and identify the possible solutions.

# PART ONE

## *Thematic and Systematic Patterns*

# 1 The Third World: Definitions and New Perspectives on Development

## Srinivas R. Melkote and Allen H. Merriam

THE TERM *Third World* represents one of the significant additions to the vocabulary of the twentieth century. The 1992–1993 edition of *Books in Print* contains 143 entries with *Third World* in the beginning of the title. But what does this term really mean? And given the dramatic changes in the geopolitical landscape in recent years, are there better words for naming various levels of human development?

In traditional usage, the First World referred to the industrialized democracies, which enjoy a relatively high standard of living. The Second World contained the countries in the Soviet sphere of influence in Eastern Europe, which, until the Gorbachev era of *glasnost* (openness) and *perestroika* (restructuring), were characterized by centralized economic control and domination by the Communist Party's political apparatus. The Third World consisted of the remaining 75 percent of humanity, from Afghanistan to Zimbabwe. This conglomerate, including most of the nations of Asia, Africa, and Latin America, generally can be characterized by relatively low per capita incomes, high rates of illiteracy, agriculturally based economies, short life expectancies, low degrees of social mobility, strong attachments to tradition, and usually, a history of colonization.[1]

*Third World* is a concept of French origin. William Safire (1978) traced the term as a label for France's political parties in the 1940s, which were distinct from de Gaulle's Rassemblement du Peuple Français (RPF) and the Fourth Republic. W. M. Clegern (1978) compared the idea to the Third Estate (*le tiers état*), the rising but underrepresented bourgeoisie contending with the clergy and the aristocracy in the French Revolution of 1789. Many scholars now credit the French demographer Alfred Sauvy with

coining the term in 1952.² Since then the phrase has gained wide acceptance as a positive concept signifying the new and experimental arena of
global politics bound to neither Western capitalism nor Soviet socialism.

It is interesting to note that near the end of his life Mao Zedong formulated a creative if unorthodox theory of three worlds. Mao viewed the
First World as consisting of the superpowers (Soviet Union and United
States), whose imperialistic policies, he felt, posed the greatest threat to
world peace. Mao (1977) placed the middle powers (Japan, Canada, and
Europe) in the Second World. Africa, Latin America, and Asia (including
China) formed the Third World, the peoples whom Mao believed to be
the best hope for revolutionary struggle. Leaders in China since Mao
have reaffirmed this linkage, as in Vice Premier Deng Xiaoping's 1975
declaration that "China is a developing socialist country belonging to the
third world."³

With the dissolution of the Soviet Union in 1991 and the attendant disintegration of the Second World, does it still make sense to speak of the
*Third World?* Francis Fukuyama, after all, even went so far as to an-
nounce an end to ideological competition. While acknowledging the continuing challenges posed by religious fundamentalism and nascent na-
tionalism around the globe, he portrayed the "emergence of Western
liberal democracy as the final form of human government."⁴ Despite
such grandiose speculation, *Third World* remains a useful and desirable
term in contemporary geopolitical vocabulary for a number of reasons.
Obviously considerable competition continues to exist between capitalistic and socialistic approaches to economic practice, among nations as
well as within individual countries. Moreover, the term allows scholars,
politicians, and development planners a way to describe and analyze
commonalties among nations as diverse as Brazil, Burundi, and Bangladesh.

Easily translatable into other languages such as Spanish (*el tercer
mundo*) and French (*le tiers monde*), *Third World* has proven effective
rhetorically as a rallying point, a persuasive slogan, a source of identity
for the peoples so designated. Whether in the speeches of Fidel Castro,
the poetry of Aimé Césaire, or the economic analyses of Mahbub ul-Haq,
the term has assumed an ideology of its own. More than a mere socioeconomic label, it connotes a psychological condition, a state of mind encompassing the hopes and aspirations of three-fourths of humanity.⁵

Another justification for *Third World* is that no alternative nomencla-
ture seems preferable. Certainly many other names have been tried, but
all have deficiencies. For example, *developing nations* is a commonly used
term. But it seems overly inclusive, for the United States is developing,
and Japan and Russia are evolving. Indeed, the devotion to technological
advancement and social change in Western countries means they may be

developing faster than many Third World nations. Acronyms such as *LDCs* (less developed countries) and *NICs* (newly industrialized countries) suffer a similar ambiguity and seem limited to a primarily economic perspective. The term *emerging nations* is vague, and designations such as *underdeveloped, backward,* and *primitive* clearly are politically incorrect given their blatantly negative connotations.

Another term often used synonymously with *Third World* is *non-aligned nations,* and the two phrases are closely related both historically and ideologically. The Non-Aligned Movement grew out of the important Bandung Conference held in Indonesia in 1955 where Afro-Asian leaders asserted solidarity with anticolonialism. The movement was institutionalized at the first Non-Aligned summit conference in Belgrade in 1961, with 25 countries represented. Impressive growth has marked successive assemblies, at Cairo in 1964, Lusaka in 1970, Algiers in 1973, Colombo in 1976, Havana in 1979, New Delhi in 1983, Harare in 1986, Belgrade in 1989, and Jakarta in 1992 when membership reached 106 nations. But *non-aligned* suffers inaccuracies: Cuba is a member state despite close alliances with the former Communist bloc, and Pakistan and Turkey were not members, due to military ties with the United States through CENTO and NATO respectively, even though both are clearly Third World countries. And the fact that non-aligned states are aligned with each other makes their name misleading if not contradictory.[6]

Other designations include several two-part names. An *East-West* dichotomy is popular, usually to contrast value differences between the intuitive, holistic, spiritual, group orientation of Eastern (Asian) cultures as distinct from the individualistic, materialistic, rational, and scientific West.[7] But while helpful in delineating Oriental and Occidental philosophical tendencies (Rosan 1962) (and even this assumption has been challenged), this term essentially ignores Africa as well as the world's aboriginal and indigenous peoples. The *North-South* designation, based on the relatively advanced economic status of Northern Hemisphere nations, fails to distinguish between northern countries as diverse as Russia and Canada, necessitates the awkward placement of Australia and New Zealand in the "North," and contains the confusing image of South Asia, much of Africa, and all of Central America and Mexico in the "South" despite their location in the Northern Hemisphere. And the *haves–have nots* division is unclear about what anybody has or even wants; to many Buddhists, for example, inner peace may be more valuable than a high gross national product (GNP).

Current geopolitical vocabulary also includes a host of specialized and regional groupings. Among these are the European Community (EC), the General Agreement on Tariffs and Trade (GATT), the Association of South-East Asian Nations (ASEAN), the Organization of American States (OAS), the Organization of African Unity (OAU), the Arab League, and the Islamic Conference. Another designation is the *Group of 77*, referring to the 77 nations that, at the first meeting of the United Nations Conference on Trade and Development (UNCTAD) in Geneva in 1964, united to press for more vigorous international development programs. But this label is cumbersome and inaccurate since more than 100 nations are now members. More recently, the *G-15* has emerged as a counterbalance to the *G-7* (seven wealthy First World nations consisting of Canada, France, Germany, Great Britain, Italy, Japan, and the United States). The *G-15* consists of Algeria, Argentina, Brazil, Chile, Egypt, India, Indonesia, Jamaica, Malaysia, Mexico, Nigeria, Peru, Senegal, Venezuela, and Zimbabwe. Formed by the Non-Aligned Movement in 1989 and known officially as the Summit Level Group on South-South Consultation and Cooperation, the *G-15* promotes sustainable economic development. At its 1994 summit conference in New Delhi, it called for an expansion of the United Nations Security Council's permanent membership to include more Third World seats, with India, Brazil, and Nigeria the most likely nominees. In general, however, the names given to specialized and regional groupings lack the conciseness, universality, and emotional power of the term *Third World*.

Inspired by a desire for global unity and humanitarian concern, some thinkers have rejected any effort to divide the world into competing segments. The seventeenth-century Czech educator Comenius affirmed: "We are all citizens of one world . . . Let us have but one end in view, and the welfare of humanity" (Fersh 1974: 119). The nineteenth-century Persian mystic Baha'ul'lah shared this sentiment and his disciple Abdul-Ba'ha declared: "All are servants of God and members of one human family . . . we are all the waves of one sea" (*Baha'i World Faith* 1976). In 1970 Tanzanian president Julius Nyerere told the United Nations: "We believe that all mankind is one" (Nyerere 1970: 824). But while such universalism represents a noble ideal, it seems too utopian to allow for the political and economic distinctions that governments, multinational corporations, and social scientists need for daily decisionmaking.

Thus, as we approach the dawn of the twenty-first century, *Third World* remains a viable and important term with which to view emerging perspectives on human development.

## Development of the Third World

In the period that followed World War II, most of the Third World achieved independence from colonization and became the focus of multilateral development assistance efforts through the United Nations (UN) and its family of specialized agencies and institutions. In the early postwar years, the attention of the UN and its most influential member, the United States, was focused on relief and rehabilitation work in Western

Europe through the Marshall Plan. But starting in the 1950s, attention turned increasingly to the Third World countries where two-thirds of the world's population resided. This population was mostly impoverished and received only 15 percent of the world's income (Van Soet 1978).

Bilateral development assistance also played an important role in Third World development. U.S. President Harry S. Truman proposed the Point Four program in 1949, thus establishing a model that most of the developed world embraced. The key to prosperity and peace, said Truman in his 1949 inaugural address, was "greater production" through "a wider and more vigorous application of modern scientific and technical knowledge" (Daniels 1951: 11). The outcome of this proposal was termed as *development*. Under this program, American advances in agriculture, commerce, industry, and health care were to be diffused to the Third World countries. Whereas the Marshall Plan involved mostly capital investment in Western Europe, assistance to Third World countries consisted of monetary aid as well as scientific and technological expertise. Thus was born Organized Development Assistance (ODA).

The task of modernizing the Third World seemed quite simple at that time: Determine appropriate innovations that promised development and then arrange to have them diffused to targeted beneficiaries (Rogers 1976a). The state of affairs in the Third World countries was attributed to the inadequate or nonexistent industrial infrastructure on the one hand and the cultures of these nations and certain characteristics of their citizens on the other. Native cultures were seen as obstacles to the type of development to be achieved. Therefore, the strategy for solving the problems of underdevelopment in Asia, Africa, and Latin America seemed simple and straightforward: Guide the Third World through the different stages of development at a rate even faster than the advanced countries experienced by retracing the development path of the Western countries (minus the colonization part). This orientation to development strategy is frequently referred to as the "orthodox paradigm."

## Orthodox Paradigm of Development

Theories and concepts that recapitulated the development of West European and North American nations were used to generate prescriptive models of development for the Third World. In these modernization theories, the definition of a developed nation resembled Western industrialized nations in terms of political and economic behavior, institutions, culture, and attitudes toward technology.

The approaches in the sociology of development emphasized the theories of social evolution. Morgan, Comte, Spencer, Kidd, Ward, and others supported the evolutionary perspective for human societies. These theories applied Darwin's ideas to the process of modernization of human societies. In their models, the highest stage of evolution was exhibited by European nations of the nineteenth and early twentieth century (Portes 1976). The theories of social evolution influenced and gave rise to important concepts in the sociology of development, including the various bipolar theories of modernization. The universal stages in the earlier theories of social evolution were reduced to ideal-typical extremes: *gemeinschaft* versus *gesellschaft*, traditional versus modern societies, and so on. The Third World nations usually represented the traditional end of the dichotomy and the industrialized nations of the West signified the modern counterpart. In summary, the sociology of development theories treated the West as a model of political, economic, social, and cultural modernization that the Third World should emulate. The Western nations had a wide range of systemic autonomy; that is, they possessed an enhanced capacity to cope with a range of social, cultural, technological, and economic issues in the process of social change (Eisenstadt 1976: 31). The Third World nations, on the other hand, lacked the higher differentiation of roles and institutions, the evolutionary universals (such as democratic association, modern organizations, markets, and legal systems), and the West's orientation to secular and universal norms rather than the narrow particularistic goals of Third World countries (Parsons 1964a,b). These deficiencies were seen as severely limiting the Third World in their capacity to cope with problems or crises or to master their environment.

At the microlevel, theories on individual psychological attributes stressed that attitudinal and value changes among individuals were prerequisites to the creation of a modern society. Although institutional development in the Third World was considered necessary for modernization to occur, it was the character of individuals and not the character of society that was important. Scholars such as David McClelland (1967), Daniel Lerner (1958), and Alex Inkeles (1969) described certain value-normative complexes (e.g., motivation for achievement, capacity to empathize with the unfamiliar, openness to innovation) that accelerated development in the Western countries and that individuals in the Third World were lacking. These scholars posited that modernization of the Third World was dependent on changing the character of individuals living there to resemble more closely the attitudinal and value characteristics of people in Western Europe and North America.

Finally, the economic model presented in the orthodox paradigm was the neoclassical approach, which had served as an important model for Western economies. Adam Smith in his *The Wealth of Nations* (1776) originally proposed this approach, which was later supported and enriched by other Western economists such as Ricardo, Schumpeter, Keynes, Hirschman, and Nurkse, among others. This approach was concerned mainly with economic growth, as measured by the GNP rates, and encouragement of all factors and institutions that accelerated and maintained high growth rates, such as capital-intensive industrialization, high technology, private ownership of factors of production, free trade, and the principle of *laissez-faire* (Weaver and Jameson 1978).

In this approach, economic growth was the key to development. Most of the problems confronting the Third World countries were identified as being economic in nature. Managed plans were launched (for example, five-year growth plans) in many countries to dovetail development activities of the state and help bring about orderly and timely economic development. Bilateral and multilateral institutions were involved in these plans. Development performance was measured by indicators such as the GNP rate and per capita income. Capital-intensive, as opposed to labor-intensive, approaches and industrial, as opposed to agricultural, development were encouraged in many developing countries.

The role of the mass media in development activities was very clearly implied in the orthodox paradigm of development. For example, Wilbur Schramm (1964) maintained that the modernization of industry or agricultural sectors in developing nations required the mobilization of human resources. Education and mass media, then, were vested with crucial responsibility in the process of mobilization of human resources.

Some scholars went further, stating that the major problem in developing countries was not a shortage of natural resources but underdevelopment of human resources. Thus, education and mass media were enlisted in the important task of building human capital (Lerner 1958; Schramm 1964; Rogers 1976c). Mass media were the vehicles for transferring new ideas and models from the developed nations to the Third World and from the urban areas to the rural countryside. Information was considered the missing link in the development chain. The quality of information available and its wide dissemination were key factors in the speed and smoothness of development (Schramm 1964). Adequate mass media outlets and information would act as a spur to education, commerce, and a chain of other related development activities.

## Criticism of the Orthodox Paradigm

The decade of the 1970s was a period of ferment in the field of Third World development. Many areas of development, such as economics, family planning, population, culture, and communication, were researched heavily. There were also many scholars from Asia and Latin America interested in development, and as they became important contributors to this field, many of the ideas and assumptions that had guided research in the preceding two decades were increasingly questioned and criticized. The process of development in Africa, Asia, and

Latin America did not exactly follow the stages that the Western European or North American countries had passed through. Thus, the development of the Third World did not fit all the assumptions implicit in the orthodox paradigm. The orthodox paradigm seemed to work better as a description of what had happened in Western Europe and North America than as a predictor of change in the Third World (Eisenstadt 1976).

The criticism of the sociology of development theories addressed several core issues. The bipolar theories were essentially post hoc analyses of development in the First World in the late nineteenth and early twentieth centuries and did not provide insight into the determinants of change in the Third World in the post–World War II period (Portes 1976). The developmental process in the Third World often ran counter to some of the empirical relationships espoused by the orthodox paradigm. For example, S. N. Eisenstadt (1976) points out that in Asia, Latin America, and Central and Eastern Europe, many nations exhibited negative correlations between demographic variables—such as literacy, spread of mass media, formal education, and urbanization—and the ability to sustain economic growth or develop libertarian or Western-type institutions. On the other hand, a country such as India was able to evolve a stable and a modern Western-type libertarian democratic political system while nevertheless exhibiting all the characteristics of underdevelopment.

Criticisms were also directed at the orthodox paradigm by several neo-Marxist scholars from Latin America, including Gunder Frank, Dos Santos, and Cardoso, among others. They argued that underdevelopment and development were not separate and autonomous processes as conceptualized earlier but constituted two facets of the same process. They contended that the *development of underdevelopment* in Third World nations was and is related to the economic development of Western Europe and North America.

The sociology of development models invoked a very limited time perspective of 25 to 100 years at most. If the time frame for an analysis of Third World development were to go back in history, it would be seen that countries such as Egypt, India, Iraq, China, Peru, Guatemala, and Mexico, among others, had been centers of sophisticated civilizations. The underdevelopment of countries in Asia, Africa, or Latin America was not necessarily by choice. Due to their colonized status much of the Third World was forced to remain unindustrialized or was kept in a state of relative underdevelopment so that colonies could provide raw materials to factories in Europe and serve as captive markets for European finished goods. The critical stimulus to investment that spurred economic growth in England was provided, to a great extent, by the surplus appropriated from the slave-plantation colonies by the British (Williams 1964). It was the unlimited overseas market captured by British commerce through empire and superior naval power that fueled the industrial revolution in England (Hobsbawn 1968).

The neoclassical economic model that predicted a trickle-down effect from development efforts started losing its credibility in the 1970s among administrators in the Third World. The trickle-down of development benefits did not meet the expectations. Many developing countries showed impressive growth in their GNP rates. However, unemployment, poverty, and income inequality (when compared to rates in the 1960s) were increasing as well (Weaver and Jameson 1978). Quite often, a substantial part of domestic funds, foreign aid, and investment was directed at capital-intensive projects. This made capital relatively cheap compared to labor. However, most developing countries were labor-rich and capital-poor (Weaver and Jameson 1978). The economic model in the orthodox paradigm was found wanting in several respects. It was criticized for defining development only in terms of quantifiable characteristics such as the GNP and per capita income, for encouraging capital-intensive techniques in capital-poor developing nations and neglecting labor-intensive strategies, and for supporting a top-down approach to planning and development.

## New Perspectives on Development

Although the newer approaches in the 1970s and 1980s did not necessarily discard the quantitative approach, there was a strengthening of the qualitative and normative modes of inquiry. Development priorities and standards became more contextual to needs and problems of individual countries or regions within them. Although economic growth and industrialization were still considered important goals of development, attention was now given to other objectives as well: meeting specific needs of particular poverty groups; fulfilling people's basic needs, such as health care, nutrition, sanitation, and shelter; placing emphasis on nonmaterial indicators of development, such as self-reliance and cultural autonomy; and putting the spotlight on human rights, such as the right to free expression and the right to equitable employment and wages.

Thus, the concept of development itself was broadened. Everett Rogers (1969), who was criticized for his earlier definition that stressed only industrialization and economic growth and neglected other human factors, summarized the newer concept of development as "a widely participatory process of social change in a society, intended to bring about both social and material advancement (including greater equality, freedom, and other valued qualities) for the majority of the people through their gaining greater control over their environment" (Rogers 1976b: 133).

Wang and Dissanayake (1984: 5) emphasized the protection of nature and culture. They defined development as "a process of social change which has as its goal the improvement in the quality of life of all or the majority of people without doing violence to the natural and cultural environment in which they exist, and which seeks to involve the majority of the people as closely as possible in this enterprise, making them the masters of their own destiny."

Other definitions of development (Hedebro 1982; Rogers 1976c) stressed the following:

1. Equity in distribution of benefits of development. The emphasis was placed on the very poor, those living in urban shanty towns, and backward rural areas. "Growth with equity" rather than trickle-down was the favorite slogan of the 1970s.
2. Active participation of people at the grassroots. The objective was to involve the input of people at the grassroots in development-related activities concerned with their welfare. It was argued that this ensured that development plans and decisions were more relevant and meaningful to the recipients.
3. Opportunities for local communities to tailor development projects to their objectives. To the extent that reliance would be on local human skills and material resources this fostered a greater degree of self-reliance in development.
4. Integration of the endogenous and exogenous elements to constitute a unique blend suited to the needs of a particular community. This approach would place emphasis on local ideas as well as exogenously diffused ideas and would consider the local culture and its native wisdom as an asset, not a detriment, to achieving a unique syncretization best suited to the tasks at hand.

## Socialistic Approach

In the early 1970s, the opening of China to the rest of the world showed that it was possible for a country to achieve its development goals using its own unique model of development. The People's Republic of China had made tangible gains in the areas of agriculture, health, and family planning and had achieved some degree of equity among its citizens in the distribution of the benefits of development. In addition, Tanzania and Cuba, who also chose not to follow the Western model, were hailed as examples of successful development. Cuba had achieved impressive gains in spreading and increasing literacy among its people, whereas Tanzania had embarked on decentralized and popular participation of the people in rural development activities through its *Ujamaa* program.

## Basic Needs Approach

The basic needs approach arose as a consequence of the disenchantment with the trickle-down concept of development. It was supported by several organizations such as the World Bank, the International Labour Organization, the United Nations Economic and Social Council, and the United States Congress and many other national governments. The basic needs approach focused on essentials such as adequate food, clean drinking water, decent shelter, adequate education, security of livelihood, and reliable transportation (Streeten 1979).

### Environmental Approach

Environment, both as a concept and as a concern, became a central issue starting with the historic United Nations Conference on Human Environment held in Stockholm in 1972. The relentless pursuit of development through economic and technological growth was recognized as a threat to the future availability of natural resources and the viability of growth itself (Oakley and Marsden 1984). Nature, as a broader notion of environment, received little mention in early literature other than as something to be exploited for growth. However, in the past decade several scholars have incorporated environmental and ecological factors in their definitions of development. The current quest for sustainable development recognizes that the relentless destruction of nature jeopardizes global ecology, the balance of which is essential for the health of our planet.

### Free Enterprise System

Curiously, there has been a rebound of this concept from its heyday in the late eighteenth century. The virtues of unrestricted commerce and free markets are emphasized in this approach, and in many ways, it discounts much of the criticism of the orthodox paradigm discussed earlier. A definite link is made between market capitalism and democracy/human rights. Thus, the free enterprise system is offered as the best system to the Third World countries (Berthoud 1993). It is being touted as the most viable path to development, and with the collapse of the centralized economies of the former Soviet Union and Eastern European countries, Third World countries are being encouraged to adopt liberal capitalist ideas and to let the free market regulate the society. The rewards for embracing the free enterprise system include greater individual freedom and collective prosperity (Berthoud 1993).

## Criticism of the Newer Perspectives to Development

Although economic growth may not be the sine qua non of development, it is nevertheless still an important objective for Third World countries to strive for. Without steady economic growth it may not be possible for a

Third World nation to afford entitlement programs for the poor, called for in the basic needs approach. Providing education to all children, ensuring adequate health care for all citizens, and providing a home to all people requires an enormous financial outlay and a strong political will, both of which are in short supply in many Third World nations.

Schemes to help the poorest of the poor, the powerless, and the disadvantaged have simply not worked. Slogans such as "growth with equity," and "empowerment" have been reduced to empty phrases. This is not to say that development of the poorest sectors of the population is unimportant. From both a moral and economic point of view, it was right for the United Nations, USAID, the World Bank, and several Third World governments in the 1970s and 1980s to stress the importance of development programs tailored to the poor and powerless. It is the implementation of these programs that is being criticized here. Paradoxically, the argument used by the critics of the orthodox model may be used against the newer approaches. The critics of the orthodox paradigm pointed out that poverty and inequality had increased in the Third World since the 1960s. The same is the case at present. The newer approaches have not brought about any significant change in the lives of millions of people in the Third World living in underdeveloped rural areas or urban slums. The rigid social and economic structure that prevented a trickle-down of benefits to the poor has also stalled newer programs such as growth with equity.

The nature of the political, economic, and social structure in many Third World countries makes development difficult regardless of which development paradigm is used. State government officials in several developing countries are extremely corrupt, inefficient, and arrogant. Government structures are unnecessarily large, taxes are usually high, and public money is routinely misused to benefit political elites. Accountability to the people is woefully lacking.

## Unequal Development

Neo-Marxist scholars and other critics of the orthodox model pointed out the unequal status accorded to Third World nations vis-à-vis the First World. Although there is some merit in that criticism, it is also the inequality of regions and groups of people within individual Third World countries that may retard growth with equity or fail to empower the powerless. Development programs at the macro-level, such as hydroelectric projects, roadways, railroads, and telecommunication links, are unequally distributed within individual Third World countries and usually favor regions that have ties with politically powerful groups; similarly people belonging to certain dominant language, ethnic, or racial groups are favored over other less-dominant groups in the distribution of development benefits. Thus, the concept of *center and periphery* defined by the dependist scholars is evident within individual Third World countries, making development progress uneven and unequal. This calls into question the relevance of terms such as self-reliance and cultural autonomy that were used by the critics of the orthodox paradigm.

## The Experience of Socialism

Although the experience of Western countries was considered inappropriate for Third World development, countries such as China and Tanzania were frequently cited as models of successful development. This may not be correct. It must be remembered that China and Tanzania followed a model rooted in socialist principles. They cannot be held out as emulative models unless other Third World countries also import their socialistic, political, and social organization philosophies (Hedebro 1982). The experiences of China and India in regard to population control provide a useful illustration. Although India was the first Third World nation to design a population control and family planning policy at the highest governmental level, its rate of achievement has been poor compared to that of China. A major reason for this is the unpopularity of the family planning program among the people in India. However, another important factor is the divergent political philosophies of these two large nations. India, under its democratic form of government, respects individual choice and freedom. Therefore, unlike China, India cannot mandate couples to limit their families to only one child.

When considering the relatively successful model of China (under both Mao and Deng) in terms of economic growth, agricultural and industrial productivity, and so forth, one must also assess the human costs of the model (Chu 1987). Berger (1976: 168) notes: "Anyone who looks at the record of the communist regime since 1949 with even a modest intention of objectivity will be impressed by the enormous quantity of human pain directly traceable to the actions of the regime. It is a record of death, anguish, and fear deliberately inflicted upon the most numerous people of earth." Thus, the Chinese model, however successful it may be, is impractical for many Third World countries, especially those that are attempting to sustain democratic political systems.

## Conclusion

Where do we stand today? The model prescribed by the West has had its critics while the newer approaches to development have their share of weaknesses. Probably, the process of development in Third World countries is so complex that there is no straightforward simple solution. The

Third World is not a monolithic entity but instead consists of countries in several continents, with different forms of political arrangements, historical experience, geographical conditions, and cultural makeup.

As we approach the next century, several ideas have been put forward and are being tested. An idea that has gained some currency is that of sustainable development. Another idea that is not so new but is finding renewed support is free market liberal capitalism.

### Sustainable Development

Although this concept has become prominent in the past decade, it has been around for some time. In the orthodox paradigm, it referred to the design and execution of economic policies that sustained long-term development. However, since the mid-1980s, this term has been used in a more holistic manner. It refers to various facets of development that ensure "real development" and its sustainability, such as community/local development, community participation in development, an inclusion of and a more prominent role for women in development, and more recently, the protection of the environment.

*Community Development and Local Participation.* In the 1980s and 1990s, there has been an increasing recognition within national governments, multilateral agencies, and nongovernmental organizations of the importance of community or local development. Concomitant areas of interest focus on participation of local people in the planning and implementation of projects, the inclusion of social analysis into development planning, and the consideration of gender issues in development project planning and policies (Bamberger 1988).

Several factors have provided impetus to the importance of community participation in development activities:

1. There has been some evidence in World Bank rural development and population/health projects of the positive impact of community participation on project efficiency.
2. State and national governments are finding it increasingly difficult to adequately manage the innumerable development projects and programs, thus paving the way for a more prominent role by nongovernmental and community organizations.
3. Nongovernmental organizations and several United Nations agencies, such as the UNICEF and ILO, have made it their development objective to *empower* the underprivileged populations by giving them greater control over resources and decisionmaking in projects and programs affecting their lives.

4. There has been a greater sensitivity to gender issues. The special needs and problems of women are being taken into account in project design and management (Bamberger 1988).

The problem in the Third World is not necessarily underdevelopment but, importantly, unequal development. There are oases of "First Worlds" within the Third World just as there are pockets of "Third Worlds" in First World countries. If individuals and local communities (rather than countries) are used as units of observation and analysis, areas of underdevelopment could probably be more accurately targeted regardless of the country in which they may be located.

*Environmental Sustainability.* The World Commission on Environment and Development has defined sustainable development as "meeting the needs and aspirations of the present generation without compromising the ability of future generations to meet their needs" (Brundtland 1989: 14). This idea of sustainable development will become an important conceptual and practical framework for all development activities in the 1990s and beyond. It puts forth the view that promotion of the environment and promotion of economic development are not separate issues. For a very long time, economic progress and growth were assigned the highest priority and the resulting environmental sacrifices were considered inconsequential (Williams 1989). However, with widespread development taking place, the environmental sacrifices are being questioned. The concerns include the destruction of rain forests; carbon emission of fossil fuels and the consequent warming of Earth's climate; land, water, and air pollution; damage to the ozone shield; and exploding world population and the consequent effects on the environment. There is a growing awareness that today's environmentally unsustainable practices may well inhibit future economic sustainability. To a great extent, the environmental approach has refocused the object of the sustainable development debate from economic outcomes to environmental outcomes.

## Free Market Capitalism

The failure of the socialistic experiment in the former Soviet Union and the East European countries has given new life to the free market concept. Since the late 1980s, "the market is not considered merely a technical device for the allocation of goods and services, but rather as the only possible way to regulate society" (Berthoud 1993). In the case of many developing countries, several factors, such as the balance of payments situation or the debt situation, have given them no choice but to restructure their economies and become a part of the global market economy. However, the concept of the free enterprise system is now unhooked from strictly economic roots: The free market system is now coupled with political ideals such as individual freedom, democracy, and human rights. Countries of the Third World are being advised (Berthoud 1993) that deregulating their markets is a sure path to development and the best available system for humankind. Whether this assertion is correct, only time will tell.

## Notes

1. For background see A. Hooqvelt, *Third World in Global Development* (Atlantic Highlands, NJ: Humanities, 1982); R. P. Misra, *Third World Peasantry: A Continuing Saga of Deprivation*, 2 vols. (New York: Apt Books, 1986); and Chandra T. Mohanty (ed.), *Third World Women and the Politics of Feminism* (Bloomington: Indiana University Press, 1991).

2. See Howard H. Frederick, *Global Communication and International Relations* (Belmont, CA: Wadsworth, 1993), 79; L. Wolf-Phillips, "Why Third World?" *Third World Quarterly* 1 (1979):105–114; and Alfred Sauvy, *General Theory of Population* (New York: Basic Books, 1970).

3. *Peking Review,* June 13, 1975, 9. See also L. C. Harris and R. L. Worden (eds.), *China and the Third World: Champion or Challenger* ? (Dover, MA: Auburn House, 1986).

4. Frederick, *Global Communication,* p. 120. See Francis Fukuyama, *The End of History and the Last Man* (New York: Free Press, 1992); and Timothy Burns (ed.), *After History: Francis Fukuyama and His Critics* (Savage, MD: Rowman and Littlefield, 1994).

5. For an analysis of the linguistic, cultural, and mythic aspects of the number "3" in human discourse, see Allen H. Merriam, "Words and Numbers: Mathematical Dimensions of Rhetoric," *Southern Communication Journal* 55 (summer 1990):337–354.

6. For background see D. R. Goyal, *Non-Alignment: Concepts and Concerns* (Columbia, MO: South Asia Books, 1986); and Odette Jankowitsch and Karl P. Sauvant (eds.), *Third World Without Superpowers: The Collected Documents of the Non-Aligned Countries*, 10 vols. (Dobbs Ferry, NY: Oceana, 1978).

7. Examples are Rabindranath Tagore, *Towards Universal Man* (New York: Asia Publishing House, 1961); D. Lawrence Kincaid (ed.), *Communication Theory: Eastern and Western Perspectives* (San Diego: Academic Press, 1987); and Young Yun Kim, "Intercultural Personhood: An Integration of Eastern and Western Perspectives," in *Intercultural Communication: A Reader,* Larry A. Samovar and Richard E. Porter (eds.), 7th ed. (Belmont, CA: Wadsworth, 1994), 415–425.

## References

*Baha'i World Faith.* (1976). Wilmette, IL: Baha'i Publishing Trust.

Bamberger, M. (1988). *The role of community participation in development planning and project management.* EDI Policy Seminar Report, No. 13. Washington, DC: World Bank.

Bellah, R. N. (ed.) (1965). *Religion and progress in modern Asia.* New York: Free Press.

Berger, P. L. (1976). *Pyramids of sacrifice.* New York: Anchor Books.

Berthoud, G. (1993). Market. In W. Sachs (ed.), *The development dictionary* (pp. 70–87). Atlantic Highlands: NJ: Zed Books.

*Blade.* (1990). Rescuing our planet. Editorial, February 25, E4.

*Books in print 1992–93.* (1992). Volume 8, "Titles R–Z." New Providence, NJ: R. R. Bowker.

Brookfield, H. (1975). *Interdependent development.* Pittsburgh, PA: University of Pittsburgh Press.

Brundtland, G. H. (1989). Sustainable development: An overview. *Development* 2 (3), 13–14.

Chu, G. C. (1987). Development communication in the year 2000. In N. Jayaweera and S. Amunugama (eds.), *Rethinking development communication* (pp. 95–107). Singapore: Asian Mass Communication Research and Information Center.

Clegern, W. M. (1978). *What is the Third World?* Paper presented to the Second National Third World Conference, Omaha, Nebraska, October 1978.

Daniels, W. M. (1951). *The Point Four program.* New York: H. W. Wilson.

Eisenstadt, S. N. (1976). The changing vision of modernization and development. In W. Schramm and D. Lerner (eds.), *Communication and change: The last ten years and the next* (pp. 31–44). Honolulu: East-West Center, University Press of Hawaii.

Fersh, S. (1974). *Learning about peoples and cultures.* Evanston, IL: McDougal & Little.

Frank, A. G. (1969). *Latin America: Underdevelopment or revolution?* New York: Monthly Review Press.

Freire, P. (1971). *Education for critical consciousness.* New York: Continuum.

Frey, F. W. (1966). *The mass media and rural development in Turkey.* Rural Development Research Report 3. Cambridge: Massachusetts Institute of Technology, Center for International Studies.

Goldthorpe, J. E. (1975). *The sociology of the Third World.* London: Cambridge University Press.

Goulet, D. (1971). *The cruel choice: A new concept in theory of development.* New York: Atheneum.

_____ . (1973). Development or liberation? In C. Wilber (ed.), *The political economy of development and underdevelopment.* New York: Random House.

Gyan-Apenteng, K. (1988). Refrigerators in China: Third World reflects on civilization vs. nature. *The Blade,* December 25, 25.

Harrison, L. E. (1985*). Underdevelopment is a state of mind: The Latin American case.* Lanham, MD: University Press of America.

Harrison, P. (1979). *Inside the Third World.* New York: Penguin Books.

Hedebro, G. (1982). *Communication and social change in developing nations: A critical view.* Ames: Iowa State University Press.

Hobsbawn, E. J. (1968). *Industry and empire: An economic history of Britain since 1750.* London: Weidenfeld and Nicolson.

Inkeles, A. (1969). Making men modern: On the causes and consequences of individual change in six countries. *American Journal of Sociology 75* (September): 208–225.

Inkeles, A., and D. H. Smith. (1974). *Becoming modern: Individual change in six developing countries*. Cambridge: Harvard University Press.

Lerner, D. (1958). *The passing of traditional society: Modernizing the Middle East*. New York: Free Press.

Linton, R. (1936). *The study of man*. New York: Appleton-Century-Crofts.

*Mao's theory of the differentiation of the three worlds is a major contribution to Marxism-Leninism*. (1977). Beijing: Foreign Languages Press.

McClelland, D. C. (1967). *The achieving society*. New York: Free Press.

Neurath, P. (1962). Radio farm forum as a tool of change in Indian villages. *Economic Development and Cultural Change* 10: 275–283.

Nyerere, J. K. (1970). All mankind is one. In M. H. Prosser, II (ed.), *Sow the wind, reap the whirlwind: Heads of state address the United Nations*. New York: Morrow.

Oakely, P., and D. Marsden. (1984). *Approaches to participation in rural development*. Geneva: International Labour Office.

Parsons, T. (1964a). *The social system*. New York: Free Press.

_____. (1964b). Evolutionary universals in society. *American Sociological Review* 29 (3): 339–356.

Portes, A. (1976). On the sociology of national development: Theories and issues. *American Journal of Sociology* 82 (1): 55–85.

Rao, Y. V. L. (1963). *Communication and development: A study of two Indian villages*. Doctoral dissertation, University of Minnesota.

Rogers, E. M. (1965). Mass media exposure and modernization among Colombian peasants. *Public Opinion Quarterly* 29: 614–625.

_____. (1969). *Modernization among peasants*. New York: Holt, Rinehart and Winston.

_____. (1976b). Where are we in understanding the diffusion of innovations? In W. Schramm and D. Lerner (eds.), *Communication and change: The last ten years and the next* (pp. 204–222). Honolulu: East-West Center, University Press of Hawaii.

_____. (1976b). Communication and development: The passing of the dominant paradigm. In E. M. Rogers (ed.), *Communication and development: Critical perspectives*. Beverly Hills, CA: Sage Publications.

_____. (1976c). The passing of the dominant paradigm: Reflections on diffusion research. In W. Schramm and D. Lerner (eds.), *Communication and change: The last ten years and the next* (pp. 49–52). Honolulu: East-West Center, University Press of Hawaii.

Rosan, L. J. (1962). Are comparisons between East and West fruitful for comparative philosophy? *Philosophy East and West* 11: 239–243.

Rose, A. M. (1970). Sociological factors affecting economic development in India. In M. Palmer (ed.), *The human factor in political development*. Waltham, MA: Ginn.

Rostow, W. W. (1960). *The stages of economic growth: A non-communist manifesto*. Cambridge, England: Cambridge University Press.

Safire, W. (1978). *Safire's political dictionary: The new language of politics*. New York: Random House.

Schramm, W. (1964). *Mass media and national development*. Stanford: Stanford University Press.

Schumacher, E. F. (1973). *Small is beautiful*. New York: Harper and Row.

Singer, M. (1972). *When a great tradition modernizes: An anthropological approach to Indian civilization*. New York: Praeger.

Srinivas, M. N. (1973). Comments on Milton Singer's industrial leadership, the Hindu ethic, and the spirit of socialism. In M. Singer (ed.), *Entrepreneurship and modernization of occupational cultures in South Asia* (pp. 279–286), Monograph No. 12. Durham, NC: Duke University Program in Comparative Studies on South Asia.

Streeten, P. (1979). Development ideas in historical perspective. In K. Q. Hill (ed.), *Toward a new strategy for development* (pp. 21–52). New York: Pergamon Press.

Van Soet, J. (1978). *The start of international development cooperation in the United Nations, 1945–1952*. Assen, The Netherlands: Van Gorcum Press.

Wang, G., and W. Dissanayake. (1984). Culture, development, and change: Some explorative observations. In G. Wang and W. Dissanayake (eds.), *Continuity and change in communication systems* (pp. 3–20). Norwood, NJ: Ablex Publishers.

Weaver, J. H., and K. Jameson. (1978). *Economic development: Competing paradigms, competing parables*. Washington, DC: Development Studies Program, Agency for International Development.

Weber, M. (1964). *The sociology of religion*. Boston: Beacon Press.

Williams, E. (1964). *Capitalism and slavery*. London: Russell.

Williams, M. (1989). Sustainable development: An SID perspective. *Development* 2 (3): 7–9.

# 2 Indexes and Trends in Socioeconomic Development

## Alfonso Gonzalez

### The Measurement of Socioeconomic Development

One of the most interesting and controversial problems in dealing with development is how to assess the level of development attained by individual countries; an associated problem is the assessment of comparative changes or progress among countries through time. The most popular method, among the many that have been proposed or used, is classification based on gross national (or domestic) product per capita. In addition, the Human Development Index (HDI) has attracted some recent attention.

The GNP is the most common method used to classify countries on a socioeconomic basis. This statistic has been utilized and popularized notably by the World Bank (*World Bank Atlas* and *World Development Report*, various years). Although the classification of countries by the World Bank has undergone some modification through time, the 1996 categorization consists of the following (based on GNP per capita):

1. low-income economies (<$750)
2. middle-income economies ($770+)
   A. lower middle-income ($770–2820)
   B. upper middle-income ($2970–8260)
3. high-income economies ($9320+)

In earlier editions the income figures were generally lower but several other categories were then included:

high-income oil exporters
industrial market economies
nonreporting nonmember economies (most of the Communist bloc)

The classification categories are based, as they have been in earlier versions, essentially on income (actually per capita GNP) and, formerly, the structure of the economy. There has been a recent modification of this index with the addition of Purchasing Power Parities (PPP). This is an attempt to compare internationally the GNP/GDP per capita based on the purchasing power (based on US$) in each country (data for many countries are still not available). The rankings of countries does vary somewhat using the PPP in comparison with the GNP per capita (Table 2.1).

In the recent past some other measures of development were devised and some attained a limited, but temporary, degree of acceptance and popularity. The Physical Quality of Life Index (PQLI) was devised by Morris David Morris and the Overseas Development Council to measure the level of living on a scale of 0 to 100 and consists of a composite of three components: infant mortality, life expectancy at age 1, and literacy (Morris 1979). This measure attained some degree of acceptance and was used by some for a time, but it is now rarely encountered.

Another measure was the Index of Social Progress (ISP) developed by Richard J. Estes (Estes 1984). The ISP consists of eleven subindexes containing a total of forty-four social, economic, physical, and political components. The subindexes include education, health, women, defense, economic, demographic, geographic, political stability, political participation, cultural diversity, and welfare effort components. This index, therefore, is considerably more complex than the GNP per capita or the PQLI.

Another noteworthy index appeared in the 1980s. The (International) Human Suffering Index (HSI) was devised in 1987 by the Population Crisis Committee. There are ten components in this index: GNP per capita, rate of inflation, growth of the labor force and of the urban population, infant mortality, food calories, drinking water, energy consumption per capita, literacy, and freedom. In contrast to all the other indexes discussed herein, the *lower* the score in the HSI the greater the degree of development or the higher the level of living, that is, the lower the human suffering. The index received some attention but only for a limited period of time was it significantly in use.

With the exception of GNP per capita, these indexes are now rarely used, in part, because most are not revised annually. In 1990 the United Nations Development Programme devised a new index, the Human Development Index (HDI), that comprises life expectancy at birth, adult literacy, mean years of schooling, and GNP per capita based on real purchasing power (PPP)(UNDP 1996). This index has been revised and updated annually since 1990.

TABLE 2.1    Indexes of Development

| | GNP/cap 1994 | PPP ($) 1994 | HDI 1993 | SEDI 1994 |
|---|---|---|---|---|
| Mexico | 4095 | 7045 | 0.845 | 55.7 |
| Guatemala | 1195 | 3465 | 0.580 | 39.6 |
| Salvador | 1420 | 2460 | 0.576 | 47.2 |
| Honduras | 590 | 1920 | 0.576 | 41.9 |
| Nicaragua | 335 | 1825 | 0.568 | 40.4 |
| Costa Rica | 2390 | 5760 | 0.884 | 58.4 |
| Panama | 2625 | 5905 | 0.859 | 53.9 |
| Cuba | 1170 | 2000 | 0.726 | 55.2 |
| Dominican Rep. | 1325 | 3775 | 0.701 | 43.4 |
| Haiti | 225 | 930 | 0.359 | 28.6 |
| Puerto Rico | 7020 | – | – | 62.1 |
| Jamaica | 1480 | 3185 | 0.702 | 49.9 |
| Trinidad/Tobago | 3740 | 8555 | 0.872 | 53.8 |
| Venezuela | 2760 | 7830 | 0.859 | 55.1 |
| Colombia | 1645 | 5650 | 0.840 | 51.2 |
| Ecuador | 1295 | 4285 | 0.764 | 48.7 |
| Peru | 2000 | 3650 | 0.694 | 45.6 |
| Bolivia | 770 | 2460 | 0.584 | 40.9 |
| Paraguay | 1575 | 3545 | 0.704 | 49.6 |
| Chile | 3540 | 8975 | 0.882 | 57.3 |
| Argentina | 8075 | 8820 | 0.885 | 64.6 |
| Uruguay | 4655 | 7280 | 0.883 | 59.5 |
| Brasil | 3170 | 5515 | 0.796 | 46.9 |
| Morocco | 1145 | 3455 | 0.534 | 43.2 |
| Algeria | 1670 | 5330 | 0.746 | 45.2 |
| Tunisia | 1795 | 4990 | 0.727 | 50.6 |
| Libya | 5310 | 7000 | 0.792 | 50.4 |
| Egypt | 715 | 3765 | 0.611 | 45.3 |
| Sudan | 620 | 1162 | 0.359 | 32.3 |
| Syria | 1160 | 5220 | 0.690 | 49.8 |
| Lebanon | 2150 | 2500 | 0.664 | 60.5 |
| Jordan | 1415 | 4195 | 0.741 | 53.7 |
| Iraq | 1500 | 3500 | 0.599 | 37.7 |
| Kuwait | 19230 | 24615 | 0.836 | 64.8 |
| Saudi Arabia | 7145 | 9480 | 0.771 | 52.8 |
| United Arab Emirates | 21420 | 23390 | 0.864 | 70.1 |
| Oman | 5170 | 8870 | 0.716 | 40.5 |
| Yemen | 280 | 1374 | 0.366 | 30.0 |

(*continues*)

TABLE 2.1 *(continued)*

|  | GNP/cap 1994 | PPP ($) 1994 | HDI 1993 | SEDI 1994 |
|---|---|---|---|---|
| Turkey | 2475 | 4660 | 0.711 | 55.2 |
| Iran | 2200 | 4650 | 0.754 | 46.0 |
| Afghanistan | 280 | 700 | 0.229 | 21.0 |
| Georgia | 580 | 1160 | 0.645 | 54.0 |
| Armenia | 675 | 2165 | 0.680 | 55.3 |
| Azerbaijan | 500 | 1720 | 0.740 | 51.5 |
| Kazakhstan | 1135 | 2820 | 0.665 | 48.8 |
| Uzbekistan | 955 | 2380 | 0.679 | 51.2 |
| Kyrgyzstan | 620 | 1720 | 0.663 | 47.8 |
| Turkmenistan | 1230 | 3540 | 0.695 | 43.5 |
| Tajikistan | 355 | 1065 | 0.616 | 45.6 |
| India | 315 | 1285 | 0.436 | 34.2 |
| Pakistan | 435 | 2170 | 0.442 | 30.3 |
| Bangladesh | 225 | 1340 | 0.365 | 27.8 |
| Nepal | 200 | 1155 | 0.332 | 25.7 |
| Sri Lanka | 640 | 3155 | 0.698 | 47.4 |
| Myanmar | 220 | 650 | 0.451 | 43.4 |
| Thailand | 2310 | 6920 | 0.832 | 50.5 |
| Vietnam | 195 | 1040 | 0.523 | 43.4 |
| Cambodia | 200 | 1250 | 0.325 | 25.3 |
| Laos | 320 | 1760 | 0.400 | 30.4 |
| Malaysia | 3500 | 8525 | 0.826 | 53.3 |
| Singapore | 22930 | 21665 | 0.881 | 76.7 |
| Indonesia | 880 | 3645 | 0.641 | 43.1 |
| Philippines | 955 | 2770 | 0.665 | 49.3 |
| China | 530 | 2510 | 0.609 | 45.9 |
| Hong Kong | 21650 | 23080 | 0.909 | 73.4 |
| Taiwan | 10850 | – | – | 68.4 |
| Korea, South | 8240 | 10435 | 0.886 | 69.3 |
| Korea, North | 970 | 1750 | 0.714 | 54.9 |
| Mongolia | 320 | 2020 | 0.578 | 42.1 |
| Papua-New Guinea | 1200 | 2555 | 0.504 | 37.9 |
| Mauritania | 480 | 1570 | 0.353 | 32.0 |
| Mali | 250 | 520 | 0.223 | 26.2 |
| Burkina Faso | 300 | 785 | 0.225 | 26.5 |
| Niger | 230 | 785 | 0.204 | 23.8 |
| Chad | 185 | 730 | 0.291 | 27.4 |

*(continues)*

TABLE 2.1   (*continued*)

| | GNP/cap 1994 | PPP ($) 1994 | HDI 1993 | SEDI 1994 |
|---|---|---|---|---|
| Senegal | 605 | 1620 | 0.331 | 31.5 |
| Guinea | 515 | 500 | 0.306 | 25.9 |
| Ivory Coast | 560 | 1355 | 0.357 | 29.5 |
| Ghana | 420 | 2035 | 0.467 | 34.5 |
| Nigeria | 280 | 1310 | 0.400 | 30.4 |
| Cameroon | 680 | 1960 | 0.481 | 34.3 |
| Ethiopia | 115 | 420 | 0.237 | 23.7 |
| Somalia | 150 | 759 | 0.221 | 21.2 |
| Kenya | 255 | 1330 | 0.473 | 36.1 |
| Uganda | 195 | 1175 | 0.326 | 28.3 |
| Tanzania | 140 | 620 | 0.364 | 29.7 |
| Zaire | 230 | 469 | 0.371 | 28.5 |
| Rwanda | 80 | 330 | 0.332 | 26.3 |
| Burundi | 155 | 640 | 0.282 | 26.1 |
| Malawi | 155 | 625 | 0.321 | 26.4 |
| Zambia | 350 | 930 | 0.411 | 30.3 |
| Zimbabwe | 495 | 2040 | 0.534 | 40.3 |
| Angola | 700 | 1000 | 0.283 | 26.2 |
| Mozambique | 85 | 705 | 0.261 | 21.6 |
| Botswana | 2800 | 5265 | 0.741 | 44.3 |
| South Africa | 3025 | 5130 | 0.649 | 48.5 |
| Madagascar | 215 | 655 | 0.349 | 33.8 |
| Ireland | 13580 | 14050 | 0.892 | 76.6 |
| Spain | 13360 | 13890 | 0.888 | 75.2 |
| Portugal | 9345 | 12185 | 0.838 | 68.8 |
| Greece | 7705 | 11165 | 0.874 | 70.8 |
| Israel | 14470 | 15495 | 0.908 | 71.4 |
| Poland | 2440 | 5430 | 0.815 | 61.6 |
| Czech Republic | 3205 | 8405 | 0.872 | 60.4 |
| Hungary | 3840 | 6195 | 0.863 | 61.4 |
| Bulgaria | 1205 | 4305 | 0.815 | 57.3 |
| Romania | 1250 | 3505 | 0.729 | 55.6 |
| Yugoslavia | 1000 | – | – | 59.2 |
| Albania | 370 | 3500 | 0.714 | 48.7 |
| Canada | 19510 | 20640 | 0.932 | 82.8 |
| U.S.A. | 25870 | 25870 | 0.925 | 87.9 |

(continues)

TABLE 2.1    (*continued*)

|  | GNP/cap 1994 | PPP ($) 1994 | HDI 1993 | SEDI 1994 |
|---|---|---|---|---|
| **MEAN:** | | | | |
| LATIN AMERICA | 2482 | 10371 | 0.826 | 58.0 |
| MIDDLE EAST | 3136 | 3691 | 0.687 | 48.0 |
| ORIENT | 3794 | 1776 | 0.508 | 39.1 |
| SUB-SAHARAN AFRICA | 215 | 939 | 0.342 | 29.2 |
| | | | | |
| LD WESTERN EUROPE | 10998 | 12823 | 0.873 | 72.8 |
| EASTERN EUROPE | 1901 | 5223 | 0.820 | 57.8 |
| | | | | |
| **MEDIAN:** | | | | |
| LATIN AMERICA | 1645 | 4285 | 0.764 | 49.9 |
| MIDDLE EAST | 1195 | 3520 | 0.685 | 49.3 |
| ORIENT | 585 | 2340 | 0.625 | 44.7 |
| SUB-SAHARAN AFRICA | 255 | 785 | 0.332 | 28.5 |
| | | | | |
| LD WESTERN EUROPE | 11353 | 13038 | 0.881 | 73.0 |
| EASTERN EUROPE | 1250 | 4868 | 0.815 | 59.2 |

Data for years indicated or for closest year available.

GNP/cap: based on *World Bank Atlas 1996, World Development Report 1996,* and *Britannica Book of the Year 1996.*

PPP: (Purchasing Power Parity) from *World Bank Atlas 1996* and *World Development Report 1996.*

HDI: (Human Development Index) based on *Human Development Report 1996,* 1994, 1993. Puerto Rico and Taiwan are not included in the Human Development Index. SEDI: (Socio-Economic Development Index) based on GNP/cap, diet, health and education components.

In my view, these measures are useful but contain inherent shortcomings, and country rankings by these indexes may not conform to the world reality (discussed later in the Summary and Conclusions). The World Bank classification relies solely on per capita GNP. This particular measure has received considerable criticism. The use of PPP may partly answer only some of the criticisms leveled at the GNP per capita.

The PQLI uses three components, one of which, life expectancy at age 1, is not readily available for country or historical comparisons. That component with another, infant mortality, measure the same factor: general health conditions. The third component, literacy, although commonly used, is probably not the best for indicating educational attainment. The net result is that when countries are ranked according to the PQLI (or according to the GNP alone), there may be too many disparities, and the rankings may not reflect real or comparative levels of development. The recent HDI follows the PQLI fairly closely, although it is somewhat more complex.

## The Socio-Economic Development Index

In order to ascertain the level of socioeconomic development, or the level of living, I have felt the need to devise a comparative index (Gonzalez 1982). The components of the index were selected on the basis of their importance, their simplicity, the widespread availability of the data, and on the needs to avoid a special cultural bias, to measure performance (rather than inputs, effort, or priorities), to present a minimum of liability, to be capable of being used for historical comparisons (both relatively and absolutely), and to reflect the reality that the index is attempting to measure. The index that I have been using relies on four basic factors—income, diet, health, and education—that I feel are fundamental in development or in the level of living.[1]

Virtually all societies endeavor to improve or to increase all of these basic factors. There are proponents of a "no-growth" economy but these hardly reflect a significant or influential segment of any society. Some traditional societies may not emphasize income expansion, but such a view is not politically dominant anywhere, nor will policies based on it produce the resources to provide significant and rapid improvement in living conditions.

It can be assumed that improved diet and health are universal aspirations of all societies. The degree of education that is thought to be desirable varies among societies, but such desires may fall far short of what is required for an industrialized and technically advanced society. Since there is a universal desire for improvement in living conditions, I feel that the four factors cited best measure the degree of accomplishment and change through time ("development").[2]

*Income*

Income is based on per capita GNP. This statistic in the post–World War II period has become increasingly available. However, the use of the GNP as an indicator of income or development has often been criticized because of inaccuracy and incompleteness of coverage (notably in the underdeveloped world). Although improvements have been made in correcting these deficiencies, objections continue. The criticisms are most often directed at the compilation of the GNP in the underdeveloped world, but omissions are generally of a minor order and do not greatly influence the overall per capita GNP for most countries. The local and subsistence producers who are sometimes omitted are of low productivity and of small volume, and they are insignificant in the national economies, contributing little, if anything, to the national welfare. A compensating factor is that population may also be underenumerated in these sectors so that the per capita GNP is probably little affected by these omissions. Further objections are raised with regard to the GNP as a measure of development. It is not an indicator of social conditions, but it is the best available measure of income. A larger per capita GNP does not indicate that more funds are available for social welfare; how that income is used, and how effectively, varies considerably among countries.

## Diet

Diet is measured as a composite of kilocalories (kcal) and protein (grams) per capita daily consumption. These are clearly the best measures of nutrition for a country. Mean figures are used for countries, and the criticism can be leveled that these mask a large proportion (especially in the underdeveloped world) of the population that consumes far less than the national average. This criticism is valid for this factor as well as for the other factors in this index—and just about everything in life. One assumption is fairly safe: All economic and social indicators of development must allow for a relatively small proportion of the population that is significantly *above* the national average and for a large mass that is *below* it.

Generally about 2,200 to 2,400 kcal and 60 grams (of protein) constitute minimal levels of daily consumption for a population. The minimum national daily requirements vary according to the age composition and the general body build of the population and according to the climate. Underdeveloped countries might require somewhat less food per capita, but high-income sectors of those societies consume about as much as in the industrial countries. However, there are maximum limits of food consumption, and these are probably being approached in the advanced world. There we can now observe various restrictions on caloric intake among an increasing share of the population. More may not be better when the national average exceeds about 3,000 kcal, but I prefer the society to set the limits (despite increasing evidence) rather than to establish my own maximum limit in the index. Certainly not all aspects of development can be considered as improvements.

There is, of course, a lower limit as well in food consumption. Undernutrition (with concomitant labor inefficiency) and eventually hunger and starvation result.

## Health

Health is represented by a composite of the infant mortality rate and life expectancy at birth. These indicators, like those for diet, are now generally available and constitute the best available evidence of general health and medical conditions.

## Education

Education is measured as a composite of literacy and the proportion of the population enrolled in higher (third-level) education. Literacy is used widely as an indicator of educational attainment but has an important shortcoming in that its definition can vary significantly and constitutes only a first step in educational achievement for development. The proportion of the population in higher education may be questioned on the basis that many underdeveloped countries place greater emphasis on eradicating literacy than on rapidly expanding higher-educational facilities. This is of course true; however, developed societies require technology and a higher order of learning. Furthermore, the index does not measure priorities but attainment, and I have no doubt that technical training, research, and development are major ingredients in the present and future development of societies.

The major country with the highest level of attainment in each of the above components (or subcomponents) is given an index of 100, and all the others are given a figure based on the proportion of their individual performance as measured against the leader.[3]

## The Index Overall

The overall index is the mean of the four basic factors; that is, all four factors are given equal weight in determining the total overall index of socioeconomic development. It would be very difficult and subjective (depending on your own value judgments) to decide which of the components—income (expressed as per capita GNP), diet, health, education—is relatively more important in development than the others.

The significant countries of the Third World were selected on the basis of their total population and GNP. In total, eighty-nine countries were chosen, slightly less than two-thirds of the Third World's sovereign countries (although two nonsovereign political entities, Puerto Rico and Hong Kong, are included among the countries) (see Table 2.2).[4] These countries account for virtually all (except for 3 percent) of the Third World's total population and GNP. The countries of southern and eastern Europe are also included in the tables because they constitute the lower portion of the advanced industrial countries. The eight Asian republics of the former Soviet Union are included since data only from about 1990 are now available and these republics would be considered within the Third World.

## Components of the Socio-Economic Development Index

The four components that compose the overall total index each have equal weight. However, the components do have different effects on the overall

TABLE 2.2　Socio-Economic Development Index

| | TOTAL | | | | | | CHANGE |
|---|---|---|---|---|---|---|---|
| | 1960 | 1970 | 1980 | 1985 | 1990 | 1994 | 1960–1994 |
| Mexico | 42.1 | 49.2 | 53.9 | 54.6 | 54.5 | 55.7 | 13.5 |
| Guatemala | 30.9 | 34.4 | 37.0 | 38.4 | 38.8 | 39.6 | 8.6 |
| Salvador | 35.8 | 38.1 | 42.6 | 35.6 | 43.6 | 47.2 | 11.4 |
| Honduras | 29.5 | 32.0 | 34.5 | 38.6 | 40.4 | 41.9 | 12.4 |
| Nicaragua | 33.7 | 37.6 | 37.7 | 44.4 | 43.1 | 40.4 | 6.7 |
| Costa Rica | 44.3 | 50.5 | 57.1 | 57.8 | 57.4 | 58.4 | 14.1 |
| Panama | 46.6 | 49.1 | 52.4 | 55.5 | 52.4 | 53.9 | 7.3 |
| Cuba | 51.3 | 54.0 | 58.9 | 62.5 | 58.8 | 55.2 | 4.0 |
| Dominican Republic | 34.5 | 35.1 | 40.6 | 43.2 | 42.9 | 43.4 | 8.9 |
| Haiti | 24.5 | 23.4 | 25.1 | 26.0 | 27.2 | 28.6 | 4.1 |
| Puerto Rico | 58.7 | 65.6 | 64.0 | 68.2 | 62.0 | 62.1 | 3.4 |
| Jamaica | 49.2 | 54.5 | 53.3 | 51.4 | 52.8 | 49.9 | 0.7 |
| Trinidad/Tobago | 53.5 | 53.9 | 61.6 | 63.2 | 52.7 | 53.8 | 0.3 |
| Venezuela | 43.8 | 52.0 | 56.7 | 56.1 | 53.2 | 55.1 | 11.3 |
| Colombia | 36.4 | 39.5 | 45.2 | 47.9 | 49.1 | 51.2 | 14.7 |
| Ecuador | 35.0 | 39.8 | 45.8 | 45.7 | 45.7 | 48.7 | 13.7 |
| Peru | 36.9 | 40.1 | 40.1 | 41.4 | 42.4 | 45.6 | 8.7 |
| Bolivia | 28.5 | 30.1 | 33.7 | 36.4 | 37.0 | 40.9 | 12.4 |
| Paraguay | 42.3 | 44.1 | 50.1 | 50.1 | 49.0 | 49.6 | 7.3 |
| Chile | 45.7 | 50.6 | 54.4 | 54.9 | 54.9 | 57.3 | 11.6 |
| Argentina | 64.8 | 63.1 | 61.3 | 62.9 | 60.2 | 64.6 | −0.3 |
| Uruguay | 61.0 | 60.5 | 58.2 | 58.9 | 57.1 | 59.5 | −1.5 |
| Brasil | 37.1 | 39.8 | 45.3 | 45.4 | 46.4 | 46.9 | 9.9 |
| Morocco | 27.4 | 29.8 | 33.0 | 36.3 | 38.8 | 43.2 | 15.8 |
| Algeria | 24.4 | 27.0 | 35.3 | 40.4 | 41.2 | 45.2 | 20.7 |
| Tunisia | 27.6 | 30.8 | 39.6 | 42.0 | 45.3 | 50.6 | 23.0 |
| Libya | 25.2 | 39.1 | 55.7 | 53.1 | 46.3 | 50.4 | 25.3 |
| Egypt | 32.2 | 34.9 | 39.1 | 40.9 | 41.9 | 45.3 | 13.1 |
| Sudan | 24.0 | 26.4 | 27.9 | 26.8 | 25.0 | 32.3 | 8.2 |
| Syria | 33.5 | 34.4 | 48.1 | 48.4 | 47.6 | 49.8 | 16.3 |
| Lebanon | 44.7 | 51.2 | 54.7 | 51.9 | 52.4 | 60.5 | 15.8 |
| Jordan | 30.1 | 32.6 | 44.4 | 46.6 | 49.7 | 53.7 | 23.6 |
| Iraq | 28.2 | 31.8 | 40.4 | 40.2 | 40.9 | 37.7 | 9.5 |
| Kuwait | 69.0 | 65.3 | 75.1 | 75.9 | 62.6 | 64.8 | −4.1 |
| Saudi Arabia | 23.6 | 25.1 | 51.1 | 53.0 | 43.3 | 52.8 | 29.2 |
| United Arab Emirates | 43.0 | 52.4 | 72.4 | 75.8 | 69.0 | 70.1 | 27.1 |
| Oman | 16.4 | 21.4 | 29.6 | 34.3 | 39.4 | 40.5 | 24.1 |
| Yemen | 23.3 | 22.1 | 22.7 | 26.8 | 23.3 | 30.0 | 6.7 |
| Turkey | 37.0 | 42.0 | 43.5 | 43.8 | 50.4 | 55.2 | 18.2 |
| Iran | 26.4 | 30.4 | 37.0 | 41.5 | 36.6 | 46.0 | 19.5 |
| Afghanistan | 23.6 | 23.4 | 24.4 | 22.7 | 19.8 | 21.0 | −2.5 |

(*continues*)

TABLE 2.2 (*continued*)

| | TOTAL | | | | | | CHANGE |
|---|---|---|---|---|---|---|---|
| | *1960* | *1970* | *1980* | *1985* | *1990* | *1994* | *1960–1994* |
| Georgia | | | | | 52.4 | 54.0 | |
| Armenia | | | | | 54.0 | 55.3 | |
| Azerbaijan | | | | | 48.4 | 48.8 | |
| Kazakhstan | | | | | 51.3 | 51.5 | |
| Uzbekistan | | | | | 46.1 | 51.2 | |
| Kyrgyzstan | | | | | 49.5 | 47.8 | |
| Turkmenistan | | | | | 38.8 | 43.5 | |
| Tajikistan | | | | | 42.5 | 45.6 | |
| India | 26.9 | 28.7 | 26.8 | 29.7 | 29.6 | 34.2 | 7.3 |
| Pakistan | 24.4 | 26.5 | 25.9 | 27.3 | 27.2 | 30.3 | 5.9 |
| Bangladesh | 24.0 | 24.5 | 23.5 | 24.6 | 23.7 | 27.8 | 3.7 |
| Nepal | 22.0 | 22.8 | 22.6 | 25.8 | 25.2 | 25.7 | 3.7 |
| Sri Lanka | 39.3 | 43.5 | 44.2 | 46.3 | 45.8 | 47.4 | 8.1 |
| Myanmar | 29.2 | 31.1 | 33.6 | 35.4 | 39.4 | 43.4 | 14.2 |
| Thailand | 33.5 | 39.7 | 44.6 | 45.9 | 48.7 | 50.5 | 17.0 |
| Vietnam | 23.7 | 31.2 | 33.3 | 41.9 | 41.3 | 43.4 | 19.8 |
| Cambodia | 28.4 | 31.5 | 25.9 | 26.6 | 26.2 | 25.3 | –3.1 |
| Laos | 25.2 | 25.4 | 29.3 | 32.3 | 34.3 | 30.4 | 5.1 |
| Malaysia | 38.1 | 36.8 | 46.3 | 48.9 | 48.8 | 53.3 | 15.2 |
| Singapore | 50.5 | 58.7 | 63.9 | 66.3 | 66.0 | 76.7 | 26.2 |
| Indonesia | 24.5 | 30.2 | 33.2 | 36.9 | 40.7 | 43.1 | 18.7 |
| Philippines | 38.6 | 41.7 | 46.1 | 47.7 | 48.5 | 49.3 | 10.7 |
| China | 25.6 | 38.0 | 41.9 | 41.4 | 44.4 | 45.9 | 20.4 |
| Hong Kong | 51.7 | 59.0 | 63.9 | 65.7 | 67.7 | 73.4 | 21.8 |
| Taiwan | 53.6 | 57.3 | 58.7 | 62.4 | 64.5 | 68.4 | 14.8 |
| Korea, South | 39.5 | 49.2 | 57.2 | 60.4 | 64.9 | 69.3 | 29.8 |
| Korea, North | 38.7 | 50.5 | 52.3 | 55.5 | 56.8 | 54.9 | 16.2 |
| Mongolia | 46.6 | 48.5 | 51.9 | 53.2 | 45.3 | 42.1 | –4.5 |
| Papua-New Guinea | 25.2 | 27.7 | 29.4 | 31.4 | 36.0 | 37.9 | 12.7 |
| Mauritania | 27.3 | 24.7 | 27.7 | 29.1 | 29.8 | 32.0 | 4.8 |
| Mali | 23.9 | 23.8 | 21.2 | 22.4 | 25.7 | 26.2 | 2.3 |
| Burkina Faso | 22.3 | 20.5 | 20.1 | 23.5 | 24.4 | 26.5 | 4.2 |
| Niger | 22.8 | 21.7 | 24.1 | 24.7 | 23.1 | 23.8 | 1.0 |
| Chad | 26.5 | 24.5 | 23.4 | 22.3 | 23.1 | 27.4 | 0.8 |
| Senegal | 26.7 | 29.4 | 26.2 | 27.3 | 31.3 | 31.5 | 4.9 |
| Guinea | 23.0 | 22.0 | 24.6 | 21.7 | 24.3 | 25.9 | 2.9 |
| Ivory Coast | 23.0 | 27.6 | 31.1 | 30.1 | 28.5 | 29.5 | 6.5 |
| Ghana | 27.1 | 26.9 | 25.0 | 27.5 | 28.2 | 34.5 | 7.4 |
| Nigeria | 24.4 | 26.8 | 26.2 | 27.6 | 25.5 | 30.4 | 6.0 |
| Cameroon | 27.8 | 25.4 | 30.7 | 27.9 | 30.9 | 34.3 | 6.4 |
| Ethiopia | 24.2 | 21.2 | 22.4 | 20.9 | 19.6 | 23.7 | –0.5 |
| Somalia | 20.7 | 22.4 | 21.3 | 23.5 | 23.4 | 21.2 | 0.5 |
| Kenya | 27.1 | 29.1 | 31.7 | 34.0 | 32.6 | 36.1 | 9.0 |
| Uganda | 26.8 | 27.2 | 29.0 | 29.6 | 27.3 | 28.3 | 1.5 |
| Tanzania | 23.0 | 22.3 | 33.5 | 33.4 | 32.2 | 29.7 | 6.8 |

(*continues*)

TABLE 2.2   (continued)

| | TOTAL | | | | | | CHANGE |
|---|---|---|---|---|---|---|---|
| | 1960 | 1970 | 1980 | 1985 | 1990 | 1994 | 1960–1994 |
| Zaire | 24.6 | 23.5 | 26.6 | 27.9 | 26.4 | 28.5 | 4.0 |
| Rwanda | 24.6 | 23.5 | 27.8 | 26.3 | 26.4 | 26.3 | 1.7 |
| Burundi | 25.8 | 25.1 | 25.8 | 28.5 | 27.8 | 26.1 | 0.3 |
| Malawi | 28.2 | 27.9 | 27.6 | 28.6 | 25.6 | 26.4 | −1.8 |
| Zambia | 31.9 | 30.8 | 29.4 | 34.9 | 32.5 | 30.3 | −1.5 |
| Zimbabwe | 31.7 | 29.6 | 37.7 | 36.5 | 39.4 | 40.3 | 8.6 |
| Angola | 20.3 | 22.6 | 23.2 | 27.6 | 23.3 | 26.2 | 5.9 |
| Mozambique | 22.1 | 21.7 | 23.3 | 21.3 | 20.4 | 21.6 | −0.5 |
| Botswana | 45.3 | 34.3 | 32.4 | 39.4 | 45.6 | 44.3 | −1.0 |
| South Africa | 41.4 | 39.4 | 41.9 | 46.2 | 47.0 | 48.5 | 7.0 |
| Madagascar | 28.2 | 29.8 | 34.2 | 36.9 | 30.0 | 33.8 | 5.6 |
| Ireland | 69.1 | 71.0 | 72.2 | 71.4 | 74.0 | 76.6 | 7.4 |
| Spain | 56.9 | 62.9 | 69.7 | 69.2 | 73.5 | 75.2 | 18.3 |
| Portugal | 46.1 | 54.0 | 55.6 | 58.5 | 64.1 | 68.8 | 22.6 |
| Greece | 59.5 | 64.8 | 66.2 | 68.2 | 68.2 | 70.8 | 11.3 |
| Israel | 69.1 | 74.5 | 72.1 | 69.4 | 74.5 | 71.4 | 2.3 |
| Poland | 65.1 | 69.5 | 69.0 | 62.4 | 60.6 | 61.6 | −3.4 |
| Czech Republic | 73.9 | 72.6 | 68.9 | 68.6 | 63.3 | 60.4 | −13.6 |
| Hungary | 64.0 | 67.2 | 62.3 | 62.0 | 61.5 | 61.4 | −2.5 |
| Romania | 53.9 | 60.2 | 62.2 | 60.6 | 57.3 | 55.6 | 1.8 |
| Bulgaria | 62.9 | 64.9 | 65.3 | 65.2 | 63.7 | 57.3 | −5.6 |
| Yugoslavia | 53.5 | 59.9 | 63.1 | 61.4 | 60.8 | 59.2 | 5.8 |
| Albania | 46.4 | 45.6 | 49.6 | 49.5 | 54.9 | 48.7 | 2.2 |
| Canada | 79.9 | 85.6 | 85.5 | 92.2 | 85.6 | 82.8 | 2.9 |
| U.S.A. | 95.6 | 96.3 | 88.6 | 95.2 | 87.3 | 87.9 | −7.7 |
| LATIN AMERICA | 42.0 | 45.1 | 48.2 | 49.5 | 48.8 | 50.0 | 8.0 |
| MIDDLE EAST | 31.1 | 34.4 | 43.0 | 44.5 | 44.5 | 48.0 | 16.9 |
| ORIENT | 34.2 | 38.8 | 41.3 | 43.7 | 44.4 | 46.7 | 12.5 |
| SUB-SAHARAN AFRICA | 26.7 | 26.1 | 27.7 | 28.9 | 28.7 | 30.1 | 3.4 |
| LD SOUTHERN EUROPE | 54.2 | 60.6 | 63.8 | 65.3 | 68.6 | 71.6 | 17.4 |
| EASTERN EUROPE | 60.0 | 62.8 | 62.9 | 61.4 | 60.3 | 57.8 | −2.2 |

index. The component of income (per capita GNP) generally depresses the overall or total index. The countries average 25 to 45 points lower in per capita GNP when compared with the overall index. This is due to the great variation in countries' incomes, with great gaps possible; virtually all Third World countries (except Kuwait, United Arab Emirates, Singapore, and Hong Kong) have incomes much below the leader in comparison to other components. Furthermore, there appears to be little limit as to how much income can be attained, so the income range among countries can widen even further, as it has been doing in all Third World regions.

In addition to significantly smaller incomes, the underdeveloped countries generally have a less egalitarian distribution of income. In the industrial countries (for which data are available), more than 6 percent of total income is accounted for by the poorest one-fifth of the population, while in the underdeveloped countries it is slightly more than 5 percent (based on data from *World Development Report* published by the World Bank).[5] The richest 10 percent of the population in the industrial countries receive a quarter of the national income, whereas in the underdeveloped countries it is more than one-third. In the underdeveloped world, the poorest group generally receives the smallest share of income in Latin America, while the rich receive a significantly smaller share of income in the Orient.

However, the uneven distribution of income is certainly not unique to the income component of the index. As indicated previously, virtually all characteristics (including the four components of this index) are very unevenly distributed not only worldwide but within virtually all countries.

The diet and health components of the index are just the opposite of the income component: They inflate the overall index by approximately an average of 10 to 30 points. The reasons for this are fairly simple: Food variability is not great because food consumption is necessarily limited (and there are some dietary restrictions in parts of the industrial world); also there is a lower threshold below which undernutrition, malnutrition, and ultimately starvation and death occur. This nutritional range is proportionately not very large. Improvements in health are progressing relatively slowly in the advanced countries in terms of infant mortality (which is now very low) and life expectancy (which is increasing very slowly). Both of these measures are about the best indicators of health conditions.

In the last component, education, overall levels generally approach most closely that of the overall index for socioeconomic development. Education consists of two elements, one (literacy) having a definite upper limit. However, in all of these components there are also significant variations among individual countries.

The literacy component of education has an upper limit (100 percent literacy) and very little discrimination is possible among advanced countries. Furthermore, there is also the question of what constitutes "literacy" and definitions vary among countries, but this component is important if one considers the emphasis that many Third World countries place on campaigns to eliminate illiteracy. The other component of education (proportion of the population in third-level or higher education) is a good measure of the degree of training occurring at a high level. No doubt one can argue about the differences among countries in the "quality" of education being dispensed. It is also true that students studying abroad are not counted and foreign students within the country are included.

There is considerable variation in almost all countries when one compares the individual components of the index. In most countries at least two components (frequently three or even all four, especially in the underdeveloped world) vary at least 10 points from the overall index. The countries of the Middle East appear to have the greatest variation, whereas the more advanced industrial countries vary considerably less. However, the less advanced industrial countries of southern and eastern Europe, included in the table, are more comparable in their variations to the Third World rather than the more advanced industrial countries. Therefore, it would appear that some countries rank relatively much higher or lower in some aspects of development, as measured by this index, than in others.

*Per Capita GNP.* Considering the general depression of this component with regard to the overall index and the overall level of socioeconomic development attained by the individual countries, per capita GNP is generally higher than expected in many of the countries of the First World and in some of the oil-rich countries of Arabia (during the 1970s and 1980s). However, incomes (or per capita GNP) are significantly *lower* in the countries of eastern Europe and also in the Third World, although the newly industrialized countries (NICs) are not as depressed relatively.

*Diet.* In most countries dietary levels are higher than their levels of development would indicate (least in Latin America), notably in parts of Sub-Saharan Africa and more generally in the Middle East.

*Health.* Variations are generally less extreme, but countries of the Middle East and Sub-Saharan Africa rank below expectations. The relatively high-ranking countries are generally in Latin America, the Orient, and eastern and southern Europe.

*Education.* In this component, more so than the others, the index generally approaches the overall index of development. The countries of Latin America generally rank slightly higher whereas the countries of the Middle East generally rank significantly lower in this component relative to the overall index.

Canada and, especially, the United States have less variation in the individual components (GNP/cap, diet, health, education) when compared to the overall index than do any of the regions of the Third World. This would appear to indicate that these highly advanced countries have a more even (or balanced) level of development in the components that are used in this index. However, the countries of southern and eastern Europe resemble the Third World far more than Anglo-America in their variations in these components.

## Levels of Socioeconomic Development

As one would expect there is a very gradual change in the level of development among the countries of the world. Differentiation between levels of socioeconomic development is often difficult and arbitrary or subjective. Furthermore, changes in rankings are also gradually occurring. Nevertheless, seven levels of development can be arbitrarily identified among the world countries on the basis of the Socio-Economic Development Index (Table 2.1) during the 1990s.

1. highly developed (indexes in the 80s): the countries of Anglo-America, many of northwestern Europe, and Japan;
2. advanced development (in the 70s): the remainder of northwestern Europe, Italy, and Spain, Australia and New Zealand, and Israel, and recently, Singapore, Hong Kong, and United Arab Emirates;
3. advanced transitional (in the 60s): the remainder of southern Europe, northern eastern Europe, the remaining "little dragons/ tigers" of Asia, Kuwait, Argentina, and Puerto Rico;
4. transitional (in the 50s): the remainder of eastern Europe, several countries of Latin America and the Middle East, North Korea, Malaysia, Thailand, and Transcaucasia;
5. less developed (in the 40s): the largest group in the Third World contains numerous countries of Latin America, the Middle East, and the Orient, the remainder of the Asian republics of the former Soviet Union (Turkestan), and in Sub-Saharan Africa, South Africa, Botswana, and Zimbabwe;
6. underdeveloped (in the 30s): Guatemala, Iraq, Yemen, Sudan, India, Pakistan, Laos, Papua-New Guinea, and more than half a dozen Sub-Saharan African countries;
7. very poor/least developed (in the 20s): Haiti, the remainder of the Indian subcontinent and Cambodia, most of Sub-Saharan Africa, with Mozambique, Somalia, and Afghanistan at the very bottom.

In overall development on a world regional basis, based on this index, Anglo-America is clearly the most advanced followed by Japan, western Europe, and Australia–New Zealand. Significantly behind these are eastern Europe and the Slavic republics of the ex-USSR, followed by a smaller gap and then Latin America, the Middle East, and the Orient. Significantly further behind is Sub-Saharan Africa.

*Comparative Levels of Development*

In analyzing the other indexes of development (Table 2.1), the regional pattern for the Third World found in the Human Development Index (HDI) is very similar to the Socio-Economic Development Index (SEDI). However, using either GNP per capita or PPP, the major regional change is that the Middle East surpasses both Transcaucasia/Turkestan and even Latin America (in the mean, but not the median). In recent decades, income (either GNP per capita or PPP) and dietary improvements have characterized the Middle East, and it formerly was much closer to Sub-Saharan Africa in educational levels than to the Orient.

The two most common indexes discussed in the early sections of this chapter (GNP per capita and the Human Development Index), as well as the Purchasing Power Parities, can be compared, along with the Socio-Economic Development Index, with regard to the world's countries and regions. The indexes are comparable for the 1993–1994 period.

When the four indexes are compared for the countries of the Third World, about a third of the countries deviate significantly (three place rankings or more from the mean of the four indexes). They provide good indicators as to what has proved successful or been given priority in individual countries.

*Latin America.* Brasil is ranked high by GNP while Costa Rica and Ecuador are ranked low. Guatemala and, in contrast, Ecuador are ranked high in the PPP while Jamaica and, especially, Cuba are ranked low. Costa Rica is ranked high by the HDI. The SEDI ranks Cuba very high, while Brasil, Guatemala, and Trinidad/Tobago rank quite low.

*Middle East.* Oman is ranked high by GNP and PPP, Turkey and Syria by the HDI, and Lebanon and Jordan by the SEDI. However, Syria is ranked low by GNP and Lebanon by the PPP, and the SEDI ranks Oman very low.

*Orient.* Myanmar ranks high in GNP per capita, with Indonesia and Bangladesh high in PPP, China and Vietnam high in the HDI, with Vietnam and North Korea high in the SEDI. Only Vietnam and Mongolia are ranked low according to the GNP with Myanmar, North Korea, and Vietnam low according to the PPP, while in the SEDI, Indonesia, Pakistan, and Bangladesh rank low.

*Sub-Saharan Africa.* The greatest deviations occur in Sub-Saharan Africa. Guinea ranks high and has the greatest deviation in the Third World in the GNP, and Angola, Mali, Burkina Faso, Ivory Coast, Niger, and Senegal are also ranked high. Ranking high in PPP is Chad (the greatest deviation in the Third World), with Niger, Ghana, Somalia, Mauritania, Uganda, and Burkina Faso all ranking high under the PPP. Zaire, Madagascar, Mozambique, Kenya, Burundi, Ethiopia, Tanzania, and Rwanda are ranked high by the HDI, while in the SEDI, Tanzania (the greatest deviation in the Third World), Madagascar, Burundi, and Mali are ranked high. Ranked low according to the GNP are Tanzania, Kenya, Uganda, Burundi, and Madagascar while in the PPP, Zaire, Madagascar, Tanzania, Mali, and Guinea are all ranked high. The HDI ranks Senegal (the largest variation in the Third World), Mauritania, Burkina Faso, Niger, Guinea, Chad, and Mali significantly lower than the average of the indexes. In the SEDI, ranking low are Chad, Ivory Coast, and Guinea.

In sum, there are eight countries (Tanzania, Madagascar, Mali, Guinea, Burkina Faso, Niger, Chad, and Burundi) in Sub-Saharan Africa that vary significantly from the average ranking in three of the four indexes used, whereas in the remainder of the Third World there are only two others (Oman and Vietnam).

### Closing the Gap with the Industrial World

Using the SEDI it appears that Latin America and Sub-Saharan Africa have been losing ground compared to the advanced industrial world in GNP per capita (i.e., income) since at least 1960. Latin America may have improved its situation slightly during the 1990s. The Middle East clearly improved with relation to the advanced world into the 1980s, but the situation has been reversed since then. By 1994, the Middle East was no better off relative to the advanced world in income than it had been in 1960. However, the Orient has exhibited fairly consistent, if slow, improvement in income relative to the First World over the past third of a century. At this rate the Orient overall (not individual countries within the region) would attain the level of southern Europe in about a century, assuming that the latter does not improve in that time.

In nutrition, over the past three decades, the Middle East improved very significantly until the 1980s, with little change since. The same holds true for the Orient, but to a lesser degree, while Latin America has remained virtually unchanged overall. However, Sub-Saharan Africa, already the poorest-fed region, has declined consistently since about 1970.

The situation in both health and education is far more favorable. In health, in all Third World regions there have been rather impressive improvements since 1960, but with the least improvement in Sub-Saharan Africa, which has the poorest health conditions. In education, improvements have also been impressive, and in this element, Sub-Saharan Africa exhibits about comparable growth to the other Third World regions despite the lowest educational levels in the world.

According to the *Human Development Report*, the developing countries appear to be narrowing the North-South gap with regard to life expectancy, under-five mortality, adult literacy, daily calorie supply, and access to safe water (UNDP 1996). Except for the latter (not included in the SEDI) this confirms what was previously stated about the changes in the

SEDI. However, the report points out that there are widening North-South gaps in real GNP per capita, mean years of schooling and overall enrollment, as well as fertility and the number of telephones. In closing the gap, it has to be remembered that the North has also greatly improved its economic and social indicators over the past few decades. Fertility is declining in all Third World regions, although the rate of decline is slowest in the Middle East and, especially, Sub-Saharan Africa where fertility rates are the world's highest. However, as pointed out previously, the gap in income (GNP/cap) has been widening, and this represents a fundamental flaw in the developmental process in most of the Third World.

### Economic Transformation of the Third World

Economic restructuring became a key word in development during the 1980s, but the process of economic transformation, of course, had been going on for quite some time before then.[6] The economic transformation of most countries of the Third World tends to follow five different stages. Countries sometimes pass over the order of these stages, but generally a pattern of economic transformation can be broadly outlined. This pattern is perhaps more closely followed in Latin America than in the other regions of the Third World (Table 2.3).

1. The percentage of population in agriculture begins to decline rapidly and eventually drops below 50 percent.
2. The value of manufacturing begins to exceed that of agriculture in the gross domestic product.
3. The absolute decline of the agricultural population begins.
4. The industrial labor force begins to exceed that in agriculture.
5. The export of manufactured goods begins to exceed that of all raw materials.

All the advanced countries have passed through the above five stages, except for Australia, Norway, and New Zealand, whose export trade is still more strongly resource-based. One should be able to assume that most of the Third World countries will, in the process of their development, also pass through the above five stages, although not necessarily in the particular order given.

The proportion of population in agriculture is universally declining, but in a few countries of the Third World, notably in Sub-Saharan Africa and the Orient, the decline is relatively slow. Most of the countries of Latin America and the Middle East have by now dropped below the 50 percent level. Less than half of the countries of the Orient have reached

TABLE 2.3  Stages in Economic Transformation

| Latin America | Middle East | Orient | Sub-Saharan Africa |
|---|---|---|---|
| **Slow Decline of Population in Agriculture** | | | |
| Paraguay (47%) | | Sri Lanka (51) | Burkina Faso |
| | | Nepal | Mozambique |
| | ~ | India | Nigeria |
| | | Laos | Niger |
| | | | Madagascar |
| | | | Kenya |
| | | | Mali |
| Argentina (10%) | | Hong Kong (1%) | Angola |
| Uruguay (13%) | | Singapore (1%) | |
| **Agricultural Population Drops Below 50% of Total Population** | | | |
| Pre-1960: | | | |
| Cuba | Jordan | (Singapore)[a] | South Africa |
| Puerto Rico | Lebanon | (Hong Kong) | |
| Jamaica | Kuwait | | |
| Trinidad/Tobago | United Arab Emirates | | |
| Venezuela | | | |
| Chile | | | |
| Argentina | | | |
| Uruguay | | | |
| Mid-1960s: | | | |
| Mexico | Tunisia | | |
| Costa Rica | Libya | | |
| Panama | Iraq | | |
| Colombia | Iran | | |
| Brasil | | | |
| 1970–75: | | | |
| Peru | Algeria | Korea, South | |
| Salvador | Syria | Mongolia | |
| Nicaragua | Egypt | Malaysia | |
| Dominican Republic | | Korea, North | |
| Ecuador | | | |
| Bolivia | | | |
| 1980: | | | |
| Paraguay | Morocco | | |
| | Saudi Arabia | | |
| | Oman | | |
| Mid-1980s: | Turkey | Myanmar | |
| | | Indonesia | |
| | | Philippines | |
| 1990s: | | | |
| Guatemala | | | Ghana |
| **Manufacturing Exceeds Agriculture in GDP** | | | |
| Pre-1960: | | (Singapore/Hong Kong) | |
| Mexico | Lebanon | | South Africa |
| Cuba (?)[b] | Kuwait (?) | | |
| Puerto Rico | United Arab Emirates (?) | | |
| Jamaica | | | |
| Trinidad/Tobago | | | |

*(continues)*

TABLE 2.3   *(continued)*

| Latin America | Middle East | Orient | Sub-Saharan Africa |
|---|---|---|---|
| Venezuela | | | |
| Chile | | | |
| Argentina | | | |
| Uruguay | | | |
| Brasil | | | |
| Late 1960s: | Saudi Arabia (?) ('90s) | Taiwan | Zimbabwe |
| 1970s: | Libya | South Korea | Zambia |
| Peru | Jordan | Mongolia (?) | |
| 1980s: | | | |
| Ecuador | Turkey | Thailand | [Botswana (?)] |
| Salvador (late '80s) | Morocco (late '80s) | China (mid-'80s) | |
| Colombia (late '80s) | | Malaysia (late '80s) | |
| c1990: | Tunisia | Indonesia | |
| | Oman (?) | Philippines | |
| | [Azerbaijan] | | |
| | [Kazakhstan] | | |
| | [Uzbekistan] | | |

Absolute Decline of Agricultural Population
Pre-1960:

| Latin America | Middle East | Orient | Sub-Saharan Africa |
|---|---|---|---|
| Cuba | Tunisia | (Singapore/Hong Kong) | |
| Puerto Rico | Lebanon | South Korea | |
| Trinidad/Tobago | Jordan (?) | (Taiwan ?) | |
| Venezuela | Algeria (?) | | |
| Argentina | | | |
| Uruguay | | | |
| Late 1960s: | | | |
| Chile | | | |
| Early 1970s: | | | |
| Costa Rica (fluct) | Iraq | Malaysia | South Africa |
| Brasil | | | |
| Late 1970s: | | | |
| Panama | | North Korea | |
| Late 1980s: | | | |
| Dominican Republic | United Arab Emirates | Mongolia | |
| Jamaica | Turkey | | |
| Colombia | | | |
| 1990s: | | | |
| Mexico | Morocco | Indonesia | |
| Ecuador | Iran | China (?) | |

Industry Exceeds Agriculture in Labor Force
Pre-1960:

| Latin America | Middle East | Orient | Sub-Saharan Africa |
|---|---|---|---|
| Trinidad/Tobago | Kuwait | (Singapore/Hong Kong) | |
| Argentina | United Arab Emirates | | |
| Uruguay | | | |

*(continues)*

TABLE 2.3   *(continued)*

| Latin America | Middle East | Orient | Sub-Saharan Africa |
|---|---|---|---|
| 1960s: | | | |
| Puerto Rico | Lebanon (late '60s) | | |
| Chile | | | |
| 1970s: | | | |
| Cuba | Libya | Taiwan (late '70s) | South Africa |
| Venezuela | Jordan | | |
| 1980s: | Algeria | South Korea | |
| | Tunisia | | |
| | Syria (?) | | |
| | Iraq | | |
| | Saudi Arabia | | |
| 1990s: | | | |
| Costa Rica | [Georgia Armenia] | | Botswana |
| Brasil | [Kazakhstan] (Azerbaijan ?, na) | | |
| **Manufactures Exceed Raw Materials Exports** | | | |
| Pre-1960: | | | |
| Puerto Rico (?) | | Hong Kong | |
| | | South Korea (early '60s) | |
| Late 1960s: | | | |
| Jamaica | | India | |
| | | Pakistan | |
| | | China | |
| | | Taiwan | |
| 1970s: | | Bangladesh | |
| | | Singapore | |
| 1980s: | Tunisia | Nepal | South Africa |
| Haiti | Lebanon | Thailand | |
| Brasil | Turkey | Philippines | |
| 1990s: | | | |
| Mexico | Morocco | Sri Lanka | |
| Dominican Republic | Jordan | Malaysia | |
| | Kuwait | Indonesia | |
| | [Georgia Azerbaijan] | | |
| | [Uzbekistan Turkmenistan] | | |

[a]Brackets represent countries that may fit into this time period.
[b]Countries with a question mark represent those that may fit into this time period but are questionable.

this level, while only South Africa and Ghana have done so in Sub-Saharan Africa.

Manufacturing already exceeds agriculture in the value of the gross domestic product in most of the countries of Latin America and the Middle East. This is the case in half the countries of the Orient, but in only a fifth of the countries of Sub-Saharan Africa.

The absolute decline of the agricultural population is now widespread in Latin America and Southeast and East Asia but less so in the Middle East. This is occurring only in South Africa among the Sub-Saharan countries. The absolute decline results in a decrease of pressure on land resources and a decrease in demands for land redistribution and reform.

The size of the labor force in industry exceeds that of agriculture in half or fewer of the countries in the Middle East and Latin America and in only about half a dozen countries in the remainder of the Third World.

The export of manufactured goods exceeds all raw material exports in only a few countries of the Middle East and Latin America and in South Africa. But in the Orient, which has strongly promoted export-oriented development, only a third of the countries do *not* export more manufactured goods than raw materials. This represents the greatest and most important deviation among Third World regions to the sequential pattern of the five stages of economic transformation.

### Economic Structure, Political Freedom, and Economic Growth

Beginning in the 1980s the belief became increasingly popular that the best approach to economic development was via an open competitive capitalist economy. This belief was later joined by the idea that democracy (political openness and competitiveness) was the best political structure for the maintenance of economic growth and social well-being. The collapse of the Soviet system and the discrediting of Marxist/state-oriented development very strongly reinforced these beliefs. The capitalist economies of the Third World consisted of eighteen countries in 1994, less than a fifth of the ninety-seven countries with significant-sized economies. The capitalist economies have not been growing significantly faster than the others nor are they the most developed countries. Furthermore, they are only slightly more free than other economies of the Third World, although they were improving notably in the 1985–1994 period. Capitalism is *not* equivalent to freedom or vice versa. The correlation between economic growth and political freedom is weak although the correlation between the level of development and political freedom is moderate. It would appear that a capitalist economy and democracy do not ensure the fastest economic growth and that other factors, namely, gross domestic investment, export orientation toward manufactured goods, and political and economic efficiency, may have a greater effect on economic growth in the Third World.

### Summary and Conclusions

Indexes or measures of socioeconomic development (quality of life or human welfare) may vary from simple and statistically unsophisticated to comprehensive, multidimensional, and statistically and methodologically rigorous. One would presume that with a greater number of indicators and increasingly sophisticated statistical analysis the index would be more valid and acceptable. The real test of these indexes, however, is how truly they reflect real world conditions, and in this, subjectivity becomes a consideration.

The use of the per capita GNP alone in ranking the major countries does bring out one major point. Since the mid-1970s when the price of petroleum began its rapid rise, the petroleum-rich countries (notably of the Middle East) have markedly increased their per capita GNP. As a consequence, some major petroleum producers, especially Saudi Arabia, Kuwait, the United Arab Emirates, Algeria, Iraq, and Iran, rank relatively higher in this index than in any of the others. However, this has lessened recently as oil revenues have declined relatively and the oil producers have improved their health, education, and nutrition indicators.

Purchasing Power Parities (PPP) may contribute a more refined measure of income. But data will be needed from even more countries than is currently available.

The use of the Socio-Economic Development Index (SEDI) is, in my view, sufficiently sophisticated, without being unduly complex and cumbersome, to allow adequate discrimination between different levels of development. Furthermore, it comes closer, in my opinion, to satisfying the ranking of countries with my own observations of the real world.

The Human Development Index (HDI) may become quite popular, especially if it is annually updated (which appears to be the trend), and appears to be a useful measure of development.

Different countries have had greater success in one field of socioeconomic development than in others, and many countries exhibit significant variation from one component to another. There are many variations in the degree of "balanced development" among countries. There are also significant variations in development between the world's major regions and within each region itself. The Third World appears to be progressing, probably not fast enough for some, in the fields of both health and education. The situation is more mixed with regard to improvements in nutrition. Above all, however, the lag in income expansion appears to be the major drawback in the development of the Third World, especially since it contributes directly to the improvement of other socioeconomic indicators.

### Notes

1. If the purpose is to measure the quality of life, I add a fifth factor, political freedom (as measured annually by Freedom House in New York).

2. Most of these components, if not all, are occasionally called into question because they are allegedly inaccurate, incomplete, or misleading. However, in my estimation these are probably the best available, and although not precisely accu-

rate, they can be used for comparative purposes. GNP data for what remains of the Communist bloc and for some other countries is provisional or not available, but the latest estimates available for those countries are presented.

3. Since there are two components in the measures of diet, health, and education, it is possible that the same country may not be the leader in both components of the same factor. This would result in no country with a ranking of 100 for that factor. This is what occurs for diet and possibly education.

4. Comparable data with regard to diet are not available for Puerto Rico and Oman. Therefore, in computing the overall index, both countries have only three of the factors instead of four. However, in diet, Puerto Rico would rank high, by the standards of the underdeveloped world.

5. Recent data are available for a total of 65 countries (44 of which are in the Third World). However, all countries have been utilized in this brief discussion of income distribution.

6. As interpreted recently, economic "restructuring" now generally refers to a collection of monetary, fiscal, business, and trade policies. As used in this study, economic "transformation" refers to the sectorial structural changes in the economy and sectorial changes in the population and labor force.

# References

Estes, R. J. 1984. *The Social Progress of Nations*. New York: Praeger.

Food and Agriculture Organization. 1994 (and earlier editions). *FAO Production Yearbook 1994*. Rome: Food and Agriculture Organization.

Gastil, Raymond D., ed. 1995. *Freedom in the World 1994–1995*. New York: Freedom House.

Gonzalez, A. 1982. "A Measure of the Level of Living or the Quality of Life." Unpublished paper. Association of American Geographers, San Antonio, Texas.

Morris, M. D. 1979. *Measuring the Condition of the World's Poor*. Washington, D.C.: Pergamon and Overseas Development Council.

Population Crisis Committee. 1987. *International Human Suffering Index*. Washington, D.C.: Population Crisis Committee.

Population Reference Bureau. 1996 (and earlier editions). *World Population Data Sheet*. Washington, D.C.: Population Reference Bureau.

Sivard, R. L. 1996 (and earlier editions). *World Military and Social Expenditures*. Leesburg, Va.: World Priorities.

United Nations Development Programme (UNDP). 1996 (and earlier editions). *Human Development Report*. New York: Oxford University Press.

United Nations Educational, Scientific, and Cultural Organization (UNESCO). 1996 (and earlier editions). *UNESCO Statistical Yearbook*. Paris: United Nations Educational, Scientific, and Cultural Organization.

World Bank. 1996 (and earlier editions). *World Bank Atlas*. Washington, D.C.: World Bank.

_____. 1996 (and earlier editions). *World Development Report*. New York: Oxford University Press.

# 3 Coming Out of the Country: Population Growth, Migration, and Urbanization

## Gary S. Elbow

CHANGE IS COMING FAST IN THE THIRD WORLD. Unprecedented population growth and its concentration in one or a few giant urban centers in each country are the most evident signs of this change. For example, the Third World's population is currently growing at a rate of about 1.9 percent per year (Population Reference Bureau 1996). Since 1950, the population of the Third World has grown by 173 percent, from 1,681 million (Merrick 1986: 12–13) to an estimated 4,600 million in 1996 (Population Reference Bureau 1996). During the same period world population rose by 129 percent, from 2,516 million to 5,771 million. Because of its faster rate of growth, the Third World's share of global population rose from 67 percent in 1950 to 81 percent in 1996.

Meanwhile, an equally striking internal shift has occurred in many Third World countries. This shift is the migration of millions of people from rural areas to the region's cities. In the same 46-year period cited previously, the percentage of urban population in the Third World rose from 17 percent (Reitsma and Kleinpenning 1985: 169) to 35 percent (Population Reference Bureau 1996). In numerical terms, this means that the number of city dwellers has increased from 286 million in 1950 to 1,610 million in 1996, an astonishing 463 percent increase! Much of this growth is concentrated in a few megacities that dominate entire countries or regions. In the coming decades the Third World will continue to be affected by high rates of population growth and its concentration in urban centers.

The three phenomena noted here—rapid population growth, migration from rural areas to the cities, and accelerated urban growth—are responses to similar conditions and they are linked. Of course, not all new population contributes to urban growth, and not all migration is to cities; but there is a clear association—as population increases, people move from rural to urban areas, and cities grow. The title of this chapter reflects this characteristic of population dynamics in the Third World during the latter half of the twentieth century.

## Population

The population of the world in 1700 was about 680 million (Demeny 1990: 42). It took the entire history of humans on earth to reach that number. Since that time, global population has grown to about 5,771 million. Depending on projections, the world will have between 7,135 and 9,135 million human inhabitants in the year 2025 (El-Badry 1991: 27). Just under 80 percent of the world's people live in the Third World, and the countries with the highest rates of population growth are part of the Third World, so that by 2025 the Third World population is projected to increase to between 82.5 and 84 percent of the world total.

### World Distribution of Population Growth

Map 3.1 shows estimated rates of natural increase for the countries of the world in 1996. Regional differences in the rate of natural increase are clearly visible on this map. The countries with the lowest rates of population growth are found in Europe, Russia and the other European members of the former Soviet Union, and Anglo-America. The main exceptions are Australia, New Zealand, and Uruguay, which are Southern Hemisphere outliers of European culture, Cuba, and Japan, which has the lowest rate of natural increase of any Asian country. Germany, Italy, Russia, the Balkan states, and several other former Soviet republics and Eastern European states have negative rates of natural increase, which means they are actually losing population if a zero migration rate is assumed. Other countries in this group are growing so slowly that it will take hundreds of years at the current rate for their population to double.

The second quartile stands out as a large belt extending from Turkey eastward to take in most of Asia, including China and India, the world's most populous countries. Israel, Lebanon, and Tunisia are Mediterranean outliers, along with the United Arab Emirates, Iceland, New Zealand, and Gabon, the only Sub-Saharan African country to fall in the lower half of countries in rate of natural increase. In the Western Hemisphere, most of the Caribbean island states, Panama, and the South American countries of Argentina, Brazil, Chile, Guyana, and Suriname fall into this category. Many of the countries in the second quartile are undergoing rapid economic development and fall into the category of "newly industrializing countries." Such countries include Brazil, Chile, China, Indonesia, Singapore, South Korea, Taiwan, Thailand, and Turkey. Argentina, Ice-

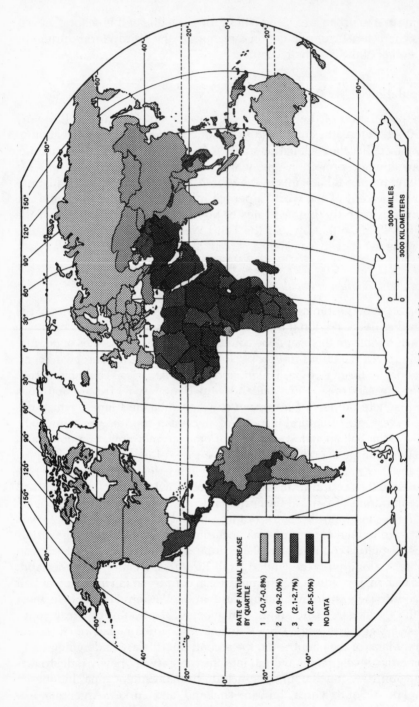

MAP 3.1   Estimated rates of natural increase for countries of the world by quartile, 1996.
SOURCE: Population Reference Bureau. *World Population Data Sheet* (Washington, D.C.: Population Reference Bureau, 1996).

land, Israel, and New Zealand are Europeanized countries in the second quartile that have well-educated populations and relatively advanced economies.

At the other extreme, the countries that make up the most rapidly growing quartile are found principally in Africa and the Middle East, with a few outliers in Central and South America, Southeast Asia, and among the Pacific Island nations. These countries all have rates of natural increase of 2.8 percent or more, and their doubling times fall at twenty-five years or less. This means they will have twice their current population in about one generation. The total estimated population of the fourth-quartile countries for 1996 was 768 million. With a doubling time of twenty-five years or less, they will account for more than 1,500 million of the earth's population in 2020 (Population Reference Bureau 1996). The third quartile countries are concentrated in Africa and Latin America, but Malaysia, Vietnam, the Philippines, New Guinea, the Himalayan countries of Nepal and Bhutan, and some former Soviet central Asian countries also fall within this rapidly growing group. If current rates of growth are sustained, the population of these countries will double in twenty-six to thirty-two years.

Many rapidly growing countries are also among the world's poorest. This contrasts with the slow-growing countries, many of which are among the world's richest. In terms of the relationship of financial resources to population, in twenty-five years, the slow-growing and well-to-do countries will be able to divide their very large economic pie among only a few more people than they have today, whereas the poverty-stricken and rapidly growing countries will have to stretch their limited resources to serve a population that may have grown to twice its current size or more. If both the population and the total national income in the rapidly growing countries were to double during the next twenty-five years, they still would have the same per capita income as they do today. If the slow-growing countries were to double their total national income during the same time period, their per capita income would be approximately twice what it is now. Seen from this perspective, rapid population growth in the Third World is a multiple liability. It places stress on limited natural resources, adds to the demand for infrastructure such as schools, hospitals, housing, roads, utilities, and other costly facilities, creates unmet demand for employment, and spreads already limited financial resources among an ever-increasing number of people.

On the other hand, some economists and many Third World government officials note that there is a historic association of rapid population growth with economic development in Europe and North America (Weir 1991: 41–44). For this reason, they believe that high rates of population growth are essential for development to be achieved in their countries, and they often interpret efforts of representatives of First World countries such as the United States to promote fertility reduction as a scheme to prevent poor countries from achieving their "natural" potential through population growth.

## The Demographic Transition Model

Around the middle of this century social scientists observed an association of population growth rates with economic development and devised a theoretical framework, known as the Demographic Transition Model, that seemed to fit the patterns they found (Chung 1970). According to this model, countries pass through four stages of population growth (see Figure 3.1).[1]

In the first stage of the model, a country has not yet begun the process of development. Health conditions are poor and family planning is limited or nonexistent, so both birth and death rates are high. Since high birth and death rates compensate for each other, the rate of natural increase is low and population grows slowly or not at all. As of 1997, no countries remained in stage 1, although wars and natural disasters may temporarily increase death rates enough in some marginal countries to move them into this category. Rwanda, an African country that suffered a devastating civil war in 1993–1994 may be one such case, as could be neighboring Zaïre, which experienced a growing conflict between rebels and the government in the spring of 1997.

Stage 2 includes countries that have just begun to receive some of the health benefits associated with development, such as uncontaminated drinking water supplies, large-scale immunization and disease control programs, and prenatal and postnatal medical care for mothers and their infants, all of which cause death rates to drop. Meanwhile, the social, economic, and cultural factors that are associated with high birth rates remain in place. The combination of declining death rates and high birth rates leads to extremely high rates of natural increase, resulting in a rapid increase in the nation's population. Some authors refer to this rapid population increase as a demographic explosion (Reitsma and Kleinpenning 1985: 33).

In stage 3, death rates are reduced about as far as possible through the institution of disease control measures and birth rates have begun to come down in response to improved economic and education levels and better access to family planning information and facilities. The result is a lower rate of natural increase. However, population continues to grow at an accelerated rate because such a high proportion of the population is young. These people, who may make up nearly half of the total population in some countries, are just entering their reproductive years. Thus,

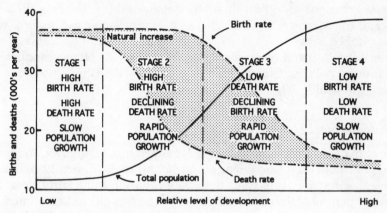

FIGURE 3.1 The demographic transition model

even if fertility rates are reduced (the number of children per reproductive age female), the population will still continue to grow rapidly because of the large base of women in their reproductive years. This phenomenon, called demographic momentum, is characterized by birth rates that must be brought down well below replacement levels if a rapidly growing country's population increase is to be stopped. The countries in the third and fourth quartiles on the map of rates of natural increase are in stage 2 or stage 3 of the demographic transition.

Stage 4, is characteristic of countries with advanced industrial economies. In this stage, birth and death rates are nearly balanced, and the rate of natural increase is again low, as it was in stage 1. The difference is, of course, that the balance is maintained by low birth and death rates, not the high birth and death rates of stage 1. The countries of the first and second quartiles of Map 3.1 are approaching or have entered stage 4 of the demographic transition.

Recently, some of the poorest and most rural countries have reduced their fertility rates, causing researchers to argue that the mainly economic-based explanations for reduced fertility of the Demographic Transition Model do not satisfactorily account for patterns of population growth in Third World countries (Robey, Rutstein, and Morris 1993). These researchers note that government policies, cultural and religious values, levels of education (especially of women), standards of living and social mobility, and access by women to family planning information and materials are all important variables in determining rates of fertility and, in turn, the rates of natural increase within individual countries. Of these factors, access to contraceptives is the most important, accounting for 90 percent of variation in fertility rates among countries. Stated in other words, a 15 percent increase in contraceptive use results in women on average bearing one less child than otherwise would be the case (Robey, Rutstein, and Morris 1993: 62). Increases in contraceptive use, in turn, are closely linked to women's economic status and level of education. Improved education and economic status for women are often a product of government policies. Clearly, there is a close relationship among these factors (Kalipeni 1995).

## Projections into the Future

Rates of natural increase are changing rapidly in many countries, and prediction of future population trends is a risky business (Cohen 1996). Nevertheless, some relatively short-term patterns seem to be fairly clear. In Africa, 44 percent of the population is under 15 years old. In Latin America the proportion of population under 15 is 35 percent, and in Asia it is 32 percent (Population Reference Bureau 1996). This youthful profile means that populations in the Third World, and Africa in particular, can be expected to grow rapidly for at least a couple of generations into the future, even if fertility rates continue to drop. In contrast, rates of natural increase in First World countries are at or close to the no growth point and only a relatively small proportion of the population is young (22 percent for Canada and the United States, 21 percent for Australia, 19 percent for Europe, and 16 percent for Japan), so their populations will grow slowly. Already, just under four out of five people live in the Third World. The stark contrast in population growth rates between the First and Third Worlds means that this proportion will inevitably increase in the future.

The unprecedented rates of population growth, combined with the ever-widening gap between rich countries and poor ones, will contribute to increasing tensions around the world. Many writers predict a Malthusian collapse some time in the next century if radical measures are not taken to reduce population growth (Ehrlich and Ehrlich 1970; Ponting 1991; Meadows, Meadows, and Randers 1992; Zuckerman and Jefferson 1996). According to this scenario, ever-increasing population, especially in Third World countries, will eventually outstrip the world's food production capacity, causing widespread famine, disease, and other disasters. At the same time, the never-ending struggle to expand agricultural land to feed the starving masses, combined with pollution from ever-increasing industrial development in First World countries, will destroy sensitive ecosystems, further reducing food-producing capacity and permanently reducing Earth's ability to support humans.

Others believe that the world can support a much larger population than at present and see maldistribution of resources rather than overpopulation as the key issue (Dickenson et al. 1983: 66–68; Reitsma and Kleinpenning 1985: 224–227; Simon 1990). Critics of the Malthusian view observe that food production has managed to keep up with rapid population growth in the past and see no reason why new advances in technology should not enable the world to feed the larger populations predicted for the future (Simon 1990: 92–102). Often the arguments are couched in terms of a conflict between biologists and ecologists, who tend to view Earth's resources as finite and diminishing through misuse, and economists, who see technology as the key to supporting a growing human population (Begley 1994: 27). Both points of view are represented in recent books by Lindahl-Liessling and Landberg (1994) and Cohen (1995) on the relationship of population to resources. Regardless of one's viewpoint on the impact of population growth, it seems safe to predict that the Third World, with its rapidly increasing share of the world's people, will demand an increasingly larger part of the world's economic pie.

## Migration

Movement is a characteristic of human populations. Until the invention of farming about 10,000 years ago, the vast majority of humans were nomadic. They lived in temporary settlements or camps and survived by collecting the products that were available in the local environment. As food supplies were exhausted in one place, people moved on to other areas to find new sources.

Human populations are still quite mobile and migration is a common process.[2] In most countries of the world there are few if any controls on internal migration, and citizens are free to move from place to place as they wish. On the other hand, all countries defend their national borders and attempt to control movement by non-nationals into their territory. Legal immigrants must qualify for visas, work permits, and other documentation. Illegal immigrants are often exploited by unscrupulous smugglers and occasionally die in the process of trying to gain entry to the country of their choice (Perlez 1995: A3). Even if they gain entry to the desired country, immigrants who lack proper documents are often forced because of their status to work for low wages at undesirable jobs, and they live in constant fear of discovery and expulsion. In addition, international migration is far more likely than internal migration to require that the immigrant learn a second language, adjust to new cultural and political conditions, and otherwise make difficult and far-reaching adaptations to the new location.

### Causal Factors in Migration

There are two classes of stimuli for voluntary migration. Conditions that cause people to leave the place where they live are push factors, and attractions that draw migrants to a particular place are pull factors. Push factors include lack of employment opportunities, political, religious, or racial persecution, warfare, famine, epidemic disease, and natural disasters. Pull factors are availability of economic opportunities, better social, educational, or health conditions, religious or political freedom, personal security, or freedom from famine, epidemic disease, or natural disasters. Pull factors may also include personal or family matters, such as a desire to live close to aging parents, siblings, or other relatives, or the wish to enjoy certain amenities, such as a mild winter climate, recreational opportunities, or retirement facilities. This latter set of pull factors is characteristic of relatively well-to-do migrants who have the means to make choices related to amenities; that is, within certain limits, they can afford to live where they want to. The first group of pull factors is related to personal security and economic conditions. They dominate among poor people from Third World countries, who tend to migrate for causes related to survival rather than to gain access to amenities. Typically, migrants are influenced by a combination of push and pull factors; that is, they have reasons for wanting to leave where they are and they believe that conditions will be better at their destination.

Examples of involuntary or forced migration include slavery, conscription for service in military or other institutions, and involuntary relocation of certain ethnic or religious groups. Slavery has largely passed from the scene, and involuntary conscription (i.e., being shanghaied) has also nearly disappeared. On the other hand, involuntary relocation still occurs. Current examples are Bosnian Moslems in former Yugoslavia who were driven from their homes as a part of ethnic cleansing, Marsh Arabs in the Tigris and Euphrates River delta who were forced to leave their homes after the deliberate drying up of the marshlands by the Iraqi government, and Hutu tribespeople from Rwanda who fled to neighboring countries because of ethnic conflict in their homeland.

Involuntary migrants fleeing political repression, warfare, or disaster may be classified as refugees. In 1993 there were an estimated 16.255 million refugees in the world (U. S. Committee for Refugees 1994: 40–41). These are mainly people who were displaced from their homes by wars, totalitarian governments, or natural disasters, and they are disproportionately located in the Third World. Palestinians who fled the newly created state of Israel after World War II are one of the longest-persisting refugee groups. Many of these refugees, now estimated to be nearly 2.8 million, still live in Jordan, Egypt, Lebanon, and the occupied territories of Israel.[3] Sub-Saharan Africa led the world with 5.693 million refugees in 1993. This included over 1.6 million refugees from Mozambique, nearly 700,000 Liberians, 420,000 Somalis, 420,000 Eritreans, and 370,000 Sudanese, but the largest bloc of African refugees in the 1990s was Rwandans, who fled the civil war in their country in the hundreds of thousands during 1994 and only began returning in large numbers during 1996. There are just under 5 million refugees in the Middle East, 2.7 million in Europe (mainly from former Yugoslavia and the former USSR), and 2.15 million in south and central Asia (over half are Afghans).

Government policies may encourage or discourage migration. For example, policies that promote concentration of land in large parcels to facilitate mechanization of agriculture may displace small farmers and force them to find new land elsewhere or to move to a city. After the end of a decade-long civil war in 1992 the government of El Salvador requested that Salvadorans who had fled the country, mainly to the United States, not return home immediately because the money they sent back to family members was an essential part of the country's foreign exchange earnings and necessary for the national reconstruction effort. For decades the government of the Soviet Union refused to allow Jewish citizens, especially scientists, to emigrate to Israel, using the argument that they had access to classified information or had jobs that were essential to the country's well being. Until 1994, the United States granted political asylum to nearly any Cuban who applied, while denying similar status to most Haitians and Salvadorans, for example (see Harris 1995: 93–109 for a lengthy discussion of government efforts to control immigration).

## International Migration

There is no hard information on the number of international migrants in the world. A 1990 study by the International Organization for Migration estimated the total number of international migrants worldwide at 80 million, including refugees. By 1992, other estimates had put the total at 100 million migrants, also including refugees. The latter estimate amounted to less than 2 percent of the world's population in 1992 (Castles and Miller 1993: 4).

Excluding refugees, the largest international migration flows are from the Third World to industrialized areas such as the United States or western Europe. Proximity and former colonial relationships are important influences on the destination of migrants from the Third World to the First World. Mexicans make up by far the largest group of foreign-born residents in the United States; Indians, Pakistanis, West Indians, and other former colonials make up a large share of migrants to the United Kingdom; Algerians, Tunisians, and black Africans from former French colonies swell the population of French cities; and the Netherlands receives migrants from its former colonies, Indonesia and Suriname.

Migration between Third World countries receives less publicity than migration to northern America or Europe. Nevertheless, such migration may be substantial. The case of Jordanian, Yemeni, Palestinian, Egyptian, Pakistani, Filipino, and other workers in the Persian Gulf states is perhaps the most notable example, but there are others. Hundreds of Bolivian workers are employed in Argentina, and that country also receives immigrants from Paraguay, Chile, and Peru. Before the collapse of the oil economy in Venezuela, thousands of Colombians migrated across the border to work in that country. In Africa, Ivory Coast and Nigeria have both been recipients of migrant laborers from neighboring countries, and South Africa depended for years on labor imported from Botswana, Lesotho, and Swaziland. Most often, as shown in these examples, migrations from one Third World country to another are to neighboring countries or nearby countries within the same region.

Finally, it is worth noting that there are small but locally important flows of permanent migrants from industrialized countries to the Third World. There are retirement communities of United States citizens numbering in the thousands in Mexico and Costa Rica. Elsewhere, military personnel, employees of multinational corporations, technicians, and skilled workers (notably, oil field workers) from industrialized countries live for years, if not permanently, in Third World countries.

International migration has impacts on both the sending and receiving countries. For the receiving country, migrants may fill essential jobs during times when labor is needed. For example, the United States allowed Mexican farmworkers to enter the country legally under the Bracero Program, which operated between 1942 and 1964. Similar examples have already been cited from the Middle East, where Kuwait, Saudi Arabia, Bahrain, and other oil-rich Persian Gulf states import large numbers of foreign workers. However, when there are economic downturns alien workers may become a liability. At such times governments may look for excuses to return migrant workers to their home countries, and prejudice and jingoism may be directed against resident foreigners. Hostility manifested against Turks living in Germany following the fall of the Berlin Wall is one example of this phenomenon, as was the expulsion of tens of thousands of Ghanaian workers from Nigeria during the mid-1980s. In 1991, thousands of Jordanian and Yemeni workers were expelled from the Persian Gulf states because their countries supported Iraq in the Gulf War.

International migrants may have other impacts on the receiving country, as well. Migrants often are among the most ambitious, best-educated, most capable, and most upwardly mobile citizens of their home country, and they may make substantial contributions to the receiving country. Some countries, including the United States, recognize this potential benefit and structure their immigration laws to favor admission of migrants with desirable training or skills.

There are multiple impacts on the migrants' home countries. The loss of skilled, well-educated young citizens who might have contributed to helping the country achieve higher levels of economic development may be the greatest impact. Often, immigrants have received higher education or advanced training in the receiving country and subsequently find employment there. The term "brain drain" came into vogue during the 1960s to describe the loss of such highly trained and skilled professionals from Third World countries to the First World. But international migration probably yields more benefits than disadvantages to the sending country. The greatest benefit is economic. It is common for international migrants to send money to relatives who remain in the home country. These remittances may make up a substantial part of the foreign exchange earnings of Third World countries. A recent report notes that the members of the Organization for Economic Cooperation and Development, which includes most developed countries, contributed an estimated US$66,000 million in migrant remittances during 1989 (Fornos and Burdett 1994: 5–6). Such funds are used for home improvements, to set up businesses, to buy or improve farmland, and for a multitude of other economically beneficial purposes. Finally, many migrants eventually return to their country of origin. These returnees may bring home useful skills that were acquired during their sojourn abroad, and most of them also bring funds with them that were saved during their time away. Like remittances, these funds may be used to acquire property or set up a business in the home country (Jones 1995).

There may be political benefits to sending countries, as well. In Mexico, for example, the proximity of the United States as a source for employment offers a safety valve that reduces political pressure on the Mexican government to institute economic reforms. Some countries may utilize international migration as a way of getting rid of political dissidents or opponents of the regime in power. The migration of approximately 800,000 mostly well-to-do and politically conservative Cubans to the United States after the Castro revolution in 1959 is but one example of many that reflect this process (West and Augelli 1989: 137).

*Internal Migration*

Until recently, data on internal migration in Third World countries were difficult to obtain (Man, Serow, and Sly 1990: 7–8). They are still hard to compare because they are collected by the government of each country and are not standardized. However, it seems likely that there are several times more people who migrate from one place to another within their country than there are international migrants. Whatever the total number of internal migrants there may be, their movement has transformed Third World countries.

Internal migration may involve several different types of move. People may move from one rural area to another, they may colonize previously undeveloped areas that are made accessible by new roads, they may move from the countryside to nearby small towns, from small towns to large cities, go directly from rural areas to cities, or migrate from large cities to small towns or rural areas. Most of the attention to internal migration focuses on rural to urban migration because of the rapid growth of cities. However, one should not overlook rural to rural migration. This form of migration is usually expressed in colonization of formerly unpopulated or relatively underutilized areas, in particular tropical forests. This has led to a general association of population growth with deforestation of tropical rain forests in Latin America, Africa, and Asia, although it should be noted that clearing of tropical forests may also be a product of lumbering or expansion of cattle ranching, and only peripherally related to population growth (Williams 1990).

One can get an impression of the extent of rural-to-urban migration in Third World countries by referring to the data in the opening paragraphs of this chapter, reflecting the unprecedented increase in urban population during the twentieth century, which can only be accounted for by massive rural-to-urban migration.

The consequences of urban migration on the receiving areas are discussed in the following section on urbanization. The impacts on the sending areas are varied. Migrants tend to be young adults in the 20–29 year age range (Man, Serow, and Sly 1990: 12). Removing sizable numbers of young men from the rural population may cause shortages of agricultural labor. On the other hand, it also relieves pressure on resources, which may be a serious problem in rural areas of some Third World countries. Since it is usually the more aggressive and adventuresome who migrate, their potential contribution is lost to the home community. Also, aged parents may be left with fewer options for survival in their old age if all or most of their children emigrate to the city. However, many of these consequences are subtle and probably have a much smaller impact on the sending area than immigration has on the cities.

## Urbanization

Fifty years ago, at the end of World War II, New York, London, Tokyo, and Paris headed the list of the world's largest urban agglomerations (Table 3.1). All of these urban centers were in industrialized countries. Only three Third World urban centers, Shanghai, Buenos Aires, and Calcutta, made the list of the ten largest cities of the world, and Buenos Aires was marginally Third World at the time. In 1989, the list of the world's largest cities included Mexico City, São Paulo, Seoul, Bombay, Calcutta, and Buenos Aires, all of which are in Third World countries. By 2035, the list will include only one city in a currently industrialized country, Tokyo/Yokohama, and it

TABLE 3.1    World's Ten Largest Urban Agglomerations, 1950, 1989, and projected to 2035

| Rank | 1950 Urban Area | Population (millions) | 1989 Urban Area | Population (millions) | 2035 Urban Area | Population (millions) |
|---|---|---|---|---|---|---|
| 1 | New York | 12.5 | Tokyo/Yokohama | 28.7 | Mexico City | 39.1 |
| 2 | London | 8.9 | Mexico City | 19.4 | Shanghai | 38.8 |
| 3 | Tokyo | 7.0 | New York | 17.4 | Beijing | 34.5 |
| 4 | Paris | 5.9 | São Paulo | 17.2 | São Paulo | 32.4 |
| 5 | Shanghai | 5.4 | Osaka/Kobe/Kyoto | 16.8 | Bombay | 30.6 |
| 6 | Moscow | 5.1 | Seoul | 15.8 | Dacca | 29.2 |
| 7 | Buenos Aires | 5.0 | Moscow | 13.2 | Calcutta | 28.9 |
| 8 | Chicago | 4.9 | Bombay | 12.9 | Jakarta | 26.8 |
| 9 | Ruhr | 4.9 | Calcutta | 12.8 | Madras | 23.3 |
| 10 | Calcutta | 4.8 | Buenos Aires | 12.4 | Tokyo/Yokohama | 19.3 |

SOURCES: 1950: T. Chandler, *Four Thousand Years of Urban Growth* (Lewiston, NY: St. David's University Press, 1987). 1989, *Cities: Life in the World's 100 Largest Metropolitan Areas* (Washington, D.C.: Population Action International, 1990). 2035, R. H. Stoddard, D. J. Wishart, and B. W. Blouet, *Human Geography: People, Places, and Cultures*, 2nd ed. (Englewood Cliffs, NJ: Prentice-Hall, 1989), p. 318.

will be the smallest of the lot (Table 3.1). As the table suggests, Third World
cities are currently growing at unprecedented rates and are projected to do
so for the next several decades. How and why has this transformation
come about and what does it mean for the countries in which these cities
are located and for the rest of the world?

## Levels of Urbanization

Map 3.2 shows the percentage of urban population for the countries of
the world by quartile. Just as with rates of natural increase, which are
discussed at the beginning of this chapter, there are striking regional differences in levels of urbanization in the Third World. Latin America
stands out as the most urbanized part of the Third World whereas Africa
and Asia are the least urbanized. The low level of urbanization in some of
the world's most populous countries—China, India, Indonesia, and
Bangladesh, for example—is striking. Not revealed in the map is a strong
correlation between per capita gross national product and percent urban
population (Gilbert and Gugler 1982: 8). This suggests a relationship between a country's level of development and growth of cities. However,
differences in regional history since the beginning of the colonial era are
also involved, along with other factors.

## Characteristics of Third World Cities

Third World cities share a number of distinguishing characteristics.
These include a tendency for primate city dominance, maintenance of established circulation patterns, high rates of urban unemployment, the
presence of squatter settlements, and an active informal economy (Jones
1990: 222–227).

*Primate Cities.*    Primate cities dominate their country or region. They are
at the top of the urban hierarchy and are at least twice as populous as the
country's next largest city.[4] National capitals are often primate cities
(some examples are London, Paris, Mexico City, Buenos Aires, Abidjan,
and Jakarta). As this list shows, not all primate cities are in the Third
World; in fact, some of the First World's most famous cities fall into this
category. Still, the phenomenon tends to be strongly identified with the
Third World.

Why does this type of urban hierarchy appear in Third World countries and what does it mean? One answer to this question is that many
Third World countries have highly centralized governments. These governments are housed in the capital and largest city. The concentration of
government activities, in itself, is a spur to urban growth because it cre-

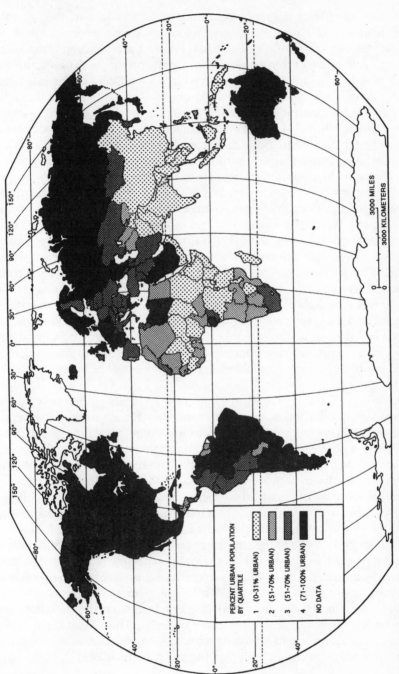

MAP 3.2   Percent urban population for countries of the world by quartile, 1996

ates jobs that attract migrants from rural areas. In addition, the national government has vast control over fiscal resources, which it tends to spend disproportionately in the capital city and surrounding areas, even though this money often comes from distant provinces. The wealthiest and most prestigious families, from which come many of the business, cultural, and political leaders of the country also tend to live in the capital city. Their economic and political power further enhances the primate city. Primate cities also offer a wide range of advantages to business and industry, which tend to locate there for access to government officials, financial backing from big city banks, skilled labor, customer access, transportation facilities, and supplies. Thus, the primate city attracts power and resources at the expense of the rural areas and smaller cities, which are isolated by poor transportation, underserved by national government institutions, lacking in educational and health facilities, and short on employment opportunities, all of which further inhibit their development.

Once a dominant primate city emerges, it is very difficult to reverse the process of accelerated and focused growth. Some countries have attempted to decentralize industry, government functions, and funds for government projects from the primate city to the provinces, but resistance is great and the results are rarely satisfactory. Putting resources into designated growth pole areas is another strategy that has been used to slow the growth of the primate cities, but this also is rarely successful. The projected 2035 populations shown in Table 3.1 suggest the extent of the problem.

*Circulation.*   Urban residents in Third World countries often retain close ties to family and friends in the places they left. Return trips on weekends and for holidays are very common, as are visits for birthdays, religious events, and other special occasions. Such movements are referred to as circulation. Circulation patterns are revealed in other ways, as well. People from the country may move temporarily to the city to live with relatives who have previously established themselves there. Teenagers or college-age youths may live with relatives while they go to school, but plan eventually to return to the smaller towns from which they came. Many unskilled workers move to the city temporarily to try their hand at finding a job. As long as they have work they stay, but when the work runs out, they return home again. Employed workers may return home on weekends to be with family and never establish a formal, permanent residence in the city. These patterns are present in industrialized countries, too, but they appear to be considerably more common in the Third World. However, data on circulation are hard to obtain because censuses fail to ask the questions that would reveal the extent of the practice (Jones 1990: 222).

*Squatter Settlements.*   High levels of unemployment, underemployment, and poverty are common to all Third World cities. Since economic necessity is the primary attraction that pulls migrants from rural areas to the city, it stands to reason that they arrive in the city with very limited financial resources. One way to cope with the problem of survival is for the migrant to live with relatives or friends who are already established. For this reason, having contacts in the city may be a key element in an individual's decision to move there. This relationship is reflected in the existence of areas in the city that house concentrations of migrants from the same village, city, or province; and regionally based social organizations may be formed to help migrants adjust to the city (Doughty 1970: 32–34). But sooner or later, the new migrant must face the problem of finding a place to live. Generally, the only choice for the new arrival, who probably is earning a marginal salary at best, is to locate an old house in a city-center slum in which to rent or share a room. In many countries, the only choice for those without a job may be to live on the street. Eventually, if the migrant stays in the city and has a family, he or she will need to find permanent quarters. For most working-class and even many marginal middle-class individuals this probably means living in a squatter settlement.

Squatters look for a vacant piece of land within the city, or more commonly, at the outskirts, and put up a shack with whatever materials may be available. A single squatter has little chance of avoiding eviction, but if dozens or even hundreds of families organize themselves and arrive at the same time on a piece of land, it can be very difficult to eject them. This applies especially to land that is owned by the government (Reitsma and Kleinpenning 1985: 193). Often, the public seeing news broadcasts or newspaper photographs of police or the army driving poverty-stricken squatters from unused government land has a higher political cost than the government is willing to pay. Even if the land taken over by squatters happens to be privately owned, the government may find it politically advantageous to expropriate the property in the name of the squatters and compensate the owners.

However, all this takes time, often many years, and sometimes it is never accomplished. In the interim, the squatters have no title to their land, and they cannot legally obtain public services such as potable water, sewers and garbage collection, paved streets and sidewalks, bus service or electricity. Sometimes such services are pirated by running electric wires from nearby power lines, tapping city water mains, or other means of access, but these temporary solutions are not really satisfactory, either for the squatters or for the city government. As a result of the lack of services and poor housing, sanitary conditions in the squatter settlements are often terrible and mortality rates high.

Squatter settlements create other problems, as well (Reitsma and Kleinpenning 1985: 192–194). Often they are built in areas that are physically unsuitable for development because they are on steep slopes, are in poorly drained marshes, along flood plains that are subject to periodic flooding, or for other reasons. As a result, squatter settlements are often the victims of natural hazards such as landslides or flooding, and they may cause problems for formal residential areas nearby. For example, squatter settlements on steep slopes may contribute to flooding of downslope areas through increased runoff. At best, the squatter settlements create a demand for services that the cities are hard-pressed to meet. Also, squatters divide up land informally in their settlements and they rarely leave sufficient land for streets, which are not very important for people who cannot afford cars and who might prefer to discourage government vehicles from entering. This may make it very difficult to lay water and sewer lines into the settlements, and it may prohibit the construction of streets. At best, the cost of providing the services may be increased by the conditions of the squatter settlement.

Despite all their problems, squatter settlements have defenders (Dickenson et al. 1983: 189–190; Turner 1970: 1–19). They provide a way of incorporating new migrants into the city, they offer low-cost housing at no direct economic cost to the state (but, as noted previously, there may eventually be considerable indirect costs), and they may contribute substantially to grassroots organization of poor urban dwellers to help themselves. In the latter case, squatter settlement residents often improve their houses, beginning with the flimsiest of shacks and ending up with relatively substantial dwellings that they could never afford to buy even in the poorest of formal neighborhoods in the city. Eventually, according to their defenders, squatter settlements evolve into stable, residential areas with longtime residents. Most social scientists seem to believe that the benefits of squatter settlements outweigh the disadvantages for Third World cities.

*The Informal Economy.* A final observation on Third World cities is that one invariably sees people on the street selling newspapers, cigarettes, candy, and other items, offering to shine shoes, watch a car or wash it, or perform other services. These street peddlers and sellers of services are part of the informal economy. Unable to find work in the formal sector (i.e., working in a store, factory, or some other regular job for a salary) they are forced to eke out a living as they can. Most members of the informal sector are poorly educated and lack skills, so they have few alternatives to living from the informal economy. However, relatively well-educated and skilled people may also be found in the informal economy. Government red tape and bureaucratic hurdles in some countries may make obtaining the business licenses required for legal operation so troublesome and time consuming that shop owners and small manufacturers ignore the law. In other cases jobs in the formal sector are so poorly paid that clever, hardworking individuals may earn more in the informal sector, and a few informal workers manage to earn quite a good living.

However, it is far more common to find that economically marginal people for whom there are no other alternative sources of income make up the vast majority of informal sector workers.

The informal sector in some countries accounts for an important part of earned income. One problem with assessing the importance of the informal sector is that income is not reported, so it is difficult to find out how many people are involved and what their incomes are. Since members of the informal sector do not report their income to the government, nor pay taxes on it, they are ineligible to receive social security and other benefits received by workers in the formal sector. Nevertheless, few would argue that informal workers are not an important part of the urban economy of Third World countries.

## Conclusion

The processes of population growth, migration, and urbanization affect the development of Third World countries in myriad ways. Rapid population growth demands scarce resources to provide schools, hospitals, houses, and other infrastructure for the ever-increasing throngs. Also, the country's limited resources must be divided among more and more individuals, which means that the national economy must grow constantly just to keep up with the increase. Population growth also places stress on natural resources such as forest land, which must be sacrificed to make way for new farms to feed additional mouths.

Migration is one result of overpopulation in rural areas. Adventurous migrants may enter the international migration stream, but most move within their home country. Urban areas receive many of these internal migrants, who contribute to growth of cities. In the cities, migrants struggle to find jobs, locate housing, and establish themselves. Common characteristics of Third World cities reflect this situation. These characteristics include the presence of squatter settlements and a large informal sector.

Primate cities are common in the Third World. These cities dominate the urban hierarchy and may absorb a disproportionate share of the national resources. As a primate city continues to grow and pull resources from outlying rural areas and smaller cities, it creates more poverty in the peripheral areas and draws even more migration to itself. Diverting more resources to peripheral areas to break this cycle has not been notably successful in the past, so new strategies will likely be needed to divert growth away from the traditional primate centers.

Meanwhile, population growth is slacking off in many Third World countries. This may mean that rates of natural increase have peaked and will slowly begin to decline. However, because of demographic momentum, Third World population will continue to increase rapidly well into the twenty-first century. Also, regional differences in rates of population growth, urbanization, and economic development will continue to differentiate Third World regions and countries. One cannot apply the same generalizations about population growth to China and India, or to Argentina and Mexico. Nor can levels of urbanization in Africa be equated with Latin America. These differences must be considered in any evaluation of future developments in the Third World. It remains to be seen if the projections of future world population and metropolitan area size presented in this chapter will prove to be accurate, and chances are they will not be. But whatever the future brings, the answers lie in the dynamics of Third World population growth, migration, and urban expansion.

### Notes

1. Some demographic transition models, such as that developed by Chung, identify three stages of population growth rather than four as used in this chapter. In those models stages 2 and 3 are combined.

2. Not all human mobility is classified as migration. Migration must include a relatively long-term change of residence. Repetitive movements, such as commuting to work or school, or temporary changes of residence to attend school, a training program, or for work do not constitute migration. These short-term and often habitual movements are referred to as circulation. Mike Parnwell (1993: 11–28) provides a comprehensive review of migration forms and the terminology applied to them.

3. As a result of negotiations between Israel and the Palestine Liberation Organization, Palestinians in Gaza and certain West Bank communities are now partly self-governing and may no longer be classified as refugees.

4. Indices of primacy are sometimes used to compare the urban primacy of countries. The index is a ratio of the population of the largest city in a country with the combined populations of the next three largest cities.

### References

Begley, S. 1994. "Can More = Better?" *Newsweek*, September 12, 27.

Castles, Stephen, and Mark J. Miller. 1993. *The Age of Migration: International Population Movements in the Modern World*. New York: Guilford Press.

Chung, Roy. 1970. "Space-Time Diffusion of the Transition Model: The Twentieth-Century Patterns." In *Population Geography: A Reader*, George J. Demko, Harold M. Rose, and George A. Schnell, eds., 220–239. New York: McGraw-Hill.

Cohen, Joel E. 1995. *How Many People Can the Earth Support?* New York, London: W. W. Norton.

————. 1996. "Ten Myths of Population." *Discover*, 17: 42–46.

Demeny, Paul. 1990. "Population." In *The Earth As Transformed by Human Action*, Billie L. Turner II, William C. Clark, Robert W. Kates, John F. Richards, Jessica T. Mathews, and William B. Meyer, eds., 41–54. Cambridge: Cambridge University Press.

Dickenson, John P., C. G. Clarke, W. T. S. Gould, R. M. Prothero, D. J. Siddle, C. T. Smith, E. M. Thomas-Hope, and A. G. Hodgkiss. 1983. *A Geography of the Third World*. London: Methuen.

Doughty, Paul L. 1970. "Behind the Back of the City: 'Provincial' Life in Lima, Peru." In *Peasants in Cities: Readings in the Anthropology of Urbanization*, William Mangin, ed., 32–34. Boston: Houghton Mifflin.

Ehrlich, Paul R., and Anne H. Ehrlich. 1970. *Population, Resources, Environment: Issues in Human Ecology*. San Francisco: Freeman.

El-Badry, M. A. 1991. "The Growth of World Population: Past, Present, and Future." In *Consequences of Rapid Population Growth in Developing Countries*. Proceedings of the United Nations/Institut national d'études démographiques Expert Group Meeting, New York, August 23–26, 1988. Pp. 15–40. New York: Taylor and Francis.

Fornos, Werner, and Hal Burdett. 1994. *Moving On: The Global Migration Problem*. Toward the Twenty-first Century, Report Number 1, 1994. Washington, D.C.: Population Institute.

Gilbert, Alan, and Josef Gugler. 1982. *Cities, Poverty, and Development: Urbanization in the Third World*. London: Oxford University Press.

Harris, Nigel. 1995. *The New Untouchables: Immigration and the New World Worker*. London: Penguin.

Jones, Huw. 1990. *Population Geography*, 2nd ed. London: Paul Chapman.

Jones, Richard C. 1995. *Ambivalent Journey: U.S. Migration and Economic Mobility in North-Central Mexico*. Tucson: University of Arizona Press.

Kalipeni, Ezekiel. 1995. "The Fertility Transition in Africa." *Geographical Review* 85: 286–299.

Lindahl-Liessling, Kerstin, and Hans Landberg, eds., 1994. *Population, Economic Development, and the Environment*. Oxford: Oxford University Press.

Man, Charles B., William J. Serow, and David L. Sly, eds. 1990. *International Handbook on Internal Migration*. New York: Greenwood Press.

Meadows, Donella H., Dennis L. Meadows, and Jørgen Randers. 1992. *Beyond the Limits: Confronting Global Collapse, Envisioning a Sustainable Future*. Post Mills, Vt.: Chelsea Green.

Merrick, Thomas W. 1986. "World Population in Transition." *Population Bulletin* 41: 1–51.

Parnwell, Mike. 1993. *Population Movements and the Third World*. London and New York: Routledge.

Perlez, Jane. 1995. "Third World Migrants Risk Hell for a Dream." *New York Times*, July 31, A3.

Ponting, Clive. 1991. *A Green History of the World: The Environment and the Collapse of Great Civilizations*. New York: St. Martins.

Population Reference Bureau. 1996. *1996 World Population Data Sheet*. Washington, D.C.: Population Reference Bureau.

Reitsma, Hendrik-Jan A., and J. M. G. Kleinpenning. 1985. *The Third World in Perspective*. Totowa, N.J.: Rowman & Allanheld.

Robey, Bryand, Shea O. Rutstein, and Leo Morris, 1993. "The Fertility Decline in Developing Countries." *Scientific American* 269: 60–67.

Simon, Julian L. 1990. *Population Matters: People, Resources, Environment, and Immigration.* New Brunswick, N.J.: Transaction Publishers.

Turner, John C. 1970. "Barriers and Channels for Housing Development in Modernizing Countries." In *Peasants in Cities: Readings in the Anthropology of Urbanization,* William Mangin, ed., 1–19. Boston: Houghton Mifflin.

U.S. Committee for Refugees. 1994. *1994 World Refugee Survey.* Washington, D.C.: American Council for Nationalities Service.

Weir, D. P. 1991. "A Historical Perspective on the Economic Consequences of Rapid Population Growth." In *Consequences of Rapid Population Growth in Developing Countries.* Proceedings of the United Nations/Institut national d'études démographiques Expert Group Meeting, New York, August 23–26, 1988. Pp. 41–67. New York: Taylor and Francis.

West, Robert C., and John P. Augelli. 1989. *Middle America: Its Lands and Peoples,* 3rd ed. Englewood Cliffs, N.J.: Prentice-Hall.

Williams, Michael. 1990. "Forests." In *The Earth As Transformed by Human Action,* Billie L. Turner II, William C. Clark, Robert W. Kates, John F. Richards, Jessica T. Mathews, and William B. Meyer, eds., 179–201. Cambridge: Cambridge University Press.

Zuckerman, Ben, and David Jefferson, eds. 1996. *Human Population and the Environmental Crisis.* Sudbury, Mass.: Jones and Bartlett Publishers.

# 4   *Health: One World or Two?*

## R. Warwick Armstrong
## and Jerome D. Fellmann

Health is part of the human condition, a quality of mind, body, and environment that supports human beings to complete their life expectancy and to function in daily living without undue mental or physical hindrance. The level of health and longevity varies greatly among individuals and among national populations, which is a reflection of variations in individual biology and behavior and in the physical, biological, and cultural environments of people. All national populations have individuals in the poorest of health and in the best of health, but the numbers and proportions of the population in these extremes and in the range between them varies greatly. Third World countries have the largest numbers and proportions of people in poor health and with the shortest life expectancies.

There are indeed at least two worlds of health. One is an affluent world where life expectancy is long and the chief killers of a mature population are heart disease, cancers, and strokes. The other is an impoverished, disease-ridden world where the deadly scourges of a youthful populace are infectious and parasitic diseases made worse by malnutrition. In 1975, the appalling disparities between the two encouraged the member countries of the World Health Organization (WHO) to endorse "Health for All by the Year 2000" as their official target. In the twenty years since this program began, there has been considerable improvement in the health of populations of many Third World countries, although some have seen very little change. In the same period, world populations have continued to grow and to consume ever greater amounts of energy, leading to further pollution and environmental degradation, which in turn cause illness and threaten health in rich and poor countries alike.

The two worlds of health are defined by changing rankings in measures of well-being, morbidity, or mortality recorded by the individual countries composing them. Such rankings are in part anticipated by generalized models that indicate where countries stand on a historical and comparative continuum of health-related development.

## Models of Development and Health

### Wealth and Health

The richest countries have created environments of health that include urban settlements for a majority of their populations, adequate food supplies, sanitation and safe water, job-producing industrialization, universal education, and the medical services essential to the well-being of their citizens. Such preconditions of health are beyond the present economic grasp of the poorest countries although some have made remarkable progress in recent years, such as China and Malaysia. The connection between national wealth and health has both logical and empirical support. Table 4.1 suggests the relationship between gross national product (GNP) per capita and three statistics of well-being. Lowest levels of health are reported among African countries, which also record the lowest per capita incomes. Latin America, with incomes among the highest in the developing world, shows health indicators closest to those of the developed world. Asia, containing great regional diversity in all health and wealth statistics, occupies a generalized middle ground. By major world regions, developed and developing, the 1995 weighted correlation coefficient for per capita GNP and life expectancy is 0.78; for 150 separate countries it is 0.60. It is therefore argued by many that a country's ranked position on an economically based scale of development should serve to measure the relative status of health of its population.

It is a persuasive argument that needs to be qualified. Countries with nearly identical per capita GNPs are by no means certain to have comparable morbidity and mortality rates or health problems, and countries with low incomes are certainly not automatically unhealthy. For example, life expectancies in Sri Lanka, a low-income country, approach those recorded in advanced industrialized states. This is due in part to different national policies of spending on health. Sri Lanka spent a larger proportion of its wealth on health, whereas other developing countries with higher rates of economic growth during the 1980s and 1990s spent proportionately less and saw less improvement in the health and well-being of the majority of their populations. Nor is income distribution a reliable predictor of such a basic health indicator as infant mortality rate. For developing countries as a group there is less than a 0.07 correlation coefficient between infant mortality and GNP per capita. Neither suggestive intercountry comparisons nor statistical economic indicators, therefore, have proved reliable as a means of categorizing countries on the basis of the quality of life or conditions of health of their citizens.

TABLE 4.1   Wealth and Health by Major World Regions

| Region | Per Capita GNP, 1994 (US $) | Life Expectancy at Birth (years) | Infant Mortality Rate (per 1,000 live births) | Crude Death Rate (per 1,000 population) |
|---|---|---|---|---|
| Less developed | 1,090 | 64 | 68 | 9 |
| Africa | 660 | 55 | 91 | 13 |
| Asia | 2,150 | 65 | 62 | 8 |
| Latin America | 3,290 | 69 | 43 | 7 |
| More developed | 18,130 | 74 | 9 | 10 |

SOURCE: Population Reference Bureau, *World Population Data Sheet* (Washington, D.C.: Population Reference Bureau, 1996).

*Transition Models*

The *demographic transition* model traces through changing population characteristics the historical progression of Western countries from conditions of "underdevelopment" to their present First World status. A first stage of high birth and death rates was succeeded, after 1650, by both an agricultural (Farb and Armelagos 1980) and an industrial revolution. Death rates were slashed, birth rates remained high, and explosive growth resulted. In stage three of the transition, urbanization and social change reduced the attractiveness of multiple child families; birth rates began to fall. Finally, with rising incomes, modern medicine, and sanitation in the twentieth century, death rates declined until old age and in this fourth stage population again stabilized, though at a much higher average age level. In population history terms, a state of "development" was achieved.

Because conditions are no longer the same, the Third World cannot exactly replicate the historical transition path traced by Western countries. Today, improved social and economic conditions, including medical technology, have resulted in plummeting death rates while cultural imperatives continue to keep birth rates high. Rapid communication, international cooperation, and application of modern technologies have jumbled the characteristics and controls of the model's transition stages. Indeed, the model itself has been rejected by some as ethnocentric and inapplicable to cultures other than European. Nonetheless, evidence of its stages can be discerned in the changing population structures of developing countries.

Table 4.2 suggests how those transition stages can identify individual countries as they pass along the model's prescribed path from demographically based underdevelopment to full development marked by mature, stable populations. Population data from developing countries are suspect and time series based on them are dubious, but we can use them with caution for the trends they suggest. For the less developed

TABLE 4.2  Vital Rates and Life Expectancies in Selected Countries

| Country | Crude Birth Rate | | | | Crude Death Rate | | | | Life Expectancy at Birth (years) | | | |
|---|---|---|---|---|---|---|---|---|---|---|---|---|
| | 1955 | 1970 | 1985 | 1996 | 1955 | 1970 | 1985 | 1996 | 1955 | 1970 | 1985 | 1996 |
| Guinea | 62 | 47 | 47 | 44 | 40 | 25 | 23 | 20 | 27 | 41 | 40 | 44 |
| Madagascar | 35 | 46 | 45 | 44 | – | 25 | 17 | 12 | – | 35 | 50 | 57 |
| Nigeria | 48 | 50 | 48 | 43 | – | 25 | 17 | 12 | – | 37 | 50 | 56 |
| Tunisia | 43 | 46 | 33 | 23 | 18 | 16 | 10 | 6 | – | 52 | 61 | 68 |
| India | 32 | 43 | 34 | 29 | 13 | 17 | 13 | 10 | 41 | – | 53 | 59 |
| Sri Lanka | 38 | 30 | 27 | 20 | 11 | 8 | 6 | 5 | 57 | 61 | 68 | 73 |
| Philippines | 34 | 45 | 32 | 30 | 10 | 12 | 7 | 9 | 51 | 58 | 64 | 65 |
| Thailand | 34 | 43 | 25 | 20 | 10 | 10 | 6 | 6 | 51 | 57 | 63 | 70 |
| Chile | 35 | 30 | 24 | 21 | 13 | 9 | 6 | 6 | 52 | 64 | 70 | 72 |
| Colombia | 41 | 41 | 28 | 27 | 13 | 9 | 7 | 6 | 45 | 61 | 64 | 69 |
| Costa Rica | 40 | 32 | 31 | 26 | 11 | 6 | 4 | 4 | 56 | 64 | 73 | 76 |
| Guatemala | 49 | 42 | 43 | 36 | 21 | 14 | 8 | 7 | 44 | 49 | 59 | 65 |
| Japan | 19 | 19 | 13 | 10 | 8 | 6 | 6 | 7 | 66 | 72 | 77 | 80 |
| United Kingdom | 15 | 15 | 13 | 13 | 12 | 12 | 12 | 11 | 70 | 71 | 73 | 77 |
| United States | 25 | 16 | 16 | 15 | 9 | 9 | 9 | 9 | 70 | 71 | 75 | 76 |

SOURCES: Population Reference Bureau, *World Population Data Sheet* (Washington, D.C.: Population Reference Bureau, 1985, 1996). United Nations, *Demographic Yearbook* (New York: United Nations, 1957, 1973).

countries shown in Table 4.2, the trends have been toward marked increases in life expectancies since 1955; apparently, most of the countries have been beneficiaries of social and economic improvement including medical technology.

For some, however, including most Sub-Saharan African countries, there has been much less progress along the transition. Continuing high birth rates and relatively high death rates indicate a first-stage position. Many of the Asian and Latin American countries show by their rapidly declining death rates and more slowly falling birth rates that they are passing into the third stage. Japan, the United Kingdom, and the United States serve as variant examples of completion of the demographic cycle; Chile, Costa Rica, and less certainly Colombia are following behind. India appears at a relative standstill in contrast to neighboring Sri Lanka.

The demographic transition summarizes effects; a parallel *epidemiologic transition* is concerned with causes (Omran 1971). It begins with the assumption that mortality is a fundamental factor in population change and that mortality patterns alter as a society makes a health-based transition from the status of underdeveloped country to advanced country. The Age of Pestilence and Famine is comparable to the first stage of the demographic transition. Infectious, respiratory, and parasitic diseases and malnutrition dominate in what is essentially the premodern pattern of health and disease still characteristic of the world's poorest countries. With modernization, the Age of Receding Pandemics is entered, mortality rates begin a progressive decline, and average life expectancy at birth begins to increase from about 30 years to about 50 years. A population explosion begins. Gradually, disease and mortality patterns start to shift. Medical and nutritional improvements control epidemics; the incidence of infectious diseases is reduced; and a moderate increase is noted in afflictions typical of a maturing population. The shift toward those conditions marks the final transition to the Age of Degenerative and Man-Made Diseases. Mortality continues to decline to a low, stable rate; average life expectancy rises to 70-plus years; and fertility becomes the key factor in sustaining population growth.

The two models summarize different aspects of the transition in the human condition that has occurred in populations in the last 300 years. But the details of the experience have differed greatly in time and in place. The experience of the United States and Europe in the eighteenth and nineteenth centuries is not transferable to Third World countries of the twentieth century (Omran 1977).

Morbidity and mortality patterns have proved to be more subject to rapidly changing social and technological conditions than to relatively stable environmental circumstances. Although this may be encouraging for the control of diseases associated with, for example, tropical regions, it also explains why declining mortality patterns in developing countries have not paralleled the Western model. In England, for example, the mortality decline during the nineteenth and early twentieth centuries was the result of generalized socioeconomic development, including improved nutrition and the creation of water-supply and sanitation systems. Only after the mid-1930s did the application of modern medical technology make a substantial contribution to life expectancy (McKeown 1976: 91–109).

Among developing countries of both Latin America and southern and eastern Asia, the sequence of events has been directly opposite. After World War II very rapid declines in mortality rates and increases in life expectancy occurred immediately after introduction of medical innovations and before there were major improvements in general socioeconomic conditions. Consequently, after a sharp initial improvement, mortality rate decreases slowed substantially (Palloni 1981; Ruzicka and Hansluwka 1982), contrary to the Western model's expectation of continuing gains in life expectancy to recognizable maximum values (UN 1980: 31).

*Derived Indexes*

Nevertheless, the epidemiologic transition model has analytical as well as predictive value. As a society progresses through the transition, degenerative diseases become predominant and an increasing proportion of deaths occur among the no-longer productive elderly rather than those actually or potentially engaged in economic activity. A measure known as potential years of life lost (PYLL) has been widely adopted as a simple indicator of the social and economic consequences of a reduction in infant and child mortality or of premature death. The calculation used by WHO and most national health agencies is a sum of all the years of life lost in a population due to deaths between the ages of 1 and 65 (U.S. Centers for Disease Control and Prevention 1986). For example, if a person dies at age 20, 45 potential years of life have been lost. Lives lost before age 65 are in theory mostly preventable and are more costly in social and economic terms than those lost at or near full life expectancy. The PYLL statistic indicates a country's position on the epidemiologic transition and, by highlighting the significance rather than the cause of death, directs national attention to health programs most beneficial to the well-being of society. For example, deaths from injuries among children, adolescents, and young adults caused by motor vehicle crashes, hazardous workplaces, or violence contributes substantially to PYLL in all countries. Similarly, the exploding epidemic of HIV-disease (AIDS) is extremely costly in terms of PYLL because it kills most of those afflicted before the age of 40.

A more sophisticated index to measure the relative burden of disease among countries, disability-adjusted life years (DALYs), was recently developed by the World Bank and WHO. This index adjusts PYLL by severity of disease and injury, by discounting future years of healthy life at progressively lower levels, and by relative value of life—rising steeply after birth, peaking at age 25, and gradually declining with increasing age (World Bank 1993: 26). The greatest burden of disease and injuries in terms of DALYs is carried by countries in Sub-Saharan Africa with 575 per 1,000 population, India with 344, and Middle Eastern countries with 286. Developed countries had 117 per 1,000 population. The proportions of DALYs in countries in Sub-Saharan Africa due to infectious diseases was 71 percent, to noninfectious diseases 19 percent, and to injuries 9 percent. In the developed countries the proportions were 10 percent infectious diseases, 78 percent noninfectious diseases, and 12 percent injuries.

An indicator introduced by the United Nations in 1990 is the Human Development Index (HDI), which seeks to measure how nearly individual countries achieve well-being by meeting the most basic needs of their citizens. Four basic variables—life expectancy, adult literacy, mean years of schooling, and income measured in "purchasing power parity" terms—have been combined to capture both the social and economic aspects of human life. Longevity and education address the formation of human capabilities, and purchasing power income per capita is the proxy measure for the choices people have in exercising their capabilities. The HDI rankings of countries differ sharply from their relative scores on single-component indexes such as GNP per capita. Costa Rica, Colombia, and Thailand, among others, do far better on their human development ranking than on their per capita income rankings, suggesting that those countries have invested their economic resources effectively toward some aspects of human well-being and progress. Libya, Gabon, Saudi Arabia, and others rank lower on the HDI than on their per capita incomes, showing that those incomes have not yet been translated into corresponding levels of human well-being. To the extent that the quality of life it seeks to measure reveals a national environment of health, the HDI is another useful device for international classification and one that sharply contrasts the two worlds of social and economic well-being.

Since 1975, WHO and other international health and development agencies have worked with national governments to improve the availability of demographic, social, health, and economic data for all Third World countries (WHO 1981). Establishing data collection systems in poorer countries where none have existed before takes time, and it is only since 1990 that most countries have been reporting comparable systematic data (World Bank 1993; WHO 1986). This richer source of information will permit more accurate assessment of the health condition of the Third World in the future.

## Third World Realities

The models and measures reviewed are useful abstractions and indicators, but they do not address the details of morbidity and mortality in developing countries. By emphasizing theoretical convergences, they gloss over the enormity of Third World divergences from patterns of health and well-being accepted as the norm in developed countries. The environment of health is a complex web of interrelationships from which isolation of individual elements is difficult and—through undue emphasis—even disruptive. Nonetheless, there is agreement that the achievement of "Health for All" must involve bringing to Third World residents First World standards of life expectancy, disease control, infrastructure improvement, nutritional levels, health care availability, and—to make those changes acceptable and practicable—near universal literacy. In each of these measures the distance between the poorest-performing LDC (less developed country) and the norms of the advanced countries is great; in each, a broad transitional zone of improvement is occupied by an ever-increasing number of countries and a greater percentage of the world population.

Life expectancy is an easily understood statistic of development. Table 4.2 suggests the range that is recorded among countries classified as less developed compared to three classified as more developed: Japan, the United Kingdom, and the United States. In general, the higher a country's average income the higher its life expectancy. Among the richer developing countries longevity approaches or equals the 75-year average in industrialized countries; in low-income countries expectancies may be only 55 years or less.

Infant and child mortality is the major contributor to low life expectancy in developing regions. Some 12 percent of children in developing countries as a whole and more than 20 percent in the poorest ones die before their fifth birthday. In industrialized countries the figure is less than 2 percent. The chief causes are diarrheal diseases, measles, pertussis, and other respiratory infections. Frequent bouts of illness and poor feeding practices lead to malnutrition which in turn greatly increases the likelihood that a given child will die from an illness such as measles (UNICEF 1990: 29). The deadly combination of diarrhea, measles, respiratory disease, and malnutrition accounts for more than half of all child mortalities. Once past the perilous childhood years, adult populations—particularly urban adults—of developing countries increasingly assume the mortality patterns of their advanced-country counterparts. Indeed, in most instances there is less distinction between the fully urban areas of developing and developed countries than there is between the urban, semi-urban, and rural districts of a single Third World country.

## Disease Patterns

Despite the wide geographical range represented by Third World countries and their separate physical and social environments, certain common disease patterns obtain. First, diseases of highest incidence are those carried in human fecal matter, including intestinal parasites, various infectious diarrheas, typhoid, cholera, hepatitis A, and poliomyelitis. They reflect unsafe water supplies and inadequate waste disposal practices. Second, diseases transmitted from person to person and often associated with crowding and poverty include tuberculosis, measles, pneumonia, influenza, pertussis, hepatitis B, and sexually transmitted diseases—all exacerbated by malnutrition. Person-to-person infectious diseases are becoming the most common in overcrowded cities where international travel, migration, and the movement of refugees promote their rapid spread. Third, the traditional vector-borne tropical diseases of malaria, yellow fever, schistosomiasis, filariasis, trypanosomiasis (sleeping sickness), and onchocerciasis (river blindness), in some instances thought under control or even subject to elimination in the 1950s and 1960s, are still serious and growing problems. Malaria continues to be one of the most serious causes of morbidity and mortality in tropical countries. It is endemic in 91 countries with about 40 percent of the world's population at risk. There are an estimated 300–500 million cases of malaria each year, 90 percent in Africa. Between 1.5 and 2.7 million people, mostly children, die from malaria each year (WHO 1996: 47). Fourth, the ultimate pattern of similarity in disease characteristics of developing countries is interconnectedness. Whatever the specific disease—localized yellow or dengue fever or cholera, or near universal tetanus, influenza, or tuberculosis—it is the product of a complex of environmental, economic, and social factors intimately interrelated (Basch 1990: 3).

Characteristic of those sociophysical environments of disease experienced by Third World peoples are (1) the specific disease conditions and health care opportunities (or their lack) associated with rural and urban-slum residence; (2) the controlling part played by safe water and sanitation; (3) the role of malnourishment as the silent accomplice of disease; and (4) the need for a literate population to understand and act upon basic measures of personal, family, and community health.

## The HIV-AIDS Epidemic and Other Emerging Diseases

About 1980, a new infection began to appear that has since exploded into a global epidemic. Caused by the human immunodeficiency virus (HIV), it leads to autoimmune deficiency syndrome (AIDS), a group of signs, symptoms, and opportunistic infections and noninfectious diseases that is 80–90 percent fatal within 3–5 years (Benenson 1995: 2). By mid-1996, 20 million people worldwide were estimated to be infected with HIV. About one-fifth (4.5 million) had developed AIDS and 85 percent (3.8 million) of these had died (WHO 1996: 31). Originating probably in central east Africa, the infection and its associated syndrome has had greatest impact in the Third World countries of Sub-Saharan Africa. More than half of all adult HIV infections in the world have so far occurred in these countries, which have only 7.5 percent of the global adult population. Latin America had 8.4 percent of the HIV infections with 7.3 percent of the global adult population, and the Caribbean 2.6 percent of the HIV infections with 0.6 percent of the adult population. North America, principally the United States, was the most affected of developed country regions with 10 percent of the world's HIV infections in 5.2 percent of the adult population. All other regions in the world so far have a smaller proportion of HIV infections than global adult population (Mann, Tarontola, and Netter 1992: 28). However, the epidemic has now reached all countries and is rapidly increasing in incidence.

Although countries in Sub-Saharan Africa are now experiencing the most severe effects of AIDS, it is clear that countries in Latin America and Asia will be affected severely in the future. Brazil, India, and Thailand all have rapidly increasing proportions of young adults with HIV infection, an ominous precursor to AIDS. This disease, for which there is yet no cure, will have an especially severe impact on Third World countries with their larger proportions and numbers of younger adults and where resources for prevention campaigns, treatment services, and social support are minimal.

Complicating the efforts to control infectious diseases worldwide is the emergence since 1970 of over thirty new diseases besides AIDS, including legionellosis, Ebola hemorrhagic fever, hepatitis C and D, and cryptosporidiosis. New strains of already well-established infections have emerged, for example, for cholera, influenza, and *Escherichia coli*, that cause more severe forms of their respective diseases. The epidemic of Ebola hemorrhagic fever in Zaire in 1995 attracted international attention because of its frightening effects including a 77 percent fatality rate. The number of cases (316) was small compared to other disease epidemics, in part due to prompt international control efforts, but it alerted WHO to the dangers associated with outbreaks of new virulent diseases. A rapid response system has been established by WHO to deal with such emergencies (WHO 1996: 16).

Perhaps the most serious public health problem emerging with infections is the evolution of resistance by many organisms to the present generation of antimicrobial drugs. Drug resistant strains of tuberculosis, shigellosis, salmonella, gonorrhea, pneumococci, haemophilus influenzae, staphylococci, and the group of streptococci that cause rheumatic fever and rheumatic heart disease have all emerged in recent years (May 1994: 167). This has come at a time when the pace of discovery and development of new drugs has slowed, and there is increasing and often indiscriminant use of existing drugs among humans and for livestock, which accelerates the evolution of resistance. Resistance by shigella and salmonella to standard low-cost drugs is particularly serious in Third World countries where these two bacteria are the major causes of death in children from diarrheal disease. Hospitals are also badly affected because with declining effectiveness of drugs to promptly control infections, the rates of nosocomial diseases (diseases that originate in hospitals or other centers of medical practice) rapidly increase. The highest rates of nosocomial infections now occur in the eastern Mediterranean, Southeast Asia, western Pacific, and Latin America, but the problem is increasing worldwide (WHO 1996: 22).

### Environmental and Behavioral Factors

Within the expanding cities of Third World countries, more than a quarter-billion people live in unsanitary and disease-ridden slums and shantytowns devoid of adequate water supply or sanitary disposal facilities. The squalor in which they exist provides—through cesspits and water-filled city litter—ideal breeding grounds for rats, flies, and mosquitoes, the carriers of diarrheal diseases and tropical fevers. Yet, despite appalling environmental conditions, it is still healthier to live in tropical Third World cities than countrysides. Most arthropod- or snail-borne infections affect primarily rural folk, who additionally endure the diseases associated with unsafe water and poor sanitation and have far less access to even rudimentary health care clinics than their urban counterparts.

Safe water and sanitary disposal of human waste are key elements in human health. Their ubiquity in the developed world and their general absence in, particularly, rural areas and urban slums in the Third World constitute a profound contrast in the conditions for health in the two realms. Despite considerable progress since 1985 to improve access to safe water supplies and more hygienic sanitary disposal methods in Third World countries, 1.7 billion people worldwide do not have access to safe drinking water, and 3.4 billion people do not have access to adequate sanitary facilities (UNICEF 1997: 98). Table 4.3 suggests the importance of access to safe water.

Malnutrition is the silent but deadly contributor to disease and death nearly everywhere in the developing world, particularly among infants and children. An estimated one-quarter of the world's children under age

TABLE 4.3    Safe Water and Measures of Health in Selected Countries, 1985–1987

| Country | Access to Safe Water (% of population) | Infant Mortality Rate (per 1,000 live births) | Life Expectancy at Birth (years) |
|---|---|---|---|
| Guinea | 55 | 128 | 44 |
| Madagascar | 29 | 100 | 57 |
| Nigeria | 51 | 114 | 56 |
| Tunisia | 98 | 30 | 68 |
| India | 81 | 76 | 59 |
| Sri Lanka | 57 | 15 | 73 |
| Philippines | 86 | 40 | 65 |
| Thailand | 89 | 27 | 70 |
| Chile | 95 | 13 | 72 |
| Colombia | 85 | 30 | 69 |
| Costa Rica | 96 | 14 | 76 |
| Guatemala | 64 | 49 | 65 |
| Japan | 98 | 4 | 80 |
| United Kingdom | 98 | 6 | 77 |
| United States | 91 | 8 | 76 |

SOURCE: UNICEF, *The State of the World's Children* (Oxford: Oxford University Press, 1997).

five and a total of some 800 million people overall suffer hunger or malnutrition; continued population growth simply compounds the numbers and the problem.

Appalling scenes of famine are common in the media, but the more insidious and hidden expressions of malnourishment are premature births; low birth weights; abnormally low weight-for-height and weight-for-age ratios; the lethargy, apathy, and low productivity associated with anemia; blindness resulting from vitamin-A deficiency; mental retardation; and a host of other impacts upon physical and mental health. Above all, malnutrition is reckoned to be a direct or indirect cause of at least 20 to 25 percent of the disease burden in children (World Bank 1993: 77).

Malnutrition frequently means more than a lack of calories and proteins; there may be crippling deficiencies in micronutrients and vitamins among, particularly, young children. Nutritional shortfalls and imbalances reflect not only family incomes too low to provide customary food in sufficient volume but also a failure to fully appreciate the role of adequate diet in the care of children and the treatment of disease.

Sexual behaviors that do not include barriers to infection account for more than 330 million new cases of sexually transmitted diseases, other than HIV infection, each year worldwide (WHO 1996: 33). These diseases

TABLE 4.4    Infant Mortality and Female Literacy in Selected Developing and More Developed Countries

| Country | Infant Mortality Rate 1995 (per 1,000 live births) | Female Literacy 1995 (%) |
|---|---|---|
| Burkina Faso | 86 | 9 |
| Afghanistan | 165 | 15 |
| Yemen Arab Republic | 76 | 26 |
| Chad | 94 | 35 |
| Mexico | 27 | 87 |
| Thailand | 27 | 92 |
| Sri Lanka | 15 | 87 |
| Malaysia | 11 | 78 |
| Hong Kong | 5 | 88 |
| Finland | 4 | 99 |
| Russian Federation | 27 | 98 |
| United Kingdom | 6 | 99 |

SOURCE: UNICEF, *The State of the World's Children* (Oxford: Oxford University Press, 1997).

include chlamydia, gonorrhea, and syphilis, which add greatly to the risk of other infections especially in pregnancy and childbirth. Their prevalence is greatest in Africa, Latin America, and some Asian countries such as India and Thailand.

Literacy, particularly female literacy, provides the surest guarantee of the eventual achievement of the "Health for All" program objectives. It is a particularly valid predictor of infant mortality rates. Numerous studies show that the more educated mothers are, the less likely are their children to die, whatever the family income. The extremes of the accepted relation between female literacy and infant mortality are shown in Table 4.4. A simple regression of infant mortality on female literacy for 150 countries reporting both sets of data for 1995 yields a correlation coefficient of –0.86. Although other factors are certainly involved, the association of low infant-mortality rates with high female literacy indicates how important for child health is a mother's awareness of (and willingness to try) recommended health, hygiene, and nutritional practices.

Injuries are major causes of death and disability in all countries of the Third World. In the poorest countries, natural hazards such as earthquakes and floods have been disasters because of such things as unsafe housing, oversettlement on floodplains, and lack of disaster control efforts. War, civil conflict, and terrorism have been major causes of death and injury in many developing countries including Afghanistan, Cambodia, Chile, El Salvador, Haiti, India, Indonesia, Iran, Iraq, Nigeria,

Rwanda, and Uganda. In the rapidly industrializing countries of the Third World, motor vehicle crashes, industrial and construction site accidents, and new consumer products account for a substantial proportion of injuries and deaths. Poorer countries are more susceptible to industrial disasters where zoning and safety regulations are nonexistent or poorly enforced. The Bhopal incident in 1984 in India, where a lethal cloud of methyl isocyanate was released by a storage plant, killed 2,250 and injured over 50,000.

Air pollution from motor vehicles and industries has reached and exceeded the levels experienced in the cities of developed countries in São Paulo, Mexico City, Kuala Lumpur, Taipei, Shanghai, and Bangkok. But the most severe air pollution in the Third World is in domestic rural settings where, women especially, are exposed to high concentrations of wood, dung, and coal smoke from cooking fires inside unventilated houses.

## Health and Medical Services

Self- and family-health care are the most important forms of health promotion and illness prevention and treatment worldwide. In the poorer countries with less literate and informed populations, and with less access to modern health and medical technology, self and family care is much less effective. Similarly, the traditional medical practitioners, who still serve the majority of the world's rural populations, while often successful in treating individual cases of illness, cannot prevent community epidemics of disease, malnutrition, or environmental pollution. Modern medical practitioners in clinics and hospitals are almost entirely confined to cities in developing countries. Only a few countries, such as China, Malaysia, and Sri Lanka, have a well-organized system of general and district hospitals and rural dispensaries serving the entire population.

The WHO program, "Health for All by the Year 2000," has encouraged all developing countries to concentrate their health development efforts on primary health care. This emphasizes health education, environmental sanitation, employment of local health workers, inclusion of traditional medicine, maternal and child health, prevention and treatment of local diseases and injuries, promotion of nutrition, and provision of essential drugs and vaccines (Basch 1990: 205). The program has had varying success depending on political, economic, and social priorities. In those countries giving priority to military expenditures there has been less development of primary health care.

The most dramatic progress since 1980 has been in reducing the impact of childhood diseases through immunizations and oral rehydration therapy (ORT). Vaccines for diptheria, whooping cough, measles, tetanus, poliomyelitis, and tuberculosis prevent the worst of childhood diseases, and ORT saves children from death by diarrhea. The result of introducing the immunization and ORT program in most developing countries was, by 1990, a saving of more than 3 million young lives each year (UNICEF 1990: 14).

## Composite Environments of Health: A World Pattern

Health is a condition of physical and mental well-being, in large part a multifactor response to spatially varied physical, biological, and socioeconomic environments. No single component measures its achievement; no single statistic indicates the failure of a country or social group to experience it. There is no mystery about the general determinants of health; equally there is no mistaking the striking world contrasts in the achievement of those determinants by different national societies.

At one extreme is the world of affluence and development where good health and long life are the currently accepted and affordable norms. At the other is the realm of malnutrition, disease, and death occupied by the poorest citizens of the poorest regions of the Third World. In between, there are the bridging worlds where some of the components of an environment of health have been achieved and the transition to modern acceptable standards of health has begun. Some countries, usually small and with more equable distribution of education and wealth, such as Singapore, Hong Kong, Taiwan, Cuba, and Costa Rica, have attained developed country standards of health. Others, disrupted by political and economic failure or violence, such as some countries in Africa and the former Soviet Union, have seen a deterioration in population health. Although a simple economic measure of the very rich and the very poor is sufficient to recognize countries at the polar extremes, the multifaceted nature of environments of disease and health demands more detailed analysis to plot the position of countries in transition and to map a global geography of the conditions of health.

Map 4.1 shows such a mapped classification. It is based upon four measures of well-being that show significant spatial variation, are reported in standardized form by international agencies, reveal conditions generally accepted as indicative of environments of health without regard to socioeconomic systems or values, and are independent, additive assessments of progress from less to more developed national health status. The components of the classification are (1) death rate for children under 5 years; (2) accessibility to safe drinking water; (3) presumed average calorie intake as a daily percentage of internationally agreed standards; and (4) female literacy.

The classification displayed in Map 4.1 is comparative. Countries were ranked from highest to lowest on each of the four factors and the ranks

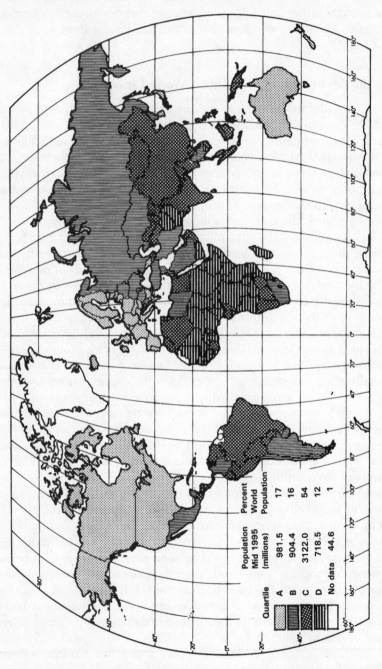

MAP 4.1  Composite environments of health

| Quartile | Population Mid 1995 (millions) | Percent World Population |
|----------|-------------------------------|--------------------------|
| A        | 981.5                         | 17                       |
| B        | 904.4                         | 16                       |
| C        | 3122.0                        | 54                       |
| D        | 718.5                         | 12                       |
| No data  | 44.6                          | 1                        |

were summed. The resulting scores were the basis for a ranked classification of conditions and potentials of health of the 150 countries for which data were available.

The spatial patterns of the extremes are expected. The advanced countries of East and West—a "First World" of health—scored well on each of the components. The poorest, least developed countries of, particularly, Africa and southern Asia clearly demonstrate the existence of a counterworld of disease and death. What is significant is the disparity in the numbers of people who reside in those worlds of extremes. Only 12 percent of global population is represented by the 38 countries of the lowest quartile, while 17 percent of the world's peoples are in the most developed upper quartile. More than two-thirds of humanity occupies transitional ground between the two extremes. Within countries, especially the larger ones, there are usually striking differences in conditions for rural and urban populations. For instance, in China, conditions in rural areas are typical of poorer developing countries; in the cities they are similar to those of developed countries such as the United States and Japan (Lawson and Lin 1994).

The appalling conditions of disease and death afflicting the poorest, least developed countries serve as a continuing reminder that much yet remains before adopted international goals of "Health for All by the Year 2000" are achieved. Nevertheless, by the multifactor evaluation of national conditions of health applied here, some two-thirds of the world's population is beginning to approach the health standards set by the most advanced countries. Although the present reality is divided, the prospect is for a converging single world of health by about 2030.

## References

Basch, P. F. 1990. *Textbook of International Health.* New York: Oxford University Press.

Benenson, A. S., ed. 1995. *Control of Communicable Diseases Manual.* 16th ed. Washington, D.C.: American Public Health Association.

Farb, P., and G. Armelagos. 1980. *Consuming Passions: The Anthropology of Eating.* Boston: Houghton Mifflin.

Lawson, J. S., and V. Lin. 1994. "Health status differentials in the People's Republic of China." *American Journal of Public Health* 84: 737–741.

Mann, J. M., D. J. M. Tarantola, and T. W. Netter, eds. 1992. *AIDS in the World.* Cambridge: Harvard University Press.

May, R. 1994. "Changing diseases in changing environments." In *Health and the Environment,* edited by B. Cartledge, pp. 150–171. Oxford: Oxford University Press.

McKeown, T. 1976. *The Modern Rise of Population.* New York: Academic Press.

Omran, A. R. 1971. "The epidemiologic transition: A theory of the epidemiology of population change." *Milbank Memorial Fund Quarterly* 49: 509–538.

_____. 1977. "Epidemiologic transition in the U.S." *Population Bulletin* 32: 2–41.

Palloni, A. 1981. "Mortality in Latin America: Emerging patterns." *Population and Development Review* 7: 623–649.

Population Reference Bureau. 1985, 1993. *World Population Data Sheet.* Washington, D.C.: Population Reference Bureau.

Ruzicka, L. T., and H. Hansluwka. 1982. "Mortality transition in South and East Asia: Technology confronts poverty." *Population and Development Review* 8: 567–588.

United Nations (UN). 1957, 1973. *Demographic Yearbook.* Department of International and Social Affairs. New York: United Nations.

_____. 1980. *The World Population Situation in 1979.* Department of International and Social Affairs, Population Studies no. 72. New York: United Nations.

United Nations Children's Fund (UNICEF). 1990, 1997. *The State of the World's Children.* Oxford: Oxford University Press.

United States Centers for Disease Control and Prevention. 1986. "Premature mortality in the United States: Public health issues in the use of years of potential life lost." *Morbidity and Mortality Weekly Report* 35: 2S.

World Bank. 1993. *World Development Report 1993: Investing in Health.* Oxford: Oxford University Press.

World Health Organization (WHO). 1981. *Development of Indicators for Monitoring Progress Towards Health for All by the Year 2000.* Geneva: World Health Organization.

_____. 1986. "Analysis of data on the global indicators." *World Health Statistics Annual 1986*, pp. 33–46. Geneva: World Health Organization.

_____. 1996. *The World Health Report 1996: Fighting Disease, Fostering Development.* Report of the Director-General. Geneva: World Health Organization.

# 5   Gender Bias
in Development

## Janet Henshall Momsen

THE DAILY LIFE OF A TAMIL WOMAN TEA PICKER on a plantation in Sri Lanka illustrates the heavy workload of many women in the developing world. She is normally the first member of the family to rise, getting up at 4:00 A.M. in order to prepare breakfast and lunch, sweep the dirt floor of her unit of plantation row housing, wash clothes and get children ready for day care and/or school before leaving for formal employment at 7:00 A.M. The paid work of such a woman involves climbing steep slopes, being exposed to rain, chill winds, and hot sun, selecting and picking the finest leaves of tea and carrying a weight of up to 25 kilos in a basket strapped to her back. She has two brief breaks during the day when she can breast-feed her baby and returns home at 5:30 P.M. to do the evening chores, finally retiring to bed at around 10:30 P.M. There is usually only one cot in the house, which is occupied by her husband, and so she sleeps on the floor. She is last to eat at family meals despite the heavy physical work she undertakes.

Women, although they have full-time paid employment, are still responsible in this patriarchal society for all tasks related to household reproduction (i.e., cooking, cleaning, child care and training children, caring for the elderly, etc.). Despite working longer hours than their husbands, contributing at least half the family income, and even having won equal pay, these women see little improvement in their own status or in their families' situation. Husbands collect their wives' wages and maternity benefits, and this money is often spent by the men on gambling and alcohol rather than on the basic needs of the family (Samarasinghe 1993). The hours women spend cooking over smoky fires encourage respiratory diseases. In addition, the physiological stress induced by the combination of malnutrition, overwork, and lack of sleep affects their reproductive health so that among these Tamil plantation workers, fertility rates are low and maternal and infant mortality rates are two to three times the level for the country as a whole.

## Gender and Development Policies

The United Nations Commission on the Status of Women, established in 1946, has helped to develop the legal basis for the promotion of equal rights for women in all countries. Over the past two decades, in response to the women's movement and to United Nations' mandates, particularly the adoption in 1979 of the Convention on the Elimination of All Forms of Discrimination against Women, measures to promote women's advancement have been widely introduced (Boutros-Ghali 1995). In 1985 only 39 states were party to this convention, but by August 1994 there were 134 states reporting regularly to the United Nations on its implementation, and remarkable progress has been achieved in providing both legal equality and equal access to education for women (World Survey 1995). Women in development (WID) and/or gender and development (GAD) policies are now on the agenda of most international development agencies and of national governments, especially those dependent on foreign aid. Whereas a WID approach seeks to make women visible within the existing development framework, a gender-aware approach brings gender relations to the forefront in order to make the development process more equitable and sustainable. GAD policies therefore challenge the existing development paradigm. The United Nations has sponsored a Decade for Women (1975–1985) and four world conferences on women: in Mexico City in 1975, in Copenhagen in 1980, in Nairobi in 1985, and Beijing 1995. It is time to consider the effectiveness of these policies and activities.

## The Feminization of Poverty

As the opening paragraphs indicate, the progress report is at best mixed. Sri Lanka has one of the best records in south Asia for gender equality, but although women tea pickers have been granted equal pay for equal work, societal norms still impose a heavy double burden on them. Nearly two decades after the Mexico City Conference on Women, the United Nations reported in 1994 (UNDP 1994) that, despite advances in labor force participation, health, and education, women still made up two-thirds of the world's illiterates, were paid half as much as men for work of equal value, and constituted only 10 percent of elected representatives to national governments.

Even the steady improvement in health and education that had been seen in the 1960s and 1970s faltered during the economic crisis and structural adjustment of the 1980s. The structural adjustment programs imposed on many countries by the World Bank and the International Monetary Fund (IMF) were not gender blind (Commonwealth Secretariat 1989;

Elson 1989; Afshar and Dennis 1992). "These rigid prescriptions have added to women's responsibilities for family survival and social reproduction, reduced the resources at our disposal, and restricted options for women's participation and leadership in public life" (Molyneux 1992: 254).

Literacy showed a big improvement in 1985 with only 40 percent of the global population unable to read compared to 54 percent in 1970, but the gender gap had grown with 54 million more illiterate women (for a total of 597 million) versus only 4 million more illiterate men (for a total of 352 million). By 1994, 39 percent of females in developing countries were illiterate as against 21 percent of males. Structural adjustment programs, with their imposition of charges for state health and education services, led to an increasing number of girls dropping out of school. These young women were thus available to take over household chores and child care, releasing their mothers to seek paid employment outside the home in order to support the family (Moser 1993). Such arrangements, found in many areas of Latin America and Africa, are ensuring the continuation of female poverty into the next generation.

In 1990 the United Nations Economic and Social Commission for Asia and the Pacific estimated that about 70 percent of the world's poor were women. In the past two decades the number of rural women living in poverty has doubled, and women now make up 60 percent of the world's rural poor (Knox 1995). The strongest direct link between gender and poverty is found in female-headed households. Globally about one-sixth of households are headed by women with such households being most prevalent in Sub-Saharan Africa and the Caribbean and least prevalent in Asia. The strong relationship between female headship and poverty reflects higher dependency ratios in such families, inadequate remittances from absent men, and gender differentials in access to resources, productive employment, and wages. However, the picture is very complex, for although "there does appear to be a rise in female headship in some countries, systematic data to verify this trend are not yet available and evidence of the association with poverty is inconsistent. Causes of female headship are political, economic, social, and demographic—including conflict, migration, divorce, teenage pregnancy, and widowhood—and the relative importance of different factors varies with the context" (Leach, Joekes, and Green 1995: 1).

Recent reports from development agencies have noted that poverty has a decided gender bias. Overlapping productive and reproductive responsibilities affect women's mobility, time allocation, and the opportunity costs of child care and employment. At the level of the household, "female members are often worse off than male members because of gender-based differences in the distribution of food and other entitlements within the family" (UNDP 1992: 22). Furthermore, "the weight of poverty falls most heavily on certain groups. Women in general are disadvantaged. In poor households they often shoulder more of the workload than men, are less educated, and have less access to remunerative activities" (World Bank 1995: 2). The complexity of the global picture of poverty, combined with the gendered institutional politics of development bureaucracies, leads to resistance by policymakers to full acceptance of information about women's different experience of poverty and of the gendered impact of development.

The advancement of women depends on economic growth, but experience shows that policies directed toward stabilization and growth resumption are not gender-neutral. Statistical analysis of data for sixty-one countries for the period 1980–1990 showed that there was a significant positive relationship between economic growth and women's participation in the labor force (World Survey 1995). The analysis also indicated that these benefits vary in relation to the level of economic development and the nature of economic growth. However, it is now also acknowledged that gender-related factors are central to the obstacles hindering development. Despite the mainstreaming of women in development policies (Jahan 1995), there is widespread evidence that gender bias in most societies has not been overcome and that there is still bias against women in the design, implementation, and impact of many projects and policy initiatives.

## Gender Bias

All societies have inequalities caused by various biases— urban, regional, class, religious, racial, and ethnic—that govern the allocation of power, authority, and resources. Different types of bias tend to be interlinked, and women may enjoy the benefits or suffer the privations, with men, of discrimination based on age, residence, class, religion, or race. However, all women will face some degree of gender bias at some time in their lives. Gender bias, based on the social construction of biological sex differences, is distinctive in that it is universal, and that those who are disadvantaged by it live in close personal relationships with those who are advantaged by it. It is paradoxical in that although gender bias may benefit individual men, it has costs for society as a whole because it distorts resource allocation by denying women adequate access to production inputs and so reduces total output.

Gender bias is reflected in unequal terms of participation in labor markets for men and women and in what Ingrid Palmer (1992) calls the reproduction tax on women. Causes of discrimination against women in the labor market are numerous and grounded in social and cultural situations. The multiple, unremunerated household tasks of women form the basis of the so-called reproduction tax, which acts as a labor tax increasing women's opportunity costs. In this way gender bias not only discriminates against individual women and women as a social group but also causes inefficiencies in the economy making development more difficult. Overcoming gender bias has been shown to have an immediate positive impact by increasing output and improving well-being.

## Gender Bias and Gender Difference

The roots of gender bias lie in both essentializing and ignoring gender differences. Essentialist views lead to a facile conflation of masculinity and femininity with biological differences. Ignoring gender differences results in the acceptance of male behavior as the norm, which in turn situates all women as deviant. Hierarchies based on a ranking of human traits, values, and activities, with those associated with men being given higher status, is an intrinsic component of gender construction in most societies. This reinforcement of masculine behavior is accompanied by a disparagement of qualities perceived as feminine. Skills associated with women, such as sewing and cooking, are considered to be innate rather than learned and thus are not generally as well rewarded in the market place as are the so-called masculine skills, such as those related to working with wood and metal. Thus women textile workers are considered unskilled whereas male steelworkers are considered skilled. However, at the high end of the market where so-called feminine skills are well rewarded as in haute cuisine and fashion, the top jobs are generally held by men.

The asymmetry of gender relations and roles is detrimental not only to women but also to men and children and so to social, economic, and political development in the wider society. Traditional child development theories based on observation of white, middle-class boys in developed countries are portrayed as both gender and culture free, giving rise to a global view of development that is reinscribed within international aid and development policies (Berman1995: 21). Erica Berman further argues (1995: 22) that even in relation to children "the geographical distribution of *psychological* development maps on to *economic* inequalities between the northern and southern hemispheres as an extension of the model's suppression of gender and cultural differences within the North." The recognition of the girl-child as a special class within the group of children arises from documentation of the link between the specific problems faced by girl-children and population growth.

*Health.* In addition to the role of reproductive technologies and national population targets in encouraging both the abortion of female fetuses and female infanticide, which is affecting the sex ratio most noticeably in

India and China (Sen 1990a,b), mortality rates for girls aged one to four years are higher than for boys in many developing countries whereas in developed countries 20 percent more boys than girls in that age group die. Studies in India and Bangladesh indicate that girls were more than forty times less likely than boys to be taken to hospital although the incidence of acute malnutrition in girls was four times that of boys (United Nations 1994). Differential feeding, nurturing, and care of female children leads not only to excess female mortality in childhood but also to lower female life expectancy. Worldwide, women generally live longer than men for hormonal reasons, but in Bangladesh, Bhutan, India, Nepal, and Pakistan they have lower life expectancies than men, reflecting the marked cultural bias against women in these countries. Among the lowest castes in India, especially in rural areas, women contribute 53 percent, men 31 percent, and children 16 percent of household energy needs, and as many as half the females but only 14 percent of the males have body weights that are 70 percent or less of expected weight (Momsen 1991: 13). In Kenya and Tanzania, women between the ages of 16 and 49 lose twice as many work days as men due to illness (Jacobsen 1992). No such difference exists for other age groups implying that the combination of heavy physical work with frequent pregnancies plays a major role in undermining women's health and productivity (see Table 5.1). Overworked, undernourished, and anemic women tend to produce smaller babies and to be more vulnerable to the dangers of childbirth. Maternal mortality is exacerbated by the dominance of traditional medicine in specialities relating only to women, such as obstetrics and gynecology. Overall only 52 percent of births in the developing world are attended by trained personnel, and in some African countries this figure falls to a mere 2 percent (United Nations 1994).

*Education.*    There is a close connection between the level of a mother's education and the size of her family yet two-thirds of the children not enrolled in school in the Third World are girls (Colclough with Lewin 1993). The World Fertility Survey noted that secondary education for women was responsible for a reduction in total fertility rates of between two and three children (Colclough with Lewin 1993: 30). Education is also associated with reduced child mortality as educated women are more likely to know how to protect their child's health. Research has shown that for every year of a mother's education, child mortality is reduced 7 to 9 percent ( United Nations 1994: 99). Reasons for underenrollment of girls in school are school facilities are considered to be inappropriate, journeys to school are thought to be too long or dangerous for girls, and future job opportunities for women are perceived as limited, which, combined with early marriage, mean uncertain economic returns to the natal family

TABLE 5.1   Regional Patterns of Gender Differences

| World Bank Group | Sex Ratio (men per 100 women) | Total Fertility Rate | | Life Expectancy 1993 (years) | | Female Adult Illiteracy Percentage | Females/100 Males in Secondary Education | Female Share of the Labor Force (%) | Female Share of the Agricultural Labor Force (%) |
| --- | --- | --- | --- | --- | --- | --- | --- | --- | --- |
| | | 1970 | 1993 | Female | Male | | | | |
| Low-income | 98.7 | 5.9 | 3.6 | 63 | 61 | 53 | 67 | 36 | 45.5 |
| Middle-income | 100.4 | 4.5 | 3.0 | 71 | 65 | 25 | 101 | 38 | 32.0 |
| Upper-mid income | 101.4 | 4.7 | 3.0 | 72 | 66 | 17 | 106 | 30 | 28.9 |
| High-income oil exporters | 145.7 | 6.9 | 5.9 | 80 | 74 | 52 | 101 | 28 | 26.0 |
| Latin America & Caribbean | 98.6 | 5.2 | 3.1 | 72 | 66 | 18 | 104 | 27 | 17.6 |
| Mid-East & North Africa | 104.5 | 6.7 | 4.7 | 67 | 65 | 57 | 79 | 16 | 30.7 |
| East Asia & Pacific | 103.1 | 5.7 | 2.3 | 70 | 66 | 34 | 78 | 42 | 47.9 |
| South Asia | 102.9 | 5.8 | 4.0 | 60 | 60 | 69 | 56 | 22 | 45.0 |
| Sub-Saharan Africa | 97.8 | 6.6 | 6.2 | 53 | 50 | 62 | 72 | 37 | 46.4 |

SOURCES: World Bank, *World Development Report 1995* (New York: Oxford University Press, 1995). United Nations, *The World's Women 1995. Trends and Statistics* (New York: United Nations, 1995).

(United Nations 1992: 17–18). Poverty, which limits the number of children for whom fees, uniforms, and books can be provided, reinforces this gender bias, but education for girls is given a higher priority in female-headed households.

## Regional Gender Differences

It has been argued that gender bias is universal, but this global view incorporates regional differences in the implementation of discrimination. Ester Boserup (1970) first drew attention to spatial differences in women's roles. She noted that the subsistence farming typical of much of Sub-Saharan agriculture was dependent on female labor and so she designated it a female agricultural system. She characterized Latin America as having a male agricultural system and Asia as having a joint system. As a result of these gender differences in labor demand in agriculture there are differences in rural to urban migration resulting in differences in urban sex ratios, which were also recognized by Boserup.

In Latin America, young women are often sent to the city to work as domestic servants since there is no role for them in the countryside. In this way they can support themselves and possibly even send some money back to their families, but they are expected to return to their natal villages for marriage (Radcliffe 1993). Many, however, choose to stay in the city because it offers a wider choice of both marital partners and employment opportunities, and thus Latin American cities tend to have female sex ratios.

In both Latin America and Asia, teenage girls are sent by their families to cities to work in factories. The globalization of production accompanied by the flexibilization of the labor market has facilitated the incorporation into the workforce of large numbers of young, unmarried women holding insecure, monotonous, and dead-end jobs, especially in the Export Production Zones (EPZs) dominated by transnational companies in Asia and Latin America. It is estimated that women constitute some 70 percent of employees in any given enterprise in these EPZs, but the proportion of women declines as the manufacturing process becomes more technologically complex. In the Mexican *maquiladores* (enterprises established by foreign firms to produce exports) the proportion of women workers fell from 77 percent in 1982 to 60 percent in 1990 (Joekes 1993). Often they are fired from these jobs when they get married or become pregnant or fail to meet increasing output quotas (Safa 1990). Although women may have benefited in terms of job creation, these benefits were confined to a few countries and were achieved in a context of rising gender inequality and a widening wage gap between men and women (Standing 1989).

In many Asian countries, poor rural families may even decide to sell girl children, who are generally seen as having little long-term economic utility for their natal family. These girls may be destined to be workers in urban families and small businesses or "housekeepers" or "brides" for older men. Often they end up in brothels which they are only allowed to leave when they become diseased. Some of this migration of women is across national borders as in the contract labor of Sri Lankan rural women for domestic service in the Middle East (Ismail 1994) or Filipinas as brides in Germany. For many years, governments of poor countries have turned a blind eye to the exploitation and sufferings of these women because of the economic importance of the earnings they remitted, but this attitude is changing largely in response to publicity given by the Western press to individual cases.

In Africa, more men than women move to towns in search of urban-based jobs in such occupations as domestic service (a male-dominated occupation in many African countries) or jobs in industry or mining, leaving families behind to be supported by women farmers. Sometimes, as in the case of Lesotho, there was a specific gender filter imposed on migration. South African authorities would allow only the immigration of men as mineworkers. These immigrants lived in single-sex hostels and returned home on annual visits. The long-term and long-distance separation of home and work often resulted in men setting up second families in the city with the consequent cutting off of remittances and other contacts with rural villages. Thus in Lesotho almost two-thirds of households are de facto female-headed, and women are better educated than men as this is their only way of obtaining urban jobs (Wilkinson 1987). In the so-called independent homelands of South Africa, women were often unable to live off the degraded farmlands and so EPZs were set up to employ them in foreign-owned factories. In the new South Africa, the ending of such gender bias is one of the main priorities (Development Bank of Southern Africa 1994; South African Ministry of Population 1995). Many changes will be precipitated by wage increases and pay equity, which is leading to the closure of marginal mines and the departure of foreign assembly industries.

Such regional differences in gender roles and characteristics have been mapped (see Sivard 1985; Seager and Olson 1986; Momsen and Townsend 1987). Table 5.1 shows these broad-brush differences by both World Bank group and world region. At this scale, it can be seen that although high national incomes are related to higher female life expectancy and education levels, these are not necessarily reflected in labor force participation or fertility rates. Women's access to higher education in Latin America and the Middle East is more related to class than to gender, and since female status in these societies has traditionally been linked to motherhood, education of women has not led to high female economic activity rates. In Sub-Saharan Africa, children are needed to assist their mothers in farmwork, to support them in their old age, and to give status. In this region, literacy rates for women over 15 years of age have risen from 13.2 percent in 1970 to 36.1 percent in 1990, but the number of births per woman also increased from 6.4 in 1950 to 6.6 in 1980 as male migration to cities made women farmers more dependent on their children's labor and infant mortality declined. By 1990 the number of births per woman had, however, fallen to 6.2, and infant mortality had declined from 126 per thousand live births in 1975 to 103, but both measures were still the highest in the world (United Nations 1994).

The figures for the Caribbean suggest commonalities with Latin America in terms of education levels and with Africa for agricultural employment. If we subdivide this region and consider only the countries of the Anglophone Caribbean, where, like Africa, there are many women farmers, literacy levels are often higher than in the United States, access to tertiary education is based more on merit than class, and more women than men have graduated from universities in the last decade. Female economic activity rates are at the same level as in North America, and fertility rates have fallen, in the case of Barbados, to below replacement level. Within regions there remain marked differences between countries. For example in Latin America and the Caribbean, the infant mortality rate is only 11 per thousand live births in Barbados whereas in Bolivia it is 110 (United Nations 1994).

Latin America, the Caribbean, and Sub-Saharan Africa all have female sex ratios reflecting gender differences in migration. All three areas have served as labor reserves for the richer countries of the North especially during the recession of the 1980s. In the Middle East, the high male sex ratio is caused mainly by the influx of male labor to the high-income oil-producing states. This ratio has declined over the past decade because of battle losses in regional wars and the related repatriation of and decline in demand for male workers. Differences in sex ratios, migration patterns, access to education, medical facilities, and job opportunities for women between rural and urban areas within countries also affect fertility rates through their influence on rates of early marriage and availability of contraception.

Thus an appreciation of scale of analysis and local culture, as well as of level of development, is vital to an understanding of regional differences in gender bias. As Table 5.1 illustrates, relationships between variables are very complex.

## Gender Division of Labor

The way in which gender bias works depends on women's role in society. Although both men and women perform a range of functions, women, in most societies, are distinctive in having many different demands on their time and capacities which often have to be dealt with simultaneously. Women's roles can be subdivided into three main aspects: a reproductive role as mothers, carers, and managers of the household; a productive role; and a community management role.

## Women and Reproduction

Women are responsible for both social and biological reproduction. They must care for their children from conception to adulthood and for elderly relatives. Most health care takes place at the family or individual level. Women have prime responsibility for this despite their heavy burden of work and often inadequate nutrition. Few societies in developing countries provide extra food for poor pregnant women, and they may in fact have taboos that prevent women consuming protein-rich foods such as eggs during pregnancy. This contributes to widespread maternal anemia and low birth-weight babies vulnerable to infection. Women also have to produce, process, and prepare food for the family, wash clothes, keep the home clean, and ensure the education of their children.

## Women as Community Managers

Women's role extends beyond the household to a network of social and community relationships. Through their work at village festivals and family events such as funerals, women maintain community culture and family cohesion. Women's cooperatives and savings groups improve community living standards by means of self-help projects for the development of schools, clinics, and communal kitchens. Women in shanty towns negotiate with government to improve community facilities such as roads, garbage collection, and water supply. These networks, built up and maintained by women, are an important source of assistance for families in times of hardship. In most developing countries the state does not provide an adequate safety net for poor families, and local community support is a vital element of household survival strategy.

## Women and Production

Millions of women have long been feeding their families and supplementing their income by tending small plots of land, raising animals, doing craftwork and petty trading, without ever being counted in official statistics. Throughout the United Nations agencies it is now accepted that it is time for women to have more access to formal employment, training, and loans and that the informal work they do should be made more visible through official recognition (United Nations 1995). It has been estimated that women's unpaid family labor within the household would add one-third to estimates of world production with an estimated value of US$4 trillion (Sivard 1985).

In all regions, women's employment outside the household, as indicated by official economic activity rates, is lower than that of men. However, one of the big changes throughout the world in recent years is the growth in the proportion of women in the labor force—from 29 percent in 1950 to 39.4 percent in Asia and from 12.7 percent in 1960 to 32.0 percent in Latin America. However, in Sub-Saharan Africa there was a decline in both male and female activity rates with women's participation falling from 30.0 percent in 1960 to 26.8 percent in 1985 followed by a rise to 38.3 percent in the following decade (United Nations 1989b: 51). Official census statistics tend to underestimate women's employment especially in agriculture, domestic service, and the informal economy. The figures in Table 5.1 are adjusted to take these omissions into account. There are also marked variations within countries, especially between rural and urban areas. In the metropolitan zone of Recife in Northeast Brazil, the economic activity rate of women increased from 35.5 percent in 1981 to 38.5 percent in 1990 when 22.45 percent of these employed women were heads of household (da Rocha 1995: 19). In a survey 100 countries, women's labor force participation rates increased in 69 countries, decreased in 8, and did not change in 22 during the 1980s (Standing 1989).

Women generally are the first to lose their jobs during a recession, and unemployment rates for women are often higher than those for men. Many women retreat to unpaid family labor, the informal economy, or flexible, contingent labor in the formal economy, all of which tend to be officially unrecorded. Table 5.2 illustrates how the classification of female employment in national censuses affects the measurement of their involvement in a single industry in the Latin American region. Women working as unpaid family helpers are most numerous in tropical South America where subsistence-level family farms and families employed as a single unit on traditional plantations are common. In Brazil and the Caribbean, the largest group of female workers is made up of laborers on modern plantations where they are often paid less than men. In Central America, Mexico, and temperate South America, over two-fifths of women agriculturalists work as partners with their husbands or as sole farm operators on family farms. The total proportion of women employed in agriculture cannot be found by adding across the three columns because individual women often work in all three ways at different times in their lives or even simultaneously.

The invisibility of much of women's work reinforces the social perception of women as dependents rather than producers. The ideology of the

TABLE 5.2   Women in Agriculture in Latin America by Occupation

| Region/Country | Percentage of Family Helpers | Percentage of Self-Employed | Percentage of Paid Laborers |
|---|---|---|---|
| Brazil | 35.7 | 17.1 | 47.2 |
| Mexico | 35.4 | 44.0 | 20.1 |
| Tropical S. America | 53.7 | 18.9 | 23.8 |
| Central America | 14.1 | 64.0 | 19.1 |
| Caribbean | 18.0 | 11.4 | 64.5 |
| Temperate S. America | 30.2 | 43.0 | 24.9 |
| Average Latin America | 32.5 | 20.9 | 44.5 |

SOURCE: Based on International Labour Office, *Yearbook of Labour Statistics* (Geneva: ILO, 1988).

male breadwinner appears to be universal, and this bias is perpetuated by government record keeping. In India, conventional measures of wage labor showed that 63 percent of men but only 34 percent of females were in the workforce. But a survey of work patterns by occupational categories including household production and domestic service revealed that in India 75 percent of females over the age of five are working as opposed to 64 percent of men (Jacobson 1992).

In rural areas of the Third World women are the main providers of food, fuel, and water for household consumption. In Sub-Saharan Africa women produce four-fifths of domestically consumed food, in the Indian subcontinent 70 to 80 percent, and in the Caribbean and Latin America about half. But in most of these areas women have no rights to land, and the distribution of the resources required for modern agriculture such as fertilizers, pesticides, hybrid seeds, and irrigation facilities reflects persistent gender bias. Agricultural extension agents, who are overwhelmingly male, tend to ignore women farmers, and women find it much harder than men to get credit. A study in Kenya showed that 49 percent of the female-managed farms were never visited by an extension agent compared to only 28 percent of the male or jointly managed farms (Staudt 1978). This bias in access to information particularly affected women's food crop productivity. Several studies have shown that where an effort is made to make even small amounts of credit available to women—either through women's affinity groups as pioneered by Bangladesh's Grameen Bank or to individual women—the positive effect, whether measured by increased output, reduction in work hours, or repayment rates, is greater than for similar grants to men (Buvinic 1995).

Much of the work done by women is low paid and offers neither employment security nor benefits. It has been estimated that half of the employed women in Quito, Ecuador, in 1985, 53 percent of those working in Zambia in 1986, and 49 percent of those in India in 1981 were in such high-risk jobs (Buvinic 1995: 2). Within the formal sector, women are paid significantly less than men in every country for which there is data. In manufacturing, women's earnings varied from 45 percent of men's in South Korea to 89 percent of men's in Burma in a survey of eighteen developing countries. Although some of this difference can be traced to women's lower levels of education and training, this does not provide a complete explanation. Data on female wages indicate that the average has fallen as a percentage of men's wages in nonagricultural production, particularly in the regions that experienced export-led growth and deregulation of labor markets (World Survey 1995). In many of these countries governments have maintained these gender differences in wage rates specifically to attract transnational firms. Brazil displays the greatest difference in earnings in Latin America: In 1988 the average salary for women was only 54 percent of men's. In Jamaica the average wage for employed males exceeded that of females by between 27 percent and 47 percent during the period 1983–1985, and 41 percent of female-headed households earned less than J$200 a month compared to only 15 percent of those headed by men (Andaiye and Antrobus 1995).

## Gender and Time Use

As the description of the Sri Lankan tea plucker's day illustrates, time is a scarce resource for many poor Third World women. The allocation of time to different tasks is constrained by competing demands, the biological necessity for time-consuming activities such as sleeping and eating, the need for groups of individuals to come together in time and space to undertake joint activities, and structural rigidities in the social system. United Nations statistics indicate that on average women work longer hours than men in every country except Australia, Canada, and the United States. In most developing countries women work 12 to 18 hours per day compared to 8 to 12 hours for men. However, Sylvia Chant found that in Mexican shantytowns there was more sharing of household tasks in female-headed households than in male-headed households (Chant 1987).

Women in the Third World are often in a zero-sum game where time and energy devoted to any additional activity must be diverted from another task. Generally sleep and leisure are first to be sacrificed. In the many countries where firewood collection is a female activity, deforestation and the related official efforts at preservation often force women to travel further, to spend more hours finding wood, and to carry heavier loads. They may have to make do with less satisfactory types of wood or find alternative sources of fuel (Sarin 1995; Ulliwishewa 1994; Ardayfio-Schandorf 1993). Poorer fuel sources may mean less cooked food, no boiling of contaminated water, and more respiratory diseases from inhaling noxious smoke.

Gender bias in entitlements to labor may affect agricultural productivity by restricting the allocation of women's time. Women's limited control over their own labor and restricted access to the labor of other family members conditions their environmental management (Leach, Joekes, and Green 1995). A study in western Sudan found that women's farms tended to have lower yields than men's farms (Gray 1993). In this region the timing of the various field operations had a major effect on output because of the unreliable and limited rainfall on which crops depended. Farm surveys revealed that women usually undertook planting and weeding of their own fields later than men. These faults of timing are not caused by women's poorer understanding of the environment but by the dual nature of their family responsibilities and by their lack of control over labor. For married women, work on their own fields is often restricted to one or two evenings a week and Friday mornings, after work on their husband's fields has been completed. Men, on the other hand, have open access to the unremunerated labor of family members and so agricultural practices on their farms are timely and their yields maximized. Thus traditional gender bias in access to labor is reducing the overall efficiency of household output. Yet studies from all over the Third World confirm that it is the mother's production and income and the degree of control she has over her own income that determines child nutrition levels.

## Conclusion

Gender bias in favor of men is widespread across the world but is especially pernicious in the Third World. In poor, developing countries women generally work longer hours than men. Much of this work is outside the monetary economy and thus is neither valued nor counted officially. Women are less likely than men to be granted entitlement to land and other resources. Men work for cash whereas women focus on subsistence production, yet men are less likely than women to spend money earned on family maintenance items such as food, health care, and education. This pattern of gendered expenditure is prevalent across most cultures and nations.

Thus it can be seen that gender bias is a primary cause of poverty since it prevents millions of girl children and women from obtaining the level of education, training, health services, child care, and legal services they need to improve their lives. It is also a major cause of high birth rates as women who have little control over family income need children to help them with their workload and to give them social status and financial security in their old age.

According to the Human Development Index, a measure created by the United Nations Development Programme (1994) to gauge the degree to which people have available to them the resources needed to attain a decent standard of living, women lagged behind men in every country for which data were available. Among developing countries the gender gap was narrowest in El Salvador, Thailand, and Paraguay and widest in Egypt, Bahrain, and Hong Kong where women's access to resources was about two-thirds that of men. These data make it clear that women's poverty is fundamentally a matter of gender bias in entitlements. Yet public action to strengthen the entitlements of poor women has been piecemeal.

The collection of data disaggregated by gender has revealed women's roles in the economies of developing countries and the differential impact of development on men and women. It is now clear that benefits accruing to the male head of household do not automatically trickle down to wives and children. Women's work and women's role in society is radically changed by development, but different groups of women are affected in opposing ways. Young educated women may be drawn into modern industrial employment whereas the work of older craftswomen becomes obsolete. Such changes upset the traditional hierarchy based on age and sex, and generational conflict may result with pressure groups urging the preservation of traditional age-sex hierarchies. This is often blamed on Western influence despite the fact that colonialism and later Western experts undermined women's traditional position and strengthened that of men.

Gender issues came into the development field largely through the influence of the women's movement in the United States, but they have become institutionalized. Only through continued pressure from both North and South will the benefits to society as a whole of ending gender bias be fully appreciated. Many of the young women in Third World countries who have completed their education and taken up employment in the industrialized economy over the past decade are unwilling to follow in the footsteps of their mothers. Global communications have brought even the most remote villages within reach of the American soap opera, and although Bolivian villagers found that the most impressive aspect of *Dallas* was the size of the cows, the overall impact of exposure to more equal gender relations and roles and to the consumption patterns of rich societies is a rapid rise in expectations. The demand for change is now coming from the grassroots, and many of today's most competent and charismatic leaders of the international movement for women and development are themselves citizens of Third World countries.

## References

Afshar, Haleh, and Carolyne Dennis, eds. 1992. *Women and Adjustment Policies in the Third World*. Basingstoke: Macmillan.

Andaiye and Antrobus, Peggy. 1995. "Towards a vision of the future: Gender issues in regional integration." *Bulletin of Eastern Caribbean Affairs* 20 (1): 17–35.

Ardayfio-Schandorf, Elizabeth. 1993. "Women and fuelwood use in Ghana." In *Different Places, Different Voices: Gender and Development in Africa, Asia, and Latin America*, edited by J. H. Momsen and Vivian Kinnaird, pp. 15–29. London: Routledge.

Association for Women in Development (AWID). 1995. *Newsletter* 9 (3): 4–5.

Beneria, Lourdes, and Shelley Feldman, eds. 1992. *Unequal Burden: Economic Crises, Persistent Poverty, and Women's Work.* Boulder: Westview Press.

Berman, Erica. 1995. "The abnormal distribution of development: Policies for southern women and children." *Gender, Place, and Culture* 2 (1): 21–36.

Boserup, Ester. 1970. *Women and Development.* New edition 1989. London: Earthscan.

Boutros-Ghali, B. 1995. *An Agenda for Development 1995.* New York: United Nations.

Buvinic, Mayra. 1995. *Investing in Women.* Washington, D.C.: International Centre for Research on Women.

Chant, Sylvia. 1987. "Family structure and female labour in Queretaro, Mexico." In *Different Places, Different Voices: Gender and Development in Africa, Asia, and Latin America*, edited by J. H. Momsen and Vivian Kinnaird, pp. 277–293. London: Routledge.

Colclough, C., with K. Lewin. 1993. *Educating All the Children: Strategies for Primary Schooling in the South.* Oxford: Clarendon Press.

Commonwealth Secretariat. 1989. *Engendering Adjustment for the 1990s: Report of a Commonwealth Expert Group on Women and Structural Adjustment.* London: Commonwealth Secretariat.

Development Bank of Southern Africa. 1994. *Gender and Development.* Development paper 32. Pretoria: Development Bank of Southern Africa.

Elson, Diane. 1989. How is structural adjustment affecting women? *Development* 1: 67–74.

———. 1992 "Male bias in structural adjustment." In *Women and Adjustment Policies in the Third World,* edited by Haleh Afshar and Carolyne Dennis, pp. 46–68. Basingstoke: Macmillan.

Elson, Diane, ed. 1991. *Male Bias in the Development Process.* Manchester: Manchester University Press.

Ferber, Marianne A., and Julie A. Nelson, eds. 1993. *Beyond Economic Man: Feminist Theory and Economics.* Chicago and London: University of Chicago Press.

Gray, Lesley. 1993 "The effect of drought and economic decline on rural women in Western Sudan." *Geoforum* 24 (1): 89–98.

International Labour Organization. 1975. *Women at Work.* Geneva: ILO.

———. 1988. *Yearbook of Labour Statistics.* Geneva: ILO.

Ismail, F. Munira. 1994. Sri Lankan women workers in the Middle East. Unpublished M.A. thesis, Department of Geography, University of California, Davis.

Jacobson, Jodi L. 1992. *Gender Bias: Roadblock to Sustainable Development.* Worldwatch paper 110. Washington, D.C.: Worldwatch Institute.

Jahan, Rounaq. 1995 *The Elusive Agenda: Mainstreaming Women in Development.* London: Zed Books.

Joekes, Susan. 1993. The influence of international trade expansion on women's work. BRIDGE paper. Brighton, England: Institute of Development Studies.

Knox, Geoffrey. 1995. Transforming development for the 21st century. *Unifem News* 3 (1): 1, 12–13.

Leach, Melissa , Susan Joekes, and Cathy Green. 1995. "Editorial: Gender relations and environmental change." *ids bulletin* 26 (1): 1–8.

Molyneux, Maxine. 1992. "Final declaration. . . . Beyond the debt crisis: Structural transformation." In *Women and Adjustment Policies in the Third World,* edited by Haleh Afshar and Carolyne Dennis, pp. 253–256. Basingstoke: Macmillan.

Momsen, Janet H. 1991. *Women and Development in the Third World.* London: Routledge.

Momsen, Janet H., and Janet Townsend, eds. 1987. *The Geography of Gender in the Third World.* London: Hutchinson and Albany: SUNY Press.

Momsen, Janet H., and Vivian Kinnaird, eds. 1993. *Different Places, Different Voices: Gender and Development in Africa, Asia, and Latin America.* London: Routledge.

Moser, Caroline O. M. 1993. "Adjustment from below: Low-income women, time, and the triple role in Guayaquil, Ecuador." In *Viva,* edited by Sarah A. Radcliffe and Sallie Westwood, pp. 197–218. London: Routledge.

Palmer, Ingrid. 1992. Gender equity and economic efficiency in adjustment programmes. In *Women and Adjustment Policies in the Third World,* edited by Haleh Afshar and Carolyne Dennis, pp. 69–83. Basingstoke: Macmillan.

Radcliffe, Sarah. 1993. The role of gender in peasant migration. In *Different Places, Different Voices: Gender and Development in Africa, Asia, and Latin America,* edited by Janet Momsen and Vivian Kinnaird, pp. 278–287. London: Routledge.

da Rocha, Edileusa. 1995. *Situação Sócio-Econômica das Mulheres-Regiäo Metropolitana do Recife.* Recife, Brazil: S.O.S. Corp.

Safa, Helen. 1990. "Women workers in the Dominican Republic." In *In the Shadows of the Sun: Caribbean Development Alternatives and U.S. policy,* edited by Carmen Diana Deere. San Francisco: Westview Press.

Samarasinghe, Vidyamali. 1993. "Access of female plantation workers in Sri Lanka to basic-needs provision." In *Different Places, Different Voices: Gender and Development in Africa, Asia, and Latin America,* edited by J. H. Momsen and Vivian Kinnaird, pp. 131–145. London: Routledge.

Sarin, Madhu. 1995. "Regenerating India's forests: Reconciling gender equity with joint forest management." *ids bulletin* 26 (1): 83–91.

Seager, Joni, and A. Olsen. 1986. *Women in the World.* London: Pan Books.

Sen, A. K. 1990a. "Gender and cooperative conflicts." In *Persistent Inequalities: Women and World Development,* edited by Irene Tinker, pp. 123–149. New York and Oxford: Oxford University Press.

_____ . 1990b. "More than 100 million women are missing." *New York Review of Books.* December 20, pp. 61–68.

Sivard, L. 1985. *Women: A World Survey.* Washington, D.C.: World Priorities.

South Africa, Ministry of Population. 1995. *Population Green Paper.* Pretoria: Ministry of Population.

South African Development Bank. 1994. *Gender and Development in South Africa.* Pretoria: South African Development Bank.

Standing, Guy. 1989. "Global feminization through flexible labor." *World Development* 17 (7): 1077–1095.

Staudt, Kathleen. 1978. "Agricultural productivity gap: A case study of male preference in government policy implementation." *Development and Change* 9: 439–457.

Ulliwishewa, Rohana. 1994. *Development Planning, Environmental Degradation, and Women's Fuelwood Crisis: A Sri Lankan Case Study.* IGU Gender Commission Working Paper no. 28. Davis: University of California.

United Nations. 1989a. *Review of Recent National Target Setting.* New York: United Nations.

_____ . 1989b. *World Survey on the Role of Women in Development.* New York: United Nations Centre for Social Development and Humanitarian Affairs.

_____ . 1992. "Gender perspective in family planning programmes." Note prepared by the Division for the Advancement of Women for the Expert Group Meeting on Family Planning, Health, and Family Well-being, Bangalore, India, October 26–30, 1992.

_____ . 1994. *World Social Situation in the 1990s.* New York: United Nations Department of Economic and Social Information and Policy Analysis.

_____ . 1995. *The World's Women 1995: Trends and Statistics.* New York: United Nations.

United Nations Development Programme (UNDP). 1992. *Human Development Report, 1992.* New York: Oxford University Press.

_____ . 1994. *Human Development Report, 1994.* New York: Oxford University Press.

United Nations Division for the Advancement of Women. 1994. *Women 2000.* No. 1. New York: United Nations.

Wilkinson, Clive. 1987. "Gender and development in Lesotho." In *Different Places, Different Voices: Gender and Development in Africa, Asia, and Latin America,* edited by J. H. Momsen and Vivian Kinnaird. London: Routledge.

World Bank. 1985. *World Development Report.* New York: Oxford University Press.

World Bank. 1995. *Women in Development: A Progress Report on the World Bank Initiative.* Washington, D.C.: World Bank.

World Survey on the Role of Women in Development 1994. 1995. *Women in a Changing Global Economy.* New York: United Nations Department for Policy Coordination and Sustainable Development.

# 6 Worlds Within Worlds: The Separate Reality of Indigenous Peoples Today

## Elmer Brian Goehring

WITHIN THE MODERN WORLD of instant telecommunications, high-speed travel, and routine global interchange of goods and services, it is now difficult to imagine a time when the world was not one. The ease with which the planetary perspective can now be adapted reflects the ultimate resolution of the "Age of Discovery," in which light-skinned men from one continent began to sail to others, and back again, in search of gain. The world today, a quarter of a century after the Apollo moon landings and now in the time of Mariner, is a finite reflection still of the hegemony of happenstance that propelled sixteenth-century Europeans, and the nascent economic enterprise they then possessed, to eventual planetary domination. Development, in its inferred forms and meanings, must still be viewed as the logical outcome of the efforts of the smallest continent to overcome the bounds that had separated it from the exploitable resources of all others.

That it is at all possible to contemplate a planetary perspective today is a direct result of the erasure of the buffers that once separated societies. Over the course of a long and varied history of occupation on the surface of the planet, many societies, many cultures have come into being and flourished for a time as adaptations to windows of opportunity. Wherever and whenever a niche appeared that allowed for the collection of resources capable of sustaining human life, unique adaptations arose. Consolidated over the course of successive generations, each such culture perfected distinct ways of knowing adapted to their individual environments.

We may never know the true extent of the numbers and types of cultures that have flourished on the planet. Most have developed in isolation, separated from all others by barriers, both real and perceived, which have kept their adaptations essentially limited to ecosystems. In this regard the expansion of the present predominant form of adaptation, that of the modern industrial world economy, can be seen to differ from all others in one crucial way: It is the first economy that is truly global in scale. The buffers that once allowed cultures to flourish in isolation have now been erased. Modern mankind has created something entirely new—an adaptation based not upon ecosystems alone, but upon the planetary ecosphere, an evolution that has now made economic margins moot and compressed previous limiting bounds of time and space.

## Indigenous Peoples: Definitions

Preexisting remnants of a time before measured time, small pockets of Indigenous Peoples remain encapsulated within the larger universalist milieu. Perceptually, from the perspective of the dominant societies, the gulf that separates may appear small. The outer trappings of modernity have an insidious allure. Most Indigenous Peoples, wherever they may live in the world, have now outwardly adopted many of the visible manifestations of the cultures of the colonizers. In many places today, Indigenous Peoples are, superficially at least, virtually indistinguishable from later arrivals.

Yet from the perspective of the original inhabitants of large areas of the earth, the effects of the large-scale intrusions have been catastrophic. It has been their societies that have borne the brunt of the displacements necessary to establish the present global economic order. For them, the arrival of industrial "homo economicus" has meant the intrusion of randomness beyond comprehension in a world that once they knew and understood in its entirety. For them, the outer trappings of visible accommodation are but an external veneer. The gulf that separates is an ocean. Very nearly all Indigenous Peoples, wherever they live, are awash today in a sea of change, struggling to stay afloat and gain direction in a world gone terribly awry.

It is difficult to establish a universally acceptable concept of "indigenousness" in the world today. The ebb and flow of peoples over the surface of the planet has placed, and continues to place, considerable legal confusion on competing claims to finite territorial sovereignty. For many peoples who considered themselves indigenous to a particular territory, titled ownership to lands and resources was an entirely alien concept. To them the land just "was," and it was theirs: a resource base to be shared equitably among those who chose to exert freely applied human labor to the satisfaction of their daily needs. To many Indigenous Peoples one could no more own the land, or parts thereof, than one could own the sky or the water.

Indigenous Peoples derived not only a livelihood, but an identity from the lands they occupied. Usurped by the imposed concept of title to much of their territory, shunted to the margins of a dominating society, preexisting peoples now find that they must define their identity in new and unfamiliar ways. Although Indigenous Peoples themselves know who they are, the semantic strictures of the Eurocentric world require formal definitions, which are difficult to formulate. A quantitative society has great difficulty in accepting qualitative concepts.

A number of terms have emerged over the years to refer to preexisting peoples. Many are place-specific, such as Indian, Eskimo, Aborigine, Indio, Adivasis, Orang Asli, Junglis, National Minorities, or Scheduled Tribes. These are terms imposed by larger societies upon the preexisting peoples within their borders. They are certainly not the terms by which these societies define themselves. Often these have evolved to have derogatory or pejorative connotations within the larger society.

In recent years the terms First Nations, Native Nations, or Founding Peoples have gained increasing regional acceptance among many Indigenous groups as they attempt to define themselves semantically. At the International Non-Governmental Organizations Conference on Indigenous Peoples and the Land, held in Geneva in 1981 under the auspices of the United Nations, the term "Fourth World" was proposed to describe the collective situation of Indigenous Peoples in the world today. Over time, however, this term has been usurped by others to describe the conditions in the sprawling slums found at the margins of major cities throughout the developing world and has lost its original etymological intent (Burger 1987: 178).

In general, the term Indigenous Populations has emerged as the most acceptable descriptor recognized today. It is the only term for which there is a precise and recognized legal description, provided by the United Nations Economic and Social Council, Commission on Human Rights (UNESCO: E/Cn.4/Sub.2/L.556, 1982) in simplified terms. It serves to identify preexisting societies that have been overrun by the forces of global economic control, that have had a long and recognized identification with land they considered as their birthright, and that have now been wholly or partially alienated from the full enjoyment of this land by usurped title or by overriding outside interference in their affairs.

## Indigenous Peoples: Distribution

Within the bounds of this somewhat arbitrary definition, there are approximately 263,891,000 Indigenous People within the world today (World Bank 1991). They can be found on six continents and in more than eighty-five countries. In total they represent about 4 percent of the total world population today (Burger 1990).

By far the largest percentage (80 percent) of Indigenous People live in the continent of Asia; India and China are home to over 60 percent of the world's Indigenous population. Spread throughout the margins of the most populous continent, hundreds of Indigenous nationalities are striving to maintain their identities against formidable odds today. In only one nation state of Asia do they form a majority of the population. Ethnic Mongols compose over 90 percent of the population in Mongolia. In all other Asian states Indigenous Peoples are minorities today, constituting approximately 7.1 percent of the total population of the continent.

In Africa, 1.2 percent of the population would be considered Indigenous by the United Nations definition. If all traditional hunting, gathering, and pastoralist people were to be included, this figure would rise to only 4.4 percent of the total population of the continent. If all preexisting peoples affected by several centuries of slavery, colonialism, and the displacement of frequent wars were included, this count would certainly increase dramatically.

Europe, the laboratory in which the nascent economic enterprise of global capitalism began, has very few Indigenous People by this definition. In absolute numbers there are approximately 80,000 Indigenous Europeans, less than 0.0002 percent of present population.

In North and South America, where Indigenous Peoples once accounted for the entire population, they have now been reduced to the status of minorities in their former homelands. In North America approximately 5.7 percent of the present population identify themselves as being of Indigenous ancestry, whereas in South America this figure has been reduced to 4 percent. It must be remembered, however, that there has been a considerable blending of peoples in the "melting pot" of the Americas. In actuality there are many places throughout the Americas where admixtures predominate. Several definable peoples, such as mestizos and metis, can trace their roots directly to consolidations of mixed ancestry.

There has been less such admixture in Australia, where the Indigenous 2 percent of the population continues to live primarily in isolated enclaves. In New Zealand (Aotearoa), approximately 10 percent of the population are direct descendants of the Indigenous Maori. If all of the scattered islands of Oceania were to be included with Australia and New Zealand, approximately one-quarter of the combined population would today be considered Indigenous.

It is in the Pacific that the processes of decolonization have recently seen the rise of a number of small yet independent island nations with Indigenous majorities: These include Tonga, Vanuatu, Kiribati, Tuvalu, Western Samoa, Papua New Guinea, the Solomon Islands, and Nauru. The colonies and protectorates of French Polynesia, Guam, and the Wallis and Fortuna Islands have Indigenous majorities that are seeking to achieve greater autonomy and independence in the future. In both Fiji and New Caledonia the Indigenous Peoples fall just short of a majority and are actively seeking to redress the demographic imbalances of recent history.

In other nations of the world there are only a few places where Indigenous Peoples are still a majority in their own homelands. The Mongol Peoples have only very recently emerged from Communist domination and are now actively pursuing their own course of self-determination. In Kalaalit Nunaat (Greenland), where Indigenous Inuit constitute 90 percent of the population, a limited form of home rule under the aegis of Denmark has been in place since 1979. In Canada, a similar form of home rule for Inuit, Nunavut ("Our Land"), is set to come into effect on April 1, 1999.

In Bolivia, where 66 percent of the population is Indigenous, and in Guatemala, where slightly over half of the population can claim Indigenous descent, these majorities have yet to translate demography into real self-determination as peoples. In both of these countries the Indigenous Peoples have been and continue to be subjected to the political and economic domination of ruling minorities.

As the postwar era of national decolonization wanes, many peoples who consider themselves to be "nations" within the borders of existing states are pressing for increased self-determination and autonomy. Especially in the recent post–Cold War period there has been an increase in small ethnic conflicts worldwide, many of which are being waged by peoples who can claim indigenousness to a particular landscape. At the same time as there is movement toward larger groupings of national blocks allied for economic reasons, a concomitant movement to more localized political autonomy can be seen to be emergent among minorities in many areas of the world. In many cases these localized struggles within borders are the struggles of original peoples pursuing paths toward self-government.

## Worlds Within Worlds

In nearly all places where Indigenous Peoples are found today, they may be considered economic remnants of a time long past. Once isolated, buffeted by barriers both real and perceptual, preexisting peoples are finding everywhere that traditional pursuits, such as hunting, fishing, gathering, and pastoralism, no longer provide the means to obtain a viable livelihood. The global enterprises of capital expansion unchecked through time and space have now encroached upon all areas of the habitable ecumene. The barriers that once kept cultures essentially localized phenomena have now been eradicated. Economically, the world is now one. Decisions taken by Japanese money managers in a boardroom in Tokyo in the morning now can have direct effects on Inuit in Tuktoyaktuk in the afternoon.

At the root of this intrusion is an economic system predicated on individual greed that has grown beyond the capacity of collective human control. Capitalism must continuously expand in order to survive. Abstracted to preindustrial terms, the basic concept on which industrial society is based—the growth of capital through the compounding of interest—is a phenomena that is virtually incomprehensible from an Indigenous perspective. When Indigenous People stored five fish for future consumption, they expected there to be five fish in the cache upon returning. When industrial "homo economicus" returns to the savings cache, he or she now fully expects there to be six fish where five were left.

At base what has changed is scale. What was once purely local may now be global. The hegemony of larger bodies politic now intrudes upon the perceptual confines of all Indigenous Peoples everywhere. On a local level, cultural adhesions consolidate shared experience and provide definitional cohesiveness: the collective "we." Often the Indigenous "we" is rural and poor. On a national level, purely localized interests must give way to the commonweal. On a global scale they are irrelevant.

For Indigenous Peoples, this intrusion has meant everywhere an imposed crisis of identity. Locally based economic systems once viable are now found to be redundant in a world of borderless capital mobility. Holistic and all-encompassing nonlinear worldviews that once extended only to the next valley and that once served to explain the benevolence of a limited landscape now fail to connect cause and effect in a new universalist order. Old ways of healing fail in the light of new maladies of body and soul. Old deities at or near the top of the perceptual order lie forgotten, supplanted now by new.

In many areas throughout the world the scales of intrusion have been far beyond the capacity of precontact cultural comprehension. Indigenous Peoples lived within the bounds of a provident natural order, which imposed limitations upon their actions. No such constraints were placed upon the European mentality. Freed by a pervasive religious belief that they were unquestionably God's chosen creation, dominant over the earth and all who lived upon it, European man and successor regimes have created an ethic of control over nature. Enforced by technological prowess, this power has had a great effect upon the Indigenous Peoples encountered in its execution. Preexisting peoples of the forest have seen their forests cut down and hauled away for profit. Hunters of the plains have seen their herds eliminated and replaced with sedentary agribusiness. River peoples have met a power great enough to deny their rivers to them. The ultimate limitations of nature have, for many Indigenous Peoples, now been replaced by the imposition of the power of Industrial "homo erectus," which knows no limitations as of yet.

The warp and weft of the cloth of cultural integrity is fragile indeed. One by one, a strand at a time in seemingly endless concerted linear progression, many of the threads that once served to unify Indigenous societies into cultural cohesiveness have now been forcibly removed. Unfortunately, some Indigenous societies have not survived. Others face inevitable collapse. No Indigenous society anywhere remains unaffected.

Faced with the might of economic domination on a grand scale, Indigenous Peoples have adopted everywhere the visible characteristics of oppressed minorities. Common symptoms are ubiquitous: pervasive fatalism, self-deprecation, horizontal violence, and an attraction to the oppressor's way of life. In all areas of the world in which they now live, and by whatever indicators one cares to use, Indigenous Peoples may be found at or near the bottom of the economic order, living in marginalized "worlds within worlds," anomalous remnants of a time that once was, but now is no more.

## Indigenous Peoples: Rebirth

There are very great differences between the multitude of Indigenous Nations on the earth. Cultures that developed, often in isolation, in adjoining valleys can have different languages, customs, and lifestyles. Differences, even subtle ones, are easily magnified and exploited. Throughout the process of economic colonization that has led to the present world order, this fact has been utilized again and again by the agents of expansionary capitalism. Wherever the enemies of one's enemy could be conscripted as allies, they were. Europeans, it seems, have through long experience become masters of the strategy known as "divide and conquer."

With one foot planted firmly in the traditions of an oft-dimly remembered past and one foot placed partly in the alien cultural and economic environment of the present, all Indigenous societies today find themselves in a world of seemingly irreconcilable opposites. Prolonged contact with the dominating societies among whom they now live has eroded the need for many of the traditional aspects of life, rendering them redundant. This past cannot be resurrected. It exists only in memory now. Nowhere today does any traditional economy of any Indigenous People exist that is viable in its entirety.

Faced with a fractured past, Indigenous Peoples must also come to terms with an ill-understood present. This presents a double difficulty. While members of the dominant society have had the benefit of generations to internalize the many necessary accommodations that this system of the control of time and space requires, Indigenous Peoples have not. Achieving any measure of success within this essentially alien system requires the forging of a whole new suite of societal values and places fundamental traditions at great risk. Seeking this accommodation, the role in which tradition can be accommodated in a world of change, is the fundamental challenge of Indigenous Peoples today.

Even if accommodation is made with some aspects of this external economic reality, Indigenous Peoples find that they are marginalized within it. Racism and discrimination exist on many levels and have become concrete realities for all Indigenous Peoples today. Often easily identifiable as racial and ethnic minorities within the larger milieu, Indigenous Peoples find they are not welcomed as full participants in the dominant societies of which they are now expected to become a part. This is the double dilemma: Channeled to the paths of assimilation, they find themselves profoundly isolated from a mainstream that has often failed to accommodate them.

Compounding this difficulty of accommodation in recent years has been the fact that, worldwide, this dominant economic system has been itself moving through subtle yet profound changes in form and character. The evolution to a postmodern economy, characterized by multinational flexible accumulation in an essentially placeless global marketplace, has meant a general upheaval, a reshuffling of the hands that economic interests play. In this reconciliation of the hegemony of capital in light of changed circumstance, it is now generally accepted that restructuring will continue to widen the gap between rich and poor. In many areas the poorest of the poor, Indigenous Peoples can now expect that their share of the global pie will continue to dwindle, compounding the problems of accommodation. Money will not buy the answers to the problems that they face.

At this crucial juncture in their history, caught between competing versions of separate realities, Indigenous Peoples must now choose their various paths to the future. There are still a great many Indigenous societies in the world today with the inherent strength to unite their members into cohesive and functional cultural entities. Yet all face the same inevitable choices in the long term. This is a game in which the stakes are high. In the face of overwhelming change, Indigenous Peoples must either now forge new and hybrid cultural and economic realities or risk losing their identities as unique societies.

Indigenous Peoples throughout the world are now discovering that, despite their differences, the consequences of the one thing that unites them are the same. Commonalty of historical circumstance has seen all of their various societies dominated by contact with the same external paradigm of economic control. From the Indigenous perspective, all of the alien invaders were essentially the same. Of whatever ilk, clothed in whatever costume or symbol of authority, there was a remarkable consistency of purpose. Whether military or industrial, resource extractive or agricultural, wave after wave of uninvited alien intrusions have affected Indigenous societies in remarkably similar ways.

In discovering that they have a common series of comparable reactions to the Eurocentric expansionism of the past several centuries, Indigenous Peoples are now beginning to ally in common purpose. In the understanding of this commonalty lies their future strength.

All over the world today there are resurgent and revitalized Indigenous societies utilizing new concepts and philosophical constructs, unrecognizable to their ancestors, to find solutions that work. Within the worlds in which they live, some are beginning to define and protect the margins of their societies from the effects of further intrusion. They are building on the shared strengths of the past to overcome the difficulties of the present and are creating new, altered, and hybridized cultures in the process.

These emergent lifeworlds are neither "traditional" cultures in the true sense of the concept, nor are they truly part of the new world order, and most will never be. The present is a time when these "new" Indigenous realities are being tested and refined in the harsh crucible of an accelerated global evolution. Some will ultimately fail. Without the critical mass, momentum, and cultural cohesiveness required to succeed, and without a valid economic or political raison d'être, many Indigenous societies will simply pass from the face of the earth.

Yet others will succeed. The healing process has begun. From their successes will come the ultimate reconciliation with modernity and its successor regimes: a shared knowledge of how to succeed. All over the world, the dominant perceptions of reality are being challenged by a rebirth of Indigenous pride and a renewal of self-worth. The postmodern world has reserved a place for new voices within it. All over the world Indigenous Peoples are saying loudly: "We are here, we cannot be destroyed, and we will be here forever."

At the local, national, and international levels a host of new and vibrant Indigenous organizations dedicated to rekindling cultural pride have begun to emerge in recent years (see Burger 1990: 178–179). By shared effort directed at common concerns, a uniformity of purpose is beginning to result in common solutions. Indigenous Peoples are now discovering that what unites them in the world today is greater than that which divides. The road to reconciliation and recovery will be long and difficult, and it will be paved with failures. Yet, in the end, it is the ability to make their own mistakes, in their own time and in their own way, and to share the knowledge learned in the process thereof, that will be the vehicle whereby Indigenous Peoples, wherever they may live in the world today, will make their way into the future.

## Conclusion

All Indigenous societies have now begun to voice their concerns. Not only are they seeking a form of accommodation from society at large, they are now demanding, in an organized and increasingly effective way and in the name of international justice, certain inherent rights from within the dominant societies in which they live. In essence, after the specifics have been distilled, most Indigenous desires and demands can be condensed into three basic requests for accommodation.

First, a secure and tenured land base, approximating as far as is possible the extent of the territories that have been alienated from them. Indigenous Peoples are connected to the land in spiritual ways that are difficult for non-Indigenous people to fathom. Without such lands on which to live and secure a livelihood, assimilation is inevitable. All Indigenous groups are willing to accept that there are competing interests in the lands they claim. Most are willing to negotiate.

Second, the desire for a viable and culturally relevant economy based on a mixture of traditional and sustainable renewable resources with nontraditional developments of their own choosing and incorporating a community-oriented approach to economic development. Indigenous Peoples are not opposed to all development, only to those aspects that are erosive to their cultures. Given the appropriate conditions, they are willing to share resources with the dominant societies, providing there are perceived benefits for both sides.

Third, the right to a measure of political self-determination as distinct peoples; this may be defined as the ability to organize to preserve valued cultural traditions, the ability to say no to outside forces and interests (and mean it), and the ability to make their own mistakes in their own time and in their own way in all relevant aspects of their life, as they themselves determine them.

There are a host of decisions to be made by Indigenous Peoples today between seemingly irreconcilable opposites that must somehow be reconciled. Faced with a common affront to their existence, Indigenous Peoples are beginning to recognize their uniformity of experience and have now begun to consolidate with common cause. They are beginning to coalesce on common fronts, to unite on many levels in mutual purpose, and to share among themselves the many commonalties and realities of Indigenous experience worldwide.

The learning curve this has entailed has been that of an alien culture, and it has been exceedingly steep. Yet the ascent has begun. The tides of change have flowed over all Indigenous societies everywhere. The alien economy and its legion metaphysical supports have intruded upon all aspects of all traditional Indigenous lifeworlds. The Indigenous 4 percent of the world's population, however, have now begun to find the will to voice their concerns loudly and have begun to demand, in the name of humanity and justice, a meaningful place as nations in their own right on the national and international stages. The voices are beginning to be heard.

## References

Australian Bureau of Statistics. 1990. *Aboriginal People in the Northern Territory.* Darwin: Government of the Northern Territory.

Beauclerk, J., J. Nerby, and J. Townshend. 1988. *Indigenous Peoples: A Field Guide for Development.* New York: Oxfam.

Berger, T. R. 1991. *A Long and Terrible Shadow: White Values, Native Rights in the Americas: 1492–1992.* Vancouver and Toronto: Douglas & McIntyre.

_____. 1981. *Fragile Freedoms.* Toronto: Clarke, Irwin.

Bodley, J. H., ed. 1988. *Tribal Peoples and Development Issues: A Global Overview.* Mountain View, Calif.: Mayfield.

Brosted, J., et al. 1985. *Power: The Quest for Autonomy and Nationhood of Indigenous Peoples.* Bergen: Univeersitats Forlaget.

Burger, J. 1990. *The Gaia Atlas of First Peoples: A Future for the Indigenous World.* New York: Anchor Books.

_____. 1987. *Report from the Frontier: The State of the World's Indigenous Peoples.* London: Zed Books.

Cobo, J. M. n.d. *Study of the Problem of Discrimination Against Indigenous Populations.* New York: UNESCO Commission on Human Rights.

Goehring, B. 1993. *Indigenous Peoples of the World: An Introduction to their Past, Present, and Future.* Saskatoon: Purich.

Goehring, B., and J. Stager. 1991. The intrusion of industrial time and space into the Inuit lifeworld. *Environment and Behavior* 23(6): 666–680.

Moody, R., ed. 1988. *The Indigenous Voice,* 2 vols. London: Zed Press.

Ortiz, R. D. 1984. *Indians of the Americas.* London: Zed Press.

Rowley, C. D. 1988. *Recoveries: The Politics of Aboriginal Reform.* New York: Penguin.

Schumacher, E. F. 1976. *Small Is Beautiful: A Study of Economics As If People Mattered.* Tiptree, Essex: Anchor Press.

United Nations. n.d. *Covenants 107 and 169 Concerning Indigenous Peoples.* New York: International Labour Organization.

_____. 1985. *Rights of Indigenous Peoples to the Earth.* Geneva: World Council of Indigenous Peoples, Commission on Human Rights.

World Bank. 1992. *Tribal Peoples and Economic Development: Human Ecological Considerations.* Washington, D.C.: World Bank.

_____. 1991. *World Data and Statistics.* Washington, D.C.: World Bank.

Wright, R. 1992. *Stolen Continents: The "New World" Through Indian Eyes Since 1492.* Toronto: Viking.

# 7  *The Global Spread of the Democratic Revolution*

## Thomas D. Anderson

### A World of Change

Since 1989 most of the Second and Third World has experienced profound political and economic change at an unprecedented pace. More striking even than these dramatic transformations is the fact that they were unanticipated. Although this brief account can only skim the list of differences between the world of January 1988 and that of mid-1997, the circumstances demand attention. This account focuses on the differing pattern of personal freedoms around the world—a world in which personal liberties are more widespread than ever before.

The most significant event was the collapse of the Soviet Union in 1989. The breakup of this powerful modern empire into fifteen new countries also ended the Cold War. No longer were there two superpowers competing on ideological and economic terms in every corner of the globe, and gone also was the collection of largely East European governments known as the Second World. (The communist governments of Asia as well as Cuba were also variously regarded as Second World or Third World depending upon who made the assessment.) Remaining were a militarily and economically predominant United States, its longtime allies of the First and Third Worlds, and a diverse assortment of other countries, many of whose leaders were left bereft of justifiable alternatives to political and economic pluralism. Within two years, all but a few governments began to abandon one-party rule and centrally planned economic systems, a process that continues. The approaches varied but the goals appear more alike than different. Stated simply, coercion from the national level in political and economic affairs was out, and political and economic choice was in. As had happened in the Soviet Union under Gorbachev, *glasnost* (openness) and *perestroika* (restructuring) diffused into a wide range of ordinary activities.

## Nationalism and Its Effects

The consequences of change have not all been welcome. All but a few countries have degrees of cultural diversity, and the easing of past restrictions on the expression of ethnicity has increased domestic tensions in many places and in several has led to bloody conflicts. Explication of several concepts from political geography can be helpful here. A *state* (or country) is a political entity with an organized government that exercises political control over a defined area and its inhabitants and whose sovereignty is recognized by other states. A *nation*, on the other hand, consists of a group of people who have a common sense of identity and who distinguish themselves from other peoples. A nation of people may or may not currently occupy a common region, although historically their sense of identity had origins in a place and time. Thus, in geography, a state (country) is defined politically and a nation culturally. A country in which nearly all inhabitants share a common ethnic identity is termed a *nation-state*. Several examples are Iceland, Poland, Cuba, Uruguay, and Ireland, but most countries do not qualify.

A country with diverse populations may be regarded as a *polyethnic state* or a *plural state*. Both terms apply to a country that has at least two different ethnic groups with significant populations within its borders, but they differ in that for polyethnic states the homelands of the ethnic groups lie within the country whereas in a plural state one or more of the ethnic groups has a homeland elsewhere. Thus the United States is a plural state because, except for the Amerindian peoples, the vast majority of its inhabitants are the result of migrations from other parts of the world. Polyethnic states are numerous: India, Nigeria, Belgium, and the United Kingdom (England, Wales, and Scotland) are several examples.

The difference between these circumstances has geopolitical significance. The Soviet Union was a polyethnic state in which the union republics had defined homelands and when the political breakup occurred the boundaries of each already were in place. Czechoslovakia was a similar case, and the peaceful establishment of separate Czech and Slovak republics represented a civilized way to resolve a perceived problem. However, in a plural state the immigrant ethnic groups do not have recognized homelands within the country, settlement patterns are mixed, and the arbitrary designation of territory exclusively for one group would of necessity entail the dislocation of others. In the mid-1990s the most vivid, and violent, examples of this circumstance were Bosnia-Herzegovina and Rwanda. In the former Yugoslavia the process acquired the euphemism "ethnic cleansing" and involved unspeakable cruelties to many longtime neighbors regarded as members of the "wrong" group.

Some unassimilated peoples with their own homelands have constituted problems to their central governments for long periods, such as the Basque of Spain and France, the Kurds in southwest Asia, and the Tibetans in China. Yet ethnic turmoil, although smoldering for generations, worsened greatly in the 1990s. The breakup of the USSR left about 25 million ethnic Russians in what became foreign countries, bordering areas that the Russians have begun to call the "near abroad." Most of these new governments have insisted on fostering their own cultures, and the Russian minorities have been pressured to conform or to leave. The reaction in Moscow was to express alarm and hint at protective actions. Whether or not these problems will be resolved peacefully remains uncertain.

Russia, like most countries, has a proportion of its population who long for a return to what are believed passionately to have been past glories. Labeled variously as reactionary, Old Guard, patriotic front, fascist, right wing, skinheads, and so forth, such groups tend to reject change and perceived foreign influences and to favor violent solutions to what they regard as nettlesome problems, especially to problems related to minority segments of their country's population. The head of such a coalition in Russia received strong support in a 1994 election, although his popularity has faded since. Should leaders of this ilk rise to power in Russia, Ukraine, or other countries during the uncertainty of a transition to functioning democracy, not only would the improvement of personal freedoms be interrupted but the chances of aggressive wars would be increased.

## The Democratic Revolution

The political dimensions of ethnicity are hardly new developments yet there has been a close correspondence between the recent increase in their expression and the drastic changes in so many established political and economic orders since 1989. It has been argued, by myself and others, that a major causative factor has been the wide appeal and increasing spread of the Democratic Revolution.

The degree of individual freedom varies widely across the world, in part because of ideological differences regarding just what is meant by freedom. Even among scholars with similar viewpoints there is no unanimity regarding the question of how best to classify and measure levels of freedom. Such a diversity of viewpoints notwithstanding, the subject has a broad popular interest and is used often to evaluate governments. Toward the end of providing a rational basis for such assessments, I have devised a system to rank each sovereign state on the basis of personal liberties perceived to be present in mid-1997.

The liberties treated here are part of the broader concept of human rights. The initial world standard in this regard was the *Universal Declara-*

*tion of Human Rights* passed by the United Nations General Assembly on December 10, 1948. This document of 30 articles and 30 subarticles is comprehensive yet constitutes essentially a statement of worthy principles believed to be applicable to all modern societies. In order to establish a legal basis for compliance by ratifying states, it was divided and passed by the General Assembly in the form of two treaty provisions in 1976. The resultant two documents are the *International Covenant on Civil and Political Rights* (ICCPR) and the *International Covenant on Economic, Social, and Cultural Rights* (ICESCR) (U.S. Department of State 1978).

Controversy regarding human rights centers mainly on the comparative significance of the content of these two covenants. In First World (Western) countries, greatest attention is on the importance of individual civil and political liberties whereas communist governments and many Third World governments have professed primary concern with collective economic and social goals. Philosophically the roots are, respectively, with the concept of the natural rights of man versus that of a naturally harmonious society, which is the intellectual foundation of Marxism. In short, should a government protect primarily individual or collective rights? A valuable critique of the two positions is part of a study by two Polish scholars (Drygalski and Kwasniewski 1986).

Critics of the Western stance often employ sophisms such as "other cultures have different views of freedom" or "hungry people don't care about civil and political rights." Such ethnocentric arguments I find unpersuasive, especially when they are not accompanied by specific examples of just who are those peoples who prefer repression over freedom. My own studies have found scant evidence that a social justice that does not include individual justice has been adopted willingly by many of the world's peoples. (See Humana 1992: 6–9, and Donnelly and Howard 1987: 16–24 for similar views on this position.)

The emphasis here is on the word "willingly," as many governments have imposed unwelcome restrictions of various kinds. Fundamental to the Western concept of civil and political rights is the notion of choice. Choice in turn encompasses individual decisions expressed periodically in collective fashion (contested elections), a diffusion of government power (checks and balances), and the mutability of government policy in response to popular will (referendum). Inextricably bound up with the notion of choice are open expression of ideas and unfettered movement. In my view, denial of any of these elements constitutes infringement of basic rights regardless of the excuses offered.

Disputes about the central content of human rights can convey the impression that the two segments are antagonistic in purpose. Yet on the assumption that social justice includes the nondiscriminatory provision of a population's needs for such as food, shelter, employment, education, medical care, and old-age security, one finds that it has been achieved widely in countries that also protect civil and political liberties. Successful examples include but are not limited to New Zealand, Austria, Japan, and the countries of Scandinavia. On the other hand, governments that proclaim a principal concern with collective rights do no better (and often less well) in social and economic areas and very much worse with respect to civil and political liberties. Examples here are Cuba, Libya, and Singapore. It is important to note at this point that the argument for an emphasis on collective benefits was the basic position of communist governments. Since 1989 most such governments have fallen due to popular repudiation, and the consequent end to censorship has revealed that actual social and economic conditions were much worse than had been acknowledged officially.

## The Evaluation System

The evaluation scheme used here has evolved gradually from one first devised in 1976. Although its focus is also on civil and political liberties, the criteria are more concise than those of the U.N. covenants. The approach is based on the concept of the Democratic Revolution articulated by the geographer Preston E. James (1964: 29–31). James, in turn, took the term and some of the ideas from the works of R. R. Palmer (1959). Six elements of freedom are identified, each of which represents radical changes in the status of the individual relative to the power of the state. Oppression by rulers has ancient origins; only its forms and justifications have been altered in modern times. On the other hand, legally protected personal rights on a mass scale are a little more than two centuries old.

James's six elements are as follows: (1) the individual is accorded equal treatment before the law; (2) the individual is protected from arbitrary acts of those in authority; (3) the individual has the right to be represented where taxes are levied or laws formulated; (4) the principle of majority rule and use of the secret ballot are accepted; (5) the rights of free access to knowledge and open discussion of policy issues are accepted; (6) the individual can exercise freedom of choice, including the right to take a job or leave it, to move from one place to another, to express religious convictions in any way—and a revolutionary new right—the right to resign (James 1974: 2).

This emphasis on personal rights is not intended to belittle the importance of economic and social needs: Their provision is essential to the maintenance of a society. Rather the liberating values of the Democratic Revolution raise the quality of human existence above that of a well-run military unit or slave plantation.

In response to protests that these are purely Western European ideas imposed on other cultures, I offer the words of Chief Joseph of the Nez

Perce American Indian nation over a century ago: "Let me be a free man—free to travel, free to stop, free to trade where I choose, free to choose my own teachers, free to follow the religion of my fathers, free to think and talk and act for myself—and I will obey every law or submit to the penalty" (as printed in the *North American Review*, April 1879). Although the elegant phrasing reflects his own genius, the nonliterate Chief Joseph merely expressed the traditional values of his own people. It seems clear that the notion that an individual has worth and a right to choose was not uniquely Western European.

The following indicators derive in part from personal perceptions and in part from Seymour Lipset (1963: 27) and were used to apply James's six elements to conditions in specific countries: (1) Did the current national leadership gain power by legal means and are there one or more recognized sets of leaders attempting to gain office by the same political process? (2) Is there an accepted legal procedure by means of which current national leaders may be removed from office or their replacements selected upon death or resignation? (3) Do the public media openly distribute views from domestic and foreign sources that are at variance with official policy, and is news of national events, favorable and unfavorable, freely available inside and outside the country? (4) Are the inhabitants allowed to move freely within the country, to emigrate and to return if they choose? A related aspect is the degree of restriction placed on foreigners who wish to leave or enter the country. (5) Do the country's courts rule against the government, and are such rulings honored by the national leadership? (6) Are there present organizations not under direct state control with which inhabitants may openly affiliate if they choose?

The thrust of these indicators is to assess the opportunities for the peaceful transfer of political power, the expression of alternative views, and freedom of movement and association. These rights are deemed prerequisite to the function of other human rights. Restriction of movement, for example, is what most distinguishes the life of a convict from those not imprisoned. In a related sense, if reporters are not permitted to seek out and publicize details about economic, civil, political, and social conditions, how else is a society to learn about them? Surely government pronouncements are not reliable sources of news. Few Americans accept at face value all claims by their public officials. Why then should they not exercise a similar caution about unverified versions of reality by those in power in other countries?

Based on James's elements of the Democratic Revolution, six categories suitable for the classification of all world countries were devised. They are as follows: (1) countries in which all elements of individual rights are specified by law and presently are extended to all inhabitants without restriction; (2) countries in which all elements of individual rights are specified by law but presently are not extended uniformly to some minorities, often due to residual prejudice; (3) countries in which most elements of individual rights are specified by law, but access by many inhabitants to one or more rights is inhibited by law, custom, or arbitrary authority; (4) countries in which most elements of individual rights are restricted by law, custom, or arbitrary authority, but at least one such element is available to nearly all inhabitants; (5) countries in which none of the elements of individual rights is available due to law, custom, or arbitrary authority, but effective political organization provides social and economic stability; (6) countries in which the status of most inhabitants with respect to all individual rights is insecure, even where specified by law, due to the capricious exercise of absolute authority or a near absence of civil organization resulting from disruptive political, social, or economic conditions.

The categories include two distinctive features. One is application to all inhabitants of a state. Many countries contain large numbers of resident aliens. To exclude such people from the national political process is fair morally and legally, but discriminatory treatment in areas of civil liberties is regarded as an infringement of human rights. Recognition of the role of tradition as a factor in discrimination in ethnically and racially diverse countries is also a part. The term custom identifies attitudes that may persistently inhibit the enjoyment of all freedoms by segments of some societies. As has been demonstrated in the United States and Canada (in the case of race) and India (in the case of caste), passage of legislation that mandates equal treatment for all does not necessarily end societal prejudice.

## Country Rankings

The ranking of every country is a difficult task. Verified information for each was used to the greatest extent possible, yet the final choice sometimes rested on intuitive judgment tempered by long experience. Known conditions were balanced and trends considered. In several instances, countries with comparable conditions were placed in separate categories based on evidence of progress or retrogression. An unavoidable shortcoming is the fact that bias-free information for many areas is incomplete or conflicting, and even where data are accurate a sudden change in circumstances can occur.

Information came from a diversity of sources, with newspapers and journals such as *The Economist* of special value in monitoring changes. *The World Factbook*, issued regularly by the U.S. Central Intelligence Agency, is a solid resource for background data for all places in the world. Comparable but different systems for rating the human condition also were gleaned. Included here were Charles Humana's *World Human Rights Guide* (1992), the U.S. Department of State's *Country Reports on Human Rights Practices* (various years), Jack Donnelly and Rhoda Howard's *International Handbook on Human Rights* (1987), and *Freedom in the World: Political Rights and Civil Liberties* (1997). The latter is prepared annually by Freedom House in New York City and, along with their bimonthly journal *Freedom Review*, is of exceptional value for this purpose. My own ratings in general conform more closely with those of Freedom House than with other ratings, mainly due to a similar emphasis on the civil and political dimensions of the human rights of individuals (see Anderson 1988). Agreement regarding conditions in certain countries was not invariable, however. Another basis for differences is that my system ranks countries by means of six categories whereas Freedom House employs three.

Some explanation of the list of countries is appropriate. As of January 1997, there were 190 independent countries, the greatest number in world history. Unlike most of the post–World War II period, more of the newest country additions were in Europe and Asia. The breakup of the Soviet Union alone created fifteen countries out of one. Five of these fifteen new countries are in central Asia and three in Transcaucasia. Czechoslovakia split into two separate countries. Yugoslavia was splintered into Slovenia, Croatia, Bosnia-Herzegovina, and Macedonia, leaving a shrunken and still polyethnic Yugoslavia. Due to an arbitrary decision to exclude countries with fewer than 100,000 population, the number ranked here is 180 countries. Those microstates excluded are Andorra, Kiribati, Liechtenstein, Marshall Islands, Monaco, Nauru, St. Kitts and Nevis, San Marino, Seychelles, and Tuvalu. Thus numerical comparisons between current rankings and those of past years are difficult, both because of roughly a score more countries and the decision to exclude several states that were ranked previously.

Also excluded are assessments of conditions in various entities under the political jurisdiction of outside governments. Depending upon the criteria used, the number of these places ranges from about fifty to perhaps a hundred. Freedom House recognizes sixty-three "related territories" that alphabetically range from the Aland Islands to Vojvodina. Uninhabited areas such as Jarvis, Baker, and Navassa islands are not included among the sixty-three, whereas several prominent places such as Tibet, Puerto Rico, and Hong Kong are. My ranking does not address circumstances in dependencies although it is fair to point out that for most the level of civil freedoms tends to resemble those of the metropole.

### Brief Analysis of Country Rankings

Perhaps the most notable difference over a quarter century of assessments is the increased number of countries in both the highest and lowest categories (see Table 7.1). The total of sixteen countries in Category 1

TABLE 7.1 Ranking of Countries by Civil and Political Liberties

| I | II | III | IV | V | VI |
|---|---|---|---|---|---|
| Austria | Argentina | Antigua | Algeria | Azerbaijan | Afghanistan |
| Barbados | Australia | Bangladesh | Armenia | Burma | Albania |
| Costa Rica | Bahamas | Brazil | Bahrain | China | Angola |
| Denmark | Belgium | Bulgaria | Belarus | Cote d'Ivoire | Burundi |
| Dominica | Belize | Colombia | Bhutan | Cuba | Liberia |
| Iceland | Benin | Comoros | Bosnia-Herz. | Gambia | Somalia |
| Ireland | Bolivia | Congo | Brunei | Iraq | Tajikistan |
| Luxembourg | Botswana | Dominican Rep. | Burkina Faso | Korea, North | Zaire |
| Malta | Canada | Ecuador | Cambodia | Laos | |
| Mauritius | Cape Verde | El Salvador | Cameroon | Libya | |
| Netherlands | Chile | Estonia | Central Afr. Rep. | Maldives | |
| New Zealand | Cyprus (Gr.) | Ghana | Chad | Mauritania | |
| Poland | Czech. Rep. | Guatemala | Croatia | Niger | |
| St. Lucia | Finland | Honduras | Dijibouti | Rwanda | |
| Switzerland | France | India | Egypt | Saudi Arabia | |
| Uruguay | Germany | Israel | Equatorial Guinea | Sudan | |
| | Greece | Jordan | Eritrea | Syria | |
| | Grenada | Macedonia | Fiji | Turkmenistan | |
| | Guyana | Madagascar | Gabon | Uzbekistan | |
| | Hungary | Malawi | Georgia | Vietnam | |
| | Italy | Malaysia | Guinea | | |
| | Jamaica | Mexico | Guinea-Bissau | | |
| | Japan | Namibia | Haiti | | |
| | Korea, South | Nicaragua | Indonesia | | |
| | Latvia | Panama | Iran | | |
| | Lithuania | Papua-New Guinea | Kazakhstan | | |
| | Mali | Paraguay | Kenya | | |
| | Mongolia | Peru | Kuwait | | |
| | Norway | Romania | Kyrgyzstan Rep. | | |
| | Philippines | Russia | Lebanon | | |
| | Portugal | Seychelles | Lesotho | | |
| | St. Vincent | Singapore | Moldova | | |
| | St. Tome-Prin. | Slovakia | Morocco | | |
| | Slovenia | South Africa | Mozambique | | |
| | Solomon Is. | Suriname | Nepal | | |
| | Spain | Thailand | Nigeria | | |
| | Sweden | Turkey | Oman | | |
| | Taiwan | Uganda | Pakistan | | |
| | Trinidad-Tobago | Ukraine | Qatar | | |
| | United Kingdom | Venezuela | Senegal | | |
| | United States | | Sierra Leone | | |
| | Vanuatu | | Sri Lanka | | |
| | West. Samoa | | Swaziland | | |
| | | | Tanzania | | |
| | | | Togo | | |
| | | | Tonga | | |
| | | | Tunisia | | |
| | | | United Arab Emirates | | |
| | | | Yemen | | |
| | | | Yugoslavia | | |
| | | | Zambia | | |
| | | | Zimbabwe | | |

NOTE: Rankings as of April 1997.

is the highest ever. This category is the most difficult to apply because in reality no country is without political and social inequities or has complete freedom for all its peoples, while at the same time a large number of countries have generally very good human conditions. In most cases the difference between a 1 and a 2 ranking is based on the presence of ethnic minorities and especially the circumstance of polyethnicity (multiple homelands). Thus Iceland and Denmark are ranked above Norway, Sweden, and Finland not because of superior virtue but because of greater ethnic homogeneity. The latter have native Sammi (Lapps) who remain unassimilated into the national ethos and the former do not. Most countries ranked highest are small, a factor that can make application of justice less complex but that did not forestall repression in places such as Singapore, Djibouti, or Brunei. It does seem worth pointing out that the countries so designated are spread widely and that cultural diversity, as in Barbados, Mauritius, and Switzerland, has not been a barrier to good government.

Most of the countries regarded as part of the First World appear in Category 2, a recognition that, despite widespread freedoms and open governments, not all inhabitants share these benefits equally. In many cases the assessment took note of discrimination against perceived minorities based on residual prejudices rather than on governmental policies. The various unassimilated elements consist of either or both indigenous peoples and recent immigrants. The inclusion of forty-three countries is a number similar to most past years, but mainly because most countries that improved to higher categories were replaced by additions from below. A trend toward greater freedom in many places is clearly evident.

The total number of countries in the lowest two categories is twenty-eight. Not only is this total lower than in the past but it also includes consideration of twenty new countries, most the result of the breakup of former federations of the Second World. Unfortunately, just as the number of freest countries is the most ever, so also is the number of lowest ranked ones. Afghanistan has been a consistent member of the lowest category for two decades. The bloody domestic strife in all of these countries is based primarily on ethnic differences. Involved were traditional animosities that became more violent with the easing of previous government repression. Even where international efforts were made to stem the slaughters, as in Somalia, Liberia, Angola, Croatia, and Bosnia-Herzegovina, some killing continued. It is important to recognize that such circumstances persist not because of poor government but because of a virtual absence of any government at all in parts of the troubled countries.

Most encouraging is the decreased number of countries in Category 5. Previously a substantial proportion of this grouping were countries governed by communist parties. By mid-1997 such parties ruled only in

Cuba, China, North Korea, Laos, and Vietnam. Communist parties hold power under the principles of Marxist-Leninism, a term in which the hyphen is important. In practice Marxism constitutes application of the economic principle of state control of virtually all national wealth, whereas Leninism signifies a political system based on the concept of "democratic centralism." This ideology limits political power to a single "vanguard" party that professes to represent the genuine interests of all the people and that tolerates no alternative views. Although Leninism is only one form of single-party governance, it constituted the most widespread opposite of what increasingly has become known as political pluralism. Its ideology includes the concepts that it is historically irreversible and should be spread to all world peoples, viewpoints that contributed greatly to the persistence of the Cold War.

The surprising, shocking to some, disintegration of Communist Party rule in Europe and the corollary disappearance of a Second World made the membership of category 5 more complex. Besides the remaining communist-led countries, the largest cluster of remaining dictatorships is in the Middle East. They range from hereditary monarchies as in Kuwait, Saudi Arabia, Oman, and Qatar to "strong man" rule in Iraq, Libya, and Syria, with all governments in the region under political pressures to varying degrees from reactionary Islamic factions. This latter influence (usually termed "fundamentalist" in press reports) may soon cause Algeria to be ranked a notch lower. A number of other repressive regimes result from military takeovers of legally elected governments, a circumstance that has long been common worldwide. Myanmar is an example. (This country traditionally was called Burma rather than Myanmar, which is the name given it by the military junta now in control. I am confident that when they are gone the Burmese will return to the traditional usage.)

Many of the governments included in the middle columns have improved the civil and political conditions of their citizens since 1990. Because previous circumstances were so poor in many cases, much remains to be changed in order for functioning democracy to prevail. Yet the trends during the period were distinctly positive. Places such as Ukraine, Moldova, and Kazakhstan have populations with no collective memory of political pluralism. This inexperience and the presence of institutions left over from recent totalitarian rule have made transitions to an open form of government difficult, as have reactionary political factions that strive for a return to the past. Overall, this total of ninety-two countries is the most diverse in terms of individual freedoms. The degree of freedom available in new countries such as Namibia, Eritrea, and Slovakia far exceeds that available in those places prior to 1989. For democrats worldwide, this has been a very exciting period in history.

## Democracy and Economics: Perceived Linkages

The end of communist rule in Europe produced widespread economic as well as political restructuring. A factor was the freer flow of information, which allowed the citizens of the countries affected and the rest of the world to learn the realities of the socioeconomic Soviet system that had been imposed throughout the region. It quickly became apparent that in matters such as health, education, and industrial development far more had been claimed by the various regimes than had been achieved.

As designed under Lenin and applied by Stalin, the essence of the system was that wealth was power; those who possess great wealth either have power or have the means to influence those who do. Examples of this principle in American culture are the fictional Daddy Warbucks from the comic pages and the very real H. Ross Perot from Texas. Thus the Soviet system insisted that only the state could be an employer and that the accumulation of personal wealth was an economic crime, with penalties as extreme as execution. The Communist Party, of course, controlled the state and its wealth, and as a consequence its higher officials became a privileged elite (a *nomenklatura*), while the bulk of the inhabitants lived in egalitarian poverty (see Anderson 1986: 135–136). Jobs and social benefits were provided by the state on its own terms and were withdrawn from political dissenters. This system of centralized control of both economy and politics proved attractive to a number of leaders in the Third World who, although often not communists, installed versions of Marxist-Leninist principles to maintain political power in their own countries.

As popular awareness of the failures of the Soviet model spread, a growing number of peoples around the world began to pressure their governments for a greater voice not only in political affairs but in economic matters as well. In practice the greatest successes of communist governments had been the enforcement of political stability, development of large military forces, success in sports, and exploitation of natural resources. In general they were mediocre in agriculture and manufacturing, and poor in technological innovation, provision of consumer products, and in commerce. Yet these last areas are often the most promising avenues toward economic improvement available to poor countries, especially to small ones.

The creation of national wealth despite a paucity of natural resources has been achieved by a remarkable number of countries in the world (Denmark, Austria, Japan, Taiwan, Singapore, etc.). However, despite the diversity of circumstances, the constant has been application of some form of a market economy. It also is true that nowhere has the Soviet model of development been successful in this regard. This reality became appreciated more widely during the 1980s, and following the collapse of the Second World, variations of market-oriented economic policies were adopted by all but a few countries.

The coincidence of the spread of the Democratic Revolution and of capitalist economic approaches suggests that the two are related. Whether or not such a linkage actually exists remains unproven (places such as Barbados, Botswana, and Mauritius support the contention, whereas others such as Singapore and Brunei do not). Yet the freedom to make personal decisions in economic matters can encourage a desire to do so in political ones as well, and perhaps the reverse also often is true. One aspect does seem clear, the right to accumulate personal wealth reduces dependency upon the state for subsistence and serves to weaken central authority. Regardless, the world of the 1990s has been marked by trends toward greater individual choice in political and economic matters nearly everywhere, and appreciation of this reality is prerequisite to understanding world conditions during this era of change.

The spread of market economies has occurred in many ways in societies with very different local circumstances. Most common has been the transfer of former state enterprises to individual, corporate, or collective regional ownership (a process usually termed "privatization"). These enterprises consisted of such economic activities as transportation systems, utilities, factories, mines, and in former communist-ruled countries, much of the agriculture. The restructuring has been most traumatic in the latter places because not only had private ownership, especially of land, been prohibited but generations of citizens had been taught that it also was immoral. Thus along with the stresses of sudden economic and political uncertainty, large segments of the populations experienced degrees of culture shock. The replacement of policies that promised employment so long as one did not challenge the status quo with those in which jobs must be sought and layoffs were possible introduced a period of exciting opportunity for some and of frightening insecurity for others.

In political atmospheres where national leaders are elected and are replaced by the same process, popular perceptions of the relative benefits of economic restructuring have created voting constituencies of fluctuating moods. What is called by economists the "pain of reform" has produced income inequities different from those of the past. Supporters of restructuring maintain that radical changes at the onset will result in a shorter and more successful transition to economic stability and growth. Critics argue that more gradual modifications will reduce the emotional and economic suffering of the poorer segments of the various societies during the period of transmutation. Thus in scores of countries worldwide, not only are differing economic policies being tried but some governments are periodically switching from one to another.

Major influences in this process have been the International Monetary Fund (IMF) and the World Bank. These nongovernmental organizations provide investment funding to developing countries but stipulate that such funding will be continued only so long as certain specific recommended economic policies are followed. In a dozen or more countries (Bolivia, Argentina, and Chile are examples) where its strictures have been heeded, inflation has been reduced and economic growth has resulted, but only after periods of economic and related social stress. Elsewhere various governments have rejected or at least criticized the IMF formula as an unwelcome foreign intrusion into their domestic affairs. During this complex series of events the only constant appears to have been that economic readjustment induces political as well as economic tensions.

## Resistances to Change

The political and economic changes described previously are indeed revolutionary for many of the societies in which they are underway. Hence neither their relative success nor eventual forms can be predicted. The resistance encountered in specific countries differs but several factors of wide scope can be identified.

In formerly communist-ruled countries, the onset of elected government left many Communist Party members in the same offices they had held previously. Ideological disagreement with political pluralism and a reluctance to give up positions that gave them prestige and influence caused many bureaucrats to impede if not openly oppose many of the new programs and policies intended to implement *perestroika*. In addition, many of the *apparatchiks* who were factory or bank managers have used personal contacts to manipulate funds and administrative decisions in order to enrich themselves at the expense of the general public. The result has been the sabotage of the transition to greater political democracy and the diversion of many of the benefits of emerging market economies to the same people who were the most privileged under the previous system (the *nomenklatura*). Such circumstances have been most common where communist government had endured longest, as in Russia, Ukraine, and Belarus, and less persistent in places such as the Baltic republics, Hungary, and Poland where it had been imposed at the end of World War II.

A different situation developed in East and Southeast Asia. Although in countries such as Japan, South Korea, Taiwan, and the Philippines both democracy and market economies have been implemented to varying degrees, leaders in countries such as China, Vietnam, and Singapore have embraced many economic changes but have rejected most of the elements of the Democratic Revolution. In China and Vietnam, for example, Communist Party rule continues but statist economic policies are being abandoned in favor of market-oriented ones. Each avidly seeks foreign investment. China in particular has become a major participant in the world economy. The governments in Singapore and Malaysia are not communist but openly reject the concepts of greater individual freedoms on the basis of what has been termed "the Asian Way," a concept that puts respect for authority above personal choices. In truth, each country in the region differs in recognizable ways and this description of current circumstances only calls attention to some generalities. Continued change, perhaps even of a radical nature, can be anticipated.

In countries with largely Muslim populations, market-oriented economic systems have long been in place, with some far more successful than others. On the other hand, few of these governments profess strong agreement with the principles of the Democratic Revolution. Only Bangladesh, Jordan, and Turkey are ranked as high as Category 3, for example. (It does seem worthy of mention at this point that Bangladesh, Pakistan, and Turkey all have elected women to positions of national leadership.) The reasons are complex and are not obvious but the record is consistent. Even though open elections have occurred with increasing frequency in such countries, the results have not always been honored.

However, since the Iranian Revolution in 1977 all Muslim societies have been subject to increasing pressures from what have been loosely termed "fundamentalist" factions to reject those social and political changes that are perceived to be "Western" in origin. Two common objectives have been a return to *purdah* (the seclusion of females) and to application of *Sharia* (the old Islamic legal code). Previously such rules were imposed widely only in Saudi Arabia but since have spread officially to Iran and Sudan and have been considered elsewhere. Terrorism directed toward such ends exists in a number of countries and perhaps most threatens unsympathetic governments in Algeria and Egypt. Future developments are difficult to predict but as of mid-1997 the prospects for greater individual freedoms in such countries were dim, especially for women.

Although the resistances identified here have wide regional distribution, for the world as a whole it is the combination of ethnic differences and traditional animosities that constitutes the greatest threat to expansion of individual political and economic freedoms. Labeled by some observers as "turf wars," the savage struggles for ethnic dominance over territory have intensified during a period in history when wars between sovereign states have virtually ended. The last decade of the twentieth century thus appears to be marked by a bloody resumption of conflicts with ancient origins and fueled more by visceral hatred than by conventional economic and political objectives. It is this fundamental irrationality that makes each clash virtually inexplicable to outsiders and hence extraordinarily difficult to resolve by disinterested mediators.

These last circumstances are operative particularly in non-Arab Africa. Along the southern fringe of the Sahara exists not only an ecological transition but also a racial and religious one. Most peoples here are Muslim but religious diversity increases as the environments become more rainy and forested southward. In Sudan and Mauritania, black Africans are minorities in countries where political and economic power is held by desert peoples. Elsewhere, however, it is ethnic identity (often termed "tribalism" by Europeans) that most hampers establishment of stable, elected governments. Other factors are also cited, such as the legacies of European colonialism, poorly developed infrastructures, disease, and the geopolitical interferences associated with the Cold War. Regardless of the significance of these various influences in a region where racial diversity is slight, the presence of an estimated 700 or more different languages complicates even sincere efforts to achieve degrees of political harmony. Openly elected governments are not common, and of these, only a few endure long. Over the past two decades only Botswana has consistently enjoyed democratic rule. Geopolitically the most significant event has been the emergence of elected black-majority government in South Africa, the richest and best-educated country in the region.

In contrast, in Latin America the impacts of the Democratic Revolution have affected every country except Cuba. As the ratings demonstrate, the spread has been uneven, and not all recent changes have been positive. Yet the long persistence of arbitrary rule by *caudillos* or military *juntas* appears to have ended. This assessment does not ignore the continuing undue influence of the military on a number of elected governments, but leaders within the region now attain office by means of ballots and not by bullets. The various current imperfections notwithstanding, in terms of political and civil liberties, for the inhabitants of Latin America the present is better than the past, and the prospects for the future appear to be even brighter.

## Summary

This assessment of human conditions has focused on individual civil and political freedoms and the degrees to which they exist in different countries around the world. The concept of the Democratic Revolution was explained and employed to rank all sovereign states of 100,000 population or more. These appraisals were presented in the context of a period of political and economic change of unprecedented magnitude and scope during which nearly every inhabited area has been affected to some extent. The circumstances that have propelled the expansions of freedoms, as well as various resistances, were identified and analyzed briefly. This treatment included explication of a number of terms and processes useful in understanding the complex events.

Although this chapter is based on several decades of research on the subject and the examination of comparable work by scores of other scholars, the ideas and interpretations presented are largely my own. Some conform with conventional evaluations and some do not. The reader is encouraged to view it all with a degree of caution and accept those aspects that appear to be most sensible in the context of personal experience and education. In addition, it must be recognized that any such evaluations are aimed at moving targets; conditions change continually and what has been true may change tomorrow. The thrust of my analyses, however, is that improvements in fundamental human conditions are spreading worldwide at an accelerating pace and that awareness of this reality enhances global understanding.

## References

Anderson, Thomas D. 1988. "Civil and Political Liberties in the World: A Geographical Analysis." Pp. 89–99 in Raymond D. Gastil, *Freedom in the World: Political Rights and Civil Liberties, 1987-1988*. Lanham, MD: University Press of America.

_____ . 1986. "Marxists and Non-Marxists in the Caribbean." In Adjit Jain and Alexander Matejko, eds., *A Critique of Marxist and Non-Marxist Thought*. New York: Praeger Publishers.

Donnelly, Jack, and Rhoda E. Howard, eds. 1987. *International Handbook of Human Rights*. New York: Greenwood Press.

Drygalski, Jerzy, and Jacek Kwasniewski. 1986. "Harmonious Society Versus Conflict-Ridden Society: Marxism and Liberalism." Pp. 259–281 in Adjit Jain and Alexander Matejko, eds., *A Critique of Marxist and Non-Marxist Thought*. New York: Praeger Publishers.

Freedom House. 1997. *Freedom in the World, Political Rights and Civil Liberties, 1996–1997*. Lanham, MD: University Press of America.

Humana, Charles. 1992. *World Human Rights Guide*, 3rd ed. New York: Oxford University Press.

James, Preston E. 1974. *One World Divided*, 2nd ed. Lexington, MA: Xerox College Publishing.

_____ . 1964. *One World Divided*. New York: Blaisdell Publishing.

Lipset, Seymour. 1963. *Political Man: The Social Basis of Politics*. Garden City, NY: Anchor Books.

Palmer, R. R. 1959. *The Challenge*, vol. 1 of *The Age of the Democratic Revolution*. Princeton, NJ: Princeton University Press.

U.S. Central Intelligence Agency. *The World Factbook*. Washington, DC: U.S. Government Printing Office.

U.S. Department of State. *Country Reports on Human Rights Practices*. Washington, DC: U.S. Government Printing Office.

_____ . 1978. *Human Rights*. Selected Documents, N. 5 (revised). Washington, DC: U.S. Government Printing Office. This source contains copies of eight selected international documents related to human rights.

# PART TWO

*Third World Regions*

# 8   The Caribbean Basin: Cultural and Political Diversity Overview

**Thomas D. Anderson**

## Introduction

The Americas consist of two broadly defined socioeconomic regions. The United States and Canada occupy most of the North American continent and are First World countries. The rest of North America, South America, and the Caribbean islands are regarded as part of the Third World. Because of differing, largely English or Iberian colonial legacies, shared cultural elements in the two segments led geographers to term them Anglo-America and Latin America, respectively. This chapter focuses on the portion of the latter that fringes on the Caribbean, termed here the Caribbean Basin.

The region's integrating element is the Caribbean Sea. This westward bulge of the Atlantic provides a maritime routeway between the two main land masses as well as with the Pacific Ocean by way of the Panama Canal. Land routes across this narrow isthmus of North America also link the two oceans, but no land route effectively connects the two continents. These circumstances have given the sea lanes and associated shore lines strategic significance during the nearly five centuries of European presence. The region is adjacent to the world's leading superpower, the United States, which historically has feared the influence of hostile powers there. This proximity and associated attitude have long affected U.S. relations with Caribbean Basin countries, and apprehension about intervention by the "Colossus of the North" is part of the political climate in nearly every country.

Several of the political entities treated as part of the Caribbean Basin do not in fact border that sea. These are El Salvador, the Guianas, the Ba-

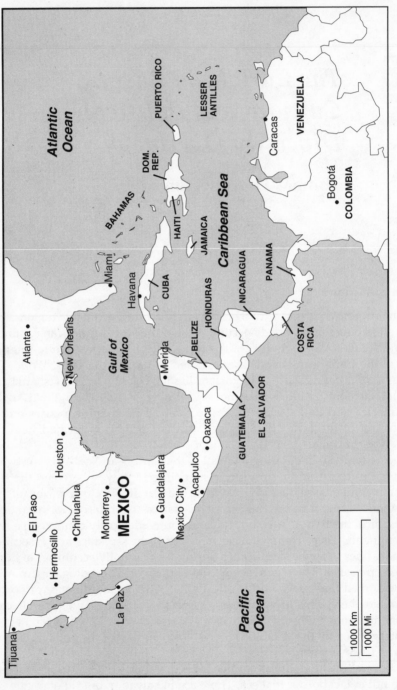

MAP 8.1  Middle America

hamas, the Turks and Caicos Islands, and in the strictest sense, Barbados. Each is included because of common history or contemporary regional interaction. Directly or indirectly all have concerns with the Caribbean. In addition to twenty-five countries, twelve dependencies—holdovers from the colonial past—help to make the region the most politically complex in the world. Because the United States, the United Kingdom, France, and the Netherlands retain territories in the region, they all have a direct interest in Caribbean affairs.

## Subregions

John Augelli (1962) divided the region into a Rimland and a Mainland on the basis of differing historical development. His Rimland consisted of the islands and the coastal margins of Central America and the Guianas. Here the early European contacts virtually destroyed native peoples, and the subsequent labor needs of large sugar plantations to serve European markets initiated a repopulation, first by slaves taken by force from Africa and later, following emancipation, by contract workers from British India or the Dutch East Indies. The current populations largely reflect these African and Asian origins, and the cultural residue of slavery and the plantation system permeates Rimland societies. The Rimland's centuries-old reliance on international commerce persists despite changes in recent decades of basic economic activities and principal trade partners.

Following massive population declines in the decades after conquest (Lovell 1992), most of the surviving native peoples on the Mainland were acculturated under Spanish rule. Mainland populations consist racially of various proportions of Amerindians, whites of Hispanic origin, and mestizos (mixtures of whites and Amerindians). The hacienda, rather than the plantation, was the most influential institution. The primary economic function of this large landholding with numerous workers was to serve local needs, not to supply a commodity for overseas markets. Its legacies include economic and class inequalities and a rural-based power structure that long dominated national affairs in most countries. Such generalizations are not meant to obscure the uniqueness of each country or the uneven spread of modernization. They are offered in order to assist recognition of interregional differences and to stimulate comparisons.

Pertinent also is a distinction between Spanish and non-Spanish areas. Countries regarded as Mainland experienced centuries of Spanish colonial rule, as did Cuba, Puerto Rico, and the Dominican Republic of the Rimland, and share a broader Latin American culture. Independence came earlier in the Spanish lands, beginning in the 1820s and ending with the separation of Panama from Colombia and Cuba from Spain around 1900.

Haiti won independence from France in 1804 and, after the United States of America, was the second country in the world to shed European colonialism. However, it was not until 1962, when Jamaica and Trinidad and Tobago were granted independence by Britain, that other non-Spanish lands of the Caribbean began a decolonization process that may not yet have ended. Languages and cultures in these various entities reflect past or present colonial affiliations. Hence governments function in Dutch in Suriname, Aruba, and the Netherlands Antilles; in French in Haiti, French Guiana, Guadeloupe, and Martinique; in Spanish in Puerto Rico, Cuba, and the Dominican Republic; and in English everywhere else.

Decolonization has created a cluster of increasingly smaller states of questionable economic and political viability (Anderson 1984: 22–25). Whether any remaining dependencies will choose independence is unclear. The French territories held the status of Overseas *Départements* (D.O.M.'s) politically equivalent to *départements* in France itself. The relation of Aruba and the five Netherlands Antilles to the Kingdom of the Netherlands was roughly similar. The British dependencies politically were Crown Colonies except for the Associated State of Anguilla. Although currently a commonwealth of the United States, Puerto Rican citizens periodically have the choice of independence, statehood, or continuation of the commonwealth. Supporters of the latter two options have in recent elections roughly split about 95 percent of the vote, with the status quo winning a plurality.

Aside from Suriname, the new Caribbean ministates are English-speaking, a factor that has geopolitical consequences. Within the Organization of American States (OAS), where each government has one vote, votes on contentious issues increasingly have split along English-Spanish lines. Another difference is in the area of mass culture in that cricket is wildly popular in the British West Indies, whereas in most of the Hispanic countries it is baseball that captures attention. Soccer, nonetheless, remains the most widely played sport everywhere within the region.

## Natural Environment

The Greater Antilles are the large islands of Cuba, Jamaica, Hispañola, and Puerto Rico whereas the Lesser Antilles refers to the arc of smaller islands that curve toward Venezuela. Other small island clusters fringe the coasts of Venezuela, Central America, and the Yucatan. The Bahamas constitute a separate archipelago east of Florida. The low islands and cays (keys) consist of raised coral or limestone whereas the high islands of the Lesser Antilles have a volcanic origin, a dimension that provides spectacular scenery and occasional dangerous eruptions. High mountains, many of volcanic origin, characterize the landscapes on the mainland from Mexico into the

Guianas, with wide coastal plains present only in Honduras-Nicaragua and in Colombia. The Greater Antilles are mainly geologic extensions of the highland structures of Central America, although most of Cuba, aside from the Sierra Maestre in the southeast, is a limestone platform similar to those of the Yucatan Peninsula and Florida.

Only the northern half of Mexico and the Bahamas lie outside the tropics, and freezing temperatures are limited to high elevations of the Mainland. All of the region is in the Northern Hemisphere, and high sun and low sun periods occur in the same months everywhere. Most temperature diversity in low latitudes is associated with mountain areas. Temperatures decline with increased elevation, and higher elevations also are generally more humid. The differing vertical ecological zones customarily are termed as follows: *tierra caliente* (sea level to 3,000 feet [915 meters]), *tierra templada* (3,000 to 6,000 feet [915 to 1,830 meters]), and *tierra fría* (6,000 to 9,500 feet [1,830 to 2,900 meters]).

Of course, no sharp changes distinguish such boundaries and the actual elevation ranges vary depending upon local circumstances. Also the upper limits of each is lower for places farther from the equator. Nonetheless they constitute recognized life zones with distinctive combinations of temperatures, moisture, vegetation, and biota and consequent different human adaptations to local habitats. The "hot" zone is noted for crops such as sugar cane, bananas, and cacao; the "temperate" zone, with its milder temperatures and lack of frost, usually is regarded as the coffee zone; and the main crops in the higher "cool" zone are often grains, with potatoes more common in the higher margins. These upper fringes usually constitute the tree line as well as the limit of crop farming. The alpine meadows above are termed *páramos* in northern South America and are used to graze livestock. The highest mountains are snowcapped above this latter zone.

Much of the region is subject to a wet-and-dry regime of rainfall, with a summer maximum, and it is this rhythm, rather than temperature changes, that most distinguishes the seasons. Lowland northern Mexico is largely desert or semi-arid, as is the narrow coastal fringe of South America centered by the Gulf of Venezuela. In Central America the Caribbean side is rainy year-round whereas the Pacific side northwest of the Panama Canal has a dry winter season. Stable, tropical easterly winds (trade winds) predominate in the Caribbean and, although humid, tend to produce heavy rainfall only where forced to rise on the east sides of highlands. As a consequence, many low islands and cays are sufficiently dry to permit the accumulation of guano (dried seabird dung), a resource for which they were valued in the latter half of the nineteenth century.

Most main cities and harbors on the islands are located on the western (leeward) sides where waters are calm. These persistent easterly winds induce westward-moving ocean currents that continue clockwise into the Gulf of Mexico and thence eastward between Cuba and Florida as the Florida Current, a flow known as the Gulf Stream when it widens in the Atlantic. This clockwise surface circulation was exploited by mariners in the days of sailing ships and continues to benefit the diesel-powered craft of today.

Just as the consistent easterly winds have affected navigation, so has a wet and dry rainfall cycle influenced agriculture. Wet season rainfall normally is sufficient to support crop growth and the dry season is ecologically favorable for the ripening of cash crops such as sugar cane, cotton, and coffee. Bananas, however, require either all-season rainfall or dry-season irrigation.

The region is subject to a variety of violent acts of nature. The tectonic displacements that produced the many highlands continues, and earthquakes can occur anywhere at any time. Depending upon the circumstances, the property damage and death toll can be severe. The distribution of volcanoes is more limited, but the effects of an eruption can be catastrophic locally due to emissions of toxic gases, lava, and/or ash. A positive aspect of volcanism is that lavas are dark-colored (chemically basic) and weather into productive soils. Hurricanes (an Arawak Indian word) are a menace to coastal areas everywhere except the more equatorial Guianas and Panama. From June to December these massive storms of violent winds, heavy rains, and ocean surges can cause major damage and death in a succession of places over a period of a week or more, and the same locality can be struck more than once during the same season. Thus their impact can be experienced far more widely and more often than those of earthquakes or volcanoes. Although they may occur on the Pacific side of Mexico, hurricanes are primarily a Rimland rather than a Mainland phenomenon, with the islands generally at greater risk.

*Resources*

In terms of sustainable development, perhaps the most important natural resources of the Caribbean Basin are its situation in the middle of the Americas, its tropical climates, and its extensive sea coasts. Since Columbus, the maritime accessibility of most areas has been an economic asset, and in the modern era the centrality in terms of air routes is an added advantage. The tropical climates and relative proximity to major markets in colder latitudes fostered sugar production during colonial times, and over the last century coffee and banana exports have expanded greatly as the economic predominance of sugar has declined everywhere but in Cuba, where it has increased.

These attributes have since midcentury enabled tourism to become the most important economic activity on most small island countries and a significant source of income even for the larger Mainland countries. Beaches, warm ocean, and winter sunshine attract tourists from higher latitudes, and the island Caribbean and coastal Rimland are well endowed with each.

Regionally, the mineral base is large and varied, but the distribution is uneven. In terms of energy, Mexico and Colombia possess the only substantial reserves of coal in Latin America. Colombia's are much the larger and it is the only exporter, largely from newly developed deposits on the Guajira Peninsula. Venezuela and Mexico have major reserves of petroleum and natural gas and are leading world producers. Trinidad and Colombia also export petroleum. Guatemala has moderate reserves, and Cuba also has prospects offshore but so far little production. Other countries have little or none, and all depend on imports.

In terms of minerals, Mexico has as great a diversity as any place in the world but is a leading exporter only of lead, silver, and mercury. Jamaica, Guyana, and Suriname have large deposits of bauxite. Exports from the latter two have declined since independence, but Jamaica remains a major exporter, especially to Anglo-America. Cuba's deposits of iron ore and nickel are substantial, but only minor quantities of nickel are exported. Venezuela has been a major exporter of iron ore since the 1950s. Except for its mineral fuels, Colombia's diverse mineral base mainly serves only national needs. Elsewhere mineral resources are minor or lacking.

The fishery resources also are uneven, with the greatest abundance in waters underlain by a relatively shallow continental shelf offshore from the discharges of large rivers. Thus the Gulf of Mexico along the margins of the United States and Mexico is exceptionally rich in marine life, with a smaller resource base present in the western Caribbean and in the western Atlantic south of Trinidad. Crustaceans are especially sought in these areas. Waters in most of the rest of the basin are quite deep, even close to shore, and have a lower biotic content. Although fishing craft roam the sea nearly everywhere, the catches are more meager elsewhere. Nonetheless, fresh fish and crustaceans are marketed along all coasts and constitute an attraction to many tourists, as does sportfishing for a more select number. Only Mexico and Cuba have large, modern fishing fleets.

*Environmental Problems*

As in most of the Third World, the flood of migration into cities within the region creates a crisis in housing quality and exacerbates the degree of water and air pollution. Mexico City, which lies in a mountain basin 7,350 feet (2,240 meters) above sea level and has a metropolitan population of 16 to 18 million, has some of the worst air pollution in the world. Since 1991 catalytic converters have been mandated on all new cars, and the worst of the polluting factories have been closed or modified. The expectation is for a substantial improvement in air quality over the next decade. Similar problems afflict large cities elsewhere but on a lesser scale.

In the island Caribbean the importance of tourism makes the quality of shorelines and seawater a major concern. A concentration of tourist accommodations close to the sea and the consequent increased need for abundant fresh water and proper sewage disposal pose problems expensive to solve. Such circumstances are not unique to the Caribbean; in April 1994 the United Nations Global Conference on Sustainable Development of Small Island Developing States was held on Barbados (*Caribbean Week*, April 1994). A conference, of course, is not a solution, but policies and methods to address what clearly are common concerns were an outcome of the conclave.

The past and present impacts of human activities upon natural vegetation are environmental issues within the Caribbean Basin as in most of the world. Tropical rain forest, light tropical forest, and savanna in their various forms were the most widespread natural vegetation types except in the arid regions and highest elevations. Savannas are believed to have expanded due to the long practice of late dry-season burning and are most extensive in the Llanos region of Venezuela and Colombia where their grasses have been exploited for cattle grazing since the Spanish conquest. Rain forests cover much of Pacific Colombia and Panama east of the Canal, the interior Guianas, and the Caribbean rim of Central America, with smaller patches in other moist sites. Tropical woods have been exports from the latter two areas for centuries, but in recent decades all rain forests have been exploited more intensively than ever before, causing their extent to diminish at alarming rates. Costa Rica is noted for having the largest proportion of its total area in national parks of any country in the world, but elsewhere legal protections are far less extensive. Light tropical forests on the Caribbean islands were largely destroyed during the colonial sugar era, and various forms of scrub growth that includes introduced species now cover most land not actually farmed (Kimber 1988: 295–316). Similar forests were cleared for farming in the more settled portions of Colombia, Venezuela, and southern Mexico and currently are being converted to cattle pasture at accelerating rates along the Pacific margins of Central America.

## The People

The population of the Caribbean Basin was about 222 million in 1996, with nearly 70 percent of the total in the countries of Mexico, Colombia, and Venezuela (see Table 8.1). Numbers of this sort mask wide differences in distribution and densities, but overall most peoples of the region

TABLE 8.1  Population Data for Caribbean Basin Countries

| Country | Total Population (millions)[1] | Natural Increase (%)[1] | Infant Mortality Rate[1] | Pop.<15/ Pop.>65+ (%)[1] | Life Expectancy at Birth (yrs.)[1] | Literacy 15+ yrs. (%)[2] | Urban Population (%)[1] | GDP per Capita (PPP$)[3] | Political/ Civil Liberty Rating[3] | Armed Forces (per 1,000 pop.)[4] |
|---|---|---|---|---|---|---|---|---|---|---|
| Antigua-Barbuda | 0.1 | 1.2 | 18.0 | 25/6 | 73 | 89 | 31 | 5,369 | 4-3 | n.a. |
| Bahamas | 0.3 | 1.3 | 23.8 | 29/5 | 72 | 90 | 84 | 16,180 | 1-2 | n.a. |
| Barbados | 0.3 | 0.5 | 9.1 | 24/12 | 76 | 99 | 38 | 10,570 | 1-1 | 0 |
| *Belize* | 0.2 | 3.3 | 34.0 | 44/4 | 72 | 91 | 48 | 4,610 | 1-1 | 4.8 |
| *Colombia* | 38.0 | 2.1 | 28.0 | 33/4 | 69 | 88 | 67 | 5,790 | 4-4 | 4.1 |
| *Costa Rica* | 3.6 | 2.2 | 13.0 | 34/5 | 76 | 93 | 44 | 5,680 | 1-2 | 2.4 |
| Cuba | 11.0 | 0.7 | 9.4 | 22/9 | 75 | 94 | 74 | 3,000 | 7-7 | 12.9 |
| Dominica | 0.1 | 1.3 | 18.4 | 32/10 | 78 | 94 | 61 | 3,810 | 1-1 | n.a. |
| Dominican Republic | 8.1 | 2.3 | 52.0 | 37/4 | 68 | 83 | 61 | 3,690 | 3-3 | 2.8 |
| *El Salvador* | 5.9 | 2.6 | 41.0 | 40/4 | 68 | 73 | 45 | 2,360 | 3-3 | 5.2 |
| Grenada | 0.1 | 2.4 | 12.0 | 43/5 | 71 | 98 | – | 3,118 | 1-2 | n.a. |
| *Guatemala* | 9.9 | 2.9 | 51.0 | 45/3 | 65 | 55 | 39 | 3,400 | 3-4 | 3.2 |
| *Guyana* | 0.7 | 1.8 | 48.0 | 38/4 | 65 | 96 | 33 | 2,140 | 2-2 | 2.7 |
| Haiti | 7.3 | 2.3 | 74.0 | 40/4 | 57 | 53 | 32 | 1,050 | 4-5 | 0 |
| *Honduras* | 5.6 | 2.8 | 50.0 | 45/3 | 68 | 73 | 47 | 2,100 | 3-3 | 3.2 |
| *Jamaica* | 2.6 | 1.8 | 24.0 | 34/7 | 74 | 98 | 53 | 3,180 | 2-3 | 1.2 |
| *Mexico* | 95.0 | 2.2 | 34.0 | 36/4 | 73 | 88 | 71 | 7,010 | 4-3 | 1.9 |
| *Nicaragua* | 4.6 | 2.7 | 49.0 | 44/3 | 65 | 57 | 63 | 2,280 | 3-3 | 3.4 |
| *Panama* | 2.7 | 1.8 | 18.0 | 33/5 | 73 | 89 | 55 | 5,890 | 2-3 | 4.2 |
| St. Kitts-Nevis | 0.04 | 1.3 | 24.0 | 37/7 | 72 | 97 | 42 | 9,340 | 1-2 | n.a. |
| St. Lucia | 0.1 | 2.0 | 23.0 | 37/7 | 72 | 67 | 48 | 3,795 | 1-2 | n.a. |
| St. Vincent & Grenadines | 0.1 | 1.8 | 17.0 | 37/6 | 73 | 96 | 25 | 3,552 | 2-1 | n.a. |
| *Suriname* | 0.4 | 1.6 | 28.0 | 35/5 | 70 | 95 | 49 | 3,670 | 3-3 | 4.7 |
| Trinidad & Tobago | 1.3 | 1.2 | 12.2 | 31/6 | 71 | 97 | 65 | 8,670 | 1-2 | 2.4 |
| *Venezuela* | 22.3 | 2.1 | 23.5 | 38/4 | 72 | 90 | 84 | 8,360 | 2-3 | 3.6 |

1. Population Reference Bureau, *World Population Data Sheet* (Washington, D.C.: Population Reference Bureau, 1996).
2. Freedom House, *Freedom in the World: The Annual Survey of Political Rights and Civil Liberties 1996–97* (Lanham, Md.: University Press of America, 1997). Political Rights–Civil Rights rated 1 to 7, 1 = most free. PPP$ = Parity Purchasing Power of GDP per capita in US$.
3. U.S. Central Intelligence Agency, *World Fact Book* (Washington, D.C.: USGPO).
4. U.S. Arms Control and Disarmament Agency, *World Military Expenditures and Arms Transfers* (Washington, D.C.: USGPO, 1995), p. 47.
NOTE: Mainland Countries in italics.

live in dense clusters separated by water or sparsely occupied territory. On the Mainland, populations tend to be greatest in the same places they were at the time of Spanish conquest. Aside from Nicaragua, Panama, Belize, and the Guianas, most people live in mountain basins in the higher environments of tierra templada and tierra fría. On the islands, densities are greatest along the coasts or in other lowlands, due in large part to the centuries-old emphasis on an export economy but also to the more recent focus by the tourist industry on ocean-side facilities.

Urbanization is increasing nearly everywhere, although the pace is slower in most of Central America where ties to the land remain strong and urban economies are growing more slowly. In the Rimland, urban populations are lowest in Antigua-Barbuda, Barbados, Guyana, Haiti, and St. Vincent where similar factors are operative (see Table 8.1). Nearly all countries have a primate city. (This geographic concept postulates a single city that is simultaneously the center of government, culture, and economic activity and is at least twice as populous as any other city in that country.) Even where official policies strive to disperse economic development and its related population growth, the primacy of a single city in most countries appears difficult to reverse. Rural-to-urban migrations are motivated both by push and pull factors. Although rural land hunger often is cited as a primary push factor, it is the large country of Venezuela that has the highest percent of urban population (84 percent). Clearly the causes vary in different countries and regions. A belief that land reform will diminish the human flows does little to explain individual circumstances, especially in a modern era of mass electronic information distribution where few youth are content with the prospects of a rural future.

Regardless, the process of urbanization has complex effects on the countryside as well as cities. Some ecological aspects on the latter were noted previously, but to the people involved, the shift from rural to urban is perceived most keenly in social and economic terms. These, in turn, tend to have political consequences as well.

## Race and Ethnicity

The initial European impact on the islands resulted in the virtual destruction of the native peoples. Even the numerous native peoples on Hispañola were reduced to mere tens of thousands within a few decades following conquest, and little of the race mixing that characterizes the Mainland had time to occur. Because of centuries of shipments of slaves to work sugar plantations, the majority of people in the Rimland have at least some African ancestry (Richardson 1992: 8). It is important to recognize that perceptions of race within the Caribbean differ from those in Anglo-America. They are so different, for example, that the U.S. Census

Bureau does not gather data by race for Puerto Rico. Even so, a lighter skin color tends to confer higher social status nearly everywhere.

In the Rimland the Caucasian proportions are small except in Cuba and include peoples of both European and Middle Eastern origins, such as Syrians and Lebanese. East Indian is a widely used term to refer to people whose ancestry is South or Southeast Asian and contrasts with the equally common application of West Indian to refer to inhabitants of the small island Caribbean, especially those who speak English. East Indians are most numerous in Trinidad, Guyana, and Suriname, with many of the latter of Javanese origins. Although traditionally these latter groups have tended to have proportionately greater economic influence in the Rimland, universal suffrage and the spread of democratic government has given the Afro-Caribbean populations a high degree of political power everywhere but in Cuba.

On the Mainland, about half of the population of Costa Rica is thought to be of European ancestry whereas more than half that of Guatemala is regarded as Amerindian. Elsewhere the majority of people are regarded as mestizo. Racially this term means a person with both white and Amerindian biological ancestry, but in practice a person is more likely to be classed on the basis of culture. Those who retain a native language and customs are classed as Indian, and those who function in the Hispanic culture are regarded as mestizo, regardless of genetic heritage. Whites and mestizos (termed "ladinos" in Guatemala) dominate the power structures in all Hispanic countries on the Mainland.

## Migration

As a region, Caribbean Basin countries are especially noted for the emigration of their peoples. Indeed, the human flow from the islands over the past century has been termed the Caribbean Diaspora. Perhaps a third of all people born since 1900 live or have lived outside their land of birth, mainly in the countries of western Europe or Anglo-America but also others within the Caribbean Basin. On the Mainland the scale of similar migration from Mexico to the United States exceeds ten million, and the numbers from Central America may be proportionally as great. Smaller numbers from Colombia, Venezuela, and the Guianas also are involved.

The movements are significant in several ways. Economically, they transfer wealth back to their families, either with returnees or through postal remittances. In foreign countries they create, sometimes sizable, communities. Return migration, visits, and correspondence enable Caribbean peoples even in small villages to be informed regarding events and conditions in distant places. Such cultural and economic linkages in-

creasingly entwine the peoples and their governments with the First
World (Western 1992), as well as with other parts of the Caribbean region.

Conversely, the accelerated scale of tourism has brought millions of
Anglo-Americans and Europeans to the Rimland and parts of the Mainland, primarily to Mexico. Such contacts are mostly brief and rarely offer
an opportunity for close personal experiences with local inhabitants, but
they are real and provide greater awareness of the characteristics of place
for an increasing number of people in First World countries. A positive
effect on both ends of the migration streams is the reduction of general
ignorance of other cultures and the conditions of life elsewhere.

## The Economy

Compared with the Third World as a whole, Caribbean Basin countries
ranked well on the basis of gross domestic product (GDP) per capita in
1993. The data listed in Table 8.1 were compiled using the recently
adopted practice of Parity Purchasing Power in dollars, an approach intended to credit differences in prices and wages among countries rather
than to apply the same monetary scale for all. These figures suggest that
of the forty-eight countries in the world with incomes less than $2,000,
only one is Caribbean—Haiti. The highest per capita GDPs in the Basin
were those of the Bahamas, Barbados, St. Kitts and Nevis, Trinidad and
Tobago, and Venezuela. The latter two benefit from petroleum exports
whereas the former three have prospered despite an absence of mineral
wealth. At the other end were El Salvador, Guyana, Haiti, Honduras, and
Nicaragua. Protracted civil war combined with politically unwise economic policies impoverished El Salvador and Nicaragua; the others have
suffered incompetent government.

Space constraints allow summaries only of selected countries, with
most grouped on the basis of collective criteria, as much to emphasize
certain themes as to describe circumstances. Several states, however,
merit individual treatment. Per capita data notwithstanding, Mexico and
Venezuela are most broadly developed and are regarded as newly industrialized countries (NICs). Home to roughly half the region's people,
both are major petroleum exporters with reserves expected to last at least
several decades at current rates of extraction. Proximity to the United
States is a marketing advantage, but price declines over the past decade
severely reduced national incomes. Both have nationalized mineral industries, and income from these sources flows directly to the government. Both invested much of this income in social programs and improvement of infrastructure, yet mismanagement and corruption has
diverted major sums from their planned purposes.

Venezuela is a founding member of OPEC whereas Mexico does not belong but usually sells at the cartel's prices. During the mid-1970s when oil prices increased dramatically, they jointly subsidized oil sales to oil-poor neighbors within the Caribbean Basin, a policy that both increased their geopolitical influence and lessened that of the United States. Heavy borrowing on the expectation of continued high oil demand left each country heavily in debt to First World banks when prices later dropped sharply.

Multinational investments combined with those of national entrepreneurs have spurred diversified industrial growth in both countries, a growth that was enhanced by mandatory domestic components. These regulations and heavy tariffs initially aided industrial development but also contributed to growing economic stagnation. Like most of the world, and Caribbean countries in particular, Mexico and Venezuela began to participate in a freeing of their economies by 1990. Such changes have stimulated total, but regionally uneven, national growth which has induced severe social strains and related political stress.

Colombia stands on the threshold of NIC status. Its assets include large size and population, strategic location, and diverse mineral and agricultural resources. It is Latin America's only, though still small-scale, coal exporter, and development of newly found petroleum reserves increased this known resource from sufficiency to an exportable surplus. Unlike mineral-rich Mexico and Venezuela, Colombia's main export traditionally had been coffee, which remains important.

It is Colombia's leading role in the hemisphere's illegal drug trade, however, that remains an economic boon and a sociopolitical curse. Massive quantities of marijuana are grown and shipped from its northeast region, and although the activity gradually has spread to other countries, Colombia has remained the major processor of cocaine from coca leaves grown mainly in Peru and Bolivia, but increasingly in Colombia as well. The enormous sums of money received by criminal elements from such shipments have profoundly disrupted the national society. The trade also has created diplomatic tensions with the United States, the main target of the drug flow.

Economic circumstances are quite different in Central America. Here neither fossil fuels nor minerals are present in quantity, and only Guatemala has prospects of greater development of its moderate petroleum reserves. Foreign exchange is earned mainly from exports of coffee, bananas, sugar, and cotton (listed in descending order of significance), except for Panama. Its region-leading GDP per capita is derived largely from Canal tolls and from commerce, manufacturing, and tourism stimulated by traffic through the Canal. Panama also is one of the leading financial centers in all Latin America. Light manufacturing enjoyed about two decades of modest growth in the region until a broad downturn in the 1980s. Efforts at a revival had shown only modest results by the late 1990s.

This period of economic sag in Central America reflected conditions worldwide but was exacerbated by the turmoil of political rebellion, natural catastrophe, and corruption in the various countries. Only Belize and Costa Rica were largely spared such internal troubles. More basic than these disruptions is the fact that Central American countries have little to sell that is not available from other sources in the Caribbean Basin. Its human resources also are not outstanding in quality (see Table 8.1). Although literacy and health levels are quite good in Belize, Costa Rica, and Panama, they are moderate at best elsewhere. Efforts to increase tourism face stiff competition from Mexico and the island Caribbean.

Historically the wealth of the islands came from exports of tropical crops, and of sugar and its derivative rum in particular. For over a century Cuba has been a leading world sugar exporter. Yet as sugar's relative economic significance declined everywhere else, Cuba in 1997 remained the only place in the Caribbean still mainly dependent upon plantation crops of sugar cane and tobacco for export earnings. Jamaica's most valuable export also was a crop—marijuana—which was neither traditional nor legal. Elsewhere on the islands sugar cane, bananas, coffee, cacao, citrus fruits, or spices remained exports of varying importance, but their former share of national economies has dwindled. Aside from Cuba, the role of small, owner-operated, commercial farms has largely displaced that of plantations.

Tourism has become the paramount industry in the Bahamas, Antigua-Barbuda, Barbados, St. Martin, the Cayman Islands, and several smaller islands. Tourism shared significance with petroleum processing in the Netherlands Antilles, U.S. and British Virgin Islands; and St. Lucia and was a major component of the more complex economies of Jamaica, Haiti, Dominican Republic, Puerto Rico, and Trinidad and Tobago. Thus far, the Guianas have not shared this boom although efforts are being made to do so.

Important causes of expanded tourism were the U.S. trade embargo of Cuba and the development of jumbo jet aircraft. Negative aspects of the industry are its seasonality, generally low wages, disproportionate foreign ownership of facilities, and the unpredictability of tourist preferences. These elements, plus a growing popular dissatisfaction with the servile nature of most jobs, have caused island political leaders to seek alternative income sources, even while promoting its improvement and expansion.

Manufacturing expansion has focused on textiles and labor-intensive, assembly-type factories (locally termed "screwdriver" industries) integrated with the world economy. Regional advantages are literate workers, underemployment, low wages, ocean transportation, tax rebates, proximity to Anglo-America, and close past and current cultural links with First World countries. Although this participation in international markets has historic roots and offers prospects for economic growth, the strategy is criticized both in and outside the region because of a concern that it fosters dependency (Erisman 1992: ix–xi). Others point out that economic growth is weakest, in the Caribbean Basin and elsewhere, in those very countries that participate *least* in a world market.

Circumstances in Cuba illustrate this last position. Until its breakup, the Soviet Union was Cuba's major trading partner, with much of the commerce highly subsidized by the USSR for Cold War purposes. With the end of this assistance, Cuba's never vibrant, centrally planned economy has become one of the weakest in the region. Although Cuba has the highest proportion of fertile land per capita of any tropical country in the world (U.S. Department of Commerce 1956), Castro's refusal to remove restrictions on production by private farmers had, by late 1994, induced widening malnutrition, and a lack of sufficient national hard currency to pay for oil imports was causing a descent into virtual preindustrial technology.

This circumstance calls attention to an important characteristic of the island Caribbean. Since the sugar plantation era that began before 1600, the region has not been self-sufficient in food production. Even islands with a substantial agricultural sector continue to grow mainly cash crops for export and to import a substantial part of basic subsistence needs. It is this dimension as much as any other that motivates governments to seek ways to continue if not to expand national participation in a world economy.

## Trade Organizations

Countries of the Caribbean Basin have been involved in a variety of international organizations intended to strengthen commerce. The British West Indies early developed a common marketing organization that evolved into the present group labeled CARICOM. Early in the 1980s all became part of the Lomé Agreements, which allow products originating in African, Caribbean, and Pacific countries to enter the European Community (EC) free of customs and duties; the arrangement, however, pointedly exempts such agricultural commodities as sugar, which competes directly for markets with crops also grown in Europe. The remaining political dependencies, on the other hand, function economically as parts of their respective metropole. On the Mainland, Venezuela and Colombia are members of the Andean Pact, which has its own customs reduction provisions. They also joined with Mexico in the early 1990s in a so-called Group of Three with the aim of fostering closer mutual trade relations.

In an effort to bolster regional economies during a period of political turmoil and for obvious Cold War purposes, in 1982 the Reagan administration launched the Caribbean Basin Initiative (CBI). Its provisions included duty-free access to the United States, tax incentives for investors in the region, economic aid, technical assistance, and cooperative policies between hemispheric countries. Although better in concept than in function, the program did identify a region where an improvement of economic conditions was in the best national interests of the United States, and hence won congressional approval (Anderson 1984: 148–149).

It is the most recent of such multinational schemes, however, that has created the greatest excitement. Late in 1993 the North American Free Trade Agreement (NAFTA) became reality. By gradually eliminating tariffs between the United States, Canada, and Mexico it became, at the time at least, the world's largest and richest single market. The inclusion of Mexico automatically reduced the advantages other Caribbean Basin countries had enjoyed under the CBI. NAFTA motivated other governments within the region to search for a way to become part of such an economic union. These efforts resulted in the creation of the Association of Caribbean States. This treaty was signed in Cartagena, Colombia, by twenty-four countries (El Salvador chose to delay its decision) on 24 July 1994, the 211th anniversary of the birth of "El Libertador," Simón Bolívar. Although more a statement of intention than a functioning system in mid-1997, the intent of the agreement was to increase international cooperation on common regional concerns, with a goal of eventual free trade between its members (*Caribbean Week*, July–August 1994). Should such objectives be achieved, a major part of the Americas would be united economically in two major free trade regions, with Mexico as the only country participating in both organizations.

## Political Development

An assessment of political development within the Caribbean Basin properly begins with a recognition of the democratic basis of nearly all current governments. The principle and practice of openly elected leaders has endured longest in Costa Rica (1889) and Venezuela (1959). Independence of parts of the British West Indies and changes within the Hispanic countries had by mid-1997 produced a region in which Cuba remained the only country without an openly chosen government. This spread of the Democratic Revolution seems likely to continue. Haiti's elected president was ousted in a military coup, but diplomatic pressures and a regional economic boycott culminated in military intervention by the United States, which brought an end to the repressive military regime in September 1994 and restored the elected President Aristide to office. He, in turn, gave way to an elected successor in 1996, the first such constitutional transfer in Haitian history.

Even the communist caudillo of Cuba—Fidel Castro—had acknowledged the popular enthusiasm for democracy and held an election, but one limited to solitary Communist Party candidates, of course. Few observers expected his dictatorship to continue in the face of economic disaster and growing popular dissatisfaction, but predictions regarding just when or how change would occur also were few.

Because circumstances differ within the region, its governments are classified here into one of four categories: (1) stable democracies, (2) established democracies under stress, (3) new democracies, and (4) authoritarian rule. Only Cuba remained in the last category, whereas the largest number of countries are considered to be stable democracies. The dozen remaining political dependencies could also be placed in this category on the basis of personal freedoms despite the absence of sovereignty. The outstanding members of this category are Barbados and Costa Rica. By nearly any criterion these states are among the best governed in the world. The others are the Bahamas, Belize, Dominica, St. Kitts and Nevis, St. Lucia, St. Vincent and the Grenadines, and Trinidad and Tobago. Each has experienced problems since independence but all have endured. In the Bahamas, corruption was endemic but had at least abated following a change in national leaders. Trinidad and Tobago gracefully changed leaders and later quickly regained stability following an attempt by a radical Muslim faction to seize power. Belize replaced one long-ruling party with an opposition party in quiet legal fashion.

For the countries placed in category 2 the details of political stress differ. Since independence, the tiny island of Antigua and Barbuda has been run by an elected family dynasty troubled in recent years by problems of leadership transition and corruption. Colombia has striven with some success to continue constitutional transfers of power and an independent judiciary in the face of armed insurrection by Marxist bands and the world's highest levels of narco-terrorism. It has been a courageous example but one flawed by corruption and poor decisions. Since 1959 Venezuela had been a model democracy for Hispanic countries until economic distress induced by economic restructuring and high-level corruption provoked two abortive military coups in the early 1990s. In my view, the attempts were less significant than was their failure. Most of the armed forces and population appeared to recognize that despite popular discontent with conditions, the plotters had no real solutions and that democracy was too valuable to lose. Regardless, by late 1997 the elected government was beset with problems and critics from all sides.

The Dominican Republic has openly elected its government since 1966, following a crisis that led to military intervention by the United States. A weakness, however, was that the same two men, quite aged, were the only main candidates, although a younger candidate of Haitian ancestry added a new option in the elections of May 1994. A resignation and special election in 1996 elevated this man to the presidency and opened a new era in the country's political leadership. A weak economy, rising crime, and corruption weaken the performance of what is in most respects a free society in which the role of the military has diminished steadily. Honduras has changed presidents three times since military rule ended in 1980. Undue influence by the military on the civilian leaders and a small band of Marxist guerrillas—circumstances that are related— make the democracy less than it could be but still a major improvement over the preceding military junta.

Mexico has had constitutional changes of presidents and a rule of law since about 1934, one of the longest such records in the world. However, concentration of political power in a single party (*Partido Revolucionario Institutional*, or PRI) has resulted in something less than open democracy even though personal freedoms have been relatively good compared with most countries in the world. Economic recession and astute leadership has led to adoption of a more competitive economy, which in turn has been accompanied by a strengthening of opposition political parties. There has been a growing popular mood in favor of greater political pluralism. Even though the PRI candidate won the 1994 presidential election, state governors and the congress represent divergent parties to a much larger extent than previously. Creation of NAFTA, as well as a Caribbean Basin Trade Agreement, is expected to accelerate liberalization both of politics and the economy.

The new democracies are a mixed bag. Grenada gained independence from Britain in 1974 but elected a popular prime minister who subsequently became authoritarian. Early in the 1980s he was overthrown in a Marxist coup, the only such armed event to occur in the West Indies. This government then suffered its own bloody Marxist change, followed by a U.S. military intrusion that restored civilian rule. An open election in 1984 produced a government that has handled political and economic difficulties in legal fashion and now stands as one of the better governments in the Caribbean.

El Salvador long was one of the stereotypical Central American right-wing dictatorships, a country with a long history of political violence. The process of competitive elections began in the late 1970s, as did a Marxist-led, Cuban-aided armed insurrection. Free elections, including a change of ruling parties, occurred three times in the 1980s, despite periods of severe fighting and the ravages of paramilitary death squads. Tens of thousands of civilians, soldiers, and guerrillas died during this period. By 1993 agreements were reached between the government and rebels, open combat ceased, and elections that included all political factions took place. The goal is a society in which free exercise of civil and political freedoms will be achieved. The prospects are good but remain unproven, although in elections in 1997 the parties of the left and the right each received about 40 percent of the vote, a circumstance that is interpreted as a popular nudge toward cooperative policies.

Nicaragua was ruled by members of the Somoza family for over five decades, a period marked by political repression, corruption, and economic stagnation. In 1979 a coalition of popular forces, quickly coopted by the Marxist Sandinista Movement, ousted the dictatorship and took control. This leadership established close relations with the Soviet Union and Cuba and supported efforts to overthrow neighboring governments. Under pressure from the OAS, a free election was held in 1990 in which the Sandinista leadership was rejected and a non-Marxist coalition put into power. As of 1994 the Sandinistas remained the largest, best-organized, single political force, held key offices in the government, and essentially controlled the army. While in power the Sandinistas had made a shambles of the economy, a condition which continued through a worldwide recession. Political and personal freedoms have generally been good, but rural guerrillas of both right- and left-wing ideology, along with mass unemployment, have made newly democratic Nicaragua a troubled country.

Guatemala emerged from a long period of military rule in the mid-1980s to elect a civilian, who served a full six-year term and then stepped aside for an elected successor. This was a good start that was accompanied by the slow scaling down of a long, Marxist-led rural insurgency that had caused tens of thousands of deaths and much population dislocation. In early 1997 a peace agreement was signed between the rebels and the government, and the bloodshed ceased. Just how and when functioning democracy can be achieved remains in doubt, but the prospects are favorable.

Panama has a long history of elections subverted by a "strong man" military commander. Its position astride the Canal has given it close attention by a succession of U.S. administrations. This concern was manifested most recently in 1990 when the United States sent military forces to arrest the ruling General Noriega on drug trade charges and to replace him with the civilian winner of the competitive election of 1989. The election of early 1994 produced another civilian president. These efforts to govern constitutionally have been hampered by corruption, various aftereffects of the U.S. invasion, and a slumping economy. Perhaps the most encouraging trend has been the weakening of the decades-old political influence of the National Guard.

Former British Guyana and Dutch Suriname achieved independence in 1966 and 1975 respectively. Both began with governmental systems modeled on that of its metropole, yet democracy was compromised early in each. In Guyana, politics coalesced around two racially based parties, black and East Indian. Both were socialist in inclination, with the latter led by a communist. During the Cold War, pressures from Britain and the United States favored the black People's National Congress Party as the lesser of the two perceived evils, even though it declared Guyana a "co-operative republic" in 1970 and remained in power by means of obviously fraudulent elections. With the dissolution of the Soviet Union this geopolitical consideration ended, the election process began to function more honestly, and the East Indian faction won power—hence the designation of new democracy for a country in which the political parties and many of the political figures are the same as in the past. The death of President Cheddi Jagan early in 1997 necessitated a change in leadership and future prospects are less clear.

In Suriname the initial elected government was ousted in 1980 in a sergeant-led military coup. By 1987 its leader agreed to an open election, which restored civilian leadership, but an insurrection movement and increasing influence by narcotics dealers induced another military takeover in 1990. In 1991, this group permitted elections on its own terms, with the effect that civilian rule returned but in weakened form. Despite its flaws the new government negotiated a reduction of internal conflict and won resumption of economic aid from the Netherlands.

Late in 1994, Haiti also became a new democracy, primarily because of an intervention by United States military forces. Leaders of the military cabal who had ousted the openly elected president left the country as a coalition of police-trained military personnel from around the Caribbean entered the country to help maintain civil order and to train a largely new Haitian police force. Because the country has had only a few short periods of democratic rule during its long history and its people are largely poor and ill-educated, the prospects for stable government are uncertain, especially for the next few decades. On the other hand, the willingness of its democratic neighbors to cooperate in the effort to establish a freer society there provides ample evidence of the regional bias toward personal freedoms in a democratic political context.

The thrust of this treatment is to call attention to the sequence of events that have changed the political character of the Caribbean Basin from one of widespread political repression to that of a region where nearly all governments are headed by civilians who attained office by constitutional means. Similar changes in Cuba are expected though neither the circumstances nor the timing can be foreseen.

## Problems and Prospects

Although the Third World countries of the Caribbean Basin faced obstacles in their efforts at greater economic development, there were regional assets as well. A basic problem has been that most national economies depended heavily on foreign trade. This dependence was magnified by the world recession of the late 1980s and early 1990s, which weakened the markets for their exports. Because the island states and Venezuela are net food importers, reduced national income brought social as well as political stress. Other Mainland states largely were able to feed themselves, but their agricultural surpluses were of nonstaple commodities such as coffee, sugar, and bananas.

Breakup of the Soviet bloc and widespread rejections of statist economic systems in favor of market approaches required fundamental restructuring of many domestic economies. Such radical changes in the status quo fractured established political coalitions, produced widening wealth disparities, and caused sharp increases in unemployment. The benefits have been a stimulus to stagnant economies, sharp reductions in inflation, and increased infusions of investment capital from both foreigners and nationals who previously had sent their wealth overseas. It can be argued that the most important economic change in the early and mid-1990s was the "coming home" of much domestic capital within the Caribbean Basin. Personal wealth used for national purposes was not a major feature of the region's economics, especially in the Hispanic countries. Unfortunately, in Venezuela political turmoil in the mid-1990s caused a sharp reversal of this trend.

Such contemporary problems notwithstanding, the regional assets are considerable. The Caribbean Basin occupies a central position in the Western Hemisphere and abuts the First World. Aside from Haiti, literacy levels are moderately good to quite high, and even in the lowest ranked countries they are rising steadily as increasing proportions of the young are attending at least elementary school and the aged illiterates are dying off. Nearly all inhabitants live in open societies with freely chosen governments periodically accountable to their constituents. Although not a quantifiable development factor, an environment of individual civil, political, and economic freedoms can be conducive to all manner of innovation.

Contrary to the image common in Anglo-America, political stability within the region is widespread despite local troubles. The spread of democracy has been a major factor in the outbreak of relative peace, as was the breakup of the Soviet Union. This latter event led to the end of the Cold War and worldwide repudiation of Soviet-style economic systems. These in turn hastened the impoverishment of Cuba and Nicaragua and virtually ended their ability to finance efforts by various insurgent Marxist bands to overthrow the region's established governments. In a national atmosphere of democracy, such groups have been forced to compete openly for popular support for their programs. Elected governments thus have the advantage that despite flaws in their policies or management, their constituents understand that they will again have an opportunity to express approval or disapproval of the standing government. In addition, the political and economic deficiencies both of military and Marxist rule are sufficiently known that their attractions have waned. Events in Venezuela also demonstrated that a president proven to be corrupt can be removed from office by constitutional means and force is not required. Such examples help to keep the military in their barracks.

An important dimension in this regard is the reality that, aside from Cuba and until recently Nicaragua, regional expenditures for military budgets have decreased and armed forces have become reasonably proportioned to populations (see Table 8.1). The rapid scaling down of armed rebellions everywhere provides even further impetus for decreasing military establishments. The new governments of the Rimland never did have large armies, and Costa Rica abolished its army in 1948. However, a corps of military officers has been traditional in Hispanic countries, a circumstance that has social and often political manifestations as well. Military coups and the consequent ruling juntas have occurred many times in countries of the Mainland. Also, past circumstances in insular Haiti give ample evidence that interference in national government does not require a large army.

Although the Caribbean Basin is one of the least militarized regions in the world, concerns about national security exist in small countries as well as large (see Griffith 1993: 19–44). The end of Cold War tensions and increased awareness of the benefits of cooperative approaches to economic development notwithstanding, there remains the necessity for protection against domestic turmoil and for safeguarding borders in these countries as in all others in the world.

Legitimately, however, the region's leaders in the mid-1990s appeared to place their main emphasis on economic issues. One can assume that the demand for public funds to address health, infrastructure, and education concerns was a strong motivation, along with awareness that greater general prosperity eases personal income disparities and defuses political discontent. A sense of national identity remains strong within the region, but growing recognition by governments that economic expansion by small developing countries is best accomplished by involvement in interdependent trade alliances has encouraged a greater receptiveness for multinational arrangements. The poor performances of alternative development approaches—military and Marxist—has led planners and economists to concentrate on devising schemes that allow each society to thrive in the competitive, swirling milieu of the world market.

For Caribbean Basin countries with and without abundant mineral or energy reserves, economic activities that offer the best prospects for sustained economic growth appear to be commerce, labor-intensive manufacturing, and technology innovation. Several places, Panama, the Bahamas, and the Cayman Islands in particular, have thrived as "offshore" banking and financial centers (an approach currently being tried in the Turks and Caicos Islands), but for most, only commerce and assembly-type manufacturing have been pursued. Yet the human resource base to expand the latter is present. How quickly the differing societies adapt to incorporate aspects of technology into their economic systems may become a measure of their relative success in a changing modern world.

## References

Anderson, Thomas D. 1984. *Geopolitics of the Caribbean: Ministates in a Wider World.* New York: Hoover Institution and Praeger Publishers.

Augelli, John P. 1962. "The Rimland-Mainland Concept of Culture Areas in Middle America," *Annals of the Association of American Geographers* 52: 119–129.

*Caribbean Week,* April 1994. St. Michael, Barbados.

*Caribbean Week,* July–August 1994. St. Michael, Barbados.

Erisman, H. Michael. 1992. *Pursuing Postdependency Politics: South-South Relations in the Caribbean.* Boulder: Lynne Rienner.

Freedom House. 1997. *Freedom in the World: The Annual Survey of Political Rights and Civil Liberties, 1996–1997.* Lanham, Md.: University Press of America.

Griffith, Ivelaw Lloyd. 1993. *The Quest for Security in the Caribbean: Problems and Promises in Subordinate States.* Armonk, N.Y.: M. E. Sharpe.

Kimber, Clarissa T. 1988. *Martinique Revisited: The Changing Plant Geographies of a West Indian Island.* College Station: Texas A&M University Press.

Lovell, W. George. 1992. "'Heavy Shadows and Black Night': Disease and Depopulation in Colonial Spanish America." *Annals of the Association of American Geographers* 82: 426–443.

Population Reference Bureau. 1994. *World Population Data Sheet.* Washington, D.C.: Population Reference Bureau.

Richardson, Bonham C. 1992. *The Caribbean in the Wider World, 1492–1992: A Regional Geography.* New York, Port Chester: Cambridge University Press.

United States Arms Control and Disarmament Agency. 1995. *World Military Expenditures and Arms Transfers.* Washington, D.C.: U.S. Government Printing Office.

United States Central Intelligence Agency. *The World Factbook.* Washington, D.C.: U.S. Government Printing Office.

United States Department of Commerce. 1956. *Investment in Cuba.* Washington, D.C.: U.S. Government Printing Office.

Western, John. 1992. *A Passage to England: Barbadian Londoners Speak of Home.* Minneapolis: University of Minnesota Press.

# 9 South America: Continent of Contrasts

## Alfonso Gonzalez

THE CONTINENT OF SOUTH AMERICA comprises the southern nearly nine-tenths of the cultural region of Latin America but contains only two-thirds of that region's total population.[1] It is a continent that exhibits a considerable diversity of physical characteristics, some of them quite unique and extreme, as well as outstanding cultural features and contrasting levels of socioeconomic development.

### Natural Environment

Almost one-third, the southern portion, of the continent ("the southern cone") lies outside the tropics.[2] Midlatitude climates extend northward to include virtually all of Paraguay (certainly the effectively settled national territory), the southern part of the Brasilian state of Mato Grosso, all of São Paulo, and southern Minas Gerais. Dry climates are found in four locations: (1) from southern coastal Ecuador through the northern third of Chile, (2) Patagonia extending into northwestern Argentina, and two smaller areas, (3) portions of the interior of Northeast Brasil, and (4) coastal Venezuela with a slight extension into adjacent Colombia.

South America possesses some truly interesting physical superlatives. It contains the highest continuous mountain barrier on earth (the Andes) with the highest summits outside of central Asia. The Andean region has a larger population residing at high altitudes than anywhere else, and it is here that some of the world's highest cultural features are found. The world's greatest river, by far, in volume, drainage basin, and navigability (the Amazon) dominates the interior of the continent. The world's highest as well as the greatest waterfalls (in volume) are found in the eastern highlands/plateaus, and one-fifth of the world's potential hydroelectric power is on the continent.

MAP 9.1    South America

No region in the world has such a high proportion (nearly one-half) of its area in forest, and within the same country, Chile, are located both the world's driest weather station and the wettest place (in number of days with precipitation). One of the direct effects of the physical environment is that the continent, like Latin America overall, is affected by natural disasters, notably earthquakes, volcanic eruptions, hurricanes, and weather disturbances associated with "El Niño" in the Pacific. Loss of life due to these natural disasters occurs to a greater degree than in any other region, except the Orient.

## Cultural Characteristics

South America also has some unique cultural features. It, along with Middle America, is the only major world region that not only has a relatively large proportion but significant numbers of all three major racial stocks.[3] It is the most complex and intermixed region racially, although race generally is not a major issue. Much of the continent is essentially mestizo (admixture of Amerindian and European), but one of the two largest blocs of Amerindian population resides in the central Andean region from southern Colombia through Bolivia. Negroid elements are prominent in Brasil, especially in the northeast, and the country has the second largest Negroid (black) population in the world (after Nigeria). Negroid elements are also significant from coastal Venezuela to coastal Ecuador. The largest bloc of European whites in the Third World resides from Southeast Brasil to Argentina and into middle Chile.

Latin America is, by far, the most Roman Catholic region on earth, and it contains nearly two-fifths of the world's Catholics. Many of these are only nominal Catholics; Protestant groups are noteworthy in Chile, Brasil, and Paraguay, and Jews in Argentina. Religion, notably the status and influence of the church, has played a major role in Latin American affairs.

South America was the first area of the underdeveloped world to attain independence, yet, like Middle America, it is the only underdeveloped region that adopted and retained European languages and religion and that contains large numbers of people of European extraction. Furthermore, in virtually all measures of development, it is the leader among underdeveloped regions.

## General Unifying Characteristics

The most outstanding common characteristic that ties the countries of the continent together is the three-century period of colonization that ended in the second and third decades of the nineteenth century. Although Brasil was under the control of Portugal and the other countries were divided among three Spanish viceroyalties, the long colonial experience was quite similar.

The colonial period resulted in the development of a number of cultural traits that distinguish virtually all of Latin America. European languages and religion were superimposed and adopted with the result that no other underdeveloped region has such a large area that is as relatively homogeneous in both language and religion or so westernized.

Population has been strongly concentrated in a small portion of each national territory, with outlying areas being generally neglected and developing a very limited infrastructure. All countries, except Uruguay, have a large proportion of their total area that is very sparsely settled or developed. The interior half of the continent contains no more than 10 to 15 percent of the total population.

The fundamental sociopolitical structure, with an established elite consisting, at least in the early stages of development, of the landed oligarchy, was also established essentially during the colonial period and was strongly reinforced after independence. The region has always been the most democratic of the Third World and significant improvements have occurred, as in much of the Third World, since the early 1980s. However, in Latin America, including South America, there has been somewhat of an erosion of freedom and democracy in this decade.

The limited development of an entrepreneurial class and restricted effective investment have characterized all countries until perhaps recently. The general absence of direct U.S. intervention, in contrast to the Caribbean Basin, has also typified the continent.

## National Differences

The physical environment of individual countries is rather varied. Coastal lowlands are everywhere rather restricted, but three great lowland river basins (the Amazon, La Plata-Paraná, and Orinoco) dominate much of the continental interior. The very high and rugged Andean cordillera on the western margin makes transportation and communication in that region difficult. Geologically older plateaus occur on the eastern margins of the continent, the Brasilian and Guiana Highlands.

South America is the wettest continent but almost all countries have areas of varying degrees of dryness. Arid conditions prevail over two large areas of the continent: (a) in the northern third of Chile and extending along the entire Peruvian littoral and somewhat into adjacent Ecuador, and (b) in Patagonia (the southern one-quarter of Argentina) extending into the northwest of Argentina and adjacent Bolivia. Smaller subhumid conditions occur in portions of northeastern Brasil and in the western coast of Venezuela and adjacent Colombia.

Vegetation types are very varied and frequently present problems to the development of agriculture and transportation. Humid tropical soils that prevail over the lowlands of most of the continent are generally low in quality and easily damaged by improper and/or frequent cultivation. However, some of the world's best soils are located in the Pampa region of Argentina. As indicated previously, midlatitude climates as well as

vegetation and soil types predominate over about the southern third of
the continent.

Resources, like all other features (physical or cultural), are unevenly
distributed in South America as elsewhere. High-quality agricultural
land occurs in Argentina, Uruguay, South and Southeast Brasil, and central Chile. Many minerals are most abundant in the central Andean region, Chile, the Brasilian plateau, and select smaller areas. Petroleum and
natural gas are most abundant in Venezuela, with smaller deposits in
Brasil, Colombia, Argentina, Ecuador, and some other countries. In addition, South America is a major world-producing region of iron ore, copper, lead, zinc, tin, and silver.

High cultural levels were attained in the pre-Columbian period in the
central and northern Andean regions. Currently, the Amerindians compose a large proportion, even a majority, of the population from southern
Colombia to Bolivia. They still resist integration into the national societies,
and these regions today are some of the least developed areas of the continent. Large numbers of Europeans (primarily from Iberia and Italy) migrated to Argentina and to São Paulo and South Brasil, with smaller numbers going to Uruguay and middle Chile. These areas are certainly the
most commercialized and industrialized in South America. Negroids are
an important component of the population, especially in Northeast Brasil
and in the coastal lowlands from Ecuador to Venezuela. Asians (Japanese)
are significant only in São Paulo (excluding, as was indicated, the
Guianas).

There are significant differences in other population characteristics as
well. Growth rates vary from the relatively slow pace in the midlatitude
countries (due essentially to lowered fertility) and the relatively fast
growth of the Andean countries and Paraguay (due to higher fertility).
Fertility rates have declined significantly in recent decades but remain
high in Bolivia, Paraguay, and to a lesser degree, Ecuador and Peru. The
degree of urbanization also varies from more than 80 percent in the slow-
growing midlatitude countries and Venezuela to somewhat more than 50
percent in Paraguay, Bolivia, and Ecuador.

Different forms of political structure have been tried by various South
American countries. Ostensibly Argentina, Brasil, and Venezuela have
federal forms of government, but in reality they are also centralized in
function. Monarchy was tried in Brasil for more than half a century after
independence; Chile experimented for a time with a parliamentary system, and Uruguay with an executive council instead of the presidential
system that has generally prevailed. A true revolution occurred in Bolivia
(1952), and major attempts at fundamental reforms have also occurred in
Peru and Chile.

Prolonged periods of democratic administration occurred in Chile and
Uruguay (both terminated in 1973), with shorter intervals in Colombia

and Argentina. At present, and South America does go through political cycles, no governments are controlled by the military, and the degree of democracy is quite high with, again, Uruguay and Chile at the highest level and Colombia at the lowest. The greatest improvements since the late 1980s have occurred in Paraguay and Chile, with Uruguay the only other country that showed any improvement. Some countries have had caudillos of relatively long duration, such as Paraguay, which had the longest-reigning (1954–1989) head of state in the Western Hemisphere in recent times. Other countries are far more unstable, such as Bolivia, which since independence in 1825 has had about 190 coups, 72 presidents, and 11 constitutions.

Some institutions that are frequently involved politically include the Catholic Church, which varies from strong in Colombia and Peru to weak in Uruguay, and labor unions, which have the strongest traditions in Bolivia, Argentina, Uruguay, and Chile.

Another factor to be taken into account is the continuing animosity between neighboring countries arising from territorial disputes. Hostilities have occasionally broken out, and the attitudes of government have been instrumental in difficult relations between neighbors, seriously hindering attempts at regional integration. The major territorial disputes involve Venezuela and Guyana, over the Essequibo region currently within Guyana; Ecuador and Peru, over the Amazonian territory and their boundary (the most recent outbreak of hostilities); Bolivia and Chile, over Bolivia's loss of its outlet to the sea in the War of Pacific, 1879–1883; Bolivia and Paraguay, over the Chaco; Argentina and Chile, over the Beagle Channel and the islands just south of Tierra del Fuego; and Argentina and the United Kingdom, over the Falkland/Malvinas Islands.

## Economic Development

The economies of the countries of South America have a number of characteristics in common: (1) they are in varying degrees of underdevelopment; (2) they place considerable emphasis on economic expansion; (3) most have programs for and all stress the need for improvement of the poor masses; (4) all are experiencing the relative decline of agriculture in employment, gross domestic production (GDP), and exports (except Bolivia and Chile); (5) they are characterized by the more rapid growth of the industrial sectors of the economy (except during the recession of the 1980s); and (6) they have experienced recent restructuring via structural adjustment programs due to external pressures and domestic economic decline. These measures are directed toward a more open and flexible economic system.

However, there are also some important differences among the countries in several areas: (1) in the stages or levels of socioeconomic development; (2) in the rates of economic growth and socioeconomic change; (3) in the relative importance of agriculture and industry; and (4) in the degree of government ownership and intervention in the economy.

There have been considerable differences in the rates of growth of the South American countries (Table 9.1). In the 1960s Argentina, Bolivia, and Brasil grew moderately whereas Uruguay remained virtually unchanged. Overall, per capita growth was faster during the 1970s in South America (in contrast to Middle America) than in the previous decade. During the 1970s, Brasil, Paraguay, and Ecuador grew rapidly; Argentina expanded very slowly overall, while Peru and Chile experienced virtually no growth or a slight decline. The 1980s was a period of relative decline ("the lost decade"), especially for manufacturing, in Latin America overall as well as in the Middle East and Sub-Saharan Africa. All the countries of South America sustained decreases in output per capita, except Chile, Colombia, and Brasil where growth was slow. By the late 1980s and into the early 1990s, the economic recovery began, and economic growth per capita resumed in all of South America, except in Brasil and, especially, Peru.

A universal trait of development or modernization is the relative decline of agriculture in an economy. All the countries of South America experienced a decrease in the proportion of the economically active population and the GDP accounted for by agriculture. The median for the South American countries of the population engaged in agriculture decreased from one-half in 1960 to about two-fifths in 1970, to one-third in 1980, and to one-quarter in the early 1990s. Presently, the more agricultural countries (with a third or more of the population in agriculture) consist only of Paraguay, Bolivia, and Peru, whereas in the southern cone countries and Venezuela, the proportion is only about a tenth of the population. Although considerable efforts were made to expand the industrial labor force in virtually all countries, by the early 1990s more people were still engaged in agriculture than in manufacturing in Colombia, Ecuador, Peru, Bolivia, Paraguay, and Brasil.

All of the countries have long reached the stage where the urban population is growing faster than that of the rural/agricultural sector. A further stage in settlement evolution occurs when the agricultural population begins to decline in absolute numbers (as has occurred in all the advanced countries). Argentina, Uruguay, and Venezuela entered this stage decades ago. In the 1960s, Chile began to experience an absolute decrease in its agricultural population followed, in the early 1970s, by Brasil. Later Colombia and, most recently, Ecuador have sustained declines in their agricultural populations. In the only other countries (Peru, Bolivia, and Paraguay), the agricultural population continues to increase but at an ever-declining rate. This slowdown or reversal of the growth of

TABLE 9.1 South America: Population and Economic Characteristics

| | Population 1996 (millions) | Population Growth 1990–1995 (%/year) | Urban (%) | GNP/cap 1994 (US$) | GNP Change per capita 1985–1994 (%/year) | Population Economically Active (%) | | Distribution of GDP (%) 1995 | | Exports (% of total) 1993 Manufactures |
|---|---|---|---|---|---|---|---|---|---|---|
| | | | | | | Agriculture (1994) | Manufacturing (1990s) | Agriculture | Manufacturing | |
| Venezuela | 22.3 | 2.3 | 84 | 2760 | 0.7 | 9.4 | 15.0 | 4.9 | 19.9 | 14 |
| Colombia | 38.0 | 1.7 | 67 | 1645 | 2.2 | 24.7 | 14.6 | 14.8 | 18.0 | 40 |
| Ecuador | 11.7 | 2.2 | 59 | 1295 | 0.9 | 27.3 | 11.7 | 12.9 | 18.8 | 7 |
| Peru | 24.0 | 1.7 | 70 | 2110 | –2.0 | 32.6 | 10.4 | 7.0 | 26.6 | 17 |
| Bolivia | 7.6 | 2.4 | 58 | 770 | 1.8 | 39.4 | 8.8 | 14.9 | 16.8 | 19 |
| Paraguay | 5.0 | 2.7 | 50 | 1575 | 1.0 | 45.2 | 12.0 | 26.8 | 16.0 | 17 |
| Chile | 14.5 | 1.6 | 85 | 3540 | 6.4 | 11.2 | 16.8 | 8.0 | 17.7 | 18 |
| Argentina | 34.7 | 1.2 | 87 | 8080 | 2.0 | 9.4 | 19.9 | 6.9 | 25.5 | 32 |
| Uruguay | 3.2 | 0.6 | 90 | 4660 | 2.9 | 12.8 | 21.3 | 11.8 | 20.5 | 43 |
| Brasil | 160.5 | 1.5 | 76 | 3170 | –0.4 | 21.9 | 15.2 | 10.6 | 24.4 | 60 |
| South America | 321.5 | 1.79 | 72.6 | 2961 | 1.55 | 23.4 | 14.5 | 11.9 | 20.4 | 26.7 |

SOURCES: Based on various editions of Population Reference Bureau: World Population Data Sheet, UN Demographic Yearbook, World Bank Atlas, FAO Production Yearbook, Britannica Book of the Year, World Development Report, Economic & Social Progress in Latin America.

South America: average of the countries, except Population, which is the sum total.

the agricultural population, along with the massive rural exodus, helps to explain, at least in part, the declining emphasis on land reform as a major issue.

As stated previously, agriculture has been in continuous decline as an economic sector in terms of employment. As is the norm, the value of agricultural production (percentage of gross domestic production) is below that of the proportion of the labor force in agriculture. Since the 1950s the value of manufacturing has exceeded that of agriculture on the continent. In 1960 agriculture provided approximately one-fifth of the continent's GDP, and by the 1990s it had declined to less than one-eighth. The value contributed by agriculture declined in all countries during the 1960s and 1970s, with a slight reversal during the deep recession of the early 1980s. Manufacturing contributed increasing proportions of national production in all countries (again, with a slight reversal in the early 1980s). Paraguay now remains the only country on the continent where agriculture continues to exceed manufacturing in value. During the 1960s and 1970s manufacturing was expanding more than 50 percent faster than agriculture (except in Chile and Argentina in the 1970s) and, obviously, was receiving priority by virtually all governments. During the recessional 1980s there was a reversal in this trend. In that decade the agricultural sector of all countries in South America performed better than manufacturing, but by the 1990s agriculture was expanding faster only in about half the countries (Ecuador, Bolivia, Uruguay, and Brasil, with both sectors about equal in Paraguay).

The increasing importance of the export of manufactured goods has also characterized South America as countries have moved from a policy of import substitution to a more externally oriented approach to industrialization. In 1960 only 1 to 2 percent of exports were manufactures; by the 1980s that had increased to almost 20 percent. By the early 1990s manufactured exports composed almost 27 percent of total exports. Only in Ecuador and Venezuela (major petroleum exporters) did manufactures constitute less than 15 percent of total exports in the early 1990s. By 1990 more than one-half of the exports of Brasil, the leading regional trader, were manufactured goods. It was the first major Latin American country to attain this level.

Agricultural products now contribute a smaller share of the export trade (almost two-fifths) but somewhat less of the imports (slightly less than 10 percent). The only net importers of agricultural products are Venezuela and Peru, with Bolivia fluctuating. However, all the countries are net importers of cereals, except Argentina and Uruguay. Most countries have increased their cereal imports due to relatively rapid population growth, the increasing importance of higher-quality livestock production, and slightly improved diets (Peru being a significant exception), but importantly not due to a shift to export crops or expansion of livestock raising.

Traditionally, the mineral-oriented economies of Venezuela, Bolivia, and Chile have been net importers of agricultural commodities. Chile and Bolivia have reduced that dependency but Peru, in the 1980s, has become a net importer. Latin America (notably South America) remains one of the two world regions (with Anglo-America) having the greatest net agricultural surpluses. South America's net surpluses are primarily in tropical products, such as coffee, sugar, cotton, bananas, cacao, and citrus, but also in meats, midlatitude fruits, tomatoes, and recently, soybeans.

U.S. direct investments are most noteworthy in Brasil, the largest in any Latin American country and about half of the South American total. Most of the remainder is in Argentina, Chile, Colombia, and Venezuela with very little in the small countries. However, the South American total is exceeded by Middle America, Canada, and four other countries.

Tourism is most important in Argentina, Brasil, Uruguay, Chile, and Colombia, but it is really not comparable with most industrialized countries or Mexico (one of the Third World's leaders).

Government was absorbing a gradually increasing share of GNP in most countries until the 1980s, but in the past decade this trend has been reversed, especially in Peru and Ecuador (an exception is Colombia). Gross domestic investment, after widespread declines in the 1980s, has had an impressive recovery in the 1990s, except for the uniquely slow growth in Paraguay (with Colombia, the only countries in the 1980s that did not register a decline). The degree of government participation in the economy also varies considerably on the continent. The economies of Chile, Argentina, and Bolivia have undergone the most restructuring, rejecting the import-substitution, government-intervention pattern that has dominated the region.

A problem that is not generally as evident in Latin America as in other regions is military expenditures. Only about 2 percent of South America's GNP is devoted to the military—the lowest proportion anywhere. However, this apparently was no restraint on military intervention in politics, as coups were more frequent in Latin America than anywhere except Sub-Saharan Africa. Military expenditures are now below that of education in every country, but they exceed health expenditures in more than half the countries, the exceptions being Brasil, Argentina, Venezuela, and Chile.

## The Economic Transformation of South America

In recent decades most of the countries of South America have undergone a rapid decline in their agricultural population, with the possible exception of Paraguay. As part of this trend, by the early 1980s, the agricultural population dropped below 50 percent in Paraguay, the last country on the continent to do so. Some countries had dropped below 50 percent before 1960: Chile, Argentina, and Uruguay. By the early 1960s, Brasil had attained the 50 percent level and Peru did so in the late 1960s. In the early 1970s, Ecuador and Bolivia attained this level and Paraguay attained 50 percent by 1980.

The second stage in the economic transformation occurs when the value of manufacturing exceeds that of agriculture in the GNP/GDP. By the 1990s all of the countries of the continent had attained this stage, except for Paraguay. All the major economies, except Peru, attained this stage before 1960. Peru did enter this level about 1970.

The third stage in the transformation occurs when the agricultural population begins an absolute decline. In South America this is especially important because demands for redistribution/agrarian reform ease in conjunction with decreases in the agricultural population. This level has not yet been attained in Peru, Bolivia, or Paraguay. Venezuela, Argentina, and Uruguay attained this level before 1960, Chile attained it in the late 1960s, and Brasil in the early 1970s. Colombia probably reached this stage in the late 1980s and was recently joined by Ecuador.

The fourth stage in the economic transformation occurs when the labor force in manufacturing exceeds that in agriculture. Only four of the countries in South America have attained this level in their structural change toward development. Argentina and Uruguay had already attained this stage before 1960 to be followed in the 1960s by Chile. In the 1970s Venezuela, the latest country so far, achieved this level.

The final stage in this process of economic transformation occurs when the export of manufactured goods exceeds that of all raw material exports. This appears to be an objective of many, if not most, of the countries of South America and of other Third World regions as well. It was not until the late 1980s that Brasil, the third Latin American country (after Puerto Rico and Jamaica) and the only South American country, attained this level.

## Problems of Development

In the process of development there are a number of persistent problems that confront South American countries, but the problems typify much of the underdeveloped world and generally become more manageable with development.

### Rapid Population Growth

Although the rate of population growth has been declining since at least the 1960s, the decrease has been more notable in the past decade or two.

However, the growth rate still exceeds 2 percent annually in nearly half the countries and is highest in Paraguay (Table 9.1). The absolute increase annually is only leveling off at the present time. Family planning programs were initiated in the late 1960s and early 1970s, and fertility has dropped significantly in the tropical countries but remains high in the fast-growing countries. Mortality has also declined to very low levels, except in Bolivia (the shortest life expectancy on the continent) and in Uruguay (an aging population comparable to Anglo-America). Although rapid population growth does not cause poverty or underdevelopment, it does present a formidable obstacle that must be overcome in order to raise the general level of living.

### Inadequate Capital Investment

Domestic capital available frequently is considered insufficient and generally conditions have not been propitious to attract foreign funds. However, most countries are now actively formulating policies to attract foreign as well as domestic capital investments. Foreign investment and assistance generate considerable controversy and are political problems that must be faced.

### External Debt

Brasil has carried the largest total external debt of any Third World country since before the debt crisis of the early 1980s. Argentina has also had one of the largest debts and in 1994 ranked sixth in the Third World in terms of the size of the external debt. In most of the other countries of South America debt continues to be a major concern, although reduced from a decade ago. All countries still have to contend with the problems of repayment or rescheduling. There are groups who place the blame (or a large part of it) on the banks of the industrialized world, but poor planning, mismanagement, and the lack of prudence on the part of the recipient underdeveloped countries certainly contributed to the problem. Although the threat of loan default appears to have passed for the present, austerity measures have resulted in a decline of real living levels and continue to pose a threat to sociopolitical instability. Periodic economic crises can arise very quickly, as occurred in Mexico in December 1994.

### Inflation

The problem of inflation is ameliorating in many countries, but even prior to the rapid inflation of the 1980s, the southern cone was the most inflationary area in the world. In the 1980s, many South American countries endured inflation rates among the highest in the world.

*Monocultural Export Economy*

The dependency on one or two export commodities (monoculture) has characterized most Latin American economies, but in recent decades there have been widespread efforts toward diversification. In addition, the focus of development is on the encouragement of exports.

In 1960, agricultural commodities accounted for approximately three-quarters of the exports of South American countries. By the early 1990s that proportion had declined to less than two-fifths. The decline has occurred in all the countries, except Bolivia and Chile, which have shown significant increases since the 1970s. In the traditional mineral-exporting countries (Venezuela, Bolivia, and Chile), there has been some decline in exports since the 1980s, and minerals are negligible in the economies of Paraguay and Uruguay. However, an important change has occurred in manufactured exports. They were very minor (approximately 1 to 2 percent of the total) in 1960, but by the 1990s manufactured goods constituted about one-quarter of all exports. They are most important in Brasil (where they compose more than half of all exports), Uruguay, Colombia, and Argentina (Table 9.1).

The leading export commodities have changed, at least somewhat, over the past three or four decades for most countries of South America. The national economies have been gradually maturing and developing, and as a result, there has been an increasing diversity in the export trade of most of the countries of the region. However, in three countries (Venezuela, Argentina, and Uruguay), the pattern of the leading export commodities has remained unchanged since at least the 1950s. The relative importance of these leading commodities, however, has declined.

In recent decades a number of nontraditional commodities have attained very prominent levels in the export trade of a number of countries of South America. These have generally been encouraged by government policy as a way to encourage diversification and reduce the customary reliance on one or two commodities dominating the export trade and commercial economies of most countries. Some of the more significant nontraditional export commodities that have emerged in recent decades include the following:

1. Petroleum has been important in Ecuador since 1975, and in Colombia it has surpassed coffee since 1990.
2. Natural gas has been important in Bolivia from approximately 1980 and surpassed tin exports in about 1985.
3. Soybeans, important in several countries, have been especially significant in Brasil since about 1980 and surpassed coffee by 1985.
4. Fisheries have been significant in Uruguay from the early 1980s.

Food imports are alleged by some to constitute a handicap to development in the Third World. Only about one-tenth of imports into South American countries is food, a slight decline since earlier decades. No other Third World region is comparable, except Middle America and recently the Orient. However, in Peru, food constitutes one-fifth of all imports. Argentina and Uruguay are the only net exporters of cereals in Latin America.

## Income Distribution

The underdeveloped world is characterized by a markedly uneven distribution of income, and Latin America, along with Sub-Saharan Africa, probably has the most uneven distribution of all. Although no country of South America for which data is available is comparable with the industrialized countries, the southern cone countries had among the least uneven distribution of all of Latin America. However, recently (at least in Chile) income has become far more unevenly distributed, and Brasil and Chile have markedly uneven distribution by any standards. Both consumer expenditures and investment potentialities are restricted by this pattern. Furthermore, it creates major social disparities that contribute to sociopolitical instability.

## Levels of Socioeconomic Development

The range of development that exists in South America is considerable as in some other subregions of the underdeveloped world. There is a marked difference between the degree of development or level of living in countries at the extremes in South America, such as Argentina and Bolivia. Based on the Socio-Economic Development Index (SEDI) (see Chapter 2), which employs four basic components (per capita GNP, diet, health, and education), the fairly broad diversity of development levels can be seen (Table 9.2), although these have narrowed since at least 1960.

Argentina has clearly been South America's most developed country. Uruguay, which earlier was closer to Argentina, is now about on a par with Chile and Venezuela. The next group comprises Colombia, Paraguay, Brasil, Ecuador, and Peru; Bolivia is at the bottom with a significantly lower rating. Since 1960 the greatest overall improvements have occurred in Colombia, Bolivia, Chile, and the beneficiaries of greatly augmented petroleum income, especially during the 1970s, Venezuela and Ecuador, when their income improvement exceeded that of the previous decade. Meanwhile, the relatively small decreases in Argentina and Uruguay are noteworthy, although both appear to have reversed the decline recently. However, in the early 1990s, all countries ap-

TABLE 9.2    South America: Comparative Socioeconomic Development (SEDI)

|               | 1960 | 1970 | 1980 | 1985 | 1990 | 1994 | Change 1960–1994 |
|---------------|------|------|------|------|------|------|------------------|
| Venezuela     | 43.8 | 52.0 | 56.7 | 56.1 | 53.2 | 55.1 | 11.3 |
| Colombia      | 36.4 | 39.5 | 45.2 | 47.9 | 49.1 | 51.2 | 14.7 |
| Ecuador       | 35.0 | 39.8 | 45.8 | 45.7 | 45.7 | 48.7 | 13.7 |
| Peru          | 36.9 | 40.1 | 40.1 | 41.4 | 42.4 | 45.6 | 8.7 |
| Bolivia       | 28.5 | 30.1 | 33.7 | 36.4 | 37.0 | 40.9 | 12.4 |
| Paraguay      | 42.3 | 44.1 | 50.1 | 50.1 | 49.0 | 49.6 | 7.3 |
| Chile         | 45.7 | 50.6 | 54.4 | 54.9 | 54.9 | 57.3 | 11.6 |
| Argentina     | 64.8 | 63.1 | 61.3 | 62.9 | 60.2 | 64.6 | –0.3 |
| Uruguay       | 61.0 | 60.5 | 58.2 | 58.9 | 57.1 | 59.5 | –1.5 |
| Brasil        | 37.1 | 39.8 | 45.3 | 45.4 | 46.4 | 46.9 | 9.9 |
| South America | 43.1 | 46.0 | 49.1 | 50.0 | 49.5 | 51.9 | 8.8 |

peared to be undergoing notable improvements, except perhaps Paraguay and Brasil.

Progress overall for South America (as measured by the individual components of the SEDI [not shown in Table 9.2]) seems to have been fairly comparable in the 1960s and the 1970s. Diets improved during the 1960s but declined during the 1980s. Health conditions have improved relatively in all decades since 1960. Education improved relatively until the mid-1980s. Incomes (i.e., per capita GNP) declined relatively in both the 1960s and, especially, the 1980s, with little overall change in the 1970s.[4] There has been some improvement overall very recently. Apparently income improvement has been very difficult for South America, like all other underdeveloped regions except for the oil-rich (until the late 1980s) and the newly industrialized countries.

In the period since 1960, although income did not improve relative to the industrialized countries in any country of South America, diet did improve somewhat in Brasil, Colombia, and Venezuela. But it has deteriorated significantly in Peru and less so in Argentina and Uruguay (which by underdeveloped world standards still have outstanding nutrition). Health improvements have been very impressive on the continent, most notably in Chile, Venezuela, Ecuador, and Colombia. Improvements in education have also been notable, although not to the level of health improvements. The greatest progress in education has occurred in Peru, Bolivia, and Venezuela.

Other indexes measuring comparative development provide almost identical results as that of the Socio-Economic Development Index. Using the Human Development Index (HDI) for 1993, Argentina, Uruguay, and Chile form the most developed group, followed by Venezuela and Colombia, and then the remainder of the countries, with Bolivia at the bottom.[5] Using Purchasing Power Parity income per capita (1994) the ranking is virtually identical, except for slight changes among the most advanced countries.[6]

## Summary and Conclusions

The continent of South America provides contrasts in both the physical landscape and cultural characteristics so that the individual countries have to contend with differing circumstances in their quest for socioeconomic development. The approaches and policies of different countries vary, as do those in the same country through time as administrations change, less frequently by coups than formerly.

Countries are confronted, to varying degrees, by population growth, inadequate capital investment, debt and inflation, a relatively narrow-based economy, and a host of social and political problems and obstacles. Some of these problems are not as severe as a decade ago and policies are now being implemented that may ameliorate conditions. Overall, there are different levels of development and the degree of change also is quite marked. Virtually all countries, as measured over the past three decades, are improving in real terms and on a per capita basis, especially in health and education; but on a relative basis, compared with the world overall and especially with the industrialized world, the results are far more mixed. By most measures of development and modernization the countries are changing, but whether the change is fast enough to satisfy social and political demands is in serious question.

There are some interesting economic points with reference to this continent that should not be overlooked. A policy of greater government intervention, to a degree unprecedented in South America, was tried in Chile in the early 1970s with unsatisfactory results, culminating in a military coup and a period of dictatorship, rare for Chile. Perhaps the greatest nationalistic fervor regarding nationalization occurred in Argentina (railroads), Bolivia (tin), and Chile (copper). All these enterprises have now been nationalized for more than two decades and none have performed well, for a variety of internal and external reasons. The trend is now toward privatization of many formerly government-owned or controlled enterprises. Regional integration has been attempted through the Latin American Free Trade Association (LAFTA, initiated in 1960) and the Andean Group (1969) and despite some initial success have foundered essentially because of internal problems. Chile is now moving to join the North American Free Trade Agreement (NAFTA). Land redistribution programs have been attempted in various countries, and invariably food production has declined and food scarcity has resulted. Emphasis on private enterprise, the open market, and foreign investment are currently being tried, with notable success (in some aspects) in the 1990s, especially in Argentina and Chile. This approach is now favored, to varying degrees, in virtually all countries of the continent and in the Third World in general.

The governments of these countries, for probably the first time without direct military control of any government, whether through the electoral system or the fiat of an elite, have some interesting questions or options to consider. Who is to develop and control the mineral resources (or other resources, for that matter)? Most countries surely would prefer to control the resource but do not possess sufficient capital or technology to develop it. In a somewhat similar vein, what about agribusiness, especially if foreign? There appeared to be a fetish in the recent past against "dependency on imported food," but if imports are less costly than local production (food or manufactured goods) the result that must be faced is that consumer prices will be higher or government subsidies will be costly. Although other considerations may be involved (encouragement of local producers, security of production, perhaps social benefits), governments must take the economic costs into account. The present trend is to allow the open market to exert a greater role in determining prices, but these policies frequently result in greater unemployment (supposedly short-term) and failed local businesses. Some countries appear to be prepared to accept the economic and social costs of restructuring their economies from government intervention and import-substitution policies to more open economies based on private initiative and investment (including foreign-based assets).

The way ahead for South America is certainly not clear. The potential is considerable but the problems are formidable. The options have to be weighed, and the question is whether the decision will be made via a free and honest electoral process or by an elite group (with or without popular support). And the basic question to be resolved regarding policy is who will benefit and who will bear the cost.

### Notes

1. "South America" as used in this chapter refers to the whole of that continent, except for the Guianas (Guyana, Suriname, and French Guiana) and the Falkland Islands, which are culturally distinct from the remainder of the continent and have a different historical background. These excluded areas constitute less than 3 percent of the area and less than one-half of 1 percent of the population of the continent.

2. The "southern cone" refers to the southern portion of the continent of South America. It comprises Chile, Argentina, Uruguay, and the south and sometimes the southeast of Brasil. In some cases even Paraguay is included. In this study, Brasil and Paraguay are not included as southern cone countries.

"Brasil" is the spelling in Portuguese for that country and, therefore, is the correct spelling rather than the Anglicized "Brazil."

3. "Middle America" refers to the northern 13 percent of the Latin American region (i.e., the southern portion of the North American continent). Middle America comprises the mainland and islands between the United States and South America, and therefore includes Mexico, Central America, and the Antilles (West Indies).

4. Although incomes, even in real terms, increased for virtually all South American countries in both decades, compared to the world leaders (in the industrialized world) all countries in South America (except Suriname, which is excluded in this study) experienced a *relative decline* in their income position from 1960 to the early 1990s overall.

5. Based on data from the *Human Development Report 1994*.

6. Based on data from the *World Bank Atlas 1995*. Purchasing Power Parities, developed by the United Nations, attempt to measure real gross domestic product per capita based on an internationally comparative scale of real purchasing power in US$. This may evolve into a new measure of comparative income between countries.

## References

Food and Agriculture Organization. 1994 and earlier editions. *FAO Production Yearbook*. Rome: Food and Agriculture Organization.

_____. 1994 and earlier editions. *FAO Trade Yearbook*. Rome: Food and Agriculture Organization.

Inter-American Development Bank. 1996 and earlier editions. *Economic and Social Progress in Latin America*. Washington, D.C.: Inter-American Development Bank.

International Labour Organization. 1995 and earlier editions. *ILO Yearbook of Labour Statistics*. Geneva: International Labour Organization.

Population Reference Bureau. 1996 and earlier editions. *World Population Data Sheet*. Washington, D.C.: Population Reference Bureau.

Sivard, R. L. 1996 and earlier editions. *World Military and Social Expenditures*. Washington, D.C.: World Priorities.

United Nations. 1994 and earlier editions. *Demographic Yearbook*. New York: United Nations.

_____. 1993 and earlier editions. *Statistical Yearbook*. New York: United Nations.

United Nations Development Programme. 1996 and earlier editions. *Human Development Report*. New York: Oxford University Press.

United Nations Educational, Scientific, and Cultural Organization (UNESCO). 1996 and earlier editions. *Statistical Yearbook*. Paris: UNESCO.

U.S. Department of Commerce. "U.S. Direct Investments Abroad." *Survey of Current Business*, September 1996.

World Bank. 1996 and earlier editions. *World Bank Atlas*. Washington, D.C.: World Bank.

_____. 1996 and earlier editions. *World Development Report*. New York: Oxford University Press.

# 10 The Arab World: Advance amid Diversity

## Raja Kamal and Souheil Moukaddem

### Background

Many mistakenly think of the Arab World as a homogeneous region unified by Islam and the Arabic language. However, reality indicates the opposite: The seventeen countries discussed in this chapter include some of the richest in the world, such as Kuwait and the United Arab Emirates (UAE), and some of the poorest (e.g., Sudan). Some are religiously diverse (e.g., Lebanon), whereas the majority are more religiously homogeneous. Some are heavily populated (e.g., Egypt), and others (e.g., Qatar) have barely a million inhabitants. Some claim a long, rich national heritage and identity (e.g., Egypt), whereas others (e.g., UAE and Oman) have existed as independent nations for fewer than three decades. The term "Arab World" is used to represent countries stretching west to east from Morocco to Oman, and north to south from Iraq to Sudan. The landscape varies tremendously from one area to another and from one country to another. The North African countries bordering the Sahara Desert are subjected to intense heat in their southern parts during the summer months; in contrast, their northern borders are tempered by the Mediterranean climate. The Gulf countries of Arabia are also subjected to high temperatures during the summer months.

The differences in the Arab World are not limited to climate and geography. Although Arabic is the predominant language and Islam the main religion, colloquial dialects can vary so widely that communication can sometimes be difficult. However, literary Arabic is universal in all Arab countries and is used in formal ceremonies and broadcasting. In some countries, ethnic differences exist; the Berbers in North Africa are a good example of an ethnic group living in Arab countries.

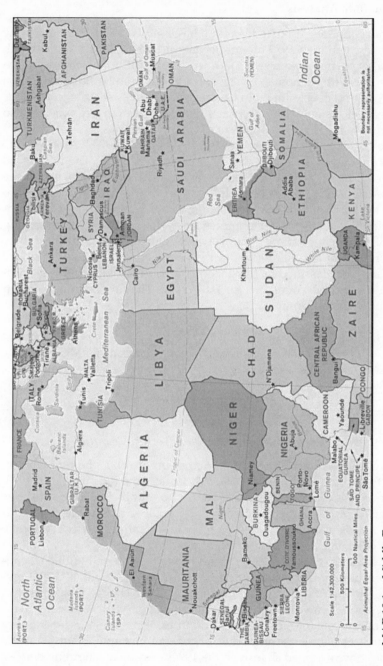

MAP 10.1   Middle East

## An Economic Analysis

The Arab countries discussed here can be classified as "developing." The oil price escalation of 1973 brought economic enhancement to many rich Arab oil-exporting countries. One finds it difficult, if not impossible, to deal simply with economic development in the Arab World: Each nation is approaching development in its own way. Usually internal conditions hinder development within the Arab World, but external causes can also contribute to the slow development of certain countries.

Since the dramatic increase in the price of oil in 1973, "Arab World" has become an economic as well as a geographic term. The flow of oil revenues from all around the world represented a turning point for the entire Arab World, but especially for the oil-producing nations, who channeled some of their surplus income to other developing Arab countries, either as loans for development or as direct grants. The emerging rich, oil-producing nations (Saudi Arabia, Oman, UAE, Kuwait, Libya, Qatar) represent a small portion of the Arab nations discussed here; the others may be classified as low-income, lower-middle-income, and upper-middle-income countries (see Table 10.1). The seventeen nations fall into four economic groups:

1. High-income (Qatar, Kuwait, and UAE);
2. Upper-middle-income (Bahrain, Libya, Oman, and Saudi Arabia);
3. Lower-middle-income (Algeria, Jordan, Iraq, Lebanon, Morocco, Syria, and Tunisia);
4. Low-income (Egypt, Sudan, and Yemen).

*High-Income and Upper-Middle-Income Oil-Exporting Countries*

Although the world price of oil started rising in 1971, the dramatic increase took place as a result of the Arab-Israeli Yom Kippur War in 1973. The price rise provided sizable revenues to all oil-exporting countries and particularly for the nations with large oil reserves, such as Saudi Arabia and Kuwait. The increased revenues became an effective source for fast economic development.

Today, the oil-exporting countries have gained virtually full cost control over their indigenous natural resources. Their immediate use of revenues generated has led to significant economic changes, especially in Saudi Arabia, Kuwait, and the UAE. However, with oil as the main source of revenue for most of these countries, this economic dependency puts them at the mercy of market prices. For example, Saudi Arabia's revenues have dropped sharply in the 1990s causing an alarming deficit.

TABLE 10.1   The Arab World: Basic Indicators

| Country | Population 1993 (m) | Population Projection 2020 (m) | GNP/Capita 1993 ($US) | 1992 Infant Mortality Rate (per 1,000) | Life Expectancy at Birth 1992 Male | Female |
|---|---|---|---|---|---|---|
| Low-income (GNP/capita < $695) | | | | | | |
| Egypt | 55.7 | 81.7 | 660 | 57 | 60 | 63 |
| Sudan | 27.3 | – | a | 99 | * | * |
| Yemen | 13.4 | 31.9 | a | 106 | 52 | 53 |
| Lower-middle-income (GNP/capital $696–$2,785) | | | | | | |
| Algeria | 26.9 | 44.3 | 1,650 | 55 | 67 | 68 |
| Jordan | 4.1 | 8.1 | 1,190 | 28 | 68 | 72 |
| Iraq | 19.8 | 40.5 | b | 58 | 62 | 68 |
| Lebanon | 3.8 | 5.5 | b | 34 | 64 | 68 |
| Morocco | 26.7 | 40.8 | 1,030 | 57 | 62 | 65 |
| Syria | 13.4 | 30.4 | b | 36 | 65 | 69 |
| Tunisia | 8.6 | 13.4 | 1,780 | 48 | 67 | 69 |
| Upper-middle-income (GNP/capita $2,786–$8,625) | | | | | | |
| Bahrain | 0.5 | 0.9 | 7,870 | 21 | 68 | 71 |
| Libya | 5.0 | 11.6 | c | 68 | 62 | 65 |
| Oman | 1.7 | 4.5 | 5,600 | 20 | 68 | 72 |
| Saudi Arabia | 17.4 | 38.8 | 7,510 | 28 | 68 | 71 |
| High-income (GNP/capita > $8,626) | | | | | | |
| Qatar | 0.5 | 0.8 | 15,140 | 26 | 68 | 73 |
| Kuwait | 1.5 | 2.6 | 23,350 | 14 | 73 | 78 |
| UAE | 1.7 | 2.6 | 22,470 | 20 | 70 | 74 |

SOURCE: World Bank, *World Bank Atlas* (Washington, D.C.: World Bank, 1995).
NOTES: *52-year life expectancy (no gender breakdown)
a. Estimated to be low-income
b. Estimated to be lower-middle-income
c. Estimated to be upper-middle-income

With the exception of Libya and recently Iraq, the Arab oil-rich nations share good political and economic relations with the United States and western Europe. Their per capita gross national products rank among the world's highest. They have chosen to use their oil revenues to develop infrastructure. For example, Saudi Arabia and Kuwait built highways and telecommunications systems, which are the best in the Middle East and among the best in the world. They built hospitals, schools, and universities in a short time. The oil exporters provide excellent health services to their citizens, as the life expectancy data in Table 10.1 reflect. Lack of blue-collar and white-collar workers did not slow development; laborers and professionals were imported from all over the world as they were needed.

Inter-Arab labor migration forms one indirect but important source of financial aid from the oil states to the other Arab countries. Again, 1973 was the turning point, and the subsequent oil price jump the reason. Oil revenues pouring into the Arab oil-exporting nations increased their need for imported labor from neighboring Arab countries. It is difficult to ascertain the magnitude of the financial flows from the Arab oil-exporting countries to others in the region. Most private transfers and some of the public expenditures are not well documented or publicized. The income earned by Arab workers in the Gulf region was a substantial aid to their home countries, and the regular transfers of funds were never disrupted until the 1991 Gulf War.

The inter-Arab labor migration was successful for the following reasons:

1.  Within the labor-importing countries, with some exceptions, the incoming laborers have melded easily into the society they entered; both already shared religion and language.
2.  The imported labor force working on infrastructures obtained experience which they later transferred to their home countries.
3.  The Arab labor force working and residing in the rich Arab nations transferred substantial amounts of their wages as savings and investments to their home countries, thus helping those economies.
4.  For the labor-exporting countries, the increase of workers laboring abroad meant a decrease in unemployment. Egypt, with the largest surplus of workers, benefited the most.

One of the legacies of the 1991 Gulf War, however, is that laborers from countries that sided with Iraq, such as Jordan, have had work visas to Saudi Arabia and Kuwait systematically denied since the end of the war. This has led to a new trend of importing foreign laborers from countries such as Pakistan and India. The benefits to the host countries are twofold:

First, the labor is cheap, and second, the political stability of the country is generally not threatened by non-Arab workers who are not politically motivated.

## Lower-Middle-Income Countries

Countries in the lower-middle-income classification have progressed well industrially and are now at similar economic levels in their development. Almost 60 percent of the entire Arab World and one-third of the Arab countries discussed here fall into the lower-middle-income economic bracket. Syria, Iraq, and Jordan, along with Lebanon and the Palestinians, all in the same geographical region, represent much of the Arab World's administrative and technical elite. In the Arab World, their share of the agricultural and industrial bases is sizable. Iraq, Syria, and Jordan advocate, in varying degrees, self-reliance strategies, depending on their economic size, resource endowment, and level of economic development. During the late 1970s, Syria and Jordan experienced high rates of growth in their gross domestic products, which reflected both increased income and higher efficiency of investment. The Arab-Israeli conflict disrupted Jordan's and Syria's economies, but they have since achieved steady growth. Syria's economy was traditionally based on agriculture and trading; today almost 30 percent of its labor force is in the industrial sector. The Jordanians working in the rich Gulf region represented a major economic base to their country in that transfers of savings to their home country offset its balance-of-payments deficit. As stated earlier, after the 1991 conflict, Jordanians had their work permits revoked and visas denied to most of the Gulf countries. This has resulted in a loss of funds transferred as well as an increased burden on the Jordanian economy as these workers find themselves unemployed or underemployed at home. Prior to the 1980 outbreak of war with Iran, Iraq's economy, based on oil, natural gas, and other minerals, showed a favorable trade balance. This situation has dramatically changed since the end of the 1991 Gulf War.

Algeria, one of the North African nations in this classification, has some of the world's largest natural gas reserves and is the continent's largest producer. Although about 40 percent of its people are engaged in agriculture, industry—primarily oil and natural gas extraction—dominates the economy.

Morocco and Tunisia have as their most important resources other minerals, notably phosphates; Morocco is the world's third-largest phosphate producer, after the United States and China. Although agriculture remains important, natural resources give Tunisia and Morocco a unique advantage that facilitates their economic development.

## Lower-Income Countries

These relatively poor nations lag behind the other Arab countries. Except for Egypt, they lack a solid industrial base; and despite partial industrialization, even Egypt's per capita income remains comparatively low. In Sudan, where agriculture dominates the economy, although only 5 percent of the land is cultivated, over 50 percent of the exports are agriculture-based. Newly united Yemen has a small agricultural base and lacks mineral resources, although significant oil resources have been recently discovered. For all three countries, the real obstacles to development of the agricultural sector include the lack of transportation and communications infrastructures, lack of land tenure, and rapidly growing populations. Improving the infrastructures would require intensive capital, which they lack. All receive some economic aid from regional and foreign sources.

## New Challenges to the Region

In the past five years the Arab countries have faced major new challenges. Once seen as a center for trade and growth, the region has slowed economically and has lost some financial credibility because of these challenges. Some factors are primarily regional, others more localized; their impact is nevertheless clear and obvious. These regional factors include the following.

*The Palestinian Issue.*   The ongoing peace process with Israel poses both considerable economic and social challenges. As the region progresses toward a comprehensive peace settlement and a permanent resolution of the Israeli-Palestinian conflict, the economic boom expected from the peace has yet to arrive. Many countries involved in the process are scrambling to set up the infrastructure required by lending institutions, such as the World Bank, before aid funds can be disbursed.

*Religious Fundamentalism.*   Religious extremism is threatening governments from Algeria to the West Bank. It is not a coincidence that religious extremism is found predominantly in areas that are economically depressed; the mosque is increasingly becoming a forum for economic frustration. It is argued that Iran and others have fueled the extremist groups in various parts of the Arab World. In such areas, these externally supported organizations are able to provide better basic services than those offered by the official governments. These organs are also politically and socially active; they run hospitals, schools, and television stations. This in turn gives them exposure and a political base. The resulting political instability has a clear economic impact in some of the more beleaguered countries as investors are wary of trusting their funds in politically volatile environments.

*Petroleum.* Due to depressed demand for oil, most producing countries have been forced to cut back on oil production. This translates into decreased revenues for the Arab oil-exporting countries. The 1990s have witnessed a decline in development; Saudi Arabia has put several large infrastructure projects on hold, and for the first time taxes are being contemplated.

*The Gulf War.* The 1991 Gulf War has had a severe financial impact on some of the wealthiest Arab countries. Saudi Arabia's per capita gross national product figures dropped from $12,230 to $7,510. Saudi Arabia and Kuwait, who were the main financiers of the war, were left with low cash reserves. This situation has had negative repercussions on lower-income countries that have relied on help from the more affluent Arab countries.

*Iraq.* An international embargo has been imposed on Iraq as a result of its invasion of Kuwait. The embargo has taken a toll on the Iraqi economy, and Iraq's ranking fell from the upper-middle-income to the lower-middle-income category. The purpose of the embargo is to weaken the Iraqi regime enough to cause the collapse of the leadership. To date, although the Iraqi economy has seen its main source of income severely curbed, the leadership seems to be well entrenched.

*Economic Systems.* Countries such as Syria have had to reshuffle their economic priorities as a result of the end of the Cold War and the collapse of the Soviet Union. Although the Syrian economic policies are unclear, there are indications of loosening of the economy and a focus on the consumer economy. The recent shift in economic structures is closely tied to the peace process and the anticipated economic competition in the region.

Many view the ongoing Middle East peace process as a vehicle for future economic development. A peace settlement would have major implications for the region: (1) It would bring greater stability, which would increase trade flows especially for Egypt, Lebanon, Jordan, and Syria. (2) Private capital and investments would also increase as a result of stability. (3) Reducing the risk of war would allow governments to reallocate resources away from military expenditures and to place a greater emphasis on sustainable economic growth, especially human resources and development. The region presently has the highest proportion of GNP devoted to military budgets. (4) Peace would enable economic cooperation in the areas of water management, the environment, and infrastructure. These expectations have yet to materialize, and the progress to date has fallen short of expectations.

## A Social Analysis

In recent decades, the Arab states have experienced accelerating social change. Arab scholars agree that the centuries-old traditional social structures of their nations are giving way to a new social order. Dynamic change is occurring, albeit at differing rates from country to country, on the social, economic, and political levels. Kerr (Kerr and Yassin 1982) has called the massive migration of workers, technicians, and other experts to the oil fields the "engine" of change. Other scholars list additional forces leading to the new social order: increased emphasis on education, external and internal conflict, travel, trade, and the impact of the outside world.

Social change began at the end of the eighteenth century when Western influences penetrated Arab society. Ibrahim (1982) attributes much of the social change to four forces: (1) colonial influences, (2) modern science and technology, (3) the struggle for independence, and (4) oil. With these impacts, the influence of traditional social orders diminished but did not disappear. Instead, the traditional structures coexist with modern concepts; their interplay has put the entire Arab World in a state of constant transition. Arab social change must therefore be seen as a process in ferment.

During the days of traditionalism, common traits characterized all the Arab nation-states and sheikhdoms. Societies were patriarchal, patrilineal, usually patrilocal, and controlled by a small ruling class. Men dominated; women served as the backbone of close-knit families. Three levels of hierarchical family structure existed: the tribe, the clan, and the extended family. Stringent religious and moral codes prevailed.

Today divergent political philosophies divide the Arab World. Some are oriented to the West, others seek a return to more traditional ways. Former "have-not" states have taken the ascendancy because of oil, natural gas, and mineral wealth (phosphates, mica, iron). Education, much of it offered free by governments, has changed attitudes and produced modernizing trends. Still, illiteracy rates are among the highest in the world in some of the Arab nations. In a few countries, resurgence of religion has led to a return to traditional values; in others, loosening of religious ties has produced secularized societies. Movement to cities has impacted social structures and has brought modernization (Table 10.2).

The diversities and accelerating change make social classification difficult. However, three social groupings are emerging, all influenced by change. The "traditionalists" represent the element most resistant to change. The "technocrats" reflect the impact of outside forces, recently

TABLE 10.2   The Arab World: Urban Population Growth

| | Percentage of Urban Population | | | |
|---|---|---|---|---|
| *Country* | *1965* | *1983* | *1992* | *1994* |
| Algeria | 38 | 46 | 54 | 50 |
| Bahrain | – | – | 84 | 81 |
| Egypt | 41 | 45 | 44 | 45 |
| Iraq | 50 | 69 | 73 | 70 |
| Jordan | 47 | 72 | 69 | 70 |
| Kuwait | 75 | 92 | 96 | – |
| Lebanon | – | – | 86 | 86 |
| Libya | 29 | 61 | 84 | 76 |
| Morocco | 32 | 43 | 47 | 47 |
| Qatar | – | – | 91 | 91 |
| Oman | 4 | 25 | 12 | 12 |
| Saudi Arabia | 39 | 71 | 78 | 79 |
| Sudan | 13 | 20 | – | 23 |
| Syria | 40 | 48 | 51 | 51 |
| Tunisia | 40 | 54 | 57 | 59 |
| United Arab Emirates | 56 | 79 | 82 | 83 |
| North Yemen | 6 | 18 | * | * |
| South Yemen | 30 | 37 | * | * |
| Yemen, Republic of | – | – | 31 | 31 |

SOURCE: World Bank, *World Bank Atlas* (Washington, D.C.: World Bank, 1994).
*See Republic of Yemen (the two Yemens unified in 1991).

discovered resources, and urbanization. The "entrepreneurs" manifest sensitivity to political ideologies and corporate business activity. These three groupings overlap considerably. Sometimes individuals or sub-groups evidence characteristics of all three, but taken together, these groups comprise the "shapers" of a new Arab social order.

### The Traditionalists

For centuries, geophysical conditions divided Arab society into three major lifestyles: (1) desert nomads, (2) farmers and villagers, and (3) urban dwellers. However, in recent decades, the discovery of oil, industrial and economic expansion, education, and foreign influences have speeded the urbanization and liberalizing tendencies, changing the nomadic-rural-urban balance. Table 10.2 illustrates the accelerating urban growth. The most significant changes in lifestyles and values have taken place in the cities. In the process, the gap between the traditional rural and modern urban lifestyles widened.

Classical traditionalists, represented by nomads and farmers not highly exposed to modernization, resist social change. Nomadic Bedouin tribes still compose over 10 percent of the population in nations with desert areas (e.g., the Gulf States). Similarly, farmers and villagers, especially the older generation, cling to strong emphases on the family, domination by the male, hard work, and traditional value systems.

Classical traditionalists also reside in urban areas. Often, they have come in search of work, bringing their conservative ways with them. They find reassurance by clinging to old values amid the confusion of liberalizing tendencies. But modernization affects most of them. Melikian and Diab (1983) found that traditional respect for the family was perceived to be the most important value among American University of Beirut students, with religious and ethnic mores second and third. In another study of social change in urbanizing Qatar, Melikian and Al Easa (1983) concluded that current trends indicate that the nuclear family will replace the traditional extended family, that couples will increasingly reject arranged marriages, that endogamy will decrease, that families will have fewer children, and that women will strive for a more equal partnership in the family.

The neotraditionalists place their faith in return to the historical achievements of Islam. Essentially, they are reactionaries who challenge secularizing influences. They revive Islamic symbols, sometimes militantly making them the framework of political opposition to the status quo. They embrace traditional lifestyles. They have revived Friday attendance at the mosque. Among female college students in Egypt, for example, there has been a return to the veil and an Islamic dress code (Fernea 1985). El Guindi (1983) believes this neotraditional surge represents a grassroots movement to revitalize Islamic values and to reintegrate Islam into a culture interwoven with people's daily lives, needs, and values.

### The Technocrats

The discovery and development of natural gas and oil reserves and industrial development in half the Arab nations have produced demands for a wide array of technical expertise (Table 10.3). Workers from many nationalities have responded. Hundreds of thousands came from other Arab countries to work in the oil-producing nations. Others came from the West or Asia, especially India, Pakistan, and the Philippines. These immigrants brought differing lifestyles and liberalizing ideas with them. Sherbiny (1984) reports that the 1980 expatriate labor ratios in the top oil-producing countries were as follows: Saudi Arabia, 53 percent; Kuwait, 79 percent; UAE, 89 percent; Iraq, 14 percent; and Libya, 34 percent.

The exodus to the oil states created labor shortages in some labor-exporting countries. Workers from other Arab nations filled the gaps. For example, in 1985 thousands of Lebanese, Palestinians, Egyptians, and Syrians had joined 300,000 Jordanians working in the oil fields (Jordan

TABLE 10.3    The Arab World: Petroleum and Natural Gas Production (1992)

| Country | Petroleum (thousand barrels/day) | Natural Gas Gross Production (billion cubic feet/year) |
|---|---|---|
| Algeria | 1,355 | 4,486 |
| Bahrain | 45 | 296 |
| Egypt | 927 | 479 |
| Iraq | 426 | 110 |
| Jordan | – | 0 |
| Kuwait | 1,096 | 127 |
| Lebanon | 0 | 0 |
| Libya | 1,473 | 503 |
| Morocco | 1 | 1 |
| Qatar | 479 | 457 |
| Oman | 746 | 215 |
| Saudi Arabia | 9,060 | 2,334 |
| Sudan | 1 | 0 |
| Syria | 483 | 177 |
| Tunisia | 114 | 15 |
| United Arab Emirates | 2,413 | 1,295 |
| Yemen, Republic of | 182 | 0 |

SOURCE: U.S. Dept. of Energy, *International Energy Annual 1993* (Washington, D.C.: USDOE, 1995).

Information Bureau 1985). Unskilled Arab replacements came principally from Egypt, the Sudan, and from the two Yemens, before their unification in 1990. In general, all earn higher wages than at home. Many bring their families or send for them when they are established in their jobs. Most settle in the cities of their host countries.

This vast migration affects individual Arabs and the social and economic development of the entire region. Jordan's Crown Prince Hassan (Bin Talal 1984) cites five results: (1) the shifting demographic balances within Arab states; (2) the influx of influence from outside the Arab World; (3) the impacts of migrants on the host countries; (4) the effects of migration on the countries of the laborers' origin; and (5) the influence of uprootedness on the migrants themselves.

First, the heaviest influx of imported technocrats has occurred in the smallest states. The World Bank (1985) indicates that more than four of every ten persons in Kuwait, Qatar, and the UAE are non-nationals, which has strong implications for the economic growth and social transformation of these small countries.

Second, the ratio of non-Arab to Arab technocrats is increasing. In 1975, 65 percent of migrants were Arab; today about half the technocrats are from outside the Arab World, with two-thirds of non-Arabs being from Asia (LaPorte 1984).

Third, the migrant technocrats are making a dramatic social impact on the oil-rich countries. The technocrats place numerous demands on host nation administration, social services, and security, sometimes causing the restructuring of such services. Their presence sometimes raises questions about national security and political balance (e.g., in Saudi Arabia and Kuwait). Since most migrants bring their families, the host nation's educational systems are often taxed beyond capacity and require expansion. The high proportion of expatriate children is certain to have a long-term effect on Kuwaiti schoolchildren. Ibrahim (1982) indicates that the migrants are virtually shaping the new institutions and infrastructures of some Arab countries. Bahry (1982) declares that the imported technocrats have expanded the horizons of Saudi families and have profoundly affected Arab lifestyles. The modernizing influences introduced by technocrats erode traditional cultures by synthesizing traditional culture with the values introduced by the technocrats. Some changes are reflected in increased divorce, crime, and social drinking. Some persons appear to have adopted double moral standards.

As discussed in the "high income" section in the earlier economic analysis, technocrats also exercise strong influences on their countries of origin.

Finally, migration strongly affects the technocrats themselves. Attitudes toward work and money often change. Since nearly all receive more wages abroad than at home, consumption patterns change. Tastes acquired while away are often difficult to sustain upon return; dissatisfaction with the home country results. Many have learned to expect the state to provide education and social services, creating new dependencies on their own government rather than on the individuals themselves. In summary, technocrat migration erodes traditional culture, introduces new and diverse lifestyles, liberalizes traditional moral and behavioral standards, and ushers in a broader "worldview."

## The Entrepreneurs

Merchants constitute much of the economic strength of the Arab World. Since the development of oil and industrialization began, a socially significant though numerically small group of business "entrepreneurs" has arisen who wield power out of proportion to their numbers. They serve both as guardians of established values and as stimulators of interaction that facilitates growth and change. The entrepreneurs fall into three classes: (1) a growing and highly influential group of Arab government–multinational corporation go-betweens, whom we label "capitalist entrepreneurs"; (2) a larger group of "sponsors" (Al-Kafil), who make middleman arrangements, mostly in the private sector; and (3) the "enterprisers," who engage in indigenous creative business investment and expansion.

The first two classes are complementary, one working at high government to conglomerate levels, and the other on the human resource plane, "enabling" government-corporation activity and the successful completion of development projects. Both groups are highly sensitive to governmental goals, political ideology, and corporate business activity. Because they hold key information or have influential personal connections, both serve as gatekeepers with a disproportionate influence on others. Both deal with foreigners. Both act as legal go-betweens. Both take personal risks but usually invest little of their own money in their activities. Both understand clearly how their own society functions. Both keep abreast of political and social developments. Ibrahim (1982) calls both groups "lumpen capitalists" since they are neither fully productive nor parasitic citizens.

The capitalist entrepreneurs, usually educated in the West, begin by taking leadership in government or business, in the latter case often by taking up partnerships with foreign businesses or agencies. With a small capital outlay and usually with a few like-minded friends, they start their own corporation with many functions—consultancies, engineering, management, research, etc. Often they have relatives or friends in government. Usually they handle contracts worth millions. The capitalist entrepreneur performs valuable social services. He organizes, establishes contacts with the outside, and gets things done. He serves as a public relations diplomat on behalf of his nation, by interpreting his country to the outside and vice versa. As a shrewd opportunist, he assures that his dealings will bring handsome profits. Without his efforts, national development projects would move at a snail's pace.

The second class of entrepreneurs, the "sponsor" or enabler, usually comes from the working class. Often he has little education, but he is shrewd, sometimes tough. Typically, he arranges for the travel, employment, and oversight of expatriate workers or businesses. He holds legal responsibility both to government and to expatriates. He clears expatriate documents, travel, entry and residence permits, and uses the law to wield power over the migrants. Or he may sponsor and give legal cover for a new expatriate business, later claiming up to 50 percent as his cut. Finally, he travels abroad to select suitable expatriate labor or professionals. Sponsors serve two key functions: (1) they help to regulate the flow of desirable import labor and business, and (2) they protect the laws, traditions, lifestyles, and cultures of their countries. Expatriates who do not heed their suggestions can be dismissed.

The third class of entrepreneurs, the "enterprisers," are alert Arab businessmen who introduce innovative ventures using indigenous resources.

Their ideas may come from the outside, but they usually depend on indigenous ingenuity to make their ventures work. One such enterpriser has been Albert Abella, whose food catering services in Saudi Arabia have now expanded worldwide. The enterpriser may not be highly educated or trained in business administration, but he is creative, he is a wise investor, and he has seemingly innate sensitivity to the right time and place for expansion. The enterprisers make significant contributions to their countries' development and economic progress.

Taken together, the three classes of entrepreneurs wield economic power disproportionate to their small numbers, they represent powerful social influences, and they contribute significantly to change and development.

## Conclusion

Although economically diverse, all Arab governments have encouraged development and modernization. Oil, the "engine" of progress, has brought social changes, some of which threaten stability and security (e.g., in Saudi Arabia and Kuwait). The emphasis on development brings internal improvement; for example, the UAE uses oil revenues to encourage local agriculture (Richey 1982). Traditionally on a one-to-one basis, the oil-rich nations have provided generous loans and grants to the less wealthy. However, the 1990s have seen a decline in this support primarily due to the drop in oil prices as well as political and ideological rifts with poorer Arab countries; these rifts were best characterized during the Gulf War when some Arab countries sided with Iraq.

During the recent growth years, expatriate workers have inflated the populations of the oil-producing nations. The production of oil has dramatically increased per capita GNP in the entire region, especially in oil-rich states. In the process, three new social groupings have arisen. Especially in the oil states, capitalist entrepreneurs have facilitated needed aid and contractors' assistance to development, making a highly significant contribution to progress. Sponsors have served a crucial social and economic role by regulating the flow of desirable labor to underpopulated countries with manpower shortages (e.g., UAE, Kuwait, and Saudi Arabia). Enterprisers, especially Lebanese, Jordanians, and Palestinians, are increasing Arab self-sufficiency by developing indigenous resources.

The Arab World is at the threshold of a new era. The Arab-Israeli peace process promises to open new avenues of economic development for the entire region. However, this fragile peace process is going through a sensitive period and is constantly threatened by extremist forces. The three key development challenges identified by the World Bank are (1) restoring sustained growth; (2) developing human resources; and (3) managing scarce natural resources, especially water.

Sustained growth in many Arab countries has been threatened by the sharp drop in oil prices on the international market, leading to decrease in exports. In much of the Arab World the GDP growth is smaller than the population growth. Historically these countries have relied heavily on public investment. Poverty and unemployment must be countered by developing private sector enterprises, mainly small and medium-size businesses.

Developing human resources will require the improvement and expansion of basic services. Most Arab countries still lag behind other middle-income countries on all basic indicators, especially adult illiteracy and infant mortality rates.

Managing environmental resources is an urgent issue for the region. The water tables are dropping in much of the Arab World due to increased urbanization and demographic growth. Technology development for the agricultural sector, demand management, desalination and wastewater plants are options that must be explored quickly before withdrawals exceed freshwater potentials. Agreements among neighboring nations will increasingly be needed due to the sharing of underground aquifers and rivers crossing national borders.

The economic development of the region is crucial if the promises of political stability and financial prosperity are to be tangible dividends of the ongoing peace process.

### References

Abed, G. T. 1983. Arab oil exporters in the world economy. *American-Arab Affairs* 3 (Winter): 26–40.

Ahrari, M. E. 1984. OPEC's widening window of vulnerability. *American-Arab Affairs* 7 (Winter): 106–119.

Ayoob, M. 1981. *The Politics of Islamic Reassertion.* New York: St. Martin's Press.

Bahry, L. 1982. The new Saudi woman: Modernizing in an Islamic framework. *Middle East Journal* 36 (4): 502–515.

Barakat, H. 1979. Arab Society: Prospects for political transformation. In *The Arab Future: Critical Issues,* M. Hudson, ed., 65–80. Washington, D.C.: Georgetown University.

Bin Talal, H. 1984. Manpower migration in the Middle East: An overview. *Middle East Journal* 38 (4): 610–614.

Dempsy, M. W. 1983. *Atlas of the Arab World.* New York: Facts on File.

Dickman, F. 1984. Economic realities in the Gulf. *American-Arab Affairs* 7 (Winter): 50–54.

El Guindi, F. 1983. The emerging Islamic order: The case of Egypt's contemporary Islamic movement. In *Political Behavior in the Arab States,* T. E. Farah, ed. Boulder: Westview Press.

Fernea, E. W. 1985. *Women and the Family in the Middle East: New Voices of Change.* Austin: University of Texas Press.

Ghantus, I. T. 1982. *Arab Industrial Integration: A Strategy for Development*. London: Croom Helm.

Hudson, M. C., ed. 1979. *The Arab Future: Critical Issues*. Washington, D.C.: Georgetown University.

Ibrahim, S. E. 1982. *The New Arab Social Order: A Study of the Social Impact of Oil Wealth*. Boulder: Westview Press.

Jordan Information Bureau. 1985. *The Hashemite Kingdom of Jordan: Facts and Figures*. Washington, D.C.: Jordan Information Bureau.

Keely, C. B., and B. Saket. 1984. Jordan migrant workers in the Arab region: A case study of consequences for labor-supplying countries. *Middle East Journal* 38 (4): 685–698.

Kerr, M. H., and El Sayeed Yassin, eds. 1982. *Rich and Poor States in the Middle East: Egypt and the New Social Order*. Boulder: Westview Press.

LaPorte, R., Jr. 1984. The ability of South and East Asia to meet the labor demands of the Middle East and North Africa. *Middle East Journal* 38 (4): 699–712.

Melikian, L. H., and J. S. Al Easa. 1983. Oil and change in the gulf. In *Political Behavior in the Arab States*, T. E. Farah, ed., 41–54. Boulder: Westview Press.

Muir, J. 1986. Iran's push into Iraq linked to plunging oil prices. *Christian Science Monitor* 78, 70 (March 7), 9.

Nimatallah, Y. A. 1984. Economic trends in the Gulf countries and their implications for relations with the West. *American-Arab Affairs* 7 (Winter): 69–75.

Richey, W. 1982. Changing the face of the desert: Farms irrigated with oil. *Christian Science Monitor* 75, 4 (December 13), B8.

Serageldin, I., J. Socknat, J. S. Birks, and C. Sinclair. 1984. Some issues related to labor migration in the Middle East and North Africa. *Middle East Journal* 38 (4): 615–642.

Sherbiny, N. A. 1984. Expatriate labor flows to the Arab oil countries in the 1980s. *Middle East Journal* 38 (4): 643–667.

Tibi, B. 1983. The renewed role of Islam in the political and social development of the Middle East. *Middle East Journal* 37 (1): 3–13.

Todaro, M. P. 1985. *Economic Development in the Third World*. New York: Longman.

United States Department of Energy. 1995. *International Energy Annual 1993*. Washington, D.C.: United States Department of Energy.

World Bank. 1985, 1993, 1994, 1995. *World Bank Atlas*. Washington, D.C.: World Bank.

World Bank. 1985, 1993, 1994. *World Bank Development Report*. New York: Oxford University Press.

Zaghal, A. S. 1984. Social change in Jordan. *Middle Eastern Studies* 20 (4): 53–75.

Zurayk, C. K. 1979. Cultural change and transformation of Arab society. In *The Arab Future: Critical Issues*, M. Hudson, ed., 9–18. Washington, D.C.: Georgetown University.

# 11 *South Asia: A Region of Conflicts and Contradictions*

Bheru Sukhwal

## Introduction

The term "South Asia" is synonymous with the Indian subcontinent, which covers 4,487.8 thousand square kilometers including India, Pakistan, Bangladesh, Sri Lanka, Nepal, Bhutan, and the Maldives. The subcontinent is bounded to the north by the Himalayas (Sanskrit word meaning "abode of snow"), the loftiest mountains in the world, by the mountains of eastern Assam and Myanmar to the east, and by the Sulaiman and Kirthar ranges as well as the Thar Desert to the west; thus South Asia is a distinct physiographic unit. It is also a peninsula, jutting into the Indian Ocean, with the Bay of Bengal on the east and the Arabian Sea on the west. Therefore, South Asia forms an integral part of Mackinder's "World Island," that is, the Euro-African-Asiatic land mass, the most important single geographical unit in the world. Its relative location with reference to other political areas gives it immense geopolitical significance. Demographically, economically, technologically, politically, culturally, and strategically, South Asia is too important for the rest of the world to ignore. The Western industrialized nations need its tea, jute, sugar, spices, minerals and precious metals, engineering goods including computer software, small arms, its culture, and much more; conversely, South Asia needs technology, capital, manufactured goods, sophisticated military hardware, and to some extent, food, in return. The interdependence of the industrialized nations and South Asia is vital for the peace and prosperity of the region and the world at large.

The evolution of the South Asian region has a long history of over 4,500 years, an even longer history than the Indus civilization of South Asia. Its

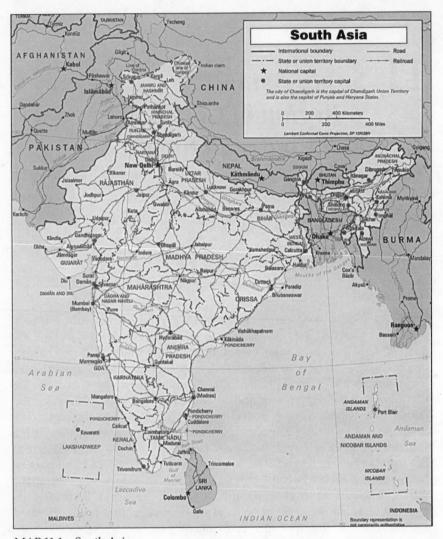

MAP 11.1    South Asia

early civilization, revealed in the cities of the Indus basin, Mohenjodaro and Harappa, dating back to 2500 B.C., had contacts with the Mesopotamian civilization. The history of the region reveals an endless succession of invasions by various peoples, all contributing in some way to the cultural growth of the land, giving a complex character to its civilization. There are many languages, several different religious groups, varied forms of art and architecture, vast regional and economic differences, diversified political ideologies, and an overall sense of social stratification.

During the periods of British colonial rule, the subcontinent was politically fragmented and economically inviable to a degree that both distressed and challenged the new national leaders of various countries of the region. To Westerners, it seemed that the nation was united, but in reality the general public was fearful of the British rulers, and as a result did not raise their voice except during the 1857 army revolt and the freedom struggle during the first half of the twentieth century. The British ruled nine large provinces, and the rest of South Asia was controlled by 565 local rajas and maharajahs who had to depend on British rulers for defense, foreign affairs, communications, and advice. The British, however, made some positive contributions to South Asian life, such as the development of systematic post and telegraph services, networks of road and railroad transportation, irrigation canals, development of urban centers and port cities, industrialization on a limited scale, higher education for a chosen few, modern practices of medicine, steam navigation, creation of a modern army, a Western-based legal system, and the system of administration services.

On the eve of British withdrawal, the subcontinent was divided into India and Pakistan; the two wings of Pakistan (West Pakistan and East Pakistan) were separated by more than 1600 kilometers of Indian territory. In 1971, after a bitter 14-day war, Bangladesh attained its independence from Pakistan. Sri Lanka gained its independence from the British in 1948. Surprisingly, postcolonial South Asia was divided into only three major nation states besides the two small mountainous countries of Nepal and Bhutan and the two island nations of Sri Lanka and the Maldives. In these South Asian states there are numerous regional, linguistic, religious, economic, and cultural differences. For example, in India there have been separatist movements in Punjab, Tamil Nadu, Assam, and Northeast India, and Jammu and Kashmir, but the country has held together for nearly half a century. Pakistan also faced persistent separatist movements in Pakhtunistan, Baluchistan, and Sind, but the nation has remained intact since the independence of Bangladesh in 1971. The majority of Singhalese Buddhists and the minority of Tamil Hindus are at odds, and the antagonism is continuing; however, the country is surviving these strains. Nepal has also experienced internal turmoil. In essence, all the South Asian nations have faced fissiparous tendencies, but states have remained intact with separate individual identities. Moreover, during the 1990s, South Asia has been a fast growing economic force in Asia, especially India due to its economic liberalization policy.

**Natural Environment**

South Asia possesses physical as well as climatic extremes. The highest mountains in the world, the Himalayas, form the northern boundary while lowland Bangladesh and the river deltas face the constant threat of flooding due to the flat nature of terrain. The variety of physical environment is evident from the snow-clad ranges of the Greater Himalayas to a belt of transitional foothills turning into a series of discontinuous longitudinal vales called "the dunes." South Asia is clearly set apart from the rest of Asia by a broad no-man's-land of mountains and jungles on the eastern frontier with Myanmar (formerly known as Burma), of snow-clad mountains on the Tibetan border, of vast deserts as well as low mountains in the west, of wide river basins in the north, and of great plateaus and spectacular shores in the south. It is the land of tropical cyclones and monsoons, of devastating droughts and destructive floods, of irrigated basins, and of unproductive uplands. The Himalayas have created a linguistic and cultural divide, as well as a natural barrier between China and central Asia in the north and South Asia in the south. The region is accessible only through the Khyber and Bolan Passes in the northwest. During the late spring and early summer (before the arrival of summer monsoons), these mountains provide valuable meltwater to the subcontinent when it is in great demand. Moreover, the cold Siberian winds are blocked by the mountains, and the climate of South Asia remains relatively moderate and dominated by the winter (land) monsoons.

The Indus and Ganges plain area has a very high density of population, the nucleus of economic activities, the center of political power, the best agricultural land, rich alluvial soils, the densest network of rail and road transportation systems, and concentrations of irrigation canals and wells; the southern peninsula, on the other hand, contains almost all the mineralized areas of the region, including iron ore, coal, mica, manganese, bauxite, diamonds, gold, thorium, lead, zinc, and uranium. In addition, it is the production center for cotton, peanuts, tropical fruits, and rice. The Deccan Plateau is the center of heavy industries including iron and steel, textiles, machine tools, shipbuilding, electronic equipment, aerospace industries, and transportation equipment. The western and eastern coastal plains are important for production of petroleum (including offshore) and various cash crops such as cashews, rubber, tropical fruits, coffee, spices, tea, coconut and coir, and rice. The Europeans first made contacts along these coastal plains at Cochin, Bombay, Madras, and Calcutta.

There are climatic extremes in South Asia: The temperatures in the Thar Desert reach over 50°C in the summer months, in direct contrast to the shimmering, ice-capped Himalayas. The region receives nearly 90 percent of its rain during the southwest monsoon season from June to September. The rainfall is torrential in nature, resulting in excessive runoff and flooding, whereas too little rain creates conditions of drought and famine. The unreliability of monsoons in their onset and departure

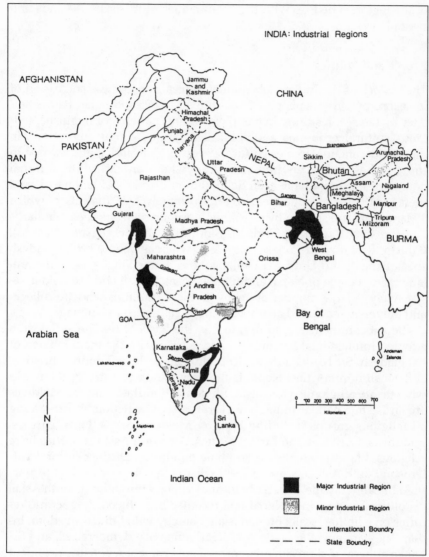

MAP 11.2   India: Industrial Regions

creates uncertainties for farmers. The unequal distribution of rainfall, with an average of 11,430 mm at Cherrapunji to less than 25 mm in the Thar Desert, creates fatalistic attitudes among the farmers. Water is a more valuable resource than land itself. Nowhere else are so many people so intimately dependent upon rainfall rhythms; the whole prosperity of the region is tied up with the eccentricities of its seasonal winds and rainfall.

## People and Politics

The history of the Indian subcontinent reveals an endless succession of invasions by various peoples through the Khyber and Bolan Passes and later by the sea, resulting in complex cultural patterns of linguistic, religious, cultural, economic, and political diversities. Barely any country in the world contains greater cultural diversity than India, and variety in India comes on a scale unmatched anywhere on earth. The internal boundaries of India have been delimited on the basis of languages, and there are 18 official languages and approximately 1,652 dialects, of which 27 languages are spoken by one million or more persons each. Similarly, Pakistan has the Urdu, Punjabi, Sindhi, Pakhtoon (Pashto/Pashtu), Baluchi, Brahui, and Pahari languages; whereas people of Bangladesh speak Bengali and Urdu. Sri Lanka adheres to the Singhalese and Tamil languages. People of Nepal and Bhutan speak Nepali and Dzongkha, respectively. A large number of people in these countries who are college- and university-educated also speak English as a second language.

The subcontinent is also divided on the basis of religions. Pakistan adopted fundamental Islamic law, and Islam is also the main religion of Bangladesh. Sri Lanka adheres to Buddhism and has Hindu, Christian, and Muslim minorities. Nepal is the only Hindu country in the world whose state religion is Hinduism. Bhutan is Buddhist, and the Maldives are an Islamic nation. India, however, is a secular nation, incorporating all religious groups including Hindus, Muslims, Sikhs, Jains, Parsees, Buddhists, Christians, and tribal groups. All South Asian countries have religious, linguistic, regional, or ethnic minorities. Distinct cultural patterns in South Asia are also evident where the caste system is still practiced in everyday life, especially in rural villages throughout South Asia.

Politically speaking, Nepal has recently introduced democratic reforms on a limited scale. Bhutan is a monarchy with limited freedom. India, Pakistan, and Bangladesh are parliamentary democracies, and Sri Lanka adheres to a presidential form of government where the president is elected for seven years and can be reelected for a second term. The Maldives have an elected government, but there are no political parties and there has been no political opposition to President Maumoon Abdul Gayoon since 1978. India constitutes the world's largest and most complex federal parliamentary state, with twenty-five states and seven union territories. Since independence, ten general elections have been held that were free and fair. It is the largest democracy in the world with an electorate of approximately 590 million voters. While many countries in the developing world and even some in Europe and Latin America have adopted other forms of government, India, in spite of the enormity of its social, economic, linguistic, religious, and regional problems, has remained wedded to the parliamentary form of government and democratic values. India has proven that successful positive changes can be brought about and that progress can be achieved through peaceful and democratic means. At present, there is a coalition government at the center and there are tensions among the various coalition partners. It is interesting to note that South Asia is considered to be a developing region, but five of its seven countries are democracies and one has introduced a limited democratic reform. In addition, at different times four major nation states have been ruled or are being ruled by female heads of state. Pakistan's former Prime Minister (Benazir Bhutto), Bangladesh's Prime Minister (Sheikh Hasina Wazed), Sri Lanka's President (Mrs. Chandrika) and Prime Minister (Mrs. Bandaranaike) are women. From 1966 to 1977 and again between 1980 and 1984, Mrs. Gandhi was the Prime Minister of India. Similarly, there are large numbers of women doctors, legislators, judges, and college and university professors, and women are employed in all different types of occupations.

## Economy and Development

At the time of independence in 1947, South Asia had a depressed economy and was considered an underdeveloped region. The economic picture of the Indian subcontinent at the time of independence was grim. Barely 5 percent of the population earned enough for a subsistence living, and millions were unemployed. Problems such as rehabilitating displaced persons from Pakistan to India and vice versa, establishing communal harmony, and increasing even slightly the economic level of the people loomed as formidable for the newly independent countries of the region. Since independence, various countries have embarked on Five Year Plans (Sri Lanka had a Ten Year Plan) initiated by the government. The utmost importance was given to agriculture, land reforms, mineral exploration, industrialization, and improving the transportation networks. Nearly 65 to 90 percent of the population is directly engaged in agriculture (it varies from country to country) with nearly two-thirds of the land under food production, especially grains. South Asia feeds and clothes its population from less than an acre of land per person. The population density of India and Bangladesh is 580 and 1,300 persons per square kilometer of cultivated land, respectively. There are few regions in the world where land is so overworked. Until recently, food shortages were common because of disastrous weather conditions, including droughts, floods, and famines, backward farming techniques, shortages of fertilizers, lack of irrigation facilities, limited and high-cost rural credit, and excessive pressure on the land by an ever-increasing population. The production per hectare was one of the lowest in the world. To improve the production per hectare, the Green Revolution was introduced in the 1960s, which bore fruit in the 1970s. Through this revolution new strains of wheat (experimentally developed in Mexico) and rice (developed in the Philippines) were introduced into South Asia, requiring heavy use of fertilizers, irrigation, small machines, and new, as well as improved, seeds. Per hectare production increased sharply; the resulting crop was called a "miracle crop." In 1995–1996 India produced 189.5 million metric tons of grain with a surplus of 40 million tons. Today India not only can feed its own growing population but is also emerging as a food exporter. During 1995–1996, India exported 5.51 million tons of rice to various countries. Pakistan and Bangladesh have reached the self-sufficiency level. Sri Lanka, Nepal, and Bhutan may remain deficient states; however, all these states have now adopted the Green Revolution so as to reach the self-sufficiency level. In this context, self-sufficiency relates to cereal production because cereals constitute a major part of the diet in South Asia.

At the time of independence in 1947, less than 2 percent of South Asian workers found employment in industry, manufacturing, and mining, producing less than 5 percent of the regional income. By 1996, industrial production had expanded elevenfold, especially in India. Highly sophisticated industrial products, at one time available only to consumers of industrial nations, are plentiful in South Asian markets. Through the planned industrialization, India has developed a high level of technological sophistication in such industries as textiles, sugar, iron and steel, machine tools, railway cars and locomotives, automobiles, television sets, electronics, computer manufacturing, chemicals and explosives, cement, transportation equipment, aircraft manufacturing, shipbuilding, and domestic goods. New industries were established according to the availability of raw material and other industrial infrastructure. All regions were given equal consideration for industrial development, and most of the states established industries appropriate to the area's resources. Currently, India is the fifth largest producer of steel in the East and ranks thirteenth among the industrialized nations of the world. Its cotton textiles, tea, fruits and vegetables, jute products, leather goods, and several agro-industrial products are among the best in the world; and the value added showed more than a thirteenfold expansion from 1947 to 1996.

In 1991, two world crises affected the Indian economy directly: (1) Iraq's occupation of Kuwait eliminated $2 billion in annual remittances from Indians working in the Gulf States, and (2) India's second-largest export market and source of cheap oil, the Soviet Union, collapsed. At this critical juncture, Narasimha Rao's government came to power in June 1991. Soon after assuming the prime ministership, he continued the market-friendly economic reform introduced by his predecessor, Rajiv Gandhi. As a result, the growth rate of gross domestic product in real terms has improved from 1.1 percent in 1991–1992 to 4 percent in 1992–1993 and to 5.2 percent in 1993–1994 ($1.17 trillion). The industrial recovery is gaining momentum with a growth rate of 6 percent in 1994–1995 and 11.6 percent during 1995–1996, and agricultural production is projected to sustain a steady growth for the seventh successive year. The foreign exchange reserves increased from $1.1 billion in 1991 to over $20 billion in 1994. The total number of projects approved from August 1991 to May 1996 under the Industrial Entrepreneurs Memorandum was 25,781, involving investment of about $144.3 billion and employment of around 3.2 million workers. Several industrial regions such as the Chota Nagpur Plateau, Bombay, Madras, and Delhi, and their surrounding areas showed phenomenal progress. In addition, the region surrounding Bangalore has attracted many foreign and Indian entrepreneurs. It is now considered the "Silicon Valley" of India, exporting computer equipment (hardware and software), electronics, and aerospace equipment. Over two hundred Indian and foreign companies have established their headquarters and plants here, including such world leaders in information technology as IBM, Motorola, Texas Instruments, Digital Equipment, Hewlett Packard, Fujitsu, Novell, Oracle, Computervision, Microsoft, INTEL, and Compaq. Indian companies located in Bangalore include Hindustan Aeronautics, Ltd. (HAL, the public sector aircraft maker), Hindustan Machine Tools (HMT), and several small and medium-sized companies manufacturing avionic equipment, small aircraft, and computer equipment. Computer software exports have improved from $2.6 million in 1991–1992 to $1.186 billion in 1995–1996, and it is expected to exceed $5 billion by 2000–2001. At present there are over 170 units operating in the area of computers comprising mini, micro, super-mini, and mainframe systems. Foreign investment, which was only $200 million in 1991–1992, increased to more than $5 billion in 1994–1995; during the first half of 1996–1997, it was $3.5 billion. It is expected to increase to $10 billion next year.

Among the multinationals are General Electric, General Motors, Texas Instruments, Motorola, Coca-Cola, Pepsi, Philip Morris, INTEL, Microsoft, IBM, Digital Equipment Corporation, and companies from Japan, the United Kingdom, Germany, and other European multinationals. In 1994 there were 565 foreign companies with 6,573 collaborations as of June 1995, and the number has sharply increased for the first half of 1997. None of the large Western companies investing in India are doing so simply for cheap labor; they are attracted by India's large and increasing open domestic market, its enormous pool of skilled labor (India as a "brain center"), and its very large and capable infrastructure of local industrial companies. India's workforce is the most attractive to foreign investors, according to a study by a Hong Kong–based consulting firm. Taking into account variables beyond the cost of labor, such as quality, availability, and stability, the average grade of India, at 2.8, is closest to zero, which is the best score. The next best score of 3.39 has been attained by Australia, followed by Britain (3.50), the Philippines (3.55), the United States (3.70), and Switzerland (3.76).

India operates within a rule of law, which makes India very stable for foreign investments. With the exception of Japan after World War II, the world has never seen such a rapid economic expansion as it is witnessing today in India. The industrial development of the last fifty years has made India a power to be reckoned with in southern, southeastern, and southwestern Asia. The growth rate in the private sector, including establishment of small-scale manufacturing units as part of the liberalization of economic policy initiated by Rajiv Gandhi and his successors, has dramatically improved the industrial climate in the last five years. China's growth rate, which is higher than India's, has been largely in the public sector, although the government has recently encouraged private and foreign investment for accelerated industrial growth. Even India's balance of trade has steadily improved since 1990–1991. It was $3,041 billion in 1990–1991 and improved to $177.4 million in 1994–1995, a seventeenfold improvement. This gap is continuing to narrow during 1996–1997. Between 1980 and 1992, China's growth rate was more than double that of India's; however, due to liberalization since 1991, India has recently improved its economic performance.

Industrial development in other South Asian countries has been slow and haphazard because of the lack of mineral resources, technological backwardness, and political inability for industrial development. Pakistan has some coal and natural gas, and Bangladesh has some natural gas; thus the major industries are agriculturally based. Textile industries have improved to satisfy home demand in Pakistan. Other industries are chemicals, cement, bicycles, fertilizers, a small steel plant, an automobile plant in Karachi, and agricultural processing plants. Bangladesh industries are cottage industries including textiles, farm implements, forestry products, fisheries, fertilizer plants, and food processing, and a major industry is jute processing. Most of Sri Lanka's industries are located in Colombo, the capital city; these industries include cement, shoes, textile, paper, china, glassware, and agro-industries. Nepal, Bhutan, and the Maldives have very little industrial development.

## Population

One of South Asia's biggest problems is the population explosion. With less than 3.3 percent of the total world area, it contains 21.5 percent of the world population (Table 11.1). South Asia has surpassed China in total

TABLE 11.1  Demographic, Political, and Economic Data for South Asia

| | India | Pakistan | Bangladesh | Sri Lanka | Nepal | Bhutan | Maldives |
|---|---|---|---|---|---|---|---|
| Area, 1000 km² | 3,204.1 | 804 | 144.0 | 65.6 | 141.0 | 46.62 | 0.3 |
| Population, 1997 millions | 966.6 | 137.2 | 124.95 | 18.7 | 23.6 | 1.83 | 0.03 |
| Life expectancy | 60 | 61 | 55 | 73 | 54 | 51 | 65 |
| Average annual growth rate (%) | 1.53 | 2.49 | 2.4 | 1.21 | 2.4 | 2.3 | 3.6 |
| Pop. density, No./km² | 301 | 171 | 867 | 286 | 168 | 182 | 1,079 |
| Form of government | Federal Republic | Islamic Republic | Republic | Socialist Republic | Constitutional Monarchy | Monarchy (Indian Protectorate) | Republic |
| Capital city | New Delhi | Islamabad | Dakha | Colombo | Kathmandu | Thimphu | Male |
| Per capita income, 1994 | $300 | $430 | $220 | $600 | $170 | $170 | $820 |
| GDP, 1994 (US$) | 1.17 trillion | 248.5 billion | 130.1 billion | 57.6 billion | 22.4 billion | 1.2 billion | .36 billion |
| Average annual growth rate, GDP, 1994, % | 5.2 | 4.0 | 4.5 | 5.0 | 5.0 | 5.0 | 9.6 |
| Average annual growth of agricultural production, 1980–92, % per year | 4.0 | 4.5 | 1.9 | 0.8 | 1.62 | – | 5.7 |
| Average annual growth rate industries, 1980–93, % | 6.2 | 6.2 | 5.2 | 5.0 | 2.2 | 2.0 | 9.1 |

Compiled from various statistical sources.

population, and by 2010 India may become the world's most populous nation, exceeding China's population. If the doubling time of population is considered as a hindrance in the improvement of living conditions, South Asia proves to be a prime example of this handicap. The region as a whole had a doubling time in 1997 of 34 years, Southeast Asia 37 years, China 62 years, Latin America 34 years, North Africa and Southwest Asia 28 years, Sub-Saharan Africa 26 years, Europe 332 years, and the world as a whole 45 years. South Asia, therefore, is growing faster than the world average and more than ten times faster than Europe. Among the three largest countries of South Asia, India's doubling time is 36 years, Pakistan 24 years, and Bangladesh 29 years. A more distressing aspect of this growth is that India alone added 135 million people between 1971 and 1981 and 163 million between 1981 and 1991, despite the fact that 74.2 million women of reproductive age were protected by various methods of family planning.

Such phenomenal growth is an extra burden on the already stressed economy. Consequently, nearly one-third of the population faces the problem of malnutrition, and some of the people are unable to secure adequate food; others live in abject poverty without proper sanitation, shelter, or health facilities—conditions that appall and depress most Western visitors. The rapid growth rate also requires additional food, housing, educational facilities, employment opportunities, clothing, and other requirements that the region cannot provide. To cope with the population problem, India started a massive family planning program under which more than 55 million sterilizations were performed between 1952 and 1992. Other family planning methods are used as well. As a result of this program, 43.5 percent of 148.4 million eligible couples whose wives are in the reproductive age group of 15–44 were protected by one of the family planning methods as of March 31, 1992, averting 143 million births since its inception in 1956—a phenomenal achievement in a developing country. India's crude birth rate was 41.2 per thousand in 1971 and its death rate was 19; that has been lowered to 29 and 10 respectively. Still, the total program of family planning needs constant encouragement for lowering the birth rate, which has to reach a zero growth rate in population. The sheer size of India's population creates a very large overall economy, the world's thirteenth-largest according to 1993 ranking. Pakistan and Bangladesh, however, have not attempted the family planning program on a national scale like India. In spite of the lack of a strong family planning program, Bangladesh is often cited as a country that lowered its fertility significantly without a drastic reduction in illiteracy.

## Development Programs

Since independence, most of the South Asian countries have embarked on planning processes of one sort or another. An extensive planning program was introduced by India, and the Government of India appointed a Planning Commission in 1950 to prepare a blueprint for development, taking an overall view of the needs and resources of the country. The First Five Year Plan (1951–1952 to 1955–1956) accorded highest priority to agriculture, including irrigation and power projects. The Second (1956–1957 to 1960–1961) and Third (1961–1962 to 1965–1966) also followed the same pattern with maximum emphasis on agriculture and basic industries. This planning process, however, did not produce balanced regional industrial and agricultural development, as each state competed for resources from the Center (central government in New Delhi). The first three five-year plans were biased toward the urban areas, except in the area of agricultural development; to compensate, the Fourth Five Year Plan (1968–1969 to 1973–1974) laid more emphasis on improving the conditions of the less privileged and weaker sections of the society, the rural population. The program, however, was carried out by several different agencies and, as a result, lacked proper coordination and implementation. The macro- and meso-level planning was unrealistic, and increased income disparities and unemployment. To correct the imbalances of development and lay more emphasis on rural development, a program of Integrated Rural Development was prepared in the Fifth Five Year Plan (1974–1975 to 1977–1978) to integrate and coordinate various development programs in rural areas, that is, to create a single strategy for development. It was based on the principle of all-round development of the rural areas through micro-level planning that included agriculture, industry, transport, commerce, health, education, market centers, urban development, and the balanced development of all regions. This process involved multi-level planning including villages, village Panchayat Samitis (elected people from the village like a municipal corporation in a city), blocks (an administrative unit of several villages), tehsils (state government agency that collects taxes and acts as a county court), districts (a large administrative unit encompassing several tehsils), states (state is equivalent to a state in the United States), and the country. The same program continued during the Sixth Five Year Plan (1980–1981 to 1984–1985).

An ambitious Seventh Five Year Plan (1984–1985 to 1989–1990) was launched by Prime Minister Rajiv Gandhi as part of the long-term strategy to virtually eliminate poverty and illiteracy, achieve near full employment, secure satisfaction of the basic food, clothing, and shelter needs, and provide health care for all by the year 2000. In absolute terms, the number of poor persons is expected to fall from 273 million in 1984–1985 to 150 million by 1995–1996. This plan was ambitious but not realistic. The new planning strategy has involved large-scale private investment more so than in previous five-year plans.

The new government of Narasimha Rao, which assumed power at the Center in June 1991, decided that the Eighth Five Year Plan would commence on April 1, 1992, and that 1990–1991 should be treated as a separate Annual Plan with a thrust on maximization of employment and transformation. The salient features of the Eighth Five Year Plan (1992–1997) are to examine the public sector and improve the performance of all public sector enterprises, to recognize the core of the plan as "human development," to be performance oriented with special attention given to employment in rural areas, and the Eighth Year Plan will be flexible with scope for change, innovation, and adjustment. The Ninth Five Year Plan was launched on April 1, 1997, which is geared toward continued industrial liberalization policies, improvement of infrastructure, and helping the poor. It is expected to increase foreign investment by $10 billion annually. Since June 1991, India's economy has grown at a faster rate, and in 1997 it is expected to grow at about 5.5 percent, with industry recording a growth rate of 8 to 10 percent. Due to liberalization of the economy, foreign investment in India was well over $5 billion in 1994–1995 and can be expected to remain at or above that level for at least the next few years. The gross national product increased at a rate of 4.93 percent, the gross domestic product increased 5.12 percent, agricultural production 3.68 percent, industrial production 6.9 percent, and electric generation 8.3 percent from 1980 to 1994. Nearly 200 million people in India live in households with annual incomes of Rupees 30,000 ($1,000) to Rs. 900,000 ($30,000); in purchasing power terms, that approximates an income of $20,000 to $600,000 in the United States. This huge middle class is increasing by 5 to 10 percent a year and should grow to households accounting for 400 million people within a decade.

Interestingly, although the GNP per capita was $350 in 1994, in terms of purchasing power parity (PPP), India's GNP per capita was $1,210 in 1992. The World Bank has derived this method as a special conversion factor designed to equalize the purchasing power of various currencies. Thus, India is the fifth-largest nation in terms of GNP as measured by PPP ($1,170 billion in 1994), preceded by the United States, China, Japan, and Germany. India ranks number one in cattle population, peanuts (in shell), tea, milk, butter and ghee, sugar, and long film production; second in population, irrigated area, rice production, and pupils at first level of education; and third in arable land, cotton, tobacco, railway passenger kilometers, cinema houses, and technical manpower. Most of India's economic growth has taken place since about 1985, and most dramatically since June 1991.

Development programs in Pakistan were initiated in 1955 with its First Five Year Plan giving a much greater role to the private sector in agriculture and industries than in India. The Pakistan Industrial Development Corporation established industries that were handed over to private firms as they became available. The development program was export-oriented and relied heavily on foreign expertise and financial aid. During the Bhutto regime, Islamic socialism and nationalization of industries were initiated, and radical land reforms were to be implemented, but Bhutto was overthrown in 1977; afterward, the earlier strategy was restored. Pakistan's development program depended more on Middle East and American aid and has not increased productivity and employment or established equitable distribution of resources and income. Overall gross domestic product per capita increased by 5.2 percent and industrial production by 6.2 percent between 1980 and 1993, a favorable growth rate.

After independence from Pakistan in 1971, Bangladesh set up a Planning Commission in 1973 to create a mixed economy and to allow for a transition to socialism. The plan laid heavy emphasis on agriculture and employment. Industries were nationalized. After the coup in 1975, socialism was no longer seen as the ultimate goal. Instead, new measures on denationalization were introduced, and agrarian reforms were proposed, including a "due share of crops to the landless." This plan did not succeed either. The long-delayed Second Five Year Plan (1980–1985) with objectives of expansion of employment, assurance of basic needs, equitable income distribution, comprehensive rural development, and self-sufficiency in foodstuffs was introduced. This has also not raised the standard of living because population growth has remained a continued impediment. The GDP increased only 4 percent and industrial production by 5.2 percent between 1980 and 1993, a moderate growth rate.

Sri Lanka's First Ten Year Plan emerged in 1959 by the Sri Lanka Freedom Party to achieve suitable industrialization progressively by importing capital goods and exporting the diversified agricultural produce as well as precious metals. In 1957 all foreign-owned estates were nationalized so that Tamil landlords would not be able to transfer their resources to India. When the United National Party came to power in 1977, a free trade zone was established in an effort to attract foreign capital on the capitalistic model of Singapore. This policy is still followed by the planning commission. The planning commission is more active on land reforms and irrigation projects, which has helped the island nation in increasing its cash-crop production and rice as a main food source. Nepal has followed the model of India in its planning programs; however, due to lack of investment and a poor natural resource endowment, the country has not made much headway on the planning and development front.

The planning process in South Asia constitutes a major part of economic development, but it has not been a balanced one. Except for India, the five year plans or ten year plans have not been administered satisfactorily and have not produced desired results. Even in India, where the planning process has been coordinated between the Center and the states, achievements have lagged behind targets, and development has produced regional imbalances and increased the gap between the rich and the poor. Overall, the governments of South Asia may continue planning processes. Future development is likely to be more balanced than what it has been during the past forty-nine years.

## International Relations

Geopolitically, South Asia will doubtlessly be among the world's most politically volatile areas and of great strategic importance to world powers. The region borders Tajikistan and Afghanistan in the west and Myanmar in the east; the Himalayan Mountains shelters it in the north, and the Indian Ocean borders it in the south. Peace and stability in Asia, particularly in South Asia, are matters of great importance to all nations of the world at large; if the Indian subcontinent remains free of tension, it could command unique weight among the community of nations.

Since its inception in 1985, the South Asian Association for Regional Cooperation (SAARC), an organization of all South Asian countries, pledged to cooperate in matters of agriculture, meteorology, telecommunications, health, education, women's issues, culture, tourism, and sports; to noninterference in each other's internal affairs; and to peaceful settlement of all outstanding regional disputes. India and Pakistan fought three wars over Kashmir and the matter is still lingering on; however, both rival nations are coming closer and have decided to settle all disputes by mutual agreement through peaceful means. This is an obvious sign of establishment of peace in the region.

Sri Lanka's newly elected President Kumaratunga has pledged to cooperate with Tamil rebels and to settle the issue peacefully, but both parties have not come to terms yet. Similarly, other South Asian nations are trying to settle their internal and regional disputes through peaceful means. Since the fracturing of the Soviet Union in 1991, most of the former republics of the former Soviet Union, including Russia, have developed close relations with India. The European Community and the Eastern European countries also desire to keep friendly relations with India and other South Asian countries.

India has always pursued friendly relations with the United States, based on shared democratic values and traditions. The changes in the international environment brought about by the end of the Cold War have provided both countries with an opportunity to reevaluate bilateral relations. India and the United States signed a defense protocol providing for joint defense exercises and the sharing of information on matters of defense. In addition, with so many U.S. firms investing in India, the United States has become the number one trading partner of India, with a 19.12 percent share of its export in 1994–1995 and steadily increasing. Second is

Japan, with 7.74 percent of exports. Japan and Southeast Asia are also wooing India for markets and technical know-how. This has greatly enhanced the status of India in the world.

## Conclusion

In summary, the conflicts and contradictions of South Asia are evident in all physical and cultural spheres. Physiographically, the north is sheltered by the high Himalayas and the south by the old Deccan Plateau, both separated by the flat Indo-Gangetic plain. South Asia experiences 50°C in the Thar Desert to below freezing weather in the Himalayas. Similarly, Assam and western Ghats receive very heavy precipitation while the Thar Desert gets very little rain. The east coast of India and Bangladesh experiences cyclones and flooding, and during the same period some parts of central India face the specter of drought. Nepal and Bhutan regularly face the horrors of landslides, whereas Sri Lanka and the Maldives are cut off from the mainland as islands, and with the continued rise of sea level, the Maldives are in serious peril of being eliminated. The environment is at times friend and foe alike.

In the north, one finds the oldest civilization centers of Mohenjodaro and Harappa, the Aryans; in the south, the Dravidians. Pakistan and Bangladesh adhere to Muslim fundamentalist religion whereas Nepal is a Hindu state with a significant Buddhist minority. Sri Lanka is predominately a Buddhist nation; on the other hand, India follows secularism with the majority consisting of Hindus. There are strict fundamentalists to atheists in South Asia. Culturally, there are caste differences among Hindus, but some Muslims and Christians also follow caste tradition. There are large urban centers such as Bombay, Calcutta, Dakha, Karachi, and Delhi, and in contrast, countless small hamlets and rural nucleated villages. Population densities in some places exceed 850 persons per km² in the rural areas of the Ganges delta and Kerala to less than 3 persons per km² in the Thar desert (excluding the Indira Gandhi Nahar Project area) and the Himalayas.

South Asia also possesses some of the best agricultural land and irrigation facilities in the Indus-Ganges basin to barren desert in the northwest. It contains the very highly industrialized regions of Chota Nagpur Plateau, Bombay, and Madras to the almost completely rural agricultural regions of Bangladesh. The region also followed varied development strategies with India being wedded to improving its economy through the planning process and recently adopting a market-friendly economic reform. Free enterprise works because, like democracy, it gives real power to the people. It is an economic democracy that limits the power of government by maximizing the power of the people. Whereas Russia has democracy but struggles for economic reform, China has economic reform but resists democracy. India has the advantages of both economic reform and an established democracy.

Bangladesh and Pakistan have used planning haphazardly without proper coordination; however, there is a marked improvement in agricultural production. The region has the landlocked countries of Nepal and Bhutan and the island nations of Sri Lanka and the Maldives and it contains the large nation states of India and Pakistan. Politically, South Asia ranges from the democracies of India, Pakistan, Bangladesh, Sri Lanka, and the Maldives (one party democracy) to the elected government of Nepal, which advises the king who has the authority to accept or reject the advice, to Bhutan, which has limited freedom. Thus, South Asia is like a museum of races and cultures, cults and customs, faiths and tongues, with a vast gap between the rich and poor and between the educated and the illiterates. Nevertheless, despite this diversity there is a considerable degree of unity due to common historical bonds, cultural similarities, economic necessities, and common interests of the region that bind all nation states together.

## References

Bhardwaj, S., ed. 1983. *Hindu Places of Pilgrimage in India: A Study in Cultural Geography.* Berkeley: University of California Press.

Chakravati, A. 1973. "Green Revolution in India." *Annals of the Association of American Geographers* 63: 319–330.

de Blij, Harm J., and Peter Muller. *Geography: Realms, Regions, and Concepts.* New York: John Wiley and Sons.

Dutt, A., et al. 1972. *India: Resources, Potentialities, and Planning.* Dubuque, Iowa: Kendall/Hunt.

Farmer, B. H. 1983. *An Introduction to South Asia.* London and New York: Methuen.

Fuhrman, Peter, and Michael Schuman. "Now We Are Our Masters." *Forbes,* May 23, 1994, 128–134.

Hall, A. 1981. *Emergence of Modern India.* New York: Columbia University Press.

*India, 1993: A Reference Annual.* 1994. New Delhi: Ministry of Information and Broadcasting, Government of India.

Johnson, B. L. C. 1982. *Bangladesh,* 2nd rev. ed. Totowa, N.J.: Barnes and Noble.

_____ . 1979. *India: Resource and Development.* Totowa, N.J.: Barnes and Noble.

Karan, P. P. 1967. *Bhutan.* Lexington: University of Kentucky Press.

_____ . 1960. *Nepal: A Cultural and Physical Geography.* Lexington: University of Kentucky Press.

Miller, E. W. 1962. *A Geography of Manufacturing.* Englewood Cliffs, N.J.: Prentice-Hall.

Myrdal, G. 1968. *Asian Drama: An Inquiry into the Poverty of Nations,* 3 vols. New York: Pantheon.

Noble, A., and A. Dutt, ed. 1982. *India: Cultural Patterns and Processes*. Boulder: Westview Press.

Nyrop, Richard F. 1984. *Pakistan: A Country Study*. Washington, D.C.: U.S. Government Printing Office.

Schwartzberg, Joseph, ed. 1978. *An Historical Atlas of South Asia*. Chicago: University of Chicago Press.

Sopher, David, ed. 1980. *An Exploration of India: Geographical Perspectives on Society and Culture*. Ithaca: Cornell University Press.

Spate, O. H. K., and A. Learmonth. 1971. *India and Pakistan: A General and Regional Geography*. London: Methuen.

*Statistical Outline of India, 1994–1995*. 1994. Bombay: Tata Services, Ltd., Department of Economics and Statistics.

Sukhwal, B. L. 1985. *Modern Political Geography of India*. New Delhi: Sterling Publishers.

_____ . 1976. *South Asia: A Systematic Geographic Bibliography*. Metuchen, N.J.: Scarecrow Press.

_____ . 1971. *India: A Political Geography*. New Delhi: Allied Publishers.

_____ . *India: Economic Resource Base and Contemporary Political Patterns*. New Delhi: Sterling Publishers and New York: APT Books, in press.

Taylor, A., ed. 1974. *Focus on South Asia*. New York: Praeger/American Geographical Society.

# 12 *East and Southeast Asia: Perspectives on Growth and Change*

**Stephen S. Chang**

## Introduction

East and Southeast Asia include eighteen political units: Japan, the Democratic People's Republic of Korea (North Korea), the Republic of Korea (South Korea), China, Hong Kong (a former British colony returned to China on July 1, 1997, which became a Special Administrative Region with broad local autonomy), Taiwan (Republic of China), Macao, Mongolia, and the ten countries in the Association of South East Asian Nations (ASEAN): Brunei, Indonesia, Singapore, Malaysia, Thailand, the Philippines, Vietnam (member since July 1995), Myanmar (Burma), and Laos (the last two admitted in July 1997). These countries constitute a dynamic region with rapid economic development and concomitant political and social changes. The term "Third World" does not fully apply here, as some countries are economically developed and others are rapidly advancing toward that status. In order to gain some perspective, various 1994 per capita GNPs (in U.S. dollars) are provided for comparison: Taiwan, $11,597 (*Far Eastern Economic Review* 1997: 14); Singapore, $22,500; Hong Kong $21,650; and South Korea, $8,260; compared to the United Kingdom, $18,340; New Zealand, $13,350; Portugal, $9,320; Greece, $7,700; and Hungary, $3,840 (World Bank 1996: 189). It is often mentioned that the Pacific Century will soon be dawning with the growing economic and geopolitical importance of the Pacific Basin.

Japan is fully developed and among the world's economic leaders. The "Four Tigers"—South Korea, Hong Kong, Taiwan, and Singapore—are developed or nearly so. Malaysia, Indonesia, and Thailand are in the ranks of newly industrializing countries. The Philippines has not kept pace because its economy has been long dominated by "crony capital-

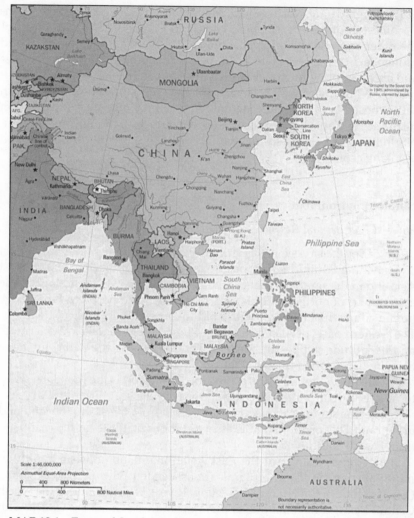

MAP 12.1   East and Southeast Asia

ism" under oligarchic rule. Brunei continues to rely on its oil and natural gas exports which make it a wealthy country.

With economic reform that began in 1978, China has experienced rapid growth in recent years. It is, however, a large and populous country; thus, economic improvement for most of its people still has a way to go. Its sheer size alone makes it a significant economic force. Macao, a Portuguese colony until its reversion to China on December 20, 1999, is small both in size and economic importance. In the last decade, it has experienced significant growth as a result of the economic boom in southern China.

The laggards are North Korea, Mongolia, Myanmar, and the three Indochinese countries of Vietnam, Laos, and Cambodia. As with many of the other centrally planned economies, Vietnam, Laos, Cambodia, and Mongolia, in the mid- to late 1980s, began changing to market economies and are attempting to attract foreign investment. In 1962, Myanmar instituted the "Burmese way to socialism" and self-sufficiency, resulting in self-imposed isolation and economic stagnation. Since 1988, it has begun introducing a market economy and encouraging foreign investment. North Korea is a closed society with its orthodox communist policies and a sinking economy.

## Natural Environment

### Physical Features and Resources

Much of Southeast Asia has humid tropical climates including rain forest and savanna. Humid subtropical climate exists in northern Southeast Asia and in the southern parts of the East Asian mainland and Japan. The eastern part of northern China, much of Korea, and northern Japan have humid continental climates with mild-to-hot summers and cold winters. The western parts of Asia in western China and Mongolia are drier with middle-latitude steppes and deserts. There is also the highland climate of the Qinghai-Xizang (Tibetan) Plateau.

One distinct climatic feature affecting this region is the monsoon. Winter winds blow from the Asian land mass to the sea during the dry season, whereas summer monsoon winds blow from the sea to the land and bring rain. This precipitation is essential for agriculture on the mainland from East to South Asia.

The geomorphology of the East Asian mainland consists mainly of mountains and hills. The plains are associated with the Chang Jiang (Yangtze River), the Huang He (Yellow River), which includes the North Central Plain, and a small delta plain in southern China associated with the Xi Jiang (West River). There is a plains area in northeast China and one on the east coast of the Korean Peninsula. Southeast Asia is made up of plains framed by mountains. The islands of Japan, the Philippines, Indonesia, and Taiwan are mountainous, with active volcanism and coastal plains of varying widths. Throughout this region, prime agricultural land, dense human settlement, and economic activities are concentrated in the plains areas.

With the exception of Hong Kong, Macao, and Singapore, most of the countries in this region have important agricultural sectors whose products figure prominently in their resource base. Rice is the major crop in the humid tropics and subtropics of East and Southeast Asia; rice and maize (corn) are important crops in North Korea, while wheat is the major crop in northern China. Major commercial crops including rubber, oil palm, coconut, coffee, pineapple, maize, and sugarcane are produced for export in the region, especially in Southeast Asia. Animal husbandry is the primary economic activity in Mongolia.

The countries also possess and exploit other renewable resources, such as tropical woods and fisheries, as well as an assemblage of nonrenewable resources. Brunei and Indonesia are important oil exporters. Malaysia, Thailand, Vietnam, and the Philippines also produce oil and natural gas. China changed from an oil exporter during the 1980s to an importer in 1993 as its consumption increased with economic growth, while the aging oil fields in eastern China are declining in yield. It is opening up the remote Tarim Basin in western Xinjiang for oil development activities. China is a major coal producer and with Indonesia leads in coal exports in the region (*Far Eastern Economic Review* 1994: 53–54). Tin is a major resource exported from Southeast Asia. Other minerals are found throughout this region.

## Environmental Issues and Problems

The countries of East and Southeast Asia have emphasized economic development, paying scant attention to resource conservation and environmental protection. The majority of people have little recognition or understanding of the processes, effects, and remedies of various forms of environmental degradation and the associated economic cost. When people are poor, they are mostly concerned about survival. With economic development increasing, the priority for people is continued progress in living standards and material abundance. Pressures on resources and the environment have been viewed as costs for economic betterment. As societies become more affluent and raise educational levels, people tend to develop an understanding of environmental issues and seek their resolution.

Economic development has relieved the poverty of millions in this region. The costs have included rapid increases in environmental degradation, such as industrial pollution, deforestation, and natural habitat destruction. Less obvious but more serious is environmental damage that is habitually ignored by governments: soil erosion; destruction of watersheds, wetlands, and fishing areas; the loss of agricultural land to urban, commercial, and industrial development; and air pollution are a few examples (*Far Eastern Economic Review* 1994: 64; Schwarz 1993b: 48).

In the long run, environmental degradation is costly in terms of money for cleanup and restoration and the threat to sustained future growth.

China serves as an example: Relative to its population and needs, much of its area is water deficient. Nevertheless, industrial waste and untreated sewage continue to pollute freshwater. In addition, water pollution endangers valuable aquatic resources.

China is consuming its resources at a rapid pace. Professor Zhou Guangzhao, the head of the Chinese Academy of Science, noted that China is ecologically fragile, yet people are blind to this serious problem. The pressure on resources and the environment will intensify with population growth. China is rapidly losing farmland to roads, industries, housing, and commercial development. Many such projects are necessary but others are merely speculative attempts by people to get rich quickly. If farmland and water resources continue to be wasted, China will have to import food to feed its people, creating worldwide pressure in supplying China's needs. The government has tried to curtail the squandering of arable land but success is not assured (Tyler 1994a,b).

Even though economic growth has the highest priority for Asian countries, there is greater recognition of the problems and costs of environmental degradation, especially among the people of better-developed countries. Japan and Singapore have long-established environmental programs. Taiwan, South Korea, and Hong Kong are spending large sums for cleanup and pollution control. Malaysia, Indonesia, and Vietnam are taking steps to slow deforestation and control toxic waste disposal. China is examining energy use, air and water standards, and wildlife trade. The Philippines plans to implement Earth Summit's Agenda 21, which calls for environmental protection measures in a country's development program. In spite of these initiatives, difficulties exist in the monitoring and enforcing of environmental laws and regulations (*Far Eastern Economic Review* 1994: 64–66 and 1996: 68; Schwarz 1993a: 58 and 1993b: 48–50).

The countries under review, reflecting their newfound confidence and assertiveness, object to being ordered about or preached to by outsiders. There is a growing awareness of the economic importance of resource conservation and environmental protection. However, these are their resources, and they want a share of the economic benefits from products made from sustainably harvested resources. They voice suspicions that the developed countries are trying to use environmental issues as a means of maintaining their own comparative advantage and promoting protectionist policies in world trade. Above all, environmental protection and economic development cannot be separated. The best way to prevent environmental degradation is to reduce poverty. Consequently, these countries seek to link environmental matters to trade and development issues when dealing with developed countries (Crovitz 1994: 20–21; *Far Eastern Economic Review* 1994: 66–67; Schwarz 1993b: 50–52).

## The People

### Ethnic and Cultural Patterns

The East and Southeast Asia region has a multitude of ethnic groups and languages, resulting in Southeast Asia's being referred to as the "shatter belt." Despite the picture of ethnic and cultural mixing presented by the broad cultural systems of individual countries, there exist groups in each country that vary in language, dietary habits, dress, social traditions, and ways of thinking and doing things. Japan and Korea are closest to being ethnically and linguistically homogeneous; however, with the political division of North and South Korea, cultural divergences are bound to occur (Spencer 1973: 20–21).

Ethnic minorities are common throughout this region. The 1990 census showed that China had fifty-five minority groups totaling 100.9 million people and accounting for 8.8 percent of the country's population (Zhao 1994: 116). In Southeast Asia, Indonesia, with its extensive archipelago, has great ethnic and linguistic diversity. In Vietnam, Laos, Cambodia, Thailand, and Myanmar, there are persistent historical conflicts between the dominant lowland groups and the ethnic minorities in the hills. Singapore and Malaysia are countries where the Chinese, Malays, and Indians must coexist.

Ethnic Chinese constitute a major minority group in all Southeast Asian countries except Singapore, where they are in the majority with over 75 percent of the total population. There are around 23 million ethnic Chinese in Southeast Asia, accounting for about 5 percent of the region's total population. Approximately 20 of the 23 million are in ASEAN countries (Hicks and Mackie 1994: 48). In Malaysia, about 30 percent of the population are ethnic Chinese, making it proportionally the largest community of its kind, next to Singapore, among ASEAN countries. However, with ongoing assimilation, it is extremely difficult to accurately determine the number of ethnic Chinese in the Southeast Asian countries.

The importance of the ethnic Chinese is due primarily to their economic success. They have endured jealousy, suspicion, discrimination, and persecution. Even today, the role of the ethnic Chinese in the countries where they settled and their relationships with people of these countries are important issues. They, along with the other overseas Chinese in East Asia, namely, in Hong Kong and Taiwan, have invested, established businesses, and contributed mightily to the economic development of East and Southeast Asia. Their impact in this region continues to expand. With burgeoning economic development and improvements in living standards, ethnic tensions in East and Southeast Asia, often borne of economic competition and jealousy, have subsided in recent years.

Many of these countries face the issue of regionalism, which has resulted from ethnic and cultural differences in the area. In China, being Chinese has traditionally been a cultural definition. When an ethnic group accepted Chinese culture, they became Chinese. Despite regional differences, such as dietary preferences and language dialects, all Chinese identify with the broader Chinese culture. Therefore, regionalism in China has been shaped primarily on political bases, with occasional economic inputs (Spencer 1973: 53). Throughout Chinese history, when central governments were weak, regionalism increased. Suffering caused by natural disasters or human-created chaos gave rise to regionally based rebellions with local leaders fighting for the "Mandate of Heaven."

East Asia and Southeast Asia have been influenced historically by Chinese and Indian cultures. East Asia is in the Chinese cultural realm, while Indonesia is in that of India. Thailand, Cambodia, and Vietnam share the influences of both. Cultural diffusion has occurred, in the modern era, through migration of ethnic Chinese to the Philippines, Thailand, Malaysia, and Indonesia, and Indians to Malaysia. Western cultures were introduced mostly through European colonial efforts. They are reflected here in their political and legal systems, some newly evolved regions and economic classes, foreign language preferences, consumer tastes, and regional ties. The Philippines, for example, exhibits strong Spanish and American cultural influences (Spencer 1973: 21–25).

One aspect of Indian cultural influence has been the spread of Hinduism, Buddhism, and Islam (Spencer 1973: 21). Malaysia, Indonesia, and Brunei are Islamic countries. Buddhism is found in much of the rest of East and Southeast Asia. Most of the people in the Philippines, with the exception of the Islamic minority in the southern islands, are Roman Catholic, a cultural vestige of Spanish influence.

In spite of Chinese influence on the region, there are no organized religions identified with China. Many researchers erroneously refer to Confucianism as the religion of China and the areas to which Chinese culture spread. Confucius is regarded as a great teacher and scholar by the Chinese whereas Confucianism is a social and political philosophy. Traditionally, when the Chinese erected a temple or shrine, invited the dead to feast, burned incense and candles, and kowtowed, they were merely honoring the dead. In the Western cultures, these acts are interpreted as worshiping, hence the mistake. Chinese ethnic religions are a mixture of several beliefs, rituals, and social philosophies, such as Buddhism, Confucianism, Taoism, and others. All types of organized religion exist today in China.

The extended-family organization is widespread in this region. Traditionally, family members did not necessarily all live under one roof, but they pooled their resources to provide everyone with a broad base of socioeconomic support because social institutions were few or nonexistent. However, with all the changes brought about by economic development—urbanization, an increase in income, and the evolution of social institutions—the extended family is slowly giving way to a nuclear family system. The Japanese extended-family organization is changing dramatically, and evolution is under way in other countries undergoing rapid development, such as South Korea, Hong Kong, Taiwan, and Singapore. As this region becomes developed, nuclear family organization will predominate in the future. Social institutions must be established to assume the functions formerly performed by the extended family. The ensuing debate is not whether such institutions are necessary, but how much is required and whether government agencies or private concerns will provide them. With a growing need for these new institutions in this region, each government increasingly will be trying to define its position on these issues.

## Population and Settlement

East and Southeast Asia is home to an estimated 34 percent of the world's population, of whom about 63 percent are in China. The rate of population growth here has been steadily declining. As shown in Table 12.1, East Asia and Southeast Asia have annual rates of natural increases of 1 percent and 1.9 percent, respectively, compared to the world average of 1.5 percent. In Southeast Asia, Singapore, Thailand, and Indonesia have natural increase rates of 1.1 percent, 1.4 percent, and 1.6 percent, respectively, and are below or near the world's average. In East Asia, Japan and Hong Kong have natural increase rates of 0.2 percent and 0.7 percent, respectively, typical of developed areas (Population Reference Bureau 1996).

The "eight economies" (term used in World Bank report *The East Asian Miracle*), Japan, South Korea, Hong Kong, Taiwan, Singapore, Thailand, Malaysia, and Indonesia, have experienced rapid declines in their birth rates, preceding and dropping further than other developing areas. Japan experienced the earliest decline shortly after World War II, whereas the others began in the 1960s or early 1970s. This came as a result of economic development and the associated socioeconomic changes, including equal educational opportunities for women (*Economist* 1993c: 6–9; World Bank 1993: 38–40).

Population size and rates of growth can provide development opportunities. For the eight economies, demographics may have given impetus to their development. A large group of productive people entering their prime working ages should provide additional fuel to a rising economy. The impressive declines in the birth rates have contributed to increased family savings, which can be invested in areas such as education and ma-

TABLE 12.1   Population and Urbanization of East Asia and Southeast Asia, 1996

| | Population Mid-1996 (Millions) | Birth Rate Per 1,000 | Death Rate Per 1,000 | Natural Increase (Annual %) | % Urban |
|---|---|---|---|---|---|
| World | 5,771.0 | 24 | 9 | 1.5 | 43 |
| More Developed | 1,171.0 | 12 | 10 | 0.1 | 75 |
| Less Developed | 4,600.0 | 27 | 9 | 1.9 | 35 |
| Less Developed (excl. China) | 3,383.0 | 31 | 10 | 2.2 | 38 |
| East Asia | 1,443.0 | 16 | 7 | 1.0 | 36 |
| China | 1,217.6 | 17 | 7 | 1.1 | 29 |
| Hong Kong | 6.4 | 12 | 5 | 0.7 | – |
| Japan | 125.8 | 10 | 7 | 0.2 | 78 |
| North Korea | 23.9 | 24 | 6 | 1.9 | 61 |
| South Korea | 45.3 | 15 | 6 | 0.9 | 74 |
| Macao | 0.4 | 15 | 3 | 1.2 | 97 |
| Mongolia | 2.3 | 22 | 8 | 1.4 | 55 |
| Taiwan | 21.4 | 15 | 5 | 1.0 | 75 |
| Southeast Asia | 496.0 | 27 | 8 | 1.9 | 30 |
| Brunei | 0.3 | 27 | 3 | 2.4 | 67 |
| Cambodia | 10.9 | 45 | 16 | 2.9 | 13 |
| Indonesia | 201.4 | 24 | 8 | 1.6 | 31 |
| Laos | 5.0 | 43 | 15 | 2.9 | 19 |
| Malaysia | 20.6 | 28 | 5 | 2.4 | 51 |
| Myanmar | 46.0 | 31 | 12 | 1.9 | 25 |
| Philippines | 72.0 | 30 | 9 | 2.1 | 49 |
| Singapore | 3.0 | 16 | 5 | 1.1 | 100 |
| Thailand | 60.7 | 20 | 6 | 1.4 | 19 |
| Vietnam | 76.6 | 30 | 7 | 2.3 | 19 |

SOURCE: *World Population Data Sheet* (Washington, DC: Population Reference Bureau, 1996). Reprinted with permission.

chinery. These investments can enhance the productivity of these young people as they enter the labor force (*Economist* 1993c: 6). Most of these eight economies, however, have faced a labor shortage since the latter part of the 1970s. This was caused by a combination of declining birth rates and reduced working hours, which typically accompany a rising living standard. The shift away from labor-intensive industries, the use of new technologies, and increased productivity alter labor needs and eliminate the shortage problem. A low birth rate is desirable because the released resources can be devoted to further investments in the economy, with concomitant increases in living standards.

Unlike the eight economies, China's large population size posed diffi-cult challenges in dealing with the bulge of young people in its age struc-ture entering the job market. In the early 1990s, about 40 percent of the population fell into the age group of 15–34 years (Population Census Office 1993). Currently, even with rapid economic growth, unemployment is still a serious problem.

The Asian population is currently young, but with the rapid decline in birth rates, the populations of countries in this region will age rapidly. In 1990, only Japan and Hong Kong had 10–20 percent of their populations above 60 years while the rest of the countries had 0–10 percent. However, it is projected that by 2030, Japan and Hong Kong will have more than 30 percent of their populations above 60 years while China, North and South Koreas, Taiwan, and Singapore will have 20–30 percent. The rest of the countries in this region will have 10–20 percent except for Laos which will have 0–10 percent (Silverman 1995: 50). Caring for aging populations will have a social and economic cost and will be part of the debate for countries in this region as social institutions evolve to assume the functions of the changing extended families.

A population phenomenon found throughout Asia is the skewing of the sex ratio at birth toward boys. A sex ratio at birth of between 105 to 106 boys for every 100 girls is normal worldwide. In China, the ratio rose from 107.2 in 1982 to 111.3 in 1989. There may be underreporting of female babies because of the one-child policy. South Korea's ratio rose from 106.9 in 1982 to 113.6 in 1988, faster than that of China, indicating that a one-child policy is not the only cause of the phenomenon (*Economist* 1993a: 38). Based on an official survey of 385,000 people in China in 1992, it was discovered that the ratio at birth rose to 118.5. The basic cause of this phenomenon throughout Asia is the cultural preference for male offspring leading to the use of medical equipment, such as ultrasound, to determine the sex of the fetus and the abortion of unwanted females (*Far Eastern Economic Review* 1994: 71). The shortage of females in the near future will have social implications, such as the inability of sons to find wives, the care of aging bachelors, and the prospect of reduced population growth.

Developing societies generally have a higher percentage of people in rural areas, but with industrialization and economic development, population shifts toward cities. Japan, South Korea, Hong Kong, Taiwan, and Singapore are highly urbanized as a result. The city-state of Singapore, the city-territories of Hong Kong, and also Macao, are almost entirely urban. Other countries in the region are not as well urbanized (Table 12.1), with China at 29 percent and Southeast Asia at 30 percent (Population Reference Bureau 1996). This generally reflects a lower level of development as compared to the more highly urbanized ones. However, rural-to-urban migration can also be caused by population growth in poor rural areas where there is a lack of land and jobs. The rural poor migrate to urban areas, hoping for improved opportunities. The Philippines, with 49 percent of its population living in urban areas (Population Reference Bureau 1996), demonstrates such a situation (*Far Eastern Economic Review* 1994: 69). About one-third (or 3.5 million) of Manila's population reside in squatter settlements with poor living conditions. However, to them and squatters in other Asian cities, this represents an improvement from conditions in the rural areas (McGurn 1997: 36).

The shift of population from rural to urban areas will continue along with economic development. The large, overcrowded cities in Asia are increasingly being challenged to provide jobs and services at a rapid rate. City planners have to make hard decisions about the allocation of scarce resources, eliminating traffic congestion, maintaining and building new infrastructure, and resettling squatters (McGurn 1997: 34). One solution is to diffuse population movements to other cities. China is encouraging rural nonagricultural enterprises, a unique idea in development, to help increase income and stabilize population in the rural areas. Such enterprises may create medium-sized towns and cities, siphoning the excess city population. Too many of these countries have their urban populations concentrated in a primate city, usually the capital, for example, Bangkok, Kuala Lumpur, Manila, Jakarta, and Seoul.

Commonly, one finds an economic gap between urban and rural populations, which in some cases is quite wide. In Thailand, much of its urban population, industries, and businesses are concentrated in overcrowded Bangkok. This creates a wide economic disparity between urban areas around Bangkok and the more distant rural locales (Fairclough and Tasker 1994: 22–23). Shanghai, with 1 percent of China's population, has about 4.3 percent of its GDP, and greater Manila accounts for 30–46 percent of the Philippines' GDP with 13 percent of its population. The economic gap between urban and rural areas will continue to attract migration to Asia's already overcrowded cities in search of better opportunities (McGurn 1997: 36). China's large "floating population" in recent years has been composed of the rural poor looking for jobs in the cities of the fast-growing coastal region. Such examples reflect uneven regional development for which no ready solution is at hand.

## The Economy

### Recent Economic History and Characteristics

Japan rebuilt its modern industries after World War II, when it was stereotyped as a producer of cheap, low-quality products. However, in the late 1960s that image began changing, ultimately to one synonymous with high-quality goods. Japan is the second-largest economy in the world, with the innovative and superior manufacturing sector as its greatest strength. Industrialization in South Korea, Hong Kong, Taiwan, and Singapore began in the 1960s and their economies grew rapidly. Economic development efforts were initiated in Malaysia, Indonesia, and Thailand in the late 1970s, and they are now in the ranks of newly industrializing countries (Table 12.2).

These eight economies achieved rapid economic growth through the exporting of manufactured products rather than through the process of import-substitution industrialization. Much of these exports went to the United States and western Europe. Their reliance on the exporting of primary products has also declined. For the three newly industrializing countries, primary products and related commodities as a percentage of their merchandise exports dropped between 1980 and 1993 approximately as follows: Indonesia 98 percent to 47 percent; Malaysia 81 percent to 30 percent; and Thailand 72 percent to 27 percent (World Bank 1996: 216–217).

Initial industries were labor-intensive, low-skill manufacturing, such as apparel and shoes, requiring cheap and abundant labor. With rising living standards and wages, industries requiring higher skills gradually replaced the low-skill ones. Their higher value products can absorb the increased labor costs. Numerous low-skill, labor-intensive businesses in Hong Kong, Taiwan, and South Korea have moved their factories abroad, with many going to China in recent years, just as Japan relocated manufacturing in other countries to achieve lower costs. The continual change to high technology and skill-intensive industries and services producing higher-value-added products is necessary to support growth.

As Japan is now manufacturing technologically sophisticated and upscale goods, South Korea, Hong Kong, Taiwan, and Singapore have shifted to the Japanese niche of high-quality, medium-priced products with efforts to develop high technological industries. Hong Kong and Singapore have also become important financial centers in Asia. In addition, Hong Kong has developed an important tertiary economy (Table 12.2), serving the Chinese hinterland (Chang 1990). Along with Macao, it is part of the fast-growing southern China region. Thailand, Malaysia, and Indonesia have assumed the production of quality, value-oriented products formerly sold by South Korea, Hong Kong, Taiwan, and Singapore.

Although the United States and western Europe continue to be important markets, the countries in this region seek to export to all areas of the world where demand exists. There is also increased intraregional trade. With the ASEAN Free Trade Area (AFTA) and the accompanying tariff reduction coming into existence in 2003, regional trade will benefit. This also changes the picture of foreign investment and competition in the ASEAN region. When it comes to doing business in much of Asia, Japanese companies are ahead of their U.S. counterparts. AFTA provides the United States with an new opportunity and, possibly, an advantage. U.S. firms can invest in one country to serve the entire ASEAN region. Japa-

TABLE 12.2  Production in East Asia and Southeast Asia, 1980 and 1994

| | GDP (US$m) | | Agriculture %GDP | | Industry* % GDP | | Manufacturing % GDP | | Services % GDP | |
|---|---|---|---|---|---|---|---|---|---|---|
| | 1980 | 1994 | 1980 | 1994 | 1980 | 1994 | 1980 | 1994 | 1980 | 1994 |
| China | 201,696 | 522,172 | 30 | 21 | 49 | 47 | 41 | 37 | 21 | 32 |
| Hong Kong | 28,496 | 131,881 | 1 | 0 | 31 | 18 | 23 | 11 | 68 | 82 |
| Japan | 1,059,257 | 4,590,971 | 4 | 2 | 42 | 40 | 29 | 27 | 54 | 58 |
| South Korea | 63,661 | 376,505 | 15 | 7 | 40 | 43 | 29 | 29 | 45 | 50 |
| Taiwan | n.a. | 240,986 | n.a. | 3.5 | n.a. | 37 | n.a. | 29 | n.a. | 59 |
| Indonesia | 78,013 | 174,640 | 24 | 17 | 42 | 41 | 13 | 24 | 34 | 42 |
| Malaysia | 24,488 | 70,626 | 22 | 14 | 38 | 43 | 21 | 32 | 40 | 42 |
| Mongolia | 2,329 | 741 | 14 | 21 | 28 | 45 | n.a. | n.a. | 57 | 34 |
| Myanmar | n.a. | n.a. | 47 | 63 | 13 | 9 | 10 | 7 | 41 | 28 |
| Philippines | 32,500 | 64,162 | 25 | 22 | 39 | 33 | 26 | 23 | 36 | 45 |
| Singapore | 11,718 | 68,949 | 1 | 0 | 38 | 36 | 29 | 27 | 61 | 64 |
| Thailand | 32,354 | 143,209 | 23 | 10 | 29 | 39 | 22 | 29 | 48 | 50 |
| Vietnam | n.a. | 15,570 | n.a. | 28 | n.a. | 30 | n.a. | 22 | n.a. | 43 |

*Industry includes value-added mining; manufacturing; construction; and electricity, water, and gas.

SOURCES: World Bank, *World Development Report* (New York: Oxford University Press, 1996), pp. 210–211. Far Eastern Economic Review, *Asia 1997 Yearbook* (Hong Kong: Far Eastern Economic Review, 1997), p. 14.

nese companies, which have already invested in several countries, may face difficulty in realigning their operations in an optimal way (Holloway 1997: 48). This illustrates that in global competition, old assumptions give way to new realities very quickly.

Tourism has been an important part of the service sector of many of the economies in East and Southeast Asia and is growing rapidly. China has become the leading tourist destination among developing countries. With increased affluence, people of this region have joined the tourist flow and have contributed to the growth of tourism here and elsewhere. The expansion of tourism will continue to benefit this region.

*Economic Development: Process of Growth*

There is no single formula to account for the rapid growth of these eight economies, but insight into the process was presented in a World Bank report (*Economist* 1993b and 1993c; World Bank 1993). There was widespread participation and sharing in the benefits of economic growth, thereby reducing poverty, raising living standards, creating a large or growing middle class, narrowing the gap between the rich and the poor, and generating support for economic policies.

The eight economies have not neglected their agricultural sectors. As their economies have grown, the portion of gross domestic product contributed by agriculture has dropped (Table 12.2). However, they have maintained investments to increase agricultural productivity, build rural infrastructure, such as roads and electrification, and improve rural living standards. They have not siphoned wealth from agriculture to support industrialization. Contributions from agriculture come largely through voluntary means, such as savings, without hurting agricultural growth. During the period between 1980 and 1992, agricultural production grew at an average annual rate as follows: Thailand 4.1 percent; Malaysia 3.6 percent; Indonesia 3.1 percent; South Korea 1.9 percent (World Bank 1994: 164–165); and Taiwan 5.9 percent (*Far Eastern Economic Review* 1995: 14).

The eight economies restrained inflation and maintained prudent fiscal policies by staying within their ability to finance deficits without excessive inflationary pressure or foreign borrowing. When borrowing abroad, they assured themselves that they could service their loans. Each of these economies has a high rate of domestic savings that generates capital for investments. Government economic interventions and policies have stayed within bounds of fiscal prudence so that the cost has not been excessive and has kept distortions of capital, labor, and goods prices to a minimum.

The eight economies have large investments in physical capital, such as infrastructure and machinery, which has increased productivity. They are friendly to the business community; private investments are encouraged. They prefer growth from increased productivity rather than from investment, indicating that capital is used to generate better economic performance. Toward this end, human capital must be developed to provide high-quality labor.

In the early stages of development, the eight economies invested most of their educational resources in primary and secondary levels, making education equally available for both sexes. The result is a well-educated citizenry and a better workforce. Equal educational opportunities for females has contributed to the rapid early decline in birth rates, which stimulates economic growth. University education, however, receives fewer resources. Entrance is based on merit and is highly competitive. This allows the poor to have greater access to higher education and to reap the rewards associated with it.

The eight economies have opened themselves to foreign ideas, which has resulted in the diffusion of new technologies and knowledge of international market conditions and business practices so important in export-oriented growth economies. Some are friendly to foreign investments. This brings in foreign capital for development and growth.

The role of government economic intervention varies on a continuum among the eight economies, from minimum to heavy involvement. The governments promote economic growth and, in general, encourage market pricing mechanisms and private initiatives. When they intervene, it is done prudently with limits on costs. Some government investments and industrial policies hasten growth while others lead to failure. Economic discipline is important to reassess, adjust, or abandon government policies and initiatives, and a competent, honest bureaucracy is essential for avoiding failure. Relying on competitive market forces reduces dependence on government capabilities. The qualities of the civil services vary from very good to those that have improved but still lag behind the leaders. Singapore is often cited for its professional, efficient, and honest civil service. The whole issue of activist government versus free market is complicated and subject to much controversy.

Some countries in this region—China, North Korea, Vietnam, Cambodia, Laos, Myanmar, and the Philippines—lagged because their policies brought stagnation. Only North Korea has remained unchanged (*Economist* 1993c: 5). The Philippine economy has been plagued by attempts to reward and enrich cronies, corruption, and the dominance of an oligarchy under the former dictator, Ferdinand Marcos. With his overthrow and the recent economic liberalization, the economy has grown steadily since 1993. The Philippines has shown renewed economic confidence and has become attractive to foreign investors (*Far Eastern Economic Review* 1995: 196 and 1997: 194–195).

Economic reform in China began in 1978 in the agricultural sector and saw crop production increase dramatically. Low-skill, labor-intensive industries followed. It has experienced rapid growth in recent years and is attracting diverse industrial investments with its economic potential. Much of this development is concentrated in the more fertile and affluent eastern coastal provinces, giving rise to increased regional disparities. With increases in per-acre yields slowing, farm income is stagnating, whereas wages of industrial workers are rising with industrial growth. The income gap is widening between urban and rural workers, especially between urban workers of the coastal areas and their rural counterparts in the inland provinces. Rural nonagricultural enterprises help by employing surplus farm labor. A reduction of farmworkers increases the per capita yield and, thus, the per capita income. Wages from rural nonagricultural enterprises further contribute to the total income of farm families. With the large Chinese population, these enterprises help but do not resolve the problem of the income gap between urban and rural workers, primarily in the eastern coastal provinces.

The nonstate sector, comprised of quasi-governmental (such as local township and village), private, and foreign ownership, contributes to much of this growth whereas the majority of the state enterprises are money-losing ventures greatly in need of reform. The support of money-losing state enterprises imposes a huge budgetary burden upon the government and contributes to difficulties in reforming the financial sector and fighting inflation. If state enterprises were made to stand on their own, many would face bankruptcy. The fear of massive unemployment and the possibility of social and political unrest make the Chinese government hesitant to reform these state enterprises. It continues to pour money into them, thus contributing to possible future inflationary pressures.

Along with rapid economic growth and rising living standards, China is approaching the stage where a mixture of state control and market mechanisms is giving rise to increased incongruities in the economy. For example, in spite of their declining share in total industrial output, from 78 percent in 1978 to less than 50 percent in 1993, state enterprises increased their claim on the financial resources in China from 61 percent in 1989 to 70 percent in 1993 through government subsidies and cheap credit, depriving the nonstate sector of its needed capital (Goldstein 1994: 60). Further economic reform, demanding difficult choices, is necessary to address issues such as the inefficient and unprofitable state enterprises, the more efficient allocation of credit, the growing income gap between urban and rural population, especially those of inland provinces, and the need to diffuse economic development inland. Success can maintain the attractive investment environment and continued growth.

Vietnam's recent change to a market economy generated significant interest as an area with investment possibilities. Only the future will reveal if rapid economic growth is possible among the laggard economies.

## Challenges to Development

China, Vietnam, and Laos are continuing their transformation to market economies, which includes freeing price controls, developing a financial system, and restructuring the state sector. The transition will not be easy or painless. China started its reform earlier than the other two and continues to face challenges. It must diffuse the growth to poorer areas. Rapid job growth is necessary to provide employment for large numbers of working-age people and help reduce urban and rural income disparities. Institutions, legal and financial, must be developed to carry out economic growth. An economic zone, involving coastal China, Hong Kong, Taiwan, Macao, and possibly South Korea is already beginning to take shape and can be expected to grow with the Chinese economy.

Japan, as a mature economy, will face economic cycles of growth and recession. Methods that worked well in a rising economy, such as lifetime employment, seeking group consensus, and interlocking ownership between companies for close financial and business relationships (*Keiretsu*), need to change. Japanese industrial efficiency is not duplicated in its service sector. The Japanese want lower prices and a better living standard. Changes have to be made in the traditional system in response to demands of a developed economy in a global setting.

With a global market, economic competition is getting more intense. Financial and trade barriers are increasingly controversial and ineffective. All countries will have to compete. Infrastructure developments in transportation, communication, and power generation have to keep pace with growth. A big challenge to be faced by all is the ability to make the transition from low-skill, labor-intensive industries to high technology ones. Low-cost labor does not last long and industries relying on it will be phased out. This occurred in Japan, Hong Kong, Singapore, Taiwan, and South Korea and is spreading to others. The belief is that growth can only be sustained if a country begins producing technologically sophisticated, knowledge-intensive and high-value-added goods and services. This requires modernization in areas such as education, industrial technology, financial systems, management methods, and research and development. Success will result in a developed economy, whereas failure will stop growth and lead to a subsequent decline. Japan has been successful. South Korea, Hong Kong, Taiwan, and Singapore are facing the challenge. The time for others will come.

## Economic Role of Confucianism

In the Confucian concept, an organization is not unlike a family. A good leader, like a good father, is just, caring, and a good provider, while a good subject or subordinate, like a good child, should be obedient, loyal, and respectful. The hierarchy of the state or organization parallels that of the family. Social harmony can only be achieved by everyone knowing and accepting his or her place in the hierarchy. As a morally superior person, the ruler sets an example for the morally inferior to follow. A good ruler will preserve the "Mandate of Heaven." In this concept, few laws and institutions are needed.

The Confucian legacy is responsible for the features often associated with Japanese management, such as life-time employment, no layoffs, dedication and loyalty to the corporation, and the hierarchical structure of management. Interestingly, similar systems are found in other areas with Chinese cultural influence. When a person becomes a member of a corporate family, the relationship between employer and employee is not defined by a written contract but instead through personal interaction. Consequently, this system of management tends to be paternalistic. In some areas of East Asia, employees view a written contract as a threat because it breaks the traditional familial relationship, which they deem as more secure.

The familial management system, unfortunately, does not withstand well the test of recession and economic change. With the phasing out of light industries based on cheap labor in places such as Taiwan and Hong Kong, factories have been closed and workers laid off. In times of labor shortages, workers willingly change jobs for better compensation. In Japan, life-time employment now exists only at elite corporations. There are now many small companies where workers do not enjoy nearly the same pay or benefits as their larger counterparts. Only a growing economy can support the life-time employment. Currently, however, with a prolonged period of very slow growth and falling corporate profits in Japan, the life-time employment system is being severely tested.

Western businesses complain that China's laws are vague. This is another legacy of Confucianism, in which there is no need for an elaborate set of laws, and those that exist are subject to personal interpretation by officials. Western legal tradition is based on clearly defined laws and legal interpretations. Perceptions of legal systems differ between cultures.

There is a widespread but erroneous tendency to attribute Chinese business success to Confucianism. Merchants were not well regarded by Confucian mandarins (government officials) and, consequently, they flourished abroad away from mandarin control, in places where laws and officials favored commerce. Values such as hard work, thrift, loyalty, trust, honesty, and family, favored by Confucian tradition, were practical and necessary for success. Business people also took risks and sought profits, values not endorsed by mandarins in the Confucian society (Wang 1991: 181–197).

## Political Development

An important change in East and Southeast Asia is the introduction of a market economy in the communist countries of China, Mongolia, Vietnam, Laos, and Cambodia, but excluding North Korea. The Communist parties, except in Mongolia and Cambodia, are willing to deviate economically from Marxism but want to maintain political control and power. Mongolia has held multiparty elections and is in the process of democratic evolution. Following elections organized by the United Nations in 1993, Cambodia's attempt to restore peace and normalcy after more than two decades of turmoil is made difficult by the rivalry between the country's ruling coalition partners, Co-Prime Ministers Prince Ranariddh of Funcinpec (the royalist party) and Hun Sen of the Cambodian People's Party (the former Vietnam-sponsored communist government party). Over the same period, the Khmer Rouge guerrillas, who were responsible for massive deaths when they ruled from 1975 to 1978, weakened. A coup in July 1997, gave Hun Sen a dominant position and ASEAN held Cambodia's admittance to the organization in abeyance. Thus, Cambodia's political future remains uncertain.

North Korea still remains a closed and repressive society, resisting any changes that threatened the power of its late leader, Kim Il Sung, who died on July 8, 1994, and those threatening his son and chosen successor, Kim Jong Il. It has become increasingly isolated following changes in the former Soviet Union and in its relationship with China. North Korea's military and nuclear stance is of concern to its neighbors and the world as a possible destabilizing force in the region. The effectiveness of a negotiated agreement with the United States in October 1994, to curtail nuclear weapons development by North Korea and its implementation remains to be seen. With poor agricultural harvests in 1995 and 1996 and the deepening food shortage, possible changes in its international behavior and political future are open to speculation.

Economic reform in China, Vietnam, and Laos requires new policies. The question is whether such changes will lead to future political liberalization and pluralism. In China, for example, among the needed changes is the development of laws and institutions to accommodate international commerce. The introduction of market mechanisms and restructuring of the state sector will bring hardship and discontent. With the growth of private enterprise, traditional controls on internal migration through household registrations are fading. The economic disparity between the wealthier eastern coastal provinces and those of the poorer interior has resulted in demands for different national economic policies and priorities. As a result of increasing provincial independence, regionalism has increased with the central government trying in recent years to reassert its control. The relationship between Beijing and the provinces is important to watch as it may affect the course of future political changes.

With about 70 percent of its population still living in rural areas, few political changes in China will occur without this strong base of support. The majority of Chinese citizens place a high value on political and social order to insure security and freedom from corrupt, unjust, and arbitrary regulations and authority. In such a setting, they can work and provide a decent living for their families. In China, societal order and economic security have always been important in maintaining stability.

China has never had a democratic tradition, thus, its people lack a fundamental understanding of what constitutes a democracy. Such a concept will take time to evolve, which requires, very importantly, the development of institutions based on laws rather than on the personalities of individual rulers. Despite counterclaims, personal freedoms in China have increased in recent years. Improvement in living standards will bring even more changes. Along with economic growth, China is an emerging global power and commands increased attention in the world. The transition to a new generation of leaders began about three years before the death on February 19, 1997, of Deng Xiaoping, the paramount leader who launched China's economic modernization in 1978. This group has formed a collective leadership that will rule in the future, with Party Chief and President Jiang Zemin as its dominant head. China's economic and political evolution is only just beginning. Change with stability is important as political chaos in China can easily destabilize both the region and the world.

Myanmar has a military government that rules over the country. It did not honor the results of the election it organized in 1990 and continues to restrict any opposition to its rule. Japan was transformed into a democracy after World War II. Other countries in this region have grown rapidly with authoritarian, but enlightened, governments that maintained stability and focused on economic growth. Asia has always placed collective welfare and social order above individual interests. With a growing middle class, people are developing political awareness and becoming personally involved in politics. South Korea and Taiwan provide examples of places that have experienced recent political evolution with attendant liberalization and pluralism. A military coup in 1992 in Thailand was negated through public demonstrations forcing the return of an elected civilian government.

A more confident, assertive region maintains that the West should not impose its definition of democracy and human rights on others. As with the environment, East and Southeast Asian countries are suspicious that various issues, such as "labor rights," are raised under the banner of "human rights" by Western industrialized countries to curtail Asia's comparative advantage while protecting their own markets from competition (Crovitz 1994: 20–21). Political change is under way with concomitant expanding personal freedoms and political liberalization. The final results and how they compare with Western definitions of democracy and human rights remain to be seen.

There are still areas of potential conflict and concern in this region. Examples include the smoldering disputes over offshore territories, such as the Spratly Islands in the South China Sea, the relationship between China and Taiwan, the role of North Korea, and ethnic issues within some countries. In geopolitical terms, China is a growing regional and global power with interests and concerns that must be considered. The countries in this region recognize that peace and political stability are important for their own continued economic growth. The overwhelming majority of them see the United States as a stabilizing force in the region and want its continued engagement in all areas—economics, politics, and the military.

## Conclusion

Both East Asia and Southeast Asia have experienced rapid economic growth, improving the livelihood of millions of their citizens. Along with this accomplishment come the challenges posed by changing societal institutions, increased urbanization, a rising demand for resources, and environmental concerns. With their growing affluence and confidence, these countries will experience more economic cooperation, an enhanced investment flow, and greater inter- and intraregional trade. As exports continue to add to their economic betterment, it is reasonable to expect them, especially those that are better developed, to play their role in contributing to global trade and economic growth. Australia and New Zealand are reorienting themselves to this region, away from their traditional British ties. The eastern portions of Russia can expand economic relationships with this region through countries bordering them. India has begun its economic reform and should increase its traditional ties to East and Southeast Asia.

If peace and political stability continues, the potential for this region and that of most of Asia is great. The key ingredient to maintaining economic dynamism is the ability of its constituent economies to continually restructure, innovate, and modernize, keeping pace with rapid global changes. Optimism for this region and the rest of Asia, therefore, must be tempered with the question of whether these countries are able to rise to the challenge.

# References

Chang, Stephen S. 1990. "China and the Economic Future of Hong Kong." *Philippine Geographical Journal* 34:77–81.

Crovitz, L. Gordon. 1994. "'Nobody Elects the Press': Mahathir Speaks Out on Media, Culture, and Trade." *Far Eastern Economic Review,* April 7:20–21.

*The Economist.* 1993a. "The Lost Girls." September 18–24:38.

_____. 1993b. "Riddle of East Asia's Success: Economic Miracle or Myth?" October 2–8:41–42.

_____. 1993c. "A Survey of Asia: A Billion Consumers." October 30–November 5:62.

Fairclough, Gordon, and Rodney Tasker. 1994. "Thailand: Separate and Unequal." *Far Eastern Economic Review,* April 14:22–23.

*Far Eastern Economic Review.* 1994. *Asia 1994 Yearbook.* Hong Kong: Far Eastern Economic Review.

_____. 1995. *Asia 1995 Yearbook.* Hong Kong: Far Eastern Economic Review.

_____. 1996. *Asia 1996 Yearbook.* Hong Kong: Far Eastern Economic Review.

_____. 1997. *Asia 1997 Yearbook.* Hong Kong: Far Eastern Economic Review.

Goldstein, Carl. 1994. "Are We There Yet? China Dangles Midway Between Statism and Capitalism." *Far Eastern Economic Review,* July 7:60–61.

Hicks, George, and J. A. C. Mackie. 1994. "Overseas Chinese a Question of Identity: Despite Media Hype, They Are Firmly Settled in Southeast Asia." *Far Eastern Economic Review,* July 14:46–48.

Holloway, Nigel. 1997. "Now's Your Chance: U.S. Consumer-Goods Firms Gird for ASEAN Single Market." *Far Eastern Economic Review,* January 30:48–49.

McGurn, William. 1997. "City Limits. In Cover Story: Urbanization." *Far Eastern Economic Review,* February 6:34–37.

Population Census Office. 1993. *1990 Population Census of the People's Republic of China.* Beijing: China Statistical Publishing House.

Population Reference Bureau. 1996. *1996 World Population Data Sheet.* Washington, D.C.: Population Reference Bureau.

Schwarz, Adam. 1993a. "Banking on Diversity. In Focus: Environment in Asia." *Far Eastern Economic Review,* October 28:55–58.

_____. 1993b. "Looking Back at Rio. In Focus: Environment in Asia." *Far Eastern Economic Review,* October 28:48–52.

Silverman, Gary. 1995. "Honour Thy Father. In Cover Story: Ageing Asia." *Far Eastern Economic Review,* March 2:50–52.

Spencer, Joseph E. 1973. *Oriental Asia: Themes Towards a Geography.* Englewood Cliffs, N.J.: Prentice-Hall.

Tyler, Patrick E. 1994a. "The Dynamic New China Still Races Against Time." *New York Times,* January 2, Section 4:4.

_____. 1994b. "Nature and Economic Boom Devouring China's Farmland." *New York Times,* March 27, Section 1:1, 4.

Wang, Gungwu. 1991. *China and the Chinese Overseas.* Singapore: Time Academic Press.

World Bank. 1993. *The East Asian Miracle.* New York: Oxford University Press.

_____. 1994. *World Development Report 1994.* New York: Oxford University Press.

_____. 1996. *World Development Report 1996.* New York: Oxford University Press.

Zhao, Songqiao. 1994. *The Geography of China.* New York: Wiley.

# 13 Sub-Saharan Africa: Problems, Progress, and Potentials

## Harold A. Fisher

### Introductory Overview

As the end of the century nears, African nations south of the Sahara Desert face discouraging and complex development problems. Recently, however, some encouraging signs have begun emerging.

Population explosion, rapid urbanization, poor infrastructures, high unemployment, massive debts, dictator or one-party governments, ethnic conflicts, wars, migration, famine, disease, low education, and other factors make the area one of crisis. Combined, these problems represent a widening gap in developmental progress between the region and more developed nations.

On the encouraging side, efforts are being made to strengthen infrastructures, improve education and health standards, embrace family planning, adopt new economic programs, liberalize political structures, and move toward democracy. Such advances are uneven and hampered by physical features, history and tradition, ethnic differences, debt, and political conditions. To date, the positive developments, while encouraging, do not dispel doubts that Sub-Saharan Africa (SSA) can some day catch up with the rest of the world. For the near future, the countries of this region must exert efforts to keep from falling farther behind other areas of the world.

Anyone wishing to grasp SSA's economic and political problems, which bridle its developmental progress, must first have a basic understanding of the physical features and the peoples who inhabit the countries of the region.

## The Physical Environment

Geographical features and natural resources affect SSA's progress toward development. As Map 13.1 shows, the region covers a vast area. Sub-Saharan Africa straddles the equator and extends north-south 3,600 miles and east-west over 4,200 miles, covering roughly the area between the Tropics of Cancer and Capricorn and encompassing a land mass larger than Canada and the United States combined. Depending on which island nations are included, the region covers up to fifty countries south of the northernmost tier of Arab nations: Egypt, Libya, Tunisia, Algeria, Morocco, and Western Sahara. Although some authors consider the Sudan as part of SSA, it is under Arab rule and is considered as part of the Middle East in this book.

### Physical Features

The region's outstanding relief features are broad plateaus, some found at high altitudes, and wide open-plain savannas or "bush country." The east is split by the Great Rift Valley, which extends from the Red Sea near the Horn to the Zambezi River in Mozambique. An eastern fissure runs across southern Ethiopia and Kenya. The larger western rift branches into Uganda, Tanzania, Zambia, and Malawi. A savanna-like region called the Sahel sprawls across most of the width of the continent just south of the Sahara. The Namib-Kalahari Desert ranges along the coast of Angola and Namibia, extends into South Africa and centers in Botswana. In South Africa, the Okavango Delta separates the Etosha Pan and Makarikari salt basins. Western equatorial SSA features rain forests and plateaus (World Bank 1997a; Oxford Press 1996a).

The Great Rift provides ample evidence of volcanic activity. Major mountain peaks, such as Mt. Kenya (16,334 feet) and Mt. Kilimanjaro (18,520 feet), jut up from near the valley floor and remain snowcapped year-round. The mile-deep Ngorogoro Crater in Tanzania testifies to a massive prehistoric eruption. Volcanism is also evident in the Ruwenzoris of central Africa, in Mt. Cameroon in the western equatorial region, with some activity in Ethiopia and on the islands of Reunion and the Comoros. A chain of large lakes, including Lakes Turkana, Albert, Tanganyika, and Nyasa, extend north-south along the western Great Rift floor. Five great river basins drain the region: the Nile, Congo, Niger, Zambezi, and Orange rivers all empty into oceans.

### Physical Resources

Marked differences in water, land, and mineral resources between the SSA countries affect their economies, development, and even politics.

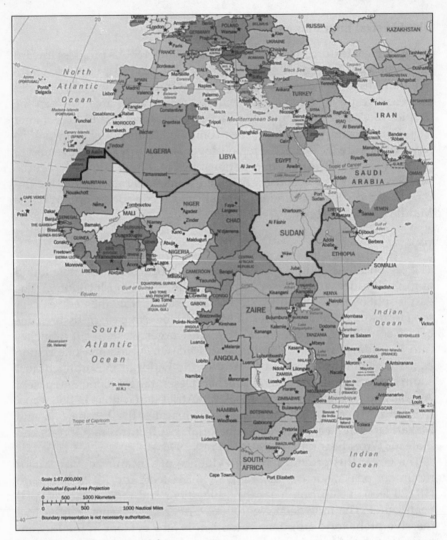

MAP 13.1    Sub-Saharan Africa

*Rainfall and Water Resources.*    Differences in rainfall vary widely across
the entire region. Annual rainfall ranges from less than 10 inches yearly
near the Sahara Desert and in the Kalahari district to 80 inches in the
equatorial region. Runoff is highest in the lower basins of the Niger and
Zaire rivers.

Lack of water resources is one of the region's most serious problems.
Overall water supply for the region is not immediately critical in most areas; with about 10 percent of the world's population, the region still has

around 15 percent of the world's available water. However, rainfall is erratic and undependable, leaving large areas arid, with insufficient water to sustain life during droughts. In the 1980s and early 1990s and again in 1997, droughts led to lost crops, famine, mass migration, starvation and death of thousands in Ethiopia and eastern Africa. In marginal tilled areas, "salinization . . . ranks among the most serious problems" (Allan and Warren 1993, 98). Nonetheless, overall food production is rising, thanks to expansion of cropland. About 7 percent of SSA is now in cropland, with continuing expansion. It is the only world region where expansion of cropland contributes nearly as much as yield increases of cereal production (Oxford University Press 1996b, 226–231).

Lack of water for food production is compounded by its poor drinking quality. According to UNICEF, 38 percent of people in SSA rural areas had access to safe drinking water; for the remainder, water is usually unfit for human consumption, leading to numerous diseases and infections (UNICEF 1994, 6).

*Land Resources.*   Nearly three-fourths of the region's people are farmers, but only some 7 percent of the area is utilized. However, the expansion of cropland may be the fastest in the world. Overall, its yields are easily the world's lowest. While some land is fertile, especially in the Rift Valley, South Africa, and parts of the west, most soils are not highly productive. Especially in west Africa, farmers must resort to "slash and burn" tactics to restore nutrients to the soil, a process in which land is allowed to lie fallow several years, after which the growth is torched to provide nutrients to provide one good harvest. Large expanses of rocky or bush country with light rainfall are suitable only for grazing.

Desertification, an increasingly serious problem, is spreading in the Sahel and the Horn of Africa, and in the Namib and Kalahari, where the raising of cattle is a mark of wealth. Overgrazing, drought, and a rapidly growing population that uses remaining trees for fuelwood all lead to soil degradation and further reduction of grazing animals the land can carry.

The United Nations Environmental Programme indicates that soil degradation derives from (1) deforestation, (2) overgrazing, (3) increased agricultural activity, (4) overexploitation of vegetation such as fuelwood for domestic use, and (5) bio-industrial activities (UNEP 1992). All but the last apply to SSA. Wind and water erosion speed the process. But the chief contributor is overgrazing due to sedentarization of nomadic herders. As a result, desertification is steadily marching southward from the Sahara, in some areas as much as 30 miles annually. Allan and Warren estimate that "a wide strip south of the Sahara . . . may be desert in 30–40 years" (1993, 97).

*Forests.* Tropical rain forests, once a prominent feature of the equatorial region, are disappearing at an alarming rate because of land clearing for agriculture, population growth, urbanization, use of firewood for cooking, and export logging. Tropical forest destruction is greater only in Latin America. But the region still contains well over one million square miles of forests which could be used to manufacture forest products.

*Mineral Resources.* The greatest concentration of mineral resources are found in the zone from Zaire to South Africa. Although unevenly distributed, they are, in general, statistically sufficient to aid development, but less so than in some other developing regions of the world.

Minerals found in greatest abundance include copper, iron ore, gypsum, and ferrochromium, with gold, diamonds, and bauxite the richest resources. Uranium, lithium, platinum, manganese, vanadium, and cobalt also exist. Africa produces approximately 41 percent of the world's diamonds, 39 percent of the world's cobalt, 31 percent of its gold; and 18 percent of its uranium (U.S. Dept. of Interior 1993). The United States gets 40 percent of its manganese from Africa, which is also its fourth-largest source of oil (National Geographic Society 1992).

## The Peoples of Sub-Saharan Africa

Archeological discoveries establish that the earliest humanoids in Africa go back over four million years and that the region was populated by great civilizations as it developed. Today SSA's population totals 597 million, with projections that it will reach 867 million by 2010 and nearly 1,250 million by 2025 (Population Reference Bureau 1996). Each of the fifty major indigenous languages is spoken by more than a million persons. Additionally, up to an estimated 1,000 ethnic languages, most unwritten, are spoken by less than a million people. Many Africans also speak European colonial languages, such as English or French.

### The Early Past: Cradle of Sub-Saharan Civilizations

Dr. Louis Leakey and his family discovered remains in eastern Africa of the oldest human creatures, called Zinjanthropus, who used crude tools and ate nuts and fruits. Later, traces of their descendants were found in South Africa. By 4000 B.C., Hamites occupied the then-fertile Sahara and Sahel areas in the north, with Negroid peoples in the southern region. In the New Stone Age, these early humans were hunters, herders, and farmers.

Scholars agree that the Bantu or Negro cultures probably originated in western Africa (now Nigeria and Cameroon), expanded gradually across the continent eastward to present-day Kenya and south toward the Cape of Good Hope. They were primarily pastoralists and hoe-cultivators. By the beginning of the Christian era, they were settling in small village communities with family or village elder leaders. As these communities grew, division of labor and new social forms developed. Kingships and even some powerful empires arose.

### Rise and Influence of Great SSA Civilizations

Great civilizations, kingdoms, and empires have flourished throughout SSA's more recent history. In several regions, kingdoms emerged during the first millennium A.D. because of ethnic migrations, trade, and expanded chiefdoms. These kingdoms exhibited increased division of labor, class distinctions, and the rise of central government. Common to all were tribal loyalties, limited technologies, and a conservatism hostile to inventive change.

One of the earliest was Ethiopia's Kingdom of Kush which arose about 1000 B.C. and existed as a powerful nation for a millennium. During the same period, the powerful Nok culture thrived in what is now northern Nigeria. Ghana in the western Sahel became the first of several medieval empires in the eleventh century. It was followed by the shorter-lived empires of Mali, Songhay, Kanem-Bornu, and the Hausa states. About 1400 A.D., the kingdoms of Guinea emerged in the coastal regions of western Africa; notable among them were the Yoruba, Ibo, Akan, and Wolof kings, and the empire of Benin.

In the seventh century A.D., Bantu people in eastern Africa migrated south of the equatorial forests with skills in farming and iron making to form powerful nation-states, such as the Kongo Kingdom and ancient Zimbabwe in southern Africa. From them, several kingdoms arose in southern Africa. The southern Bantus then formed entire states, out of which grew the Zulu empire in the early nineteenth century. The Bantu cultures were altered by regional differences in ecology, trading across the continent for commodities such as salt and gold, and the influx of Arab cultures from the north and Asian influences from the Indian Ocean. Despite these diversities, Bantu attitudes and beliefs have remained basically similar during the past 1,500 years (Davidson 1989, 9).

### Sub-Saharan African Peoples Today

Early migrations led to ethnic diversity and a linguistic polyglot, which is reflected in today's many ethnic groups. Despite their diversity, nearly all ethnic groups hold two characteristics in common—a strong extended family and respect for elders. However, impacts of modernity are making inroads into these strengths. Since independence, changing social patterns are impacting all the peoples of the entire region.

*Religion.*   Belief in gods and spirits have long characterized SSA peoples. Today, many still cling to animistic beliefs. Others worship a benevolent god; in Kenya, for example, a beneficent god Ngei dwells atop Mt. Kenya. The primitive religions made them amenable to the appeals of faiths brought by Muslims and Christians. Christianity first appeared in Ethiopia early in the Christian era. During colonial times, missionaries established churches, schools, and hospitals throughout the SSA region, winning many to their Catholic and Protestant faiths. Today, Christianity continues to grow. Pentecostalism, by its invocation of spirits, is rapidly gaining new adherents. Islam began its conquest for followers about 800 A.D., as Muslims spread southward in west Africa and into the Horn and southward along the Indian Ocean. As with Christianity, its teaching of submission to a sovereign God has attracted numerous converts, especially in west Africa.

## Colonial Legacies

After the 1880s, European colonial powers expanded into SSA, bringing changes, the effects of which still persist. They often ignored African ethnic boundaries as they carved out new national entities. In most cases, Africans were made subservient to their rule. Davidson says the new divisions "erected artificial boundaries that still cause violent disputes" (1989, 11). But the colonial powers also brought some beneficial change and progress. They "brought the beginnings of modern transportation and communication systems, increased contacts with the outside world, introduced the civil service system in which selected Africans participated, expanded external markets for basic raw materials, and improved education and medical conditions for some" (Fisher 1988, 231).

Sometimes the negative effects of colonialism appear to outweigh positive benefits. Agunga points out that the colonial relationship was marked by domination and exploitation, the desire to provide material and human resources for themselves, and mercantilism and "laissez faire" profit-motivated free trade. But exploitation was not "only one-way. . . . The mother countries also provided protection and the provision of basic services, such as schools and health centers from the colonizers" (1997, 26). There is little doubt, however, that colonial policies tended to make the Africans dependent on the colonizers.

Certain repercussions of colonialism have lingered after independence. For example, to satisfy colonial demands for raw materials, roads and railways almost invariably went from inland to ports, with few cross linkages. Rail gauges often differed, sometimes even within colonial territories. Villages were left isolated. Today's rail systems of Zambia, Zaire, Nigeria, Sierra Leone, Mali, Togo, and Senegal all reflect this phenomenon. In Liberia, multinational corporations built transport systems to export rubber and iron ore that had little relationship to the nation's internal development. Ake (1996) calls this haphazard development of transport systems "disarticulation." Such conditions prevail today partly because new nations lack financial resources to build better systems or fail to plan well.

Communication infrastructures—telephony, telex, microwave, broadcasting technologies—were also often built for colonial needs rather than improving African exchange of information. Telephoning a neighboring country required connecting through London or Paris. Today, the region's telecommunication infrastructures remain among the world's poorest; however, African governments and international corporations are cooperating to correct such problems. The greatest media concentration still prevails in cities; media distribution systems often do not reach villages, contributing to rural isolation.

Colonialism's policies reflected a lack of identification with their African subjects. Colonial overlords generally ignored the traditions of bazaar trading, failed to build up the indigenous merchant class or to utilize skilled indigenous craftsmen, and provided little labor specialization—all of which are reflected in present-day slowness to industrialize. Nor did they provide appropriate agricultural technologies or use cultivatable land or mineral resources efficiently, the price for which Africans are still paying.

The colonial powers also fostered economic dependence by encouraging a single export commodity and discouraging founding of local industries. Their legal structures clashed with indigenous forms of justice; their monetary systems promoted dependence on Western currency. Even worse, they failed to provide adequate training for development after independence, a deficiency that led many Africans to seek overseas education, which often was poorly adaptable to national development needs. This in turn often resulted in a "brain drain" of potential leadership. Unfortunately, some African nations have been slow to correct such technological and economic deficiencies to meet their own needs and progress.

### Cultural and Social Conditions

Social conditions vary widely across SSA countries, depending on the tightly intertwined histories, economics, and political backgrounds of each nation. Ethnic strife, civil wars, refugees, availability of natural and economic resources, differences in educational opportunities, health care

and problems, political policies and leadership are among the forces that
impinge on social conditions. But the greatest social impacts in SSA have
stemmed from a burgeoning population explosion, rapid urbanization,
and an AIDS epidemic.

*The Population Explosion.* In 1996, SSA's natural population growth was
reported to be 2.9 percent per annum, down from earlier estimates but
still high compared with other regions of the world (Population Reference Bureau 1996). The 1997 *World Bank Atlas* indicates ten SSA countries
had more than a 3 percent annual growth in 1996: Congo, Djibouti, Gambia, Ivory Coast, Madagascar, Malawi, Niger, Swaziland, Tanzania, and
Zaire, while most of the other SSA nations have a per annum increase of
between 2.5 and 3.0 percent (World Bank 1997a, 10). Like all lesser-devel-
oped areas, SSA countries are young. In 1996, the median age was 17
years, in contrast to 36 years for developed nations; by USAID projections, the median will be only 19 years in 2020, compared to 42 for developed areas (USAID 1996, 20). Thanks to better health standards, people
in the region are living longer; however, life expectancy remains far behind much of the world. Estimates for 1995 show that the average person
will live less than 55 years in twenty-eight countries, and between 55 and
64 years for another eleven. Only Botswana has a life expectancy over 65
years—a contrast to the 75-plus years for the United States, Canada, and
western Europe (USAID 1996, 12).

Although population growths are slowing, statistics predict the populations of twenty-four countries in the region will double their numbers
within the next quarter century as health measures improve, infant mortality falls, and life expectancy increases. Although current estimates indicate
the region's present population of nearly 600 million will increase to nearly
one and a quarter billion by 2020, the inroads of the AIDS epidemic may
slow that increase (Population Reference Bureau 1996). However, SSA will
remain "the region with the highest growth rates during the coming 25-
year period" (USAID 1996, 10). That prediction is supported by the fact
that SSA women have high fertility rates—in 1996, women in twenty-three
countries had four to six babies on average, with no country averaging under three births per woman. The population explosion contains strong economic and political implications. Hanley notes that "basic resources are being depleted and environmental pollution is intensifying as a result of
unprecedented population growth" (1994, A3). Darnton (1994) says economics will have to move full steam ahead just to avoid standing still because of the population explosion. Carr-Hill (1990) observes that, although
agricultural production has been improving, the rapid growth is bringing
a steady decline in per capita food availability that could lead to malnutrition, hunger, and even famine.

This situation demands strong measures to slow population growth. At present rates of increase, for example, Nigeria's 104 million people will rise to 162 million by 2025, Ethiopia's 57 million will be 90 million, and Kenya's 28 million will reach 49 million (Population Reference Bureau 1996). With increased numbers of young women of childbearing age, birth control measures must improve and fertility rates must come down. Hanley (1994) says population growth can be stabilized only if births come down to two per couple and crash educational programs are mounted to accomplish this goal.

*Rapid Urbanization.* The rapid population growth coupled with migration from rural areas has swelled SSA's cities. Heavy rural migration to urban centers began in the 1960s. A rough positive correlation of population increase and rate of urbanization exists. Annual urban growth, long at 6 percent, was down to 4.8 percent between 1990 and 1995 and is predicted to be 4 percent for the next quarter century. USAID projects that the SSA region will increase at the most rapid rate of all regions of the world, "growing from 31% urban today to 48% by the year 2020" (USAID 1996, 22).

Today, slums and shantytowns with minimal services surround every city. Millions live in windowless shacks, often without electricity and amid open sewers and piled-up garbage. Most get their drinking water, often polluted, from communal standpipes. A high percentage of these dwellers come from rural villages, seeking work. Relatives frequently provide free food and lodging for them; however, a tacit agreement usually exists that if a job is not secured within a specified period, the unemployed must return to the village.

Stren and White (1989), after study of urbanization in seven SSA nations, listed major factors that influence city growth: rural exodus, population growth, drought, adverse trade for exporters of agricultural goods, and domestic policies that favor urbanites over rural residents. Other forces that draw people to cities include construction activities, better education and health facilities, job opportunities, and the bright lights.

The speedy growth has produced chronic problems for urban governments. Burdened by heavy national debt, national governments turn urban maintenance over to city administrators, who may lack managerial capacity and financial resources. Stren and White also found that most governments no longer provide "free services to the poor (such as standpipes) and the middle-class (subsidized housing), leaving individuals and communities to meet their own needs" (1989, 19). This leads to profiteering. In Nigeria, most urbanites buy water from private sellers at ten times the cost of piped water. Water from a donkey cart in Nouakchott, Mauritania, costs thirty times that from the mains.

Sanitation measures vary widely from city to city; in Dar es Salaam, for example, only 15 percent of urbanites are connected to the central sewage system. Other urban problems include the failure of public transport; private taxis, minibuses, and vans now carry half of all passengers—at higher cost. Public housing schemes have had to be supplemented by corporation and individual housing. In every case, the poor have suffered the most.

*Diseases and Health Care.*   In the 1960s and 1970s, newly independent countries were building clinics, vaccinating children, and educating citizens about health care. In the 1980s, as national debts rose, health services declined. In 1994, Darnton claimed nearly one-third of SSA children were severely malnourished. Because of poor health education and social conditions, infant mortality remains high; in 1996, the rate was 96 deaths per 1,000 in the first year of children's lives (Population Reference Bureau 1996). More resistant strains of malaria, tuberculosis, diarrhea, cholera, yellow fever, and meningitis are striking children and even older people.

The Human Immunodeficiency Virus (HIV) and an AIDS (Acquired Immune Deficiency Syndrome) crisis of catastrophic proportions are adding to SSA's social burdens. Estimates of the number infected by the virus, which is spread mostly by heterosexual contact, vary widely. According to World Health Organization data, in 1996 there were about 440 thousand reported cases of AIDS; however, many go unreported. Already in 1995, estimates of cases were over three million. In addition, there were over 14 million HIV cases in the region in 1996, two-thirds of the world's total and three million more than reported in 1995 (National Research Council 1996).

HIV/AIDS were first detected in 1982 in Uganda; by 1989, all districts had reported cases. Men and women were equally affected. By 1990, an increasing number of babies were born HIV-positive. In Tanzania, a Dar es Salaam University 1994 study reported 24 percent of adults were HIV-positive and 19 percent of pregnant women infected with AIDS (Flint 1994). The epidemic has struck hardest in eastern Africa and in the Ivory Coast. HIV infections have produced a new class of poor—orphans under ten years old, many of whom are forced to live on the streets or who become wards of older siblings because parents have died of AIDS. Experts predict growth of AIDS "will slow, but not halt, population growth in affected countries because most AIDS mortality occurs after the age of childbearing" (USAID 1996, 46). Ironically, while the disease is slowing population growth, it further burdens the debt-ridden economies of the region.

*Educational Disparities.*   After independence, most SSA states increased expenditures on education. Kenya, for example, put one-third of its budget into education; however, it faced an uphill battle due to population growth, overcrowded classrooms, and lack of trained teachers (Fisher 1988). Other national governments want to provide universal primary education. There has been a dramatic increase in the number of teachers. Such efforts have markedly reduced illiteracy; in 1994, only fourteen countries topped 60 percent, with three—South Africa, Mauritius, and Madagascar—reporting less than 20 percent (Sivard 1994). In 1996, while the region was still the world's lowest in educational attainment, it was making "rapid progress in its educational achievements, especially in girl enrollees" (Tarver 1996, 206).

Secondary schools lack resources for effective training. In the past, African universities provided training for civil service. But cash-strapped governments can only minimally finance them. However, universities are responding to the challenge to provide the practical training needed for development by raising funds through higher tuition, renting facilities, and tapping alumni for donations (Morna 1995). At a time of rapid population growth, training of professionals, technicians, and managers is especially needed, as well as basic education in hygiene, health, family planning, sex education, and budgeting.

*The Rural Scene.* About three-fourths of Sub-Saharans are subsistence farmers or villagers. Little of their produce goes to urban markets, but it comprises the bulk of national food supply because large farms and corporate farming are limited. With greater urbanization, demand and consumption patterns are changing. Other food production variables include differences in soil quality and rainfall. As a result, three types of food inadequacy exist in the region—malnutrition, seasonal hunger, and famine.

Between 1961 and 1994, food production per capita fell, but by 1996, cropland expansion was changing the equation. This recent expansion of cropland is now contributing as much as yield increases of cereal production. Per capita food production is again rising. However, the potential of cropland expansion to meet burgeoning population growth is limited by high costs of developing areas that are usually not prime cropland capable of producing heavy yields (Oxford University Press 1996b, 231). Better farming practices and distribution systems are clearly still needed for healthy sustained development.

## Economies of Sub-Saharan Nations: Debts and Recovery Efforts

Nearly all Sub-Saharan countries entered independence with barely viable economies. Most had and still have a single raw material export commodity and weak industries, weaknesses that precipitate deficit spending and huge debts.

*The Deficit Crisis*

SSA countries began their independence at an economic disadvantage. Most colonial overlords had exported a single commodity for their own industries, paid little for raw materials, failed to develop indigenous industries, imposed expensive infrastructures, and neglected to train African entrepreneurs and economists. African governments compounded the economic woes by poor planning and management. Drought, wars, refugees, migration, disease, and poverty added to their problems. Slow agricultural growth, poor import-export balances, eroding social conditions, and inflation all contributed to a growing economic crisis.

The result: spiraling debts, which rose from $5 billion in 1970 to $174 billion in 1990. By 1987, the SSA nations had accrued a debt of nearly $129 billion, more than their collective gross national product. By 1990, they were making debt payments of over $20 billion to creditor nations annually (Agunga 1997, 72). By 1994, only nine countries had an external debt less than their GNP (World Bank 1996). Economic growth was not keeping up with population expansion.

But the situation is changing. By 1995, the World Bank was saying that in SSA, "there was positive per capita growth for the first time in many years, associated with trade gains and better policies in a growing number of countries" (World Bank 1997a, 28). By 1995, two countries, South Africa and Gabon, were ranked in the upper-middle income class with per capita GNPs over $3,036, four more in the lower-middle income class of $766 to $3,035, and thirty-four other SSA nations with per capita GNPs of less than $765 annual income.

As the long slide had progressed, two major studies gave divergent advice. The 1979 Lagos Plan, an African approach, recommended long-range recovery through economic self-reliance, regional integration, and de-emphasizing exports. The Berg Plan urged more exports, maximized profits, and free trade. In 1986, the United Nations adopted a program that combined international aid to relieve crises and the responsibility of African governments to assist.

*Structural Adjustment*

In the worsening economic crisis, the longest in the Third World, the SSA nations sought help from the World Bank (WB) and the International Monetary Fund (IMF). Both bodies advised strict economic "structural adjustment" with donor loans based on free market enterprise and minimal African interference as the escape from deep debt. Their prescription: reduce state intervention in markets, impose financial discipline, free up prices, and promote exports. Some African leaders perceived the remedy as neocolonialistic. But they had few alternatives. So, beginning in 1980, at least thirty SSA countries adopted IMF stabilization policies or WB structural adjustment programs.

The rigorous WB and IMF programs proved to be financially rigorous and difficult for nations already under heavy debt. Both programs sparked hot debate. Critics said the donors were "calling the shots" (Lewis 1994, 48), or the programs were a tragedy. They listed damaging effects to Africans: increased inequality of incomes and reliance on export of primary products. The World Bank, on the other hand, cited improvements in countries that pursued currency devaluation, trade liberalization, and fiscal restraint. It listed six nations that were making "large improvements" in the 1980s under structural adjustments. Critics vociferously called those programs disasters. In the early 1990s, several countries that had adopted either the WB or IMF programs, according to the critics, either "deteriorated" or made only small improvements. Some nations even abandoned the programs or fulfilled only portions of them (Lewis 1994).

Several developments in 1995 and 1996 signaled the beginnings of an economic turnaround for many SSA countries. Part of the good news came from agriculture, which "accounts for about 35 percent of total GDP, 40 percent of exports, and 70 percent of employment" across the region (World Bank 1997b, 48). Southern Africa had excellent rains. Commodity prices for Africa's exports were higher, resulting in a 5.7 percent expansion of exports. Grassroots credit unions developed. Military expenditures slowly fell. Perhaps most important, donor agencies agreed to intensify their efforts for the region's development. The World Bank has been studying systematic participatory approaches, development of indigenous human resources, and has held a hunger workshop. These and other factors combined to bring higher GDPs; in at least fifteen countries GDP grew by 5 percent or more in 1995, with rates of over 10 percent in four—Angola, Lesotho, Malawi, and Uganda. On the negative side, declines were still registered in eight countries. However, the improvements have not yet been sufficient to make significant reductions in poverty. GDP and export growth rates, savings and investment levels, and social indicators all remain below other regions of the world.

Perhaps hope for enduring economic reforms lies in a combination of greater commitment by African policymakers to economic growth, provision of a better environment for the private sector, indigenous support of sustainable participatory development, and more flexible and generous international aid agency prescriptions.

That is already happening in an increasing number of SSA nations. Benno Ndulu of the African Economic Research Consortium cites five recent encouraging economic policy developments in SSA: (1) moves toward a more open and market-oriented approach to managing economies; (2) liberalization of political systems; (3) the rising influence of economic technocrats; (4) growing donor dispositions to give recipients more say in aid strategies; and (5) an increased media role in heightening public awareness of economic policy issues (Ndulu 1997, 5).

## Political Development

The independence gained by most SSA countries in the 1960s and 1970s freed them from direct political dominance by colonial powers. Their new governance and political structures moved to various forms of autocracy, such as one-party states or dictatorial regimes, to socialism and more recently to, first, tentative steps, then strides toward democracy. As the new states formed their political structures, they had to overcome glaring weaknesses: frequent use of ethnic divisions by colonial powers; strong cultural and tribal differences; fragile business, industrial, and communication infrastructures; and their own inexperience with and training in statesmanship. In many new SSA countries, Africans had been privileged to hold lower civil service positions under the colonial powers.

### *Early Self-Rule: Political Struggles and Weak Governance*

Kunz (1991) indicates that, until recently, SSA independent statehood was "state-centric"; state consolidation had priority. Early strong leaders, such as Kenyatta, Kaunda, and at first, Banda worked to unify their diverse new nations and to gain greater political and cultural freedom. Others, like Nyerere, championed grassroots socialism, which seemed attractive as an outgrowth of the tribe or extended family. Most early leaders were educated elites who led liberation movements and initially gained internal unity.

But expectations turned to disappointment. Governance in most countries was too weak, too poorly organized, or lacked the economic power to succeed. Numerous development problems swamped inexperienced leaders. Desire for power possessed others. Frequently, the base of trained leadership was too small. Consequently, the states often became more authoritarian, lessening their will to risk volatile political adjustments to bring progress (Lewis 1994). The new governments' inability to resolve problems resulting from ethnic wars, refugees, droughts, population growth, urbanization, lack of industrialization, and mounting debts only led to further cycles of distrust of government, coups d'état, and chaos. Each new nation had its own combination of foibles.

### *Moves Toward Democracy*

Amid SSA's economic and political woes, popular desire for democratic reforms has been growing since independence. Multiple political parties have appeared in many states. Over half have held or have promised multiparty elections. In 1992, Decalo concluded that most democratic advances were still embryonic and had a long way to go to prove themselves. That is changing, but experts caution that full democracy still lies in the future.

*Defining "Democracy" in the SSA Setting.* To study critical variables that cause political change in SSA, Segal (1996) lists ten economic, social, and political factors, then singles out three quantifiable variables: (1) ideology, (2) leadership, and (3) political succession of leadership. He observes that, since 1988, eight contested elections have produced political successions in Africa (Malawi, Zambia, Madagascar, Benin [twice], South Africa, Mauritius, and Cape Verde). The means of succession include death in office, assassination, coups, electoral succession, power sharing, and civil wars. Electoral successions usually reintroduce opposition leaders. To Segal, the first election after an electoral succession is critical. Power sharing rarely works. He concludes that "weak, poor, ethnically divided states need strong presidencies" (1996, 372) and that better-trained leadership is emerging.

Dr. Adedeji, former executive secretary of the U.N. Economic Commission for Africa, adds that African democracy is not mere pluralism or voting, but "cultivating a culture, a way of life which builds into it accountability, transparency, good governance, integrity, and enables one to arrive at decisions through consultation, through consensus" (Novicki 1993, 59). It thrives by gaining the commitment of people in a diversified economy.

*Moves Toward Democracy: Independence to 1992.* Wiseman says that, since independence, "the failure of authoritarian alternatives has kept democracy alive in the region"(1990, 185). To him, opposition parties have been too divisive, single-party states have failed to produce solutions, and military coups have usually resulted in sacrifice of political rights and freedoms. He cites eighteen states that had experienced periods of multiparty democracy prior to 1990. Among them, Botswana has had continuous democracy since the mid-1960s, and Mali, Gambia, and Mauritius for the full 1970–1990 period. Zimbabwe has had uninterrupted but very limited democracy since its 1980 independence. Other nations experienced periods of democracy interspersed with military or single-party rule. Since 1988, Mali, Malawi, South Africa, Ghana, Mozambique, Burkina Faso, Ethiopia, and Eritrea have made the greatest advances.

*Recent Moves Toward Democracy: 1992–Present.* Several factors have accelerated the democratization process in the early 1990s. Following the colonial model of control, most African nations became authoritarian shortly after independence, but in the early 1990s a "rapid and nearly pervasive implosion of democracy swept across the continent" (Diamond 1994, 50). In 1995, Wiseman identified three factors that have sped demands for multiparty democracy: (1) the end of the Cold War and the fall of communism meant less support for authoritarianism; (2) debts and economic crises led to rejection of absolute political controls; and (3) the mix of styles and social makeup of states led to rejection of harsh political rule in favor in liberalization (1995, 3–6). By 1996, Ake could assure that in Africa there is "a growing realization that there is no alternative to participative development" (1996, 134) and that a strong movement for democracy was in place. Table 13.1 illustrates the recent surge toward democratization.

In the five-year period, 1992 through 1996, at least twenty-seven countries held elections, a "first step" indicator of democracy. The diversity of political histories and the continuum of passage from closed to more open rule make it difficult to precisely categorize advances. However, the trend is clear. Not only has the number of open elections grown rapidly during the past five years, but also an increasing number of states have moved further into the process.

As Table 13.1 shows, at least four countries held their first multiparty elections during the five-year period: Angola (1992), and Guinea-Bissau, Togo, and South Africa (1994). Of the four, South Africa's transition from apartheid rule to self-rule is the most dramatic. Under President Mandela's leadership, significant healing steps are being taken, including a Truth and Reconciliation Commission that forgives confessed aggression against the black majority (Matloff 1997b). Unfortunately, some apartheid offenders are taking advantage of the policy. Sisk declares, "The transition is not an easy one" (1995, 293). Some ethnic rivalry, poverty, inequality, and abuses of free speech persist.

As Table 13.1 further reveals, Malawi (1994) and Ethiopia (1995) held their first open elections after dictatorial rulers. Several countries— Benin, Seychelles, Cameroon, Mauritius, Gabon, and Senegal—opted for solidifying their democracies with peaceful open elections. For others (Ghana, Lesotho, Chad, Gambia, and Sierra Leone), leaders were reelected after they had gained power in coups d'état; the question remains whether they will now feel confident enough to opt for more democratic rule. It appears that Ghana, under President Rawlings, and Benin, under reinstated President Kerekou, are moving toward a more open system. One country, the Central African Republic, was assisted in its bid for open elections by the presence of French troops. In Tanzania and Equatorial Guinea, elections were held, but the opposition charged fraud—a sign that could predict political health or presage strife.

TABLE 13.1   Elections in Major Sub-Saharan Countries, 1992–1996

| 1992 | Angola | First multiparty elections end in renewed civil war. |
|------|--------|------|
| | Cameroon | Pres. Biya reelected; municipal elections due 1997. |
| | Ghana | Pres. Rawlins elected; had seized power in 1979 coup. |
| 1993 | Central African Republic | Pres. Patasse elected with support of French troops. |
| | Seychelles | Open elections held after 13 years of one-party rule. |
| 1994 | Guinea-Bissau | Pres. Vieira won first multiparty election; in power since 1980 coup. |
| | Lesotho | Elections after failed palace coup led to smooth transition to more democratic government. |
| | Malawi | Multiparty elections overturned Banda regime. |
| | Mozambique | Multiparty elections, but FRELIMO, which has ruled since 1975, retained strong influence; opposition weak. |
| | Namibia | After open elections, SWAPO party holds one-party power. |
| | So. Africa | Multiparty elections leading to open democracy with shared power. Peaceful local elections in 1996. |
| | Togo | Successful multiparty elections held. |
| 1995 | Ethiopia | After fall of Communist regime, opposition boycotted elections; ruling EPRDF wins 90% of vote. |
| | Ivory Coast | Elections won by Pres. Bedie; government remains an intolerant one-party state. |
| | Mauritius | Free, fair elections. Moving toward democracy backed by strong economic growth. |
| | Tanzania | Popular elections, but opposition claimed fraud. |
| 1996 | Benin | Open elections held; strong transition to pluralism from dictatorship. |
| | Chad | Pres. Deby won open elections; had come to power in 1990 coup. |
| | East Guinea | Pres. Obiang won election boycotted by opposition. |
| | Gabon | Held successful local elections; government pluralistic. |
| | Gambia | Presidential and legislative elections held late 1996. |
| | Niger | After taking power in January coup, Pres. Mainassara narrowly won elections, despite strong opposition. |
| | Senegal | Successful regional elections; long multiparty rule. |
| | Sierra Leone | Elections held despite earlier military coup. |
| | Uganda | Pres. Museveni won elections, but rejects power sharing. His economic policy is bringing stability. |
| | Zambia | Pres. Chiluba won election after disqualifying most opponents. |
| | Zimbabwe | Pres. Mugabe won national election. His ZANU party, in power since 1980, holds 98% of parliamentary seats. |

NOTE: Does not include successful popular elections of small island nations: Cape Verde in 1991, São Tomé and Príncipe and Comoros. (Compiled from Judith Matloff, "Suddenly Africa's Conflicts Aren't So Local," *Christian Science Monitor,* August 7, 1996, p. 6 and other recent sources.

Less encouraging are those who held multiparty elections, but still find themselves under military or single-party control. Mozambique, Ivory Coast, Namibia, Niger, Uganda, and Zambia all fall in this category (see Table 13.1). Zimbabwe appears to be experiencing a retrogression from earlier freedoms.

Several countries are not considered in Table 13.1, which covers only a limited five-year period. Superficially democratic nations, such as Burkina Faso and the Congo, are holding elections in 1997. Eritrea, independent since 1993, has not declared for elections, but a healthy pro-democracy movement is gathering strength. Swaziland remains a benevolent monarchy.

## Current Problems, Progress, and Prospects

Several Sub-Saharan nations were not cited in Table 13.1 because they made little or no progress toward democracy during the 1992–1996 period. There are also recent encouraging advances within the region and on the part of donor bodies. Yet other countries display retrogression. These changes are leading to fresh assessments of SSA's prospects for democratic rule.

*States Demonstrating Tentative Steps Toward Democracy.* Perhaps the most notable recent struggle has been the civil strife in Zaire, now called the Democratic Republic of the Congo. Conflict had arisen from divergent causes—the rapacious rule of dictator Mobutu Sese Seko; influx of thousands of Hutu refugees fleeing from Rwandan Watutsis; breakdown of civil order; and the rapid advance of a small rebel army led by Laurent Kabila. The army easily captured the capital of Kinshasa as Mobutu fled. Kabila promised elections within a year; however, the jury is still out on whether or how he will honor his word. Many steps must first be taken to prepare for a viable democracy.

Liberia recently held monitored multiparty elections that former rebel leader Charles Taylor won by a wide margin, possibly because of his wealth and help from Nigerian forces. Under Taylor, democracy may be slow to come.

Although still under one-party rule, Uganda is enjoying both a free market economy and many benefits of multiparty democracy under the benevolent leadership of President Yoweri Museveni. There is full freedom of press and speech; radio talk hosts are ruthless but fearless in their criticisms of the government (Santoro 1997). However, rebel teens still cause trouble in the north and the question of how far reforms will go under one-party rule remains. There are encouraging signs that other African leaders will back more open trade.

On the part of donors, there are some strong signs of support for change toward democracy. Late in 1996, the World Bank, IMF, and leading creditor nations initiated a program to forgive up to 80 percent of debts, which have crushed some African states. The first to benefit was Uganda, but help may also go to former socialist nations, as Tanzania and Ethiopia are now courting free markets. The U.S. Congress and administration recently passed the Africa Growth and Opportunity Act to aid nations willing to consider free trade and democracy.

*Problem States.* In some countries, the leadership seems unwilling to share power. Nigeria, under military dictatorship, is besieged with ethnic divisions and rampant corruption. At present, there is little hope for democratic rule. The Kenyan government has become increasingly dictatorial under nineteen years of President arap Moi's rule. He wants to change the constitution so that he can run again. Opposition is growing and violence has erupted. Recently, the National Council of Churches has been asked to mediate. Kenya's once bright future is now dark. Despite a U.N. and American military intervention, Somalia remains a patchwork of ethnic factions. The French military still protects Djibouti citizens.

*Reassessment.* The recent changes—or lack of them—have caused leaders to reassess how conditions for democracy can be improved. USAID chief Brian Atwood believes African freedom and stability depend on deepening economic and political reforms and that continuing donor-supported investments in health, education, and social needs are key to such stability and growth (Atwood 1997). Others say free trade and self-reliance will bring prosperity and democracy.

Much will depend on the will of Africans themselves. The continuing threats of ethnic violence and intransigence of single parties and military rulers does not overshadow advances toward pluralism in over half of the countries. The tide of democracy is slowly, but surely, turning in Sub-Saharan Africa.

## Conclusion

Sub-Saharan Africa, a mostly rural area nearly as large as North America, straddles the equator. A cradle of human civilization, its diverse peoples represent over 800 ethnic and lingual entities. It has endured a period of colonialism, of which some legacies still exist.

The region continues to face numerous serious social, economic, and political problems, among them poverty, illiteracy, ethnic wars, a population explosion, lack of an industrial base and infrastructure, massive debts, and weak governments. Initial restrictive donor aid efforts met resistance; donors are now adjusting programs to reward progress.

Since independence, the region's politics have been dominated by military dictatorship and one-party rule. But recent moves toward liberalization and democracy are gaining strength; over half of the region's countries have now held elections and are moving toward pluralism.

What is the region's potential for the future? First, economic recovery and political freedoms are already gaining ground. Second, its diverse peoples are energetic and resourceful. The area contains rich mineral resources; land is still available. Given their initial moves toward democracy, Sub-Saharan Africans will surely move to improve their lot with benefits they have long yearned for—better education and health, expanded industries and trade, enlightened government, and other advancements that self-rule brings.

## References

Agunga, Robert A. 1997. *Developing the Third World: A Communication Approach.* Commack, N.Y.: Nova Science Publishers.

Ake, Claude. 1996. *Democracy and Development in Africa.* Washington, D.C.: Brookings Institution.

_____. 1991. "Rethinking African Democracy." *Journal of Democracy* (Winter): 32–44.

Allan, T., and A. Warren, eds. 1993. *Deserts: The Encroaching Wilderness.* New York: Oxford University Press.

Atwood, J. Brian. 1997. "Toward a Brighter Horizon for Africa." *Christian Science Monitor*, August 4, 19.

Carr-Hill, R. 1990. *Social Conditions in Sub-Sahara Africa.* London: Macmillan Academic and Professional.

Darnton, J. 1994. "Survival Test: Can Africa Rebound?" Series of three New York Times News Service articles. *Portland Oregonian*, June 26–28, A4.

Davidson, Basil. 1989. "Africa in Historical Perspective." In *Africa South of the Sahara*, 18th edition (annual yearbook). London: Europa Publications.

Decalo, S. 1992. "The Process, Prospects, and Constraints of Democratization in Africa." *African Affairs* 91: 7–35.

Diamond, Larry. 1994. "The New Wind." *Africa Report* 40 (1): 50–53.

Fisher, Harold A. 1988. "Development in Sub-Saharan Africa: Barriers and Prospects. In *The Third World: States of Mind and Being*, J. Norwine and A. Gonzalez, eds., 231–242. Boston: Unwin Hyman.

Flint, Julie. 1994. "The Plague Years." *Africa Report* 39 (3): 27–29.

Hanley, C. 1994. "The Human Tide." Series of three Associated Press articles in *Portland Oregonian*, August 31, September 1 and 2, A3.

Kunz, F. 1991. "Liberalization in Africa: Some Preliminary Reflections." *African Affairs* 90: 223–235.

Lewis, Peter. 1994. "Politics of Economics." *Africa Report* 39 (3): 47–49.

Matloff, Judith. 1997a. "Suddenly Africa's Conflicts Aren't So Local." *Christian Science Monitor*, February 7, 6.

_____. 1997b. "In South Africa, to Forgive is to Find Out." *Christian Science Monitor*, January 30, 1, 7.

_____. 1996. "Democracy, of a Sort, Sweeps Africa." *Christian Science Monitor*, August 7, 10–11.

Morna, Colleen L. 1995. "The Plight of the Universities." *Africa Report* 40 (2): 30–33.

National Geographic Society. 1992. *National Geographic Atlas of the World*, sixth edition. Washington, D.C.: National Geographic Society.

National Research Council. 1996. *Preventing and Mitigating AIDS in Sub-Saharan Africa*. Washington, D.C.: National Academy Press.

Ndulu, Benno. 1997. Editorial. *World Development* 25 (5): 627–630.

Novicki, Margaret A. 1993. "Democracy and Development: Interview with Adebayo Adedeji." *Africa Report* 38 (5): 58–60.

Oxford University Press. 1996a. *Oxford Atlas of the World*. 4th ed. New York: Oxford University Press.

_____. 1996b. *World Resources, 1996–1997*. New York: Oxford University Press.

Population Reference Bureau. June 1996. *World Population Data Sheet*. Washington, D.C.: Population Reference Bureau.

Santoro, Lara. 1997. "Road to Riches or Ruin: One Nation Taps Africa's Potential, Another Squanders It." *Christian Science Monitor*, July 18, 1.

Segal, Aaron. 1996. "Can Democratic Transitions Tame Political Successions?" *Africa Today* 43 (4): 369–384.

Sisk, Timothy. 1995. *Democratization in South Africa: The Exclusive Social Contract*. Princeton, N.J.: Princeton University Press.

Sivard, Ruth. 1994. *World Military and Social Expenditures*. Leesburg, Va.: World Priorities.

Stren, R., and R. White, eds. 1989. *African Cities in Crisis: Managing Rapid Urban Growth*. Boulder: Westview Press.

Tarver, James. 1996. *The Demography of Africa*. Westport, Conn.: Praeger.

United Nations Conference on Trade and Development (UNCTAD). 1996. *The Least Developed Countries: 1996 Report*. New York: UNCTAD.

United Nations Environmental Programme (UNEP). 1992. *World Atlas of Desertification*. London: Edward Arnold.

United Nations International Children's Emergency Fund (UNICEF). 1994. *The State of the World's Children*. New York: Oxford University Press.

U.S. Agency for International Development/U.S. Department of Commerce. 1996. *World Population Profile*. Washington, D.C.: USAID.

U.S. Department of Interior. 1993. *Minerals Yearbook, Africa*. Washington, D.C.: U.S. Department of Interior.

Wiseman, John A., ed. 1995. *Democracy and Political Change in Sub-Saharan Africa*. London and New York: Routledge.

World Bank. 1997a. *World Bank Atlas*. Washington, D.C.: World Bank.

_____. 1997b. *World Development Report*. New York: Oxford University Press.

_____. 1996. *World Development Report*. New York: Oxford University Press.

_____. 1992. *Trends in Developing Economies, 1992*. Washington, D.C.: World Bank.

# 14 *Newly Industrializing Countries: A Discussion of Terms*

**Stephen S. Chang and Joseph G. Spinelli**

## Introduction

The term "newly industrializing countries" (NICs) is found in the literature on development describing countries in the process of industrializing whose industries are making important contributions to economic growth as traditional reliance on primary products decreases. Most NICs assemble products providing good value and quality, both for domestic and foreign consumption. The expressions "economic development" and "economic growth" are both used in the literature discussing the changes necessary for improvement in a country's level of living. "Economic growth" is the more restricted term and refers to an increase in output and productivity, whereas "economic development" includes "growth" along with broad societal and industrial changes necessary to facilitate increases in output (Kindleberger 1965:3). Today's expression "newly industrializing countries" is similar to the "takeoff stage," a term proposed by W. W. Rostow in his theory of stages of economic growth (Rostow 1971:36–58). Economic development is a sustained dynamic process.

This chapter uses several expressions when referring to different stages of economic development. "Less developed" (or "developing") economies lack a well-established industrial base; the primary sector is the driving force. Examples include countries such as Bangladesh, Myanmar, Mozambique, and Honduras. "Future" (or "emerging") NICs are those that are beginning to implement economic measures leading to an increase in industrial output and have the requisite foundations for becoming NICs. Vietnam is an example. Countries considered as NICs are industrializing and exporting their goods to the global market, achieving rapid economic growth and rising levels of development, political stability, and fairly effective policies to attract investment through domestic savings and foreign capital. Thailand, Malaysia, and Indonesia are commonly acknowledged as examples of today's NICs. Hong Kong, Taiwan, Republic of Korea (South Korea), and Singapore were considered to be NICs in the 1960s and 1970s but have moved beyond this stage and are now moving toward skill- and knowledge-intensive manufacturing and services, signs pointing toward "maturing" NICs. They are on the threshold of becoming "developed" economies. In "developed" economies, countries such as the United States, Japan, and Germany demonstrate a competitiveness and sustained growth dependent upon skill, knowledge, and innovation in all sectors of their economies. There are other socioeconomic characteristics associated with each stage, and when a country moves from one stage to another in its economic development, it will experience changes in them. They serve as useful indicators in measuring a country's stage of development and are discussed later in an examination of "newly industrializing" status.

### Defining "Newly Industrializing Countries"

Sustained economic development is unlikely without industrialization as the term NIC suggests in its reference to this gradual and evolving process. In the same way that unanimity is absent on proposed paths to economic development, it is also impossible to provide universally acceptable, objective criteria measuring these processes.

With this in mind, it is helpful to possess an intuitive feeling for the development process and to try to measure it before and while it occurs. It is a truism that poor countries are more likely to have scarce, unreliable, or invalid data, which is a hindrance to economic advancement because it is precisely these countries that are most in need of help on the road to expanding economies and wider distributions of increased income. As much as one might desire to measure development quantitatively, such data have to be evaluated through the filter of a keen understanding of the dynamics of a country or region. In fact, the "quantitative" must be subjected to a "qualitative" appraisal in order to avoid misconceptions about the degree of development currently under way or possible in the future.

In dealing with human endeavors, it is impossible to create detailed and concrete criteria and use them to evaluate every country. There are diverse cultures and varying regional conditions. Thus, flexibility is necessary in evaluating the level of development of a country.

There are indicators signaling when a country becomes a NIC and when it has matured into a developed economy. Such indicators are good

TABLE 14.1   Economic Indicators for Selected Newly Industrializing Countries

| Country | Total GDP, 1994 (Million US$) | % Average Annual Growth Rate in GDP, 1980–90 | % Average Annual Growth Rate in GDP, 1990–94 | GNP per Capita 1994 (US$) | % GDP Agriculture (1994) | % Change GDP Agriculture (1970–94) | % GDP Industry** (1994) |
|---|---|---|---|---|---|---|---|
| South Africa | 121,888 | 1.3 | –0.1 | 3,040 | 5 | –3 | 31 |
| Mexico | 377,115 | 1.0 | 2.5 | 4,180 | 8 | –4 | 28 |
| Costa Rica | 8,281 | 3.0 | 5.6 | 2,400 | 15 | –8 | 24 |
| Argentina | 281,922 | –0.3 | 7.6 | 8,110 | 5 | –5 | 30 |
| Brazil | 554,587 | 2.7 | 2.2 | 2,970 | 13 | 1 | 39 |
| Chile | 51,957 | 4.1 | 7.5 | 3,520 | 7 in '80 | n.a. | 37 in '80 |
| Colombia | 67,266 | 3.7 | 4.3 | 1,670 | 14 | –11 | 32 |
| Uruguay | 15,539 | 0.4 | 4.4 | 4,660 | 8 | –8 | 23 |
| Venezuela | 58,257 | 1.1 | 3.2 | 2,760 | 5 | –1 | 42 |
| Turkey | 131,014 | 5.6 | 3.2 | 2,500 | 16 | –14 | 31 |
| India | 293,606 | 5.8 | 3.8 | 320 | 30 | –15 | 28 |
| Indonesia | 174,640 | 6.1 | 7.6 | 880 | 17 | –28 | 41 |
| Malaysia | 70,626 | 5.2 | 8.4 | 3,480 | 14 | –15 | 43 |
| Philippines | 64,162 | 1.0 | 1.6 | 950 | 22 | –8 | 33 |
| Singapore | 68,949 | 6.4 | 8.3 | 22,500 | 0 | –2 | 36 |
| Thailand | 143,209 | 7.6 | 8.2 | 2,410 | 10 | –16 | 39 |
| China | 522,172 | 10.2 | 12.9 | 530 | 21 | –9 (1980–94) | 47 |
| Hong Kong | 131,881 | 6.9 | 5.7 | 21,650 | 0 | –2 | 18 |
| Korea, Rep. of | 376,505 | 9.4 | 6.6 | 8,260 | 7 | –19 | 43 |
| Taiwan | 240,986 | 7.6* | 11.0 | 11,597 | 3.5 | –11.5 | 37 |

*1980–91.
**Industry includes value-added mining; manufacturing; construction; and electricjty, water, and gas.
  SOURCES: World Bank 1980: 190; World Bank 1994: 166–167; World Bank 1996: 188–189, 202–203, and
208–211; *Far Eastern Economic Review* 1994: 14 and 1997: 14 and 18. Reprinted by permission.

and necessary but not absolute and involve subjective or intuitive interpretations. It is difficult to determine precisely when a country becomes a
NIC. As it enters into the process of development, the skilled observer,
using a bit of hindsight, can spot a trend whereby certain indicators point
to the status of a NIC. This is similarly true in judging when the country
passes from the ranks of the NICs to those of developed economies. Acknowledging this, key indicators used to gauge when a struggling, traditional economy metamorphoses into a NIC and later when it matures
and evolves into a developed country will be discussed. A note of caution is warranted here. Some observers of the international development
scene may disagree with the interpretation of these indicators or may
wish to include additional signaling characteristics.

### Economic Indicators

A developing country tends to have a slow rate of economic growth. It
relies mainly on its primary producing and exporting sector which accounts for a large proportion of its gross domestic product (GDP). The

TABLE 14.1   (*continued*)

| % Change GDP Industry (1970–94) | % GDP Manufacturing (1994) | % Change GDP Manufacturing (1970–94) | % GDP Services (1994) | % Change GDP Services (1970–94) | Energy Use per Capita (kg. oil equiv) '94 | % Change Energy Use per Capita 1980–94 |
|---|---|---|---|---|---|---|
| –9 | 23 | –1 | 65 | 13 | 2,253 | 9 |
| –1 | 20 | –2 | 64 | 5 | 1,577 | 9 |
| 0 | 19 | 0 (1980–94) | 61 | 8 | 558 | n.a. |
| –14 | 20 | –12 | 65 | 18 | 1,399 | –1 |
| 1 | 25 | –4 | 49 | 0 | 691 | 16 |
| n.a. | 21 in '80 | n.a. | 55 in '80 | n.a. | 943 | 36 |
| 4 | 18 | –3 | 54 | 7 | 613 | 22 |
| –8 | 17 | –9 (1980–94) | 69 | 16 | 623 | –18 |
| 3 | 14 | –2 | 53 | –1 | 2,331 | –1 |
| 4 | 20 | 3 | 52 | 9 | 955 | 35 |
| 6 | 18 | 3 | 42 | 9 | 243 | 77 |
| 22 | 24 | 14 | 42 | 6 | 393 | 133 |
| 18 | 32 | 20 | 42 | –4 | 1,711 | 147 |
| 1 | 23 | –2 | 45 | 6 | 364 | 31 |
| 6 | 27 | 7 | 64 | –4 | 6,556 | 147 |
| 14 | 29 | 13 | 50 | 1 | 770 | 197 |
| –2 (1980–94) | 37 | –4 (1980–94) | 32 | 11 (1980–94) | 647 | 54 |
| –18 | 11 | –18 | 82 | 20 | 2,280 | 104 |
| 14 | 29 | 8 | 50 | 5 | 3,000 | 176 |
| –4 | 29 | –4 | 59 | 15 | 3,110 | n.a. |

growth rate of the GDP for a country as it becomes a NIC tends to be rapid—approximately 5 to 10 percent growth per year is common—because the economy is starting at such a low level; hence, its gains are often spectacular. These growth rates may be interrupted at times by fluctuating economic circumstances such as recessions. For NICs in general, the percentage of GDP contributed by the manufacturing sector should increase while the contribution from the primary sector, although still growing in absolute terms, begins a proportionate decline. With continued economic growth, the manufacturing portion increases along with a general rise in the GDP. This indicates that a country is becoming a NIC with a diminishing reliance on primary products as the driving force of the economy (Table 14.1). Ideally, as the industrialization process continues, an increasingly larger proportion of annual economic growth should be achieved through increases in labor productivity.

The general pattern in the recent past has shown that successful NICs relied upon exporting manufactured products as their stimulus to economic growth and were receptive to investment capital, business practices, and technology introduced from abroad. Prior to these examples of rapid growth, the prevalent economic philosophy looked to "import substitution" (whereby domestic production is substituted for foreign imports) as the preferred path to rapid industrialization. This approach did not yield long-term results and subsequently has been discarded (World Bank 1991:4). In recent decades, countries that chose an "export-oriented" philosophy, such as Taiwan, South Korea, Hong Kong, Singapore, Indonesia, Malaysia, and Thailand, have achieved rapid industrialization and concomitant rapid economic growth. To participate in the global market, a country must adopt current international business practices and open itself to new ideas and technology as a means to produce and sell more competitive products.

Foreign investment can quicken the pace of industrialization by bringing with it technological change either directly or through adaptation of the techniques used in the developed countries. Hand in hand with the global market, such investment serves as a stimulus to domestic industries, preventing them from growing complacent because of the specter of competition. There have been numerous discussions about the role and desirability of foreign investments in developing countries. Foreign investors naturally seek a profitable economic return on their capital. If a country attracts foreign investment for desirable projects, such as machinery, manufacturing plants, and infrastructure, these investments facilitate economic development. However, speculative, short-term investments in an immature financial market can be disruptive. Countries can protect themselves against sudden changes in capital flows by prudent fiscal management so they do not have to rely upon excessive foreign borrowing to finance government budgets or current accounts (trade in goods and services and financial transfers such as foreign aid). High rates of domestic savings should be encouraged so that funds can be made available for investments to foster economic growth, reducing the need for foreign capital. Reasonable measures can be instituted to moderate capital movements, especially short-term flows (Carrington 1995:1).

As the process of development continues and the economy matures, the rate of economic growth usually moderates, averaging about 5 percent or less per year. This slower annual growth rate may closely resemble that of many poor, developing countries but differs in significance because it is a percentage—even though a diminishing one—of a much larger, expanding economy. The proportion of GDP accounted for by the manufacturing sector begins to level off or even decline, while the service sector often increases its share of GDP. A large portion of this increase in the service sector's contribution is caused by an increase in higher-skilled, higher-paid jobs. Such sectoral changes signal the evolution from newly industrializing status to that of a developed country. One should note that in some developing economies, service sector GDP can be quite high, such as when an economy has overcrowding in cities with resultant underemployment and low-paying jobs.

Other economic indicators help paint a picture of genuine, sustained economic development. There are changes from low-skill industries to technologically sophisticated, knowledge-intensive manufacturing and service enterprises. An expansion in labor productivity becomes an important component in the development process. Professor Krugman, in his article "The Myth of Asia's Miracle," made the point that advances in knowledge and technology that contribute to continuous gains in productivity through increased efficiency are important for sustained economic growth and per capita income (Krugman 1994:66–68). There is an expansion in participation in the global economy, which includes more bilateral trade, investment, and technological exchanges. Financial systems must become fully mature as a way of facilitating capital inflows and investment and of providing necessary macroeconomic adjustments. Modern business management practices have to be adopted to permit continued integration into the world of international competition.

With the continued maturing of NICs, there is growth in GDP and a widening participation of the labor force in the economy accompanied by an increase in personal income which is a prerequisite to a rise in the real level of living of the population and a broad-spectrum reduction in poverty. With economic maturity comes a concomitant growth of the middle class, which spreads beyond the urban environment where it is isolated in traditional societies, and it becomes the dominant social class. The income gap between rich and poor declines while both groups experience greater wealth.

## Resource Indicators

With economic development comes a greater consumption of natural resources reflected in higher consumption rates of both food and nonanimate energy sources. What is noticeable is a switch in the type of food being consumed, namely, the inclusion of more meat in the diet. This reflects a change from being a primary consumer in the food chain (e.g., vegetarian) to being a secondary consumer (e.g., meat eater), which puts a higher demand on food resources.

The rising consumption of energy resources is another good indicator of a NIC (Table 14.1). There is a concomitant demand placed on the primary energy resources of coal, oil, natural gas, and material for nuclear energy. For example, China was an oil exporter during the 1980s, but since 1993, it has become an oil importer. This is not from any oil extraction declines, but from China's oil production falling behind demand. Indonesia may likely be an oil importer at the turn of the twenty-first century, owing to a combination of increasing demand and the prospect of declining oil resources over the coming years (*Far Eastern Economic Review* 1994:53–54 and 1995:51–54).

Very likely there will be more demand for other industrial resources such as wood, paper, pulp, and metals. Consumption of these products serves as a useful indicator of development. However, one must not consider resource consumption in isolation because demand depends on a number of variables, among which are the types of growth industries, the economic cycle, manufacturing and other technologies, consumer preferences, and substitute materials. Thus, a decrease in consumption alone does not necessarily mean a regression in economic growth.

### Infrastructure Indicators

The availability of sufficient infrastructure and social overhead capital (transportation, telecommunications, water, and adequate power supplies) is vital as a stimulus to industrialization. This, in turn, compels a NIC to develop further its infrastructure. The pressure to keep up with demand, along with the need for continued investment and building of infrastructure points to a NIC's expanding economy. Such pressure is often intense, especially during periods of rapid economic growth. An offshoot of this may be an inability to keep pace with demand which can truncate development.

Providing for growth in infrastructure requires huge, lump sums of investment capital. Owing to the nature of such projects, they often cannot be provided in a piecemeal fashion. It requires technology, resources, material, and a whole array of products, parts, tools, and machinery coming at one time. Supplying these can stimulate industrial development, create jobs, and contribute to economic growth.

Regarding the maintenance of infrastructure as well as other types of facilities and equipment in general, one observes that commonly in the early phases of industrialization, new facilities are built and equipment purchased, but they deteriorate at an equally fast rate due to the absence of proper maintenance. As the NIC's industrialization begins to mature, maintenance also grows, which is sometimes seen as a surrogate measurement of economic development.

### Social Indicators

With the status of NIC will come increased urbanization and a decline in the percentage of rural people. A true picture of incipient industrialization shows that urbanization of the population results from a growing la-

TABLE 14.2    Population and Urbanization of Selected Newly Industrialized
Countries, 1996

| | Birth Rate Per 1,000 | Total Fertility Rate | Death Rate Per 1,000 | Infant Mortality Rate | Life Expectancy M/F | % Urban |
|---|---|---|---|---|---|---|
| More Developed | 12 | 1.6 | 10 | 9.0 | 70/78 | 75 |
| Less Developed | 27 | 3.4 | 9 | 68.0 | 62/65 | 35 |
| Less Developed (Excl. China) | 31 | 4.0 | 10 | 73.0 | 60/63 | 38 |
| South Africa | 31 | 4.1 | 8 | 46.0 | 63/68 | 57 |
| Mexico | 27 | 3.1 | 5 | 34.0 | 70/76 | 71 |
| Costa Rica | 26 | 3.1 | 4 | 13.0 | 74/79 | 44 |
| Argentina | 20 | 2.7 | 8 | 22.9 | 69/76 | 87 |
| Brazil | 25 | 2.8 | 8 | 58.0 | 64/69 | 76 |
| Chile | 21 | 2.5 | 6 | 13.1 | 69/76 | 85 |
| Colombia | 27 | 3.0 | 6 | 28.0 | 66/72 | 67 |
| Uruguay | 18 | 2.3 | 10 | 20.1 | 69/76 | 90 |
| Venezuela | 26 | 3.1 | 5 | 23.5 | 69/75 | 84 |
| Turkey | 23 | 2.7 | 7 | 47.0 | 65/70 | 63 |
| India | 29 | 3.4 | 10 | 79.0 | 58/59 | 26 |
| Indonesia | 24 | 2.9 | 8 | 66.0 | 61/65 | 31 |
| Malaysia | 28 | 3.3 | 5 | 11.0 | 70/75 | 51 |
| Philippines | 30 | 4.1 | 9 | 34.0 | 63/66 | 49 |
| Singapore | 16 | 1.8 | 5 | 4.0 | 74/79 | 100 |
| Thailand | 20 | 2.2 | 6 | 35.0 | 68/72 | 19 |
| China | 17 | 1.8 | 7 | 44.0 | 68/72 | 29 |
| Hong Kong | 12 | 1.2 | 5 | 5.0 | 75/81 | – |
| South Korea | 15 | 1.7 | 6 | 11.0 | 68/76 | 74 |
| Taiwan | 15 | 1.8 | 5 | 5.1 | 72/78 | 75 |

SOURCE: Population Reference Bureau, *World Population Data Sheet* (Washington, D.C.: Population Reference Bureau, 1996). Reprinted with permission.

bor demand in urban-based economic activities. Urbanization, however, is not solely the result of industrialization but may occur because of the expulsive force of rural poverty. For example, Table 14.2 shows that the Philippines has 49 percent of its population living in urban areas largely as a consequence of migrants fleeing rural poverty (*Far Eastern Economic Review* 1994:69; McGurn 1997:36). In contrast to developing countries and even NICs, developed economies have high proportions of their populations living in urban agglomerations.

Even with growing urbanization and budding industrialization, the dominance of primate cities—usually capital cities or major industrial centers—continues. They are the concentration points for scarce resources needed for economic growth, such as skilled labor, investment capital, managerial personnel, and research institutions. Once maturity is reached in the industrialization process, the degree of primacy declines as other cities become focal points or growth poles attracting workers and resources; urbanization spreads across the country. One must be cognizant of the fact, however, that primate cities occur in some but not all industrialized countries. In developing countries, it is nearly a universal phenomenon.

Along with increased urbanization, changes involving social institutions, social behavior, and attitudes also occur. With more exposure to other cultures, people become more cosmopolitan in their behavior and outlook. An important social change that serves as an indicator of the economic development process is the gradual evolution of the family system from extended to nuclear.

Demographic characteristics also demonstrate the evolution to the status of a NIC. Along with industrialization and economic development comes a decline in the annual rate of population growth brought about mostly by falling total fertility rates. The NICs of the 1960s and 1970s—Singapore, Hong Kong, Taiwan, and South Korea—have total fertility rates that have fallen below the replacement level of 2.1 births per woman during reproductive life (Table 14.2). Developed countries exhibit very low natural increase rates, often less than 1 percent with some experiencing even negative rates. Death rates are similarly low as a result of a rapid reduction in infant and child mortality caused by improvements in health care, nutrition levels, and public health measures. The outcome of reduced mortality levels is a concomitant increase in life expectancy and an increase in the average age of populations. Aging poses its own problems as Japan has learned from the growth of its elderly population. A similar readjustment in age-sex composition following in the wake of their demographic transitions faces Hong Kong, Taiwan, South Korea, and Singapore in the near future.

## Government Policies

Government policies are not indicators of whether a country is a NIC. In addition to political stability, they have an important effect on the probable success or failure of a country in its quest to industrialize and ultimately to become a mature economy. They are predictors of possible economic growth, thus, a brief discussion is warranted.

The role of government is subject to debate with evidence showing that economies such as Chile, China, and India have made important gains when government intervention was reduced. Hong Kong developed successfully following a policy of minimal government involvement, while Japan and Singapore performed equally well with government intervention. In successful NICs, both past and present, governments are reasonably competent and efficient. They favor market mechanisms and intervene in moderation only to an extent required. When they act, they take precautions against distorting market mechanisms and pricing. Their intervention is subject to and tested by the forces of domestic and international market competition. Any problematical actions or policies are usually quickly corrected or abandoned. Governments in successful economies most importantly encourage private initiatives and investments by pursuing policies to support them. They provide needed investments for developing human resources and infrastructure. Prudent fiscal management is needed to curtail budget deficits, avoid excessive foreign borrowing, encourage domestic savings, and restrain inflation. The successful economies are open to international trade, investment, technology, ideas, and competition and are part of an expanding global market (World Bank 1991:5–11). Despite an open acceptance of international trade some countries, such as Taiwan, South Korea, and Japan, are more disposed to exporting while also trying to protect their domestic enterprises with import impediments, including tariffs, regulations, and strict monitoring of quality inspections.

The economies of China and India serve as recent examples of successful attempts at market reform and economic growth. China began its reform in 1978 by allowing private initiatives, reducing government controls, introducing market mechanisms, and opening itself to the outside world. It has experienced rapid economic growth. India's economy performed poorly under its socialist policies of excessive government intervention and unfriendliness to private and foreign investments. When its policy changed in 1991 to one of encouraging private initiatives and market mechanisms and offering a friendlier face toward foreign investors, the economy grew at a healthy rate. If it maintains political stability and sustains its policies of encouragement, India's future development looks bright.

The issue of corruption has gained recent attention. Observers suggest that government regulations and controls offer ample opportunities for corruption, especially when the rule of law is weak. Yet, even with democratic reform and economic liberalization, corruption continues unabated in some countries. This may be attributed to an incomplete removal of economic controls by bureaucrats and an absence of total openness in decisionmaking. Under such circumstances, corrupt officials will find ways to exploit the system (Ghosh et al. 1997:18–19).

## Models for Development?

In the 1990s, the economies of the early NICs—Hong Kong, Taiwan, South Korea, and Singapore—are maturing and on the brink of entering into the ranks of the developed countries. Their economic and social variables point in this direction: For example, compare the per capita GNPs (for 1994 in U.S. dollars) for Singapore, $22,500; and Hong Kong, $21,650; to the United States, $25,880; Germany, $25,580; Italy, $19,300; United Kingdom, $18,340; Hungary, $3,840; and Czech Republic, $3,200 (World Bank 1996:189). Their successes have led to discussions as to whether they can serve as models of development for other developing and newly industrializing countries. Some of their policies make good economic sense and can be emulated by others. These include reliance on market mechanisms and private initiatives, prudent economic involvement by government, promotion of a high rate of domestic savings, encouragement of foreign and domestic capital in long-term productive investments, development of human resources and infrastructure, efforts to increase productivity, and willingness to deal with the outside world. These policies provide a broad general framework for economic growth and development. Each country has to devise an individualized plan in accordance with its unique situation.

However, it is unrealistic to expect other countries to follow the details of the development process demonstrated by these four economies. The paths to development vary according to local, regional, and global circumstances. For example, textile and apparel manufacturing and exporting played a vital role in the economic development of Hong Kong, Taiwan, and South Korea. Such industries maintained a leading role for fifteen to twenty years after their initial contributions to growth. However, today's NICs cannot rely upon the same textile and apparel industries to play a similarly critical role as a stimulus to development. The import quota placed upon these products in recent years by the United States and western European countries limits their contribution to growth; NICs necessarily must seek alternative industries.

Learning from the experience of other countries, the rapid change in technology and know-how, the need for industrial diversification, and the increased international movement of capital, it is evident that the value of a cheap labor supply is much more transitory today than in the 1960s and 1970s. There have been many changes in global political and economic conditions since those decades. Political and economic changes brewing in the former communist countries of Eastern Europe and the former Soviet Union have put an added strain on the supply of economic aid from granting countries. The need for capital investment funds for these and other countries such as China and India, for example, are stressing limited available funds. The result is scarcity and intense rivalry. There is increased competition in world trade making export growth more difficult. These are a few of the many changes creating different and perhaps less favorable challenges than those faced by the earlier NICs—Hong Kong, Taiwan, South Korea, and Singapore. Their performance, therefore, should not be taken as the "norm." Today's NICs may lack the sustained improvements in annual growth rates of their predecessors. They may experience intermittent periods of stagnation and regression on their path to development.

Krugman made the point that the rapid growth in Asian economies resulted more from large investments of capital and labor rather than from increased efficiency through advancements in knowledge and technology. A rise in productivity does not necessarily connote an increase in efficiency, that is, increased output per unit of input. Capital investments such as better machines or more infrastructure lead to one-time gains in productivity. Knowledge and technological advances that improve productivity through efficiency are critical to the continued increase in economic growth and per capita income (Krugman 1994:66–72). Krugman maintained that the "Asian miracle" is a myth—economic growth cannot be sustained once the one-time effect of capital investment is fully realized (Krugman 1994).

Professor Krugman's article generated considerable debate. Some observers dispute the statistics on which he based his arguments. In capital investments, he failed to take into account that Asian "miracle" economies have invested effectively to generate more benefits. Even if his conclusions are valid, growth in these economies will continue for some time. He has been too quick to cast doubt upon the future of these Asian economies by underestimating their ability to learn, adjust, and keep pace (*Economist* 1997:23–24).

Hong Kong, Taiwan, South Korea, and Singapore have made remarkable economic progress; however, their transformation to "developed" economies is by no means complete. Most noticeable is the metamorphosis from labor-intensive, low-skill manufacturing entities to those utilizing knowledge-intensive, technologically demanding, and high-value-added industries and services. Many of their labor-intensive manufacturing industries have been shifted abroad to places such as coastal China and countries in Southeast Asia. Hong Kong and Singapore are competing for the title of leading financial center in Asia. All these four economies are making every effort to nourish technology and innovation to produce globally competitive products and services. Despite arguments about Krugman's conclusions, these economies must acknowledge that his suggestion of improved productivity through efficiency is necessary. Success will bring continued growth and prosperity while failure can lead to stagnation and decline. Optimism and euphoria should be tempered with caution. Their paths to development can serve as useful experiences but not as detailed models for all to follow.

## Examples of Newly Industrializing Countries

Table 14.1 provides a partial list of countries that are considered to be NICs. South Africa, taken as a whole, is probably a mature NIC. In the recent past, large segments of its society were disenfranchised to the point where both leading and lagging sectors existed simultaneously. This was the legacy of its apartheid policy. The white minority community enjoyed a developed economy, in contrast to the nonwhite groups. With reversion to majority rule and continued political, economic, and social stability, South Africa may evolve into a developed economy in the not too distant future. Chile resembles Hong Kong, Taiwan, South Korea, and Singapore in its stage of development. Its economy has made impressive strides in the last decade. Likewise, Argentina is a mature NIC; however, it still lacks the economic foundation necessary to turn it into a fully developed economy. To do less is to doom itself to stagnation.

Countries such as Thailand, Malaysia, Indonesia, India, Philippines, Brazil, Mexico, Uruguay, Venezuela, Colombia, Costa Rica, and Turkey are among the current crop of NICs. Thailand, Malaysia, and Indonesia have performed very well in recent years. In southwest Asia, Turkey can be counted as one of the better-developed countries. It is seeking membership in the European Union. With different cultural and political views from the other members of the European Union and a lower level of economic development, its admission to that body in the near future is doubtful. However, there are measures aimed at freeing trade between Turkey and the European Union in advance of its possible future membership. Turkey's growing middle class is showing signs of being more politically active. As the largest economy in the Middle East—an important "emerging market"—whose business people are playing a major role in the development of the newly independent countries of central Asia, a stable Turkey can have a significant impact in this region (Pope 1997).

Mexico's economy has made gains in recent years by encouraging private initiatives and reducing the degree of government control and intervention. Despite the pessimism generated by the early 1995 currency crisis, one must recognize that the Mexican economy has made improvements. The high current account deficit and low level of domestic savings forced Mexico to seek help through inflows of foreign capital. When Mexico's currency crisis occurred, confidence in the economy waned and foreign capital departed, especially short-term investment money. Unfortunately for many Latin American countries, they also suffer from a low domestic savings rate (Carrington 1995:1). In addition to increasing domestic savings, some Latin American governments need to curtail excessive governmental intervention, pursue prudent fiscal policies, and keep inflation in check, all useful to their economic growth.

As mentioned earlier, India's reforms have brought it economic growth, which if sustained will demonstrate great strength and promise. In the Philippines, the effects of "crony capitalism" under the former dictator Ferdinand Marcos and the dominance of an oligarchy hampered its economic development. It has since undertaken economic and govern-

mental reforms. The economy has grown consistently since 1993 resulting in increased confidence that it has achieved stability and long-term
growth (*Far Eastern Economic Review* 1995:196 and 1997:194). Both can be
regarded as regular NICs or minimally as emerging ones and have the
potential to become mature NICs quickly.

China is a country whose impact on the world scene can be enormous
merely by virtue of its geographic extent and huge population. Although
some data show that it is still a developing country, it is already one of
the world's largest economies. The coastal regions of China can be classified unquestionably as newly industrializing or even equivalent to a mature NIC, whereas the interior regions are less developed.

In the former communist countries of Eastern Europe and in the former Soviet Union, manufacturing industries were in existence for many
decades prior to and following World War II, but they have been essentially government-directed and inefficient, unable to face competition in
the world marketplace. In effect, they must re-industrialize in the context
of a global market economy. There is pain associated with this change,
for example, unemployment from the restructuring of unprofitable industries and rising costs resulting from the removal of price controls and
government subsidies. Therefore, the question facing these governments
is the pace of privatization and market reforms. With these economic reforms, the Czech Republic and Slovenia (considered advanced NICs) will
further enhance their economic performances. Similarly, Poland, Hungary, Estonia, Latvia, and the Slovak Republic may be considered NICs,
while Belarus, Bulgaria, Romania, Lithuania, Moldova, and Ukraine are
possible future NICs. The classification of these countries is subjective
owing to the meagerness and reliability of available data. The future of
the former communist countries of Eastern Europe and the newly independent former Soviet republics is far from certain; everything depends
upon regional and internal political stability as well as the implementation of necessary economic reforms.

## Conclusion

As mentioned earlier, newly industrialized countries most likely will face
intermittent periods of growth, stagnation, and regression on their way to
economic development. Fluctuations in global market forces such as economic recessions and competition are inevitable. The key to minimizing in-
terruptions to growth rests with a country's ability to respond quickly to
changing domestic and international conditions. As noted in a World Bank
study, this rapid adjustment contributed to the successful growth of Hong
Kong, Taiwan, South Korea, Singapore, Thailand, Malaysia, and Indonesia
(World Bank 1993:115–121). When a country is slow in recognizing and ad-

justing to global fluctuations and its own weaknesses, it is very vulnerable
to stagnation and regression in its economic growth.

In the final analysis, it must be emphasized that there are numerous indicators of economic development with disagreement on what should be
considered and their relative importance. Logically, there will always be
differing opinions about which countries are NICs. There are countries
other than those mentioned earlier that can be discussed. The tables presented here can be expanded to include more countries, but countries
have been omitted owing to a lack of published, reliable data describing
them. Even if such information were available, there are domestic factors
through which such statistical information must be filtered qualitatively
to gain an appreciation of the underlying conditions. In addition, there
are qualitative indicators such as acceptance of foreign ideas and changing perceptions that are useful in contributing to an assessment of the
level of development. This provocative thought speaks to the need for
expanded field observations and in-country experience required to ren-
der a credible interpretation of the data.

## References

Carrington, Tim. 1995. "The Outlook: Private-Capital Flows Can Hurt Poor Na-
   tions." *Wall Street Journal*, January 30: A1.
*The Economist*. 1997. "The Asian Miracle: Is It Over?" March 1–7: 23–25.
*Far Eastern Economic Review*. 1994. *Asia 1994 Yearbook*. Hong Kong: Far Eastern
   Economic Review.
_____. 1995. *Asia 1995 Yearbook*. Hong Kong: Far Eastern Economic Review.
_____. 1997. *Asia 1997 Yearbook*. Hong Kong: Far Eastern Economic Review.
Ghosh, Aparisim, et al. 1997. "Reform's Dark Side. In Cover Story: Corruption."
   *Far Eastern Economic Review*, March 20: 18–20.
Kindleberger, C. P. 1965. *Economic Development*. 2d ed. New York: McGraw-Hill.
Krugman, Paul. 1994. "The Myth of Asia's Miracle." *Foreign Affairs* 73 (Novem-
   ber/December): 62–78.
McGurn, William. 1997. "City Limits. In Cover Story: Urbanization." *Far Eastern
   Economic Review*, February 6: 34–37.
Pope, Hugh. 1997. "The New Middle: Turks Add Their Voices to Contest of Gen-
   erals and Fundamentalists." *Wall Street Journal*, March 14: A1 and A8.
Population Reference Bureau. 1996. *1996 World Population Data Sheet*. Washing-
   ton, D.C.: Population Reference Bureau.
Rostow, W. W. 1971. *The Stages of Economic Growth*, 2d ed. New York: Cambridge
   University Press.
World Bank. 1980. *World Tables*, 2nd ed. Baltimore: Johns Hopkins University Press.
_____. 1991. *World Development Report 1991*. New York: Oxford University Press.
_____. 1993. *The East Asian Miracle*. New York: Oxford University Press.
_____. 1994. *World Development Report 1994*. New York: Oxford University Press.
_____. 1996. *World Development Report 1996*. New York: Oxford University Press.

# 15 USA: Is There Room for the Third World?

## Joel Lieske

$F$OR OVER TWO HUNDRED YEARS there has been an ongoing conflict in the United States between the ideals and reality of the American democratic experiment. Fundamentally, it is a cultural conflict over who we are, how we should act, and what is legitimate. But it is also an ideological conflict, one that reflects our changing states of mind and being over the proper order of society and how to achieve it.

### Founding Ideals

The central or organizing ideal of the American Revolution was liberty. But this concept meant different things to the British streams who brought their beliefs and ways of life to the American colonies between 1620 and 1775 (Fischer 1989). For the New England Puritans, who arrived in large numbers from 1629 to 1640, the emphasis was on "ordered liberty," that is, a freedom that was held in check by powerful religious and social norms. For the southern plantation gentry, who came over from 1642 to 1675, it was "hegemonic liberty," or the freedom to replicate the manorial lifestyle and feudal social order their Cavalier forebears enjoyed in the rural English countryside. For the early settlers of the mid-Atlantic States, many of whom traced their origins to the north Midlands, such as the Quakers, and reached the new land from 1675 to 1725, the stress was on "individual liberty." And for the "border people," such as the Scotch-Irish, who migrated in large numbers from northern England, Scotland, and northern Ireland to the Appalachian backcountry and border states from 1718 to 1775, the accent was on "natural liberty." Although "ordered liberty" was the preferred ideal among the Founding Fathers (Wilson and DiIulio 1995), the core value that ultimately came to dominate American life was the concept of "individual liberty" (Elazar 1994).

A derivative or corollary value that shaped the American experiment is the notion of rights—both civil and contractual. In Lockean democratic theory the basis of civil society is the social contract. This idea is perhaps best embodied, as Abraham Lincoln contended, in the U.S. Constitution. But since contracts are essentially bilateral agreements, requiring the *consent* of both parties, it was perhaps inevitable that much American history would come to focus on the struggle of different groups outside the economic and social mainstreams for their "unalienable" (read civil) rights.

Another deeply rooted value in the American political psyche is the notion of equality. But the emphasis on equality historically has always been on equality of treatment and opportunity, not results (Ladd 1978).

Rounding out the American belief system are two other core values. But they are grounded more in the economic aspirations of Americans and their enduring attachments to the free market system than to American political traditions. The first is the belief in privatism and property rights. The second is the expectation of material progress, that is, the belief that life must be better for Americans and their posterity than it was before.

Collectively, these core values form what is commonly labeled "classical liberalism" and what Everett Carll Ladd (1978) has called America's constitutive sociopolitical ideology. Fundamentally, it is an ideology that has helped define the American Dream. But it is also one that is deficient and incomplete.

In theory, the political order was to be founded on representative democracy or what the Founding Fathers called "republican government." The economic order, in turn, was to be based on capitalism—first the free and then later the regulated pursuit of material progress and therefore happiness. Finally, the social order was to be based on two organizing precepts. The first was a preference for legal, orderly change that would protect individual rights. The second was the hope, in hindsight a naive one, that one nation could be *democratically* forged from a diverse immigrant experience. This wish was perhaps best expressed in the motto: *E Pluribus Unum*—out of many, one. But how do you create social and political unity out of cultural diversity? Even more than race, this truly has been the American dilemma.

## Political Compromises

The focus, originally, was on political unity, uniting the thirteen colonies into one nation. But to create the first new nation, certain compromises had to be struck. The first was the Connecticut Compromise over popular versus state representation. But the greatest compromise was with slavery, ostensibly to win southern support for the new constitution. Others included the Missouri Compromise of 1820, which was intended to maintain a southern balance of power in the U.S. Senate, and the Dred Scott decision of 1857, which denied the rights of citizenship to black

Americans. Neither could prevent the outbreak of the Civil War, the costliest and bloodiest conflict in American history.

But even this conflict and the passage of the Thirteenth, Fourteenth, and Fifteenth Amendments could not guarantee blacks their civil rights. After the contested election of Rutherford Hayes in 1876, which was made possible by yet another compromise with southern segregationists, northern states acceded to a new system of racial subjugation in Dixie that would last until the middle of the twentieth century.

This was not the only compromise, however, that would come full circle to haunt future generations. The persistent denial of equal opportunities and rights—legal, civil, and voting—to women is one. Another was the denial of aboriginal land rights to American Indians and their forced deportation to the western territories along the "trail of tears."

Still another compromise is the nation's mostly one-sided contract with industrial capitalism. For the better part of our history, we have generally accepted the free market axiom that the primary creators of wealth are not the hardworking men and women who toil on the farms, in the factories, and in their homes and communities, but industrial entrepreneurs and financial investors. Another is the presumed trade-off between material progress and a healthy environment. Working in tandem with the nation's racial-ethnic and regional divisions, capitalists have helped to undermine many social reform movements, despoil the environment, foster the movement of industry to more profitable locations, deprive cities and public school systems of necessary revenue, and create the largest income inequalities of any industrial democracy. As a result, demands for justice, equality, and a better life *for all* have too often been silenced by promises of *individual* economic opportunity, material progress, and the accumulation of private wealth. Unfortunately, the economic promise of the American Dream may be most elusive to Third World countries, who are trying to emulate the American model, and the new waves of immigrants who are clamoring to enter through the Golden Door.

## The Golden Door

The second major wave to enter after the mainline groups—the British followed by the Germans and Scandinavians—was the celebrated "huddled masses" of eastern and southern Europe, that is, the "white ethnics." They arrived, for the most part, during the takeoff stage of the American industrial revolution, about 1880 to 1929, when the demand for labor was virtually insatiable. But this flow was dramatically interrupted by the immigration reform acts of 1921 and 1924, which imposed strict national quotas.

The last waves to enter, and by far the most controversial, have been the huddled masses of Latin America and Asia (Miles 1995, 132). Their entry was made possible by the Immigration and Nationality Act Amendments of 1965, which ended national quotas and introduced the family-reunification principle. Along with special congressional amnesties and group preferences enacted during the last decade, as well as differential fertility rates among the races, these amendments have produced dramatic increases in immigration and permanently altered the current and future ethnic composition of the United States. In 1960, the United States was 88.6 percent white, 10.5 percent black, and less than 1 percent Asian and other. By 1979, nine of the ten leading countries of origin for new immigrants to the United States were from the Third World (Fallows 1983). By 1990, the percentage of whites had dropped to 80.3 percent, while the percentage of blacks, Hispanics, and Asians had increased to 12.1 percent, 7.0 percent and 2.9 percent respectively. The Bureau of the Census predicts that by the year 2000, whites will constitute less than 74 percent of the population, while blacks, Hispanics, and Asians will constitute another 13 percent, 9 percent, and 4 percent respectively. It estimates the percentage of whites will drop to 64 percent by 2020 and 53 percent by 2050. But so far its forecasts have not been able to keep pace with changes both in the pace of immigration and the country's ethnic makeup.

In 1990 the United States admitted more than 1.5 million immigrants. Currently, about 830,000 legal immigrants enter the United States each year, more than all of the other countries in the world combined (Pear 1995). In addition, an estimated 300,000 immigrants enter illegally.[1] Since most immigrants seek safety and refuge in the nation's metropolitan areas, the United States is essentially trying to absorb—assimilation is probably culturally and politically out of the question—a metropolitan area of over one million people each year.

According to Daniel James (1995), some 20 million immigrants entered the United States between 1965 and 1990. Another 15–18 million are projected to arrive in the 1990s. And another 30–36 million are forecast to arrive in the first two decades of the twenty-first century. Unless America's immigration policies are changed, he predicts that "between 45 million and 54 million people—almost equal to the population of Great Britain—will be entering the U.S. in little more than a generation" (1995, 177).

But many critics wonder how the United States can provide all the education, jobs, housing, and public services these immigrants need, as well as the welfare benefits they are currently entitled to receive, especially in the face of the nation's other mounting burdens. For unlike yesteryear's immigrants from Castro's Cuba—mostly educated professionals, businessmen, and skilled workers—today's immigrants bring widely disparate levels of education and job skills. Some, especially legal immigrants with education and job skills, can make it on their own. But many cannot (Beck 1994). And who, critics ask, is going to pay the seemingly endless economic and social costs of family reunification (Miles 1995)?

Current immigration policies may also epitomize American optimism and cultural naivete. In theory, the principle is laudable. It would indeed be wonderful if the Golden Door could fulfill the Dream not just for all American citizens but also for the "homeless" and "tempest-tossed" from all over the world. But in reality, the Dream is beginning to fade and lose its luster for many Americans. And significant parts are no longer being realized by a growing minority, particularly those who trace their ancestries immediately or ultimately to Third World countries.

## The Fading Dream, The Unreachable Dream

How and in what sense has the Dream eroded? Signs are everywhere and palpable. They can be seen in the evasive eyes and fearful faces of pedestrians scurrying about large central cities filled with strangers. But they are also evident in all the other attendant problems of overpopulation, urban congestion, and cultural diversity. About three-fourths of all Americans, about 195 million people, are crammed into some 341 metropolitan areas. Perhaps the worst-case scenarios are to be found in the largest megalopolises where, even in the Sunbelt, people are packed into confined urban spaces like gridlocked cars on expressways during rush hour.

The typical worker in southern California, for example, must spend one and one-half hours to complete a 55-mile trek to work. He wakes up early and gets home late, leaving little time for family life and household chores. This hectic work schedule also leaves little time for being a good neighbor and getting involved in church and community activities. Some commentators have suggested that southern Californians may want privacy and their walled-in patios, in part, because they do not particularly like each other, especially if their neighbors happen to be racially or ethnically different (Davis 1991).

But there are other and more ominous signs of the American future that can be seen in the southern California landscape. One is the total breakdown in community life that unfolded during the 1992 Los Angeles race riot, the most costly civil disorder of the twentieth century. A second is a growing cultural separatism and conflict among America's racial and ethnic groups. For some years, demographers have noticed an exodus of white, largely native-born and middle-class families from southern California to less congested and troubled locations in the Pacific Northwest and interior Southwest. Now there is a significant black out-migration as well. A worsening economy, an influx of Latinos, and a deteriorating quality of life are reportedly driving growing numbers of black families to friendlier and more familiar terrain, often to southern cities, such as Atlanta, where blacks are more numerous and culturally dominant. Based on U.S. census data, an estimated 6.9 percent of the African American population left Los Angeles County between 1985 and 1990 (Noble 1995).

Another portent of an eroding Dream is the continuing loss of manufacturing jobs and a decline in living standards, especially for the middle class. According to data compiled by Kevin Phillips (1990, 17), real family income declined for the bottom eight deciles of the income distribution (those making less than $50,000 a year in 1987 dollars) between 1977 and 1988. To make up for the loss of family income, more and more housewives and mothers have been forced into part-time and full-time employment, some by their own choosing, but many because of the rising costs of home ownership and raising a family. Currently, some 62 percent of all American mothers with children under the age of five work at jobs outside the home.

One more omen of decline is the omnipresent crime problem. It has consistently ranked among the top concerns of Americans in national opinion polls and is clearly related to objective increases in the overall crime rate, which is the sum of seven indexed crimes—homicide, forcible rape, aggravated assault, robbery, burglary, grand larceny, and auto theft—adjusted for population. The overall rate increased by 120 percent during the 1960s and continued to go up during the 1970s. It decreased slightly during the early 1980s because of a decrease in the relative numbers of teenagers and young adults in the U.S. population but then continued to increase during the late 1980s. Although violent crime has decreased slightly in the past couple of years because of a slight drop in the proportion of teenagers and young adults, it is expected to increase once again by the end of the century.

Strictly speaking, crime does not threaten all Americans equally. Even in cities with high rates of crime, such as Miami or Houston, the rich can largely escape the problem by living in gated communities, the practice that is common among Western businessmen and their families who temporarily reside in Third World countries. Crime constitutes the greatest menace to urban residents who are poor, young, or people of color. It is also related to regional and cultural differences (Lieske 1993).

The most disquieting signs of decline, however, may lie in the reigning perceptions of American life and the diminished expectations that Americans now hold out for the future. Although the life expectancy of Americans has gone up in recent years, public satisfaction with the quality of life has gone down. According to a recent *Money* magazine poll, three out of five Americans thought the quality of life in the United States was getting worse. And nearly as many (58 percent) expressed similar feelings about economic and job opportunities. Other polls have detected a growing concern among parents that life for their children may not be as good and filled with opportunities as for themselves. Still others show that two-thirds to three-quarters of all Americans believe the country is headed in the wrong direction (Belsky 1994), although more recent polls are more optimistic.

Given recent economic and social developments, public pessimism about the American future should come as no surprise. What may come as a shock is new evidence of a growing exodus of Americans, mostly whites, to other countries. According to government estimates, some 250,000 Americans are leaving the United States each year, up from an annual average of 160,000, to pursue their hopes and dreams in other countries (Belsky 1994). But since most countries have very restrictive, if not closed, immigration policies, there are obvious limits both on this strategy and the magnitude of the out-migration.

This brings us to America's own huddled masses, not just those who are mired in the so-called underclass—including some two million homeless, another two million in prison or jail,[2] and the three of every ten African Americans who fall below the poverty level—but also those who are rapidly joining their ranks as newly arrived immigrants, namely, the one of every four Hispanic Americans who work as unskilled laborers and domestics and the two of every three Southeast Asian immigrants, many of them illiterate Hmongs, who have entered the country since 1986 and are still on welfare (Beck 1994). What are their chances of attaining the American Dream?

In composition, the American underclass is disproportionately, but not exclusively, made up of poor blacks and Latinos (there are still more poor whites), many of whom are caught up in a tangle of social pathologies—poverty, family breakdown and welfare dependency, educational failure, and rising levels of crime and social disorder. The size of this underclass, an estimated 39 million Americans who fall below the poverty level, about one-half of whom are black and Hispanic, as well as the apparent intractability of the pathologies that restrict their access to the American Dream can only be viewed with alarm.

But what can and should the nation *legitimately* do that has not already been tried? During the 1960s the War on Poverty and a plethora of other Great Society programs were specifically directed at the manifold problems of the American underclass. During the 1970s public assistance was channeled into block grants, revenue sharing, and public-private partnerships. But only a few of these programs, such as Head Start, appear to have made any significant, if only temporary, impact. And most have been dismissed by conservative critics as a political payoff to Democratic constituencies. Perhaps the most positive feature of these programs at the time was an official unwillingness to reconcile the presence of a large underclass with the American Dream. On the negative side, they have doubtlessly contributed to a conservative national consensus that government programs, especially social welfare programs directed toward the poor, do not work.

In sum, the challenge confronting the United States is twofold: (1) to reclaim the American Dream for the growing numbers of Americans who have become disillusioned or disenchanted with the current state of the union, and (2) to extend it to those groups who are still outside the social and economic mainstream. Regrettably, a successful and happy outcome is becoming more remote for reasons that relate to America's diminishing natural resources and environment, its changing population and culture, economic decline, and the long-term corruption of its democratic processes and institutions.

## The Natural Environment: Scarcity and the Limits to Growth

Americans like to think of the United States as a mature developed country. But most seem unwilling to recognize and accept the natural limits to *sustainable* growth that go along with modernity. This can be seen in our reluctance to conserve scarce nonrenewable resources, such as oil, and to become self-sufficient; in the failure of Jimmy Carter's Project Independence; and the readiness of the nation to go to war in 1991 over continued access to Persian Gulf oil. But it is also apparent in a general unwillingness to limit consumption and waste; a lack of concern about the giant landfills and mountains of garbage that are being deposited within large metropolitan areas; the hesitancy of local officials to restrict and regulate the use of land and to control galloping urban sprawl; and finally, in the tepid response of the Congress to the immigration problem.

But what exactly is a "sustainable" population? Earlier in this century, demographers thought that the population of the United States would stabilize at around 160 million by 1960 (Sears 1974, vi.). However, in 1970 it surpassed George Kennan's (1993) projected "ideal" of 200 million. And now, it is over 266 million and growing over 1 percent a year, a rate that is generally double those found in Western industrial democracies, but still less than India's growth rate of 1.5 to 2 percent.

One indisputable limit on further growth is America's rapidly dwindling reserves of nonrenewable resources. Compared to other developed countries, the United States is still a rich and bountiful country. But it must now import over 50 percent of the oil it consumes—a dependency that may help explain why the nation spent some $86 billion to intervene in the Persian Gulf War—and about 25 percent of the iron that is required to make steel.

A second limit is the growing population pressures on the nation's fixed supply of renewable resources, especially water. And water shortages, as well as population pressures, are unfortunately most severe in the growing Western states that encompass the Great American Desert. Although California is coming off a seven-year drought, the state has been forced to cut back dramatically on agricultural water quotas and impose strict rationing in urbanized areas because it is without sufficient reserves to sustain its large and growing population of some 31 million people (Brazil 1995).

Another rapidly depleting resource is the nation's fisheries. During the 1950s the fish population in New England's famed Grand Banks was thought to be virtually inexhaustible. Now, because of overfishing by domestic boats and foreign trawlers, catches are dramatically down. And strict government restrictions have forced many U.S. fishermen out of business.

Much the same story has been repeated on the other side of the continent in the Pacific Northwest. There ocean catches of the mighty chinook and sockeye salmon were once thought to be inexhaustible. But now the cumulative effects of several largely man-made developments have combined to threaten their continued existence. One has been overfishing by commercial and sports fishermen as well as some federally protected Indian tribes who are not subject to government regulations. A second has been the protracted drought in the Pacific Northwest and other Western states. But the major cause seems to be a network of hydroelectric dams that girdle rivers such as the Columbia and the Snake. They were originally constructed to provide water for irrigated farming in semiarid areas, deep-channel ports for shipping inland goods on ocean vessels, and electric power for an ever-growing urban population. But now they also serve to prevent adult salmon from spawning upriver and fingerlings from reaching the sea, the life cycle that must be repeated if the fish are to survive.

Unfortunately, the types of government action that have been taken and are being contemplated to save these endangered species—the imposition of strict fishing restrictions, the periodic release of dammed-up water to improve river flow, and assisted stocking schemes—are not nearly enough. Five years ago, the last sockeye salmon to reach Salmon, Idaho, the town that took its name from the thousands of salmon that used to make their way up the Columbia River system to spawn each year, was caught and mounted. His name, "Lonesome Larry," has become a rallying cry for conservationists like former Idaho Governor and Interior Secretary Cecil Andrus. But so far, they (and the salmon) have been effectively stymied by the long and arduous fish ladders that pyramid up alongside the Columbia River dams (Eagan 1994).

By comparison, conservationists have waged a much more successful campaign against air and water pollution. With the exception of the acid rain problem, environmental laws and regulations have unquestionably made a difference. But even here there is still a strong correlation between people and environmental degradation: the more people, the more degradation. Therefore, just to maintain current air and water quality, environmental regulations must of necessity become more stringent as the population of a state or region grows. This is why the U.S. Environmental Protection Agency has pressured California and twelve eastern states to require cleaner cars. In fact, the new clean air standards for California are so strict they require a 90 percent reduction in auto emissions and a 2 percent quota for the sale of emission-free (i.e., electric-powered) cars by 1997 (Wald 1994).

In the long run, however, the ultimate environmental problems are those that produce irreversible changes in the physical landscape: deforestation and desertification, soil degradation, the destruction of coastal and prairie wetlands, and urban sprawl. Deforestation, desertification, and a lack of rainfall, of course, go hand in hand. And therefore it is perhaps no accident that the most deforested and desertified regions of the United States lie west of the Mississippi (McKibben 1995). Thus U.S. government data reveal moderate deforestation (0.5 percent to 1.5 percent of total land area per year) in the Pacific Northwest, moderate desertification (less than 0.5 percent of total land area per year) in the upper part of the Great Basin and southern California, and severe desertification (greater than 0.5 percent of total land area per year) in the lower part of the Great Basin and the desert Southwest (Allen 1994, 84–85).

Soil degradation, by comparison, is almost national in scope. With the exception of New England, the coastal areas of the Pacific Northwest, and Florida, most of the continental United States has suffered moderate soil erosion (Allen 1994, 86–87) But millions of additional acres—at least one-third of all U.S. land including the nation's breadbasket and parts of Pennsylvania, Michigan, the upper Great Basin, and the Southwest— have experienced severe soil degradation. These lands have been primarily degraded by the overgrazing of cattle and destructive agricultural practices that promote wind erosion and salinization of the soil. According to one authoritative estimate, up to 85 percent of the rangeland in the western United States—some 685 million acres—is being turned into desert by overgrazing and land mismanagement. These include about 430 million acres that have experienced a 25 to 50 percent reduction in crop yield and natural vegetation from a healthy state and 13 million acres that are considered "irreversibly degraded" (Klockenbrink 1991).

Two additional man-made pressures that contribute to soil degradation are urban sprawl and the destruction of coastal and prairie wetlands (Eagan 1995). Each year, an estimated one million or more acres are being taken out of production for roads and industrial and urban development (Sears 1974, 214). The destruction of coastal wetlands is accelerating along both seaboards because of urban population pressures. The draining of prairie wetlands began during the 1970s when the federal government encouraged farmers in the Midwest to dramatically increase agricultural production. By getting farmers to boost production, federal officials hoped to reduce the nation's rising trade deficit and meet what they thought would be a growing demand for agricultural products in Second and Third World countries such as the former Soviet Union and China. Both developments—sprawl and the loss of wetlands—are now threatening entire ecosystems as they deprive plants and animals of their natural habitats. They are also rapidly despoiling the American landscape. In the upper Midwest, for instance, the aesthetic cost has been a systematic denuding of a land that once teemed with ducks, geese, and pheasants.

## The People: Cultural Diversity and Decline

Is cultural diversity a blessing or a bane? In the biological world, diversity is thought to promote the survival of a species through symbiosis or mutual interdependence. But in the social and political worlds, diversity seems to be the source of much conflict. Indeed, the best predictor of conflict across nation-states and within the American states is the degree of cultural heterogeneity or diversity ( Dye 1994; Woshinsky 1995).

Compared to most other countries, the United States is a cultural mosaic that is becoming evermore diverse—racially, ethnically, religiously, and socially (Elazar 1994). It is also becoming a balkanized country of contending regional interests and subcultures (Lieske 1993).

Currently, about 15 percent of all Americans live in poverty, up from the 1971 low of 11 percent. Poverty is still more common among racial minorities. But it is also more prevalent in female-headed households. In fact, the best predictor of being poor in America is not being black or Latino but being a member of a female-headed household. The unusually high rate of poverty among American children—one out of every five—partly reflects the growing incidence of female-headed households and the higher fertility rates of colored people.

The breakdown of the American family, which first attracted national attention following publication of the Moynihan Report (1965), has not only worsened for the black underclass but also broadened to include significant segments of the white race. Today about one-half of all black and one-quarter of all white households are female-headed. And family breakdown appears to be closely linked not only with poverty but also with a host of other social problems including educational failure, juvenile delinquency, crime, and welfare dependency.

Welfare dependency, of course, represents the antithesis of the American Dream. But what seems to trouble Americans most about welfare is the perception that hard-earned tax dollars are being squandered on loose and undeserving men and women who have flouted traditional sexual mores and exploited public altruism. What is perhaps equally galling is the belief that government welfare programs are actually encouraging dependency and that a disproportionate number of recipients are people of color who have made welfare a way of life (Murray 1984). In 1994, over 31 percent of all babies in the United States—20 percent of all white, 37 percent of all Hispanic, and 62 percent of all black—were born out of wedlock (Holmes 1994), with more recent years showing only slight improvement. And although blacks constitute 12 percent of the U.S. population, they compose almost 40 percent of the welfare recipients. A growing proportion are young women who were born out of wedlock, have now mothered children out of wedlock, and are still "trapped" in poverty.

In the past, Americans believed there was a long-term solution to poverty. Anyone could escape. All you had to do was get a good education or marketable job skills and work hard. Now the path to success is seen to be blocked with persistent racial, ethnic, and social barriers that are rooted in cultural and subcultural differences (Sowell 1994). One modern dilemma has been a long-term decline in SAT math and verbal scores. U.S. scores are lower than those of most advanced industrial countries. Scores have mostly been falling for every racial and ethnic group for several decades, with some small improvements reported. Controversially, they have been linked in particular to differences in IQ (Herrnstein and Murray 1994) and to the poor performance of students from lower-income and minority backgrounds (Coleman et al. 1966; Jencks et al. 1972). However, some cultures and subcultures seem to do better than others in supporting the values, dispositions, and character traits—hard work, rational thinking, the ability to organize others, and an eagerness to learn from "superior" cultures—that produce educational and material success (Sowell 1994; Neuhaus 1995, 56).

One cultural trait that clearly impedes educational achievement and material success is the social acceptability of dropping out of school. Unfortunately, in many cities with large minority populations, high school dropout rates approach 40 percent by the tenth grade. Being a high school dropout is also the best predictor of landing in prison. Currently, about 80 percent of all U.S. prisoners are high school dropouts.

But the lack of parental and peer support are not the only cultural traits that hold back poor and minority children. Racial segregation and separatism as well as social stratification also limit their access to the American Dream (Coleman et al. 1966). While defenders of diversity like to portray the United States as a great melting pot, there has always been more myth than reality to this metaphor. Even before the onslaught of the new immigrant waves, the only groups who had been fully assimilated into the American mainstream were European in ancestry. Today the pot con-

tinues to boil but racial and social differences have not melted away
(Glazer and Moynihan 1970). And our cities and metropolitan areas are
as segregated as ever (Gillmor and Doig 1992).

Perhaps the greatest cost of diversity is the nation's unacceptably high
levels of crime and social disorder. The United States is one of the most
culturally diverse countries in the world. But it is also one of the most violent and crime-prone. At the state and local levels, the correlation persists. It is the states and cities with the greatest cultural diversity that
have the highest levels of crime and racial strife.

Rioting has been in evidence throughout our history, but it is a problem that seems to have gotten worse. The worst riot of this century
erupted in Los Angeles in 1992 following an acquittal, handed down by
an all-white jury, of four white police officers who were charged with
brutally beating a convicted black felon after he tried to elude them in a
high-speed car chase (Mydans 1993). Ironically, riot arrest data suggest
that over half of the rioters were not African American but Hispanic,
many of them newly arrived immigrants from Mexico. Some commentators have questioned whether ethnic polyglots, such as Los Angeles, represent the future or terminus of American history (Davis 1991).

Urban mass terrorism, on the other hand, has been a more recent and
frightening development. The bombings of New York's World Trade Center in 1994 and Oklahoma City's Federal Building in 1995 may on first
glance seem unrelated. But both involve dilemmas of American cultural
pluralism. The first by Islamic extremists, all recent immigrants, illustrate
profound Arab American dissatisfaction with U.S. foreign and military
aid to Israel and its anti-Arab resettlement policies on the West Bank. The
latter by paramilitary fanatics appears to have been an anniversary act of
reprisal for perceived massacres of "innocent" civilians by federal law enforcement officers at Ruby Ridge, Idaho, and Waco, Texas.

These incendiary acts may be deviant and isolated. But they could also
foretell of a more troubled American future. For history often reads like
the obituary of nations. And ultimately, the future of any nation surely
depends on the character and quality of its people. Hence it seems prudent to consider two other modern developments.

The first concerns the emergence of a new social ethic of materialism
and instant self-gratification that the ancients simply knew as mammon.
Today, Americans save only 3–4 percent of their income and give about 1
percent to charity. By comparison, Germans save at least 10–15 percent of
their income, and the Japanese have been averaging almost 20 percent.
Whether Americans save and invest in their future or spend and live for
the moment depends in part on their psychological time horizon. And
some observers have even extended this logic to the social problems of
the urban underclass. Thus, one alleged cause of poverty is the poor's

predominantly present-oriented time horizon (Banfield 1968). This logic has also been used to explain much of the rapid increase in illegitimate births and welfare dependency over the past several decades.

In the puritanical social climate of the 1940s and 1950s, the passage to the American Dream was as straight and narrow as the path that guided Pilgrim to the kingdom of heaven. To succeed one first had to get a good education, next a job, then marry and establish a home, and finally have children. During the next several decades this cultural ideal was increasingly compromised and eventually short-circuited so that by the 1990s the cultural reality was the arrival of a new subculture of dropout mothers who birthed their and the state's children out of wedlock.

The second development concerns a growing lust for pleasure which religious moralists have condemned through the ages as hedonism. This reputed vice can be seen in, among other things, the exaltation of a sensate sports culture that shortchanges family life and values, community institutions, and vital public services such as education. As residents and taxpayers in many metropolitan areas have discovered, its bitter fruits are growing public subsidies, often hundreds of millions of dollars, to fund the construction of new sports arenas and sate the greed of wealthy franchise owners and players. And for better or worse, the United States has turned into a nation of spectators and sports junkies where an estimated one-third of all Americans are obese (defined as 20 percent or more above a medically desirable weight), one-half of the population suffers and dies from heart disease or cancer (both of which are related to weight), over 18 million are alcoholics, and another 5 million are drug addicts (Quindlen 1994; *New York Times* Editorial 1994). Currently, the average American watches seven hours of television each day. And this addiction is one reason why some major league sports figures can command 160 times as much money in salary and endorsements as the president of the United States earns in an entire year.

## The Economy: Decline and Uneven Development

With a gross domestic product of over $6 trillion, the American economy is the largest in the world by far. But it has long ceased to be the fastest growing. And although it is still very dynamic, its manufacturing sector has been in long-term decline.

One way to understand its growth and decline can be found in development theory (Dahrendorf 1959). By the 1960s the American economy had evolved to a new stage of postindustrial development. Higher and higher wages were being paid to people with technical and managerial skills. But technological changes were leaving behind those who could not or would not keep up. And it was making those individuals without a basic education or marketable skills increasingly irrelevant and superfluous. This theory, at least, seems to offer a partial explanation for the rise of the new technical-managerial class, the downward spiral of the old industrial proletariat, and the travails of the underclass.

A second approach is to cast these developments within a broader historical-cultural framework (Elazar 1994). Thus Daniel Elazar's frontier theory sees the nation's economy developing and moving with its peoples from a rural-land and urban-industrial past to a metropolitan-postindustrial and "rurban-cybernetic" future. Although his theory attempts to link economic and social changes with historical-cultural developments—for example, the emergence of "rurban" high-tech enclaves such as Silicon Valley—it assumes a healthy and growing national economy. In addition, cultural and subcultural values are assumed to be relatively constant and enduring.

Other projections of the nation's economic future, however, are less optimistic. Lester Thurow (1980) predicts that many Americans will experience a real decline in their standard of living as the nation moves from a manufacturing to a services economy. Robert Reich (1984) sees new dislocations emerging from (1) the onset of global competition; (2) the nation's increasing lack of competitiveness in fixed, standardized modes of production; and (3) the generalized move of business and government to paper entrepreneurialism. Paul Kennedy (1987) warns that all superpowers eventually drive their economies into the ground as they allocate larger and larger shares of their economic wealth to military spending and foreign aid. And Walter Rostow (1960) theorizes that all industrial societies pass through a fairly standard developmental sequence that ultimately culminates in a stage of mass consumption and long-term economic decline.

Although these issues and their ramifications are still being debated, there is little doubt about the present state of the American economy. Over the past several decades the U.S. economy has experienced long-term decline and uneven development. From 1948 to 1965, the gross national product (GNP) expanded at an overall average rate of 3.2 percent. But growth in the GNP peaked during the economic expansion of the 1960s and since then has been in a long-term decline (Frumkin 1987, 39). Overall, its rise and fall resembles a damped convex parabola, growing at an average annual rate of 3.6 percent from 1948 to 1959, rising to a 4.1 percent rate of growth from 1959 to 1969, falling to a 2.8 percent rate from 1969 to 1979, declining to a 2.0 percent rate from 1979 to 1985, rising slightly to a 2.9 percent rate from 1986 to 1990, and then falling again to a 1.9 percent rate from 1991 to 1996. As a result, the nation's economy is growing only 1 percent faster than its population.

Another indicator of decline is an upward shift in the U.S. unemployment rate. Following Okun's Law, a long-term decline in economic growth has been matched by an upward drift in unemployment. After an upward creep in the 1950s and then a sharp decline in the 1960s, the U.S. unemployment rate generally rose during the 1970s and 1980s (Frumkin 1987, 143–144). Although the trend recently has been toward declining rates of unemployment, the official rate now seems to have bottomed out at between 4.5 and 6 percent. In the near term are possibly inflationary wage increases due to labor shortages during an expanding economy. However, there remains in the long term the challenge of a large and growing global surplus labor force that has driven down real wages for many occupational groups and promises more of the same with further economic "globalization."

Other negative trends can be spotted in the growing volatility of the nation's manufacturing sector and merchandise trade balance. Since 1960, there has been a long-term decline in the utilization of corporate plants and equipment within the manufacturing sector. And since 1976, the U.S. merchandise trade balance—exports minus imports—has literally "fallen off a cliff" (Nelson 1987, 173). In 1994, it reached an estimated $152 billion, the highest trade deficit ever.

But the major strains on the national economy appear to be the omnipresent budget deficit and ever-growing national debt. The last year the federal government balanced its budget was 1969. Following the implementation of the 1981 Tax Recovery Act, the national budget deficit quickly ballooned to over $200 billion a year and the national debt quintupled to over $5 trillion by 1992. Although the 1993 Budget Agreement has cut the budget deficit almost in half, the national debt continues to grow and the debt ratio (total debt as a percentage of GNP) is expected to exceed 100 percent before the end of the century. Currently the national debt gobbles up some $230 billion in annual interest payments.

As a result, the United States is no longer the richest country in the world but now ranks in GNP per capita behind such countries as Japan and Sweden (Allen 1994, 38–40). Most such countries have more culturally homogeneous populations and fewer disparities in the distribution of income and wealth. (This same homogeneity may inhibit internal dynamism and thus over the longer term prove as disadvantageous as it has temporarily been advantageous.)

While uneven economic development is generally associated with the economies of Third World countries, it has always been a characteristic feature of American society. Historically, the economies of the border and Deep South states have lagged behind the rest of the country. But now the debate has shifted to the much-heralded rise of the Sunbelt and corresponding decline of the Frostbelt states. This economic shift was made possible by a host of developments, some of which were foreseen, but many that were not, including regional differences in defense spending, federal "cheap energy" policies, lower land and labor costs, irrigated farming and federally subsidized water development projects, tourism and the creation of a retirement class, federally guaranteed real estate ventures (that were covered by the recent savings and loan bailout), and technological advances in air conditioning and telecommunications (Perry and Watkins 1977; Weinstein and Firestine 1978). Most of these developments owe their existence, either directly or indirectly, to federal intervention. Ironically, Sunbelt voters are generally the most conservative and vocal in their opposition to "big government" and the "intrusive" policies of the federal government.

Another change that has hurt the Frostbelt is the growing loss of manufacturing jobs, originally to the South but now also to Third World countries such as Mexico. The enfeebled condition of the American labor movement was perhaps most starkly revealed in its unsuccessful attempt to defeat passage of the 1993 North American Free Trade Agreement (NAFTA) by a Democrat-controlled Congress. Since NAFTA was passed with bipartisan support, the continuing hemorrhage of the nation's manufacturing base is not likely to abate. Free trade has always been an American political icon. But now conservative, as well as liberal, critics are wondering at what price. One frequently mentioned cost is the loss of high-wage jobs and an eroding standard of living for the urban middle class. A second is the loss of job opportunities for the urban underclass. And a third is the conversion of old Fortune 500 companies into downsized management holding companies that offer changing and often completely new product lines, depending on the foreign companies they buy out in the new global competition.

But U.S. trade agreements are not the only types of federal action that distort the American labor market. One less direct, but by no means inadvertent, intrusion is produced by America's permissive immigration laws, which have the effect of creating "scab" and surplus labor, not just for domestic but also for agricultural and industrial work. Another is the start-and-stop spending policies of the federal government, especially for defense, which consumes about $280 billion annually. Neither influence can be dismissed any longer as minor or inconsequential. Acting in concert with other economic and social trends, their cumulative effect is to exacerbate and accelerate the long-term processes of economic decline and uneven development.

## The State of the Union: Corruption and Discontent

The United States is the oldest democracy in the world and its two-party system stands out as one of the most stable and enduring. Perhaps the singular genius of the American experiment was the creation of a democratic system that would do what the Founding Fathers wanted: preserve social order, safeguard individual liberties, and prevent the tyranny of a political majority. Thus the emergence of a stable two-party system was not accidental. It is almost guaranteed by an electoral system of single-member districts and plurality elections in congressional races and winner-take-all in presidential contests. Regrettably, these electoral arrangements also tend to undermine third party movements and reduce political debate to the lowest common denominator. To safeguard liberty and prevent political tyranny, the Founders devised a complicated system of checks and balances that divides power among three separate branches of government as well as the national and state governments. Working in tandem, these features have nurtured a distinctive national politics that is moderate not only in tone but also in substance.

## Liberal Action

This legacy of political stability, however, should not be confused with the absence of political change. Like other industrial democracies, the United States is still developing, not just economically and socially, but also politically. The first major changes occurred in response to a national reform movement around the turn of the century when political progressives, mostly liberal Republicans, achieved some success in eliminating politics and corruption from state and local government, reforming the party system, curbing the power and greed of the trusts, and introducing direct forms of democracy, such as the direct primary, that provided voters with the means to bypass representative institutions that were no longer responsive to their needs and concerns.

A second window for change was opened by the Great Depression. This economic crisis brought to power liberal Democrats who proposed a new social contract, or "New Deal," with the American people. The New Deal required the federal government to regulate the economy and erect a social safety net for individuals and families who could not provide for their own needs. Under a new system of cooperative federalism, the national government, in partnership with state and local governments, would intervene and take remedial and corrective action to relieve economic and social problems. But this second transformation of American government and politics was not without cost. The price that had to be paid was an expansion in the scope and powers of the federal government at the expense of state and local governments and submission to the principle of federal intervention and guidelines. But by the early 1950s most programs associated with the New Deal had been implemented and most federal spending for programs such as Social Security and federally insured mortgages was directed toward insuring middle-class access to the American Dream.

A third opportunity for change was made possible by the pivotal election of 1964, which provided liberals within the Democratic Party super-majority status. Using Lyndon Johnson's landslide (61–39 percent) defeat of Republican conservative Barry Goldwater and the more than two-to-one advantage their party held in both houses of Congress as a mandate for change, liberal Democrats enacted a new set of federal programs that radically expanded the scope and powers of the federal government. Although some (for example, Medicare and Medicaid) represented progressive extensions of the New Deal, many if not most exemplified an entirely new liberal agenda that has dominated American politics for the last thirty years.

A major part of this agenda has been directed toward using the powers of the federal government to secure the civil rights of socially marginal groups within the Democratic coalition: racial minorities, the poor, women, criminal defendants and prisoners, homosexuals, the handicapped and mentally ill, and students. A second component has focused on maintaining and expanding the social safety net that was set in place during the New Deal. And a third has aimed, in the names of diversity and equality, at extending the American Dream not only to the downtrodden of America but also to the oppressed peoples of the Third World.

To achieve these goals, liberals have employed several different but complementary strategies. The most controversial remedy has used the legal and moral authority of the state to enforce race- and gender-conscious policies of active government intervention, most notably affirmative action and minority set-aside programs. Another has employed the judicial branch to mandate the political representation of racial minorities through the creation of racially and (for Hispanics) ethnically gerrymandered districts. A less controversial approach has promoted the enactment of compensatory programs for the poor and racial minorities. Perhaps the only interventionist strategies that now enjoy widespread public support are those that provide statutory and constitutional protections for victims of race, gender, or age discrimination.

### Conservative Reaction

The seeds for a conservative counterrevolution were sown in the 1964 Goldwater debacle, when white southern and northern white ethnic voters began to vote Republican in significant numbers. This movement gathered momentum during the 1966 midterm elections when the Republican Party gained 47 seats in the U.S. House of Representatives and 6 seats in the U.S. Senate. And it gained political currency when the electorate rejected the New Dealer, Hubert Humphrey, by a 57–43 percent majority in 1968 and then repudiated his ultra-liberal compatriot, George

McGovern, by an even greater 61–39 percent margin in 1972. Following Watergate, however, the Democrats made a temporary resurgence by gaining 52 seats in the House (4 in the Senate) and then winning back the White House in 1976 by backing a white southerner, Jimmy Carter.

But by 1979, opinion polls revealed a national mood of discontent and a growing distrust of government. In a nationwide address, President Carter took note of polling trends that pointed to a dramatic decline in the proportion of Americans who said they had a great deal of confidence in their social and political institutions. Besides being the messenger of bad tidings, Carter compounded his blunder by misinterpreting the public's growing unease as an American "malaise."

What few politicians realized at the time was the existence of a growing public sentiment that the real malaise resided in government itself. For those who had become disillusioned or alienated, it was a government that had foolishly squandered the wealth of the nation and the valor of its young men and women by taking sides in an insignificant civil war in Vietnam. It was also a government riddled with vain and self-seeking career politicians who would do anything to win. Moreover, it was a government in which virtually everyone was bought in varying degrees by campaign contributions from political action committees (PACs). Finally, it was a government that had become too big, too costly, and too intrusive.

The solution offered by Ronald Reagan and Republican conservatives was simple and appealing. If government was the problem, then the answer was to reduce its size and power, cut taxes and spending, and get it off the backs of ordinary Americans. Since big government was consuming so much of the national wealth, these measures would also get the economy moving again. By comparison, the Democratic response was weak and tepid. But there was not much that could be said in defense of the party's stewardship. The economy was stagnant, unemployment and inflation were at double digits, U.S. foreign policy was adrift in a sea of "human rights" violations, and fifty-two American embassy personnel in Teheran had been incarcerated for an entire year by student militants as the Carter administration looked on in anguish.

The judgment delivered by the electorate in 1980 was swift and certain. In a stunning landslide election, Carter was remorselessly dumped. Republicans were handed control of the U.S. Senate for the first time since 1954. And the Reagan Revolution was on. Taxes were slashed by 23 percent. Spending on defense, in real dollars, increased an average of more than 7 percent annually. Tax reform favored the rich at the expense of every other group. And regulatory agencies such as the Environmental Protection Agency were put on notice that their days were numbered. But since Democrats still controlled the House, domestic spending held relatively constant. And budget deficits, as well as the national debt, quickly escalated over time. It was the era of the new "free lunch." Buy now and let your posterity pay later.

By the late 1980s, however, the Reagan juggernaut was running out of steam. In the 1986 midterm elections, voters turned control of the Senate back to the Democrats. And though Reagan's understudy, George Bush, ran successfully in 1988 as a social and economic conservative, he did not keep the conservative faith. In 1990 he violated his pledge not to raise taxes. And in 1991 he signed a civil rights bill that he had vetoed in 1990 on the grounds that it established implicit, or de facto, affirmative action quotas. By this time his "me-too" brand of Republicanism had also become a source of disappointment and embarrassment among conservatives within his own party.

And so as the 1992 elections approached, the Republican Party was a house divided. What ultimately doomed Bush, however, was not the candidacy of Bill Clinton so much as the splintering of the Republican coalition by Ross Perot, a billionaire Republican and political maverick from Dallas who spent $60 million of his own money running as a third-party candidate. Perot campaigned as a progressive populist, calling for political reform and national sacrifice to balance the budget and eliminate the national debt. To the surprise of most pundits, he garnered 19 percent of the vote, the second-highest percentage received by a third party candidate.

But Clinton's "New Covenant" with the American people was misdirected almost from the start. Instead of focusing "like a laser beam" on the economic and social problems of the "forgotten middle class," his administration got sidetracked by a series of political fumbles that damaged his popularity and frustrated his presidency. These included the much publicized failure to lift the long-standing ban on gays and lesbians in the military, the public outcry that erupted over several controversial nominations to his cabinet and the Supreme Court, and his alienation of the National Rifle Association over gun control and his falling out with the Christian Coalition over partial-birth abortion. Both groups were instrumental in targeting liberal Democrats for defeat in the pivotal 1994 midterm elections that gave Republicans control of both houses of Congress for the first time in forty years (Theiss 1994).

## The Earthquake Election

Outside of the new House Speaker, Newt Gingrich, there were few who predicted the dimensions of this earthquake election. The Democrats lost 52 seats in the House and 8 in the Senate. To make matters worse, three Democratic representatives and two Democratic Senators crossed over to the Republican side of the aisle. But if the 1994 elections are viewed within the context of a protracted chain reaction to a liberal Democratic agenda, perhaps the outcome is not that surprising.

First, the time was ripe. By the late 1980s, a Democratic-controlled Congress had become a bastion of privilege and corruption. And in the face of eroding public support, Democratic members of the House, as Thomas and Mary Edsall (1992, 26) note, "were forced to rely excessively on an essentially corrupt system of campaign finance, on gerrymandering, on pork barrel spending, on weak Republican challengers, and on assorted manipulations of the elective process in order to thwart continuing ideological and demographic shifts favoring their opponents."

Second, a growing revolt of white voters against the liberal social agenda of the Democratic Party had been building for some thirty years. Democratic policies of preferential treatment, guaranteed representation, protected group status, and compensatory programs had spawned smoldering racial-ethnic resentments and political backlash. And many whites, especially males who felt disenfranchised by the new liberal agenda and forsaken by the Democratic Party, were angry. With the exception of voting returns from culturally homogeneous states in New England and the upper Midwest, the dominant message of the 1994 midterm elections was a racial one: 62 percent of all white males and 57 percent of all white females voted for Republican congressional candidates.

Third, by fielding an unusually attractive slate of candidates and offering voters a new "Contract with America," the Republicans provided a clear and focused alternative. Among other things, the Contract promised political reform, welfare reform, a balanced budget amendment, term limits on members of Congress, selective tax cuts, and bills to fight crime and strengthen the military.

Finally, Clinton's vigorous campaigning on behalf of liberal Democrats played into Gingrich's strategy of turning the election into a referendum on an unpopular president and his socially disruptive policies. By this time even national health care had become suspect as polls revealed widespread public relief over Congress's failure to enact some version of Clinton's health care plan.

After taking control of Congress, Republican legislative leaders in both houses moved quickly to fulfill their Contract with America. And within the first 100 days House Republicans passed all of the legislation they had promised with the exception of the balanced budget amendment. But moderate Republicans in the Senate were not as eager to embrace all provisions of the Contract. Neither was a chastened President Clinton ready to capitulate to conservative demands for fiscal austerity. In frustration and to the dismay of many Americans who had come to depend on federal benefits and services, conservatives succeeded in shutting down the national government not once but twice.

Using Republican arrogance as a springboard, Clinton shrewdly cast himself as the champion and defender of social security, Medicare, education, and the oppressed. He and the Democrats then launched a preemptive strike against the Republicans, a well-orchestrated media campaign that was designed to refurbish his tarnished image, resuscitate his popularity, and paint Republican conservatives as political extremists who were insensitive to social needs. The campaign was paid for by a wellspring of "soft" money that was solicited from wealthy donors who wanted to buy access to the White House. And the tide seemed to turn. On the eve of the 1996 elections, the House Speaker was a political pariah, unemployment and inflation were both low, the president stood tall, and the Republican presidential candidate, Bob Dole, looked weak, ineffectual, and out of touch. Moreover, his flat tax proposal was not resonating with the voters, especially women, who seemed much more concerned with social than economic issues.

Clinton won handily, mostly because of a 17 percent gender gap, but failed to get an absolute majority because of independent voters who stayed with Ross Perot and voter concerns about possible improper campaign contributions from foreign donors. And Democratic hopes for retaking control of Congress were dashed when Republicans lost only five seats in the House and picked up one additional seat in the Senate. The mandate, if any, was to stand guard, keep a watchful eye on the political opposition, and somehow get along.

## The Future Struggle

For now there is a political standoff. What remains to be seen is whether (1) the Republicans can implement the broader, long-range objectives of their conservative counterrevolution, (2) the Democrats can put together a new political coalition that will once again be dominant in national politics, or (3) the "vital center" will rally behind a new progressive reform party. How these issues play out is crucially important, both in terms of the relations between the United States and the developing world and in determining how well the American democratic experiment accommodates itself to the changing national complexion and culture.

Philosophically, conservative Republicans are Jeffersonian in outlook. They generally want less government, less spending, more individual responsibility, fewer government "handouts," and a return to traditional (agrarian) values. By comparison, their political adversaries, the liberal Democrats, are Hamiltonian in philosophy. They generally prefer more government (and government programs), more spending (for worthwhile programs), more government assistance to meet individual needs, and cosmopolitan (urban) values. In between are the growing numbers of disgruntled independents, mostly white and middle-class, who find themselves without a home in either party.

All three groups are currently engaged in a great political struggle that will shape the direction and course of the American democratic experiment well into the twenty-first century. Perhaps the greatest issue of contention is over the scope and size of the welfare state. Which is better able to deliver on the American Dream, big or small government? Who is ultimately responsible for individual success and failure, society as a whole or the individual? When and under what conditions should government intervene to insure "justice for all"? How big does the social safety net need to be? Who pays the bills? And to what extent can the free market be left alone?

Another contested issue is the future of American culture and civilization, especially the ways of life and values that will come to dominate and therefore define the new social order. Will they continue to be largely derived from the European experience, the Judeo-Christian tradition, and English conceptions of common law and jurisprudence? Or will they be increasingly drawn from non-Western cultures, religions, and civilizations? And how will these different traditions affect how Americans feel toward each other, the cultural norms that unite or divide them, and the kinds of struggles that develop among different racial and ethnic groups for cultural dominance? Finally, what kinds of public policies will be pursued? Those that favor family or individual values, strict or permissive moral standards, and culturally orthodox or deviant behavior?

One issue that looms large on the political horizon is the developing crisis of political representation. Levels of public trust in the nation's political and social institutions are much lower today than they were midway through the twentieth century. And feelings of political efficacy have also sharply declined. Today, most Americans no longer believe they can trust the federal government to do what is right. And most no longer believe that government is run for the benefit of all (Luttbeg and Gant 1995, 137–138). In addition, most Americans no longer believe that public officials care much what people like themselves think (Wilson and DiIulio 1995, 96). Finally, rates of voting turnout in presidential elections, where rates of participation are the highest, have declined from a high of 63 percent in 1960 to less than 50 percent in 1996.

No one really knows what is behind these disturbing trends. Certainly, public dissatisfaction with unpopular domestic and foreign policies is one reason. So is public disgust with the self-serving performance of many elected officials. But part of the answer may also lie in the growing size, diversity, and urbanization of the nation's population. The United States is almost twice as large now as it was at the end of World War II. Moreover, its makeup is much more racially and ethnically diverse. And most Americans no longer feel the same sense of place and community that prevailed then. So perhaps it is not surprising that with some 575,000 people in each congressional district, only slightly more than half of all Americans know who their congressman is.

Another emerging issue concerns the future role and responsibilities of the United States in world affairs. The forty-two-year-old Cold War with the former Soviet Union and its Eastern bloc allies officially ended in 1989, but there is still the accumulated debt of this protracted conflict that needs to be paid off. And there are plenty of conflicts in other countries, as well as humanitarian relief efforts, mainly in the Third World, that continue to make claims on the resources of the most powerful country in the world. But are they legitimate, not only in the sense of being right and proper but also in the national interest? Is it patriotic to fight and die in someone else's civil war? Do the poor in other lands have greater claim to the nation's wealth than the poor who live in America? And does U.S. aid create and perpetuate dependency and population growth in the Third World (Connelly and Kennedy 1995)? Clearly, the United States and other developed countries have entered a new age of limits. And their leaders are no longer able to do all the good things they would like to do.

In the long run, however, the issue that will likely generate the most conflict is the debate on citizenship, in particular, as it concerns what it means to be an American, the nation's immigrant tradition, and the rights and obligations of citizenship. The outlines of this struggle are already visible in the Proposition 187 movement in California and other rapidly growing states like Florida and Texas where many residents feel besieged by the new immigrants and where the most recent extension of the Golden Door has now been met by a growing firestorm of controversy over what the new immigrants are costing taxpayers and what they are doing to the "American" way of life. Similar resentments toward racial minorities may underlie passage of the 1996 California Civil Rights Initiative, which prohibits affirmative action programs in state agencies and public higher education.

But the public debate on citizenship is not limited to those states that have borne a disproportionate share of the economic and social costs of immigration. Today the debate is national in scope. Political cartoons lampoon Emma Lazarus's well-known paean to American immigrants inscribed on the pedestal of the Statue of Liberty—"Give me your tired, your poor, your huddled masses yearning to breathe free . . . *And let them take advantage of me*." Economic studies substantiate the growing costs of legal and illegal immigration to American taxpayers. Educational reports show how some groups, most notably foreign graduate students, are educated at the expense of American taxpayers and then compete with

American students for a scarce supply of highly prized scientific and technical positions. Feature articles in national newspapers and magazines document abuses of state welfare systems and public generosity by the new immigrants (Beck 1994; Gross 1991; Rensberger 1995; James 1995). And national news reports reveal the uglier side of nativist resentments: from skinhead attacks on Asian Americans in the Portland area to black vandalism of Asian-owned stores during the 1992 Los Angeles riot and alleged Border Patrol beatings and rapes of Mexicans who cross into the United States illegally.

Overall, opinion polls show a readiness by most Americans to restrict further immigration and to cut off welfare benefits to illegal aliens (James 1995). But so far congressional Republicans have been reluctant to curtail the flood of legal immigrants, and Democrats in the Clinton administration have been unwilling to control the tide of illegal immigrants. Unfortunately, the issues of legal and illegal immigration appear to be inextricably linked. If our political leaders want federal immigration laws to be taken seriously, then surely they must take steps not only to stop the flow of illegal immigrants but also to stanch the flood of legal immigrants (James 1995). But issuing these signals is something that leaders in neither party seem willing to do.

### Conclusions

In the minds of most Americans, the United States is still "the greatest country in the world" (Williams 1995). But this is not to deny several fundamental problems that continue to erode the Dream and subvert the democratic experiment. One is the failure of most Americans to recognize the "limits to growth" that must be faced by mature developed countries. A second is a rampant cultural diversity, fed by a growing infusion of "Third World" peoples, that is undermining not only the nation's social contract but also the kinds of political support and activity that are necessary to sustain its democratic institutions. And a third is the inability of the new liberal ideals to bridge our growing racial and ethnic divisions and forge a unifying social ethic and political consensus.

What are the prospects? It is never easy to predict the American future, especially under conditions of rapid demographic and cultural change. But given the current social and political climate, it seems likely there will be rising racial and ethnic resentments and conflict, a continuing erosion of the social contract, and sharp cutbacks in domestic welfare spending and foreign aid as Americans learn to live within their means. In addition, it seems likely that historical distinctions between social welfare and social-cultural issues will become increasingly blurred as the nation divides itself into warring cultural camps. Thus, it will become increasingly difficult for politicians to divorce the issue of big versus small government from the corollary issue of "who pays" and "who benefits," "us" or "them"? Barring the emergence of a new progressive reform movement, perhaps the most likely scenario is continued population growth, environmental degradation, social and economic decline, and political fragmentation and conflict.

## Notes

1. Immigration experts now believe that almost as many illegals enter the U.S. as tourists as those who cross the border illegally. If true, then perhaps as many as 600,000 illegals and up to 1.5 million total new immigrants are actually entering the country each year (Dunn 1995).

2. About one million Americans are incarcerated in prisons, another million in jails. The prison population is double what it was in 1985. Moreover, about one-half the prison population is black.

## References

Allen, John L. 1994. *Student Atlas of World Politics*. Guilford, Conn.: Dushkin.

Banfield, Edward C. 1968. *The Unheavenly City*. Boston: Little, Brown.

Beck, Roy. 1994. The Ordeal of Immigration in Wausau. *Atlantic Monthly* (April): 84–97.

Belsky, Gary. 1994. Escape From America. *Money* (July): 60–70.

Brazil, Eric. 1995. California Downpour Fails to Resolve Water Shortage. *Cleveland Plain Dealer*, January 14.

Coleman, James, et al. 1966. *Equality of Educational Opportunity*. Washington, D.C.: Government Printing Office.

Connelly, Matthew, and Paul Kennedy. 1994. Must It Be the Rest Against the West? *Atlantic Monthly* 274: 61–84.

Dahrendorf, Ralph. 1959. *Class and Class Conflict in Industrial Society*. Stanford: Stanford University Press.

Davis, Mike. 1991. *City of Quartz*. New York: Verso.

Dunn, Ashley. 1995. Greeted at Nation's Front Door, Many Visitors Stay on Illegally. *New York Times*, January 3.

Dye, Thomas R. 1994. *Politics in States and Communities*, 8th ed. Englewood Cliffs, N.J.: Prentice Hall.

Eagan, Timothy. 1994. Governor's Quest for the Fish of Memory. *New York Times*, January 2.

_____. 1995. California Storm Brings Rethinking of Development. *New York Times*, January 15.

Edsall, Thomas Byrne, with Mary D. Edsall. 1992. *Chain Reaction: The Impact of Race, Rights, and Taxes on American Politics*. New York: W. W. Norton.

Elazar, Daniel J. 1994. *The American Mosaic*. Boulder: Westview.

Fallows, James. 1983. The New Immigrants: How They Are Affecting Us. *Atlantic Monthly* 257 (November): 45–103.

Fischer, David Hackett. 1989. *Albion's Seed*. Oxford: Oxford University Press.

Frumkin, Norman. 1987. *Tracking America's Economy*. Armonk, N.Y.: M. E. Sharpe.

Gillmor, Dan, and Stephen K. Doig. 1992. Segregation Forever? *American Demographics* (January): 48–51.

Glazer, Nathan, and Daniel P. Moynihan. 1970. *Beyond the Melting Pot*. Cambridge: MIT Press.

Gross, Jane. 1991. Poor Seekers of Good Life Flock to California, as Middle Class Moves Away. *New York Times*, December 21.

Herrnstein, Richard J., and Charles A. Murray. 1994. *The Bell Curve*. New York: Free Press.

Holmes, Steven A. 1994. Out-of-Wedlock Births Up Since '85, Report Indicates. *New York Times*, July 20.

James, Daniel. 1995. Close the Borders to All Newcomers. In *Taking Sides*, eds. George McKenna and Stanley Feingold. Guilford, Conn.: Dushkin.

Jencks, Christopher, et al. 1972. *Inequality: A Reassessment of the Effect of Family and Schooling in America*. New York: Basic.

Kennan, George F. 1993. *Around the Cragged Hill*. New York: W. W. Norton.

Kennedy, Paul. 1987. *The Rise and Fall of Great Powers*. New York: Random House.

Klockenbrink, Myra. 1991. The New Range War Has the Desert as Foe. *New York Times*, August 20.

Ladd, Everett Carll. 1978. Traditional Values Regnant. *Public Opinion* 1: 45–49.

Lieske, Joel A. 1978. The Conditions of Racial Violence in American Cities. *American Political Science Review* 72: 1324–1340.

_____ . 1993. Regional Subcultures of the United States. *Journal of Politics* 55: 888–913.

Long, Karen R. 1995. Giving Is Going Away in America. *Cleveland Plain Dealer*, February 19.

Luttbeg, Norman R., and Michael M. Gant. 1995. *American Electoral Behavior*, 2nd ed. Itasca, Ill.: Peacock.

McKibben, Bill. 1995. An Explosion of Green. *Atlantic Monthly* 275: 61–83.

Miles, James. 1995. The Coming Immigration Debate. *Atlantic Monthly* 275: 130–140.

Moynihan, Daniel P. 1965. *The Negro Family: The Case for National Action*. U.S. Department of Labor. Washington, D.C.: Government Printing Office.

Murray, Charles. 1984. *Losing Ground*. New York: Basic.

Mydans, Seth. 1993. Los Angeles Lays Plans to Avoid Repeat of '92 Riots. *New York Times*, March 30.

Nelson, Charles R. 1987. *The Investor's Guide to Economic Indicators*. New York: Wiley.

Neuhaus, Richard John. 1995. The Public Square. *First Things* (April): 56–68.

*New York Times* Editorial. 1994. Trimming the Nation's Fat. *New York Times*, December 11.

Noble, Kenneth B. 1995. Los Angeles Loses Economic Allure for Some Blacks. *New York Times*, January 8.

Pear, Robert. 1995. Change of Policy on U.S. Immigrants Is Urged by Panel. *New York Times*, June 5.

Perry, David C., and Alfred J. Watkins. 1977. *The Rise of the Sunbelt Cities*. Beverly Hills, Calif.: Sage.

Phillips, Kevin. 1990. *The Politics of Rich and Poor*. New York: Random House.

Quindlen, Anna. 1994. Public and Private: The Legal Drug. *New York Times*, June 11.

Reich, Robert B. 1984. *The Next American Frontier*. New York: Penguin.

Rensberger, Royce. 1995. No Help Wanted: Young U.S. Scientists Go Begging with Serious Consequences for the Future. *Washington Post National Weekly Edition*, January 9–15.

Rostow, W. W. 1960. *The Stages of Economic Growth*. Cambridge: Cambridge University Press.

Sears, Paul B. 1974. *Deserts on the March*. Norman, Okla.: University of Oklahoma Press.

Sowell, Thomas. 1994. *Race and Culture: A World View*. New York: Basic.

Theiss, Evelyn. 1994. Clinton Blames Losses on NRA. *Cleveland Plain Dealer*, October 25.

Thurow, Lester. 1980. *The Zero-Sum Society*. New York: Basic.

Wald, Matthew L. 1994. California Car Rules Set as Model for the East. *New York Times*, December 20.

Weinstein, Bernard L., and Robert E. Firestine. 1978. *Regional Growth and Decline in the United States*. New York: Praeger.

Williams, Daniel. 1995. Downed Flier Got By on Brains, Bugs, and Beacons. *Cleveland Plain Dealer*, June 9.

Wilson, James Q., and John J. DiIulio, Jr. 1995. *American Government*, 6th ed. Lexington, Mass.: D. C. Heath.

Woshinsky, Oliver H. 1995. *Culture and Politics*. Englewood Cliffs, N.J.: Prentice-Hall.

# About the Editors and Contributors

**Thomas D. Anderson** is Professor of Geography Emeritus at Bowling Green State University in Bowling Green, Ohio. His bachelors and masters degrees are from Kent State University and his Ph.D. degree is from the University of Nebraska in Lincoln. He is a cultural geographer, with emphasis on political geography and the geography of the Caribbean.

**R. Warwick Armstrong** is professor of community health at the University of Illinois at Urbana-Champaign. He has conducted epidemiological and geographical research in Iceland, Illinois, Hawaii, Malaysia, and New Zealand. He specializes in epidemiology, geographical epidemiology, and public health.

**Stephen S. Chang** is associate professor of geography at Bowling Green State University. His interests include cultural geography, problems of development, issues of cultural change, and the geography of East and Southeast Asia.

**Gary S. Elbow** is professor of geography at Texas Tech University in Lubbock. He has conducted research on agricultural and urban development, marketing, boundary conflicts, and economic integration in Colombia, Costa Rica, Ecuador, Guatemala, Jordan, Mexico, and the Caribbean.

**Jerome D. Fellmann** is Professor Emeritus at the University of Illinois. His professional career, except for visiting professorships at various universities, was spent at the University of Illinois at Urbana-Champaign. Teaching and research interests have been concentrated in the areas of human geography in general and urban and economic geography in particular, in geographic bibliography, geography of Russia and the Commonwealth of Independent States, and geographic education. His varied interests have been reflected in articles published in the *Annals* of the Association of American Geographers, *Professional Geographer, Journal of Geography,* the *Geographical Review,* and elsewhere. In addition to teaching and research, he has held administrative appointments at the University of Illinois and served as a consultant to private corporations on matters of economic and community development.

**Harold A. Fisher** is Professor Emeritus of journalism and international communication at Bowling Green State University School of Mass Communication in Ohio. He has done fieldwork in university-level education and national development projects in the Middle East and Sub-Saharan Africa.

**Elmer Brian Goehring** holds a Ph.D. from the University of British Columbia. He specializes in the Canadian Arctic and Nunavut and is the author of *Indigenous Peoples of the World* (Purich Publishing, 1993).

**Alfonso Gonzalez** is retired professor of geography at the University of Calgary. He specializes in population, socioeconomic development, the Third World (especially Latin America), and Spain. He has conducted field studies in all of Latin America, Europe (especially Spain), the old USSR, the Middle East, and Oceania.

**Raja M. Kamal** is the director of international development at the John F. Kennedy School of Government, Harvard University. He is also adjunct professor of economics at Wheelock College in Boston.

**Joel Lieske** is professor of political science at Cleveland State University. In his spare time he likes to play basketball with his students and coach his kids' basketball, soccer, and baseball teams.

**Srinivas R. Melkote** is professor of communication studies at Bowling Green State University. His fields of specialization include mass communication, development support communication, and health communication.

**Allen H. Merriam** is professor of speech communication at Missouri Southern State College in Joplin. He has published twenty-five articles or book chapters on intercultural communication and rhetorical studies and is the author of *Gandhi vs. Jinnah: The Debate over the Partition of India.*

**Janet Henshall Momsen** is a professor in the Department of Human and Community Development at the University of California, Davis. She has taught in Canada, England, Brazil, Costa Rica, and Nigeria and carried out research on gender and agricultural development in China, Ghana, Brazil, the Caribbean, Costa Rica, and Hungary. She has also published several books on gender and development.

**Souheil A. Moukaddem** is senior consultant at Booz Allen and Hamilton. He specializes in management consulting in the fields of business process reengineering and change management, primarily in government agencies.

**Jim Norwine** is Regents Professor of Geography at Texas A&M University–Kingsville. Trained in climatology, much of his scholarly work in recent years has been in cultural geography. These studies have focused in general on the nature and consequences of the "postmodern condition," on the character of the ongoing shift from modernity to postmodernity, and more particularly, on the implications of that change for personal worldviews and values around the world. He invites comments on this book and may be reached by e-mail at kfjrn00@tamuk.edu.

**Joseph G. Spinelli** is associate professor of geography at Bowling Green State University in Ohio. His fields of interest include the geography of Latin America, issues related to population geography including various aspects of changing population composition in the Caribbean, and geographic pedagogy.

**Bheru Sukhwal** is professor of geography at the University of Wisconsin–Platteville. He specializes in South Asia and political geography and has published numerous books on these topics.

# Index